EARTH'S LAST
EMPIRE

EARTH'S LAST EMPIRE

THE FINAL GAME OF THRONES

JOHN HAGEE

WORTHY®
PUBLISHING

Library of Congress Cataloging-in-Publication Data

Names: Hagee, John, author.
Title: Earth's last empire : the final game of thrones / John Hagee.
Description: Franklin, TN : Worthy Publishing, 2018. | Includes
  bibliographical references and index.
Identifiers: LCCN 2018033915 | ISBN 9781683972761 (hardcover : alk. paper)
Subjects: LCSH: End of the world--Biblical teaching. | Eschatology--Biblical
  teaching. | Bible--Prophecies. | Bible--Prophecies--End of the world. |
  Bible--Prophecies--International organization. |
  Bible--Prophecies--Armageddon.
Classification: LCC BS649.E63 H324 2018 | DDC 236/.9--dc23
LC record available at https://lccn.loc.gov/2018033915

For foreign and subsidiary rights, contact rights@worthypublishing.com

Published in association with Ted Squires Agency, Nashville, Tennessee

ISBN: 978-1-68397-276-1 (Hardcover)
ISBN: 978-1-68397-289-1 (Signed Edition)
ISBN: 978-1-68397-295-2 (International Tradepaper)

Cover and Interior Design by Bart Dawson

Printed in the United States of America
18 19 20 21 22 LBM 8 7 6 5 4 3 2 1

He who gives a book
gives more than cloth, paper, and ink.
He gives more than leather, parchment, and words.
He reveals a foreword of his thoughts,
a dedication of his friendship,
a page of his presence,
a chapter of himself,
and an index of his love.
Author Unknown

———————

It is my great privilege to dedicate this book
to one of the most beloved friends of my life,
Rabbi Aryeh Scheinberg.

With gratitude to my wife, Diana; my executive assistant, Jo-Ann Coffey; and Kelsey Potter, whose love and passion for Israel and the Jewish people are reflected in this work.

Special Acknowledgment

Special thanks to Dr. David Crockett for his invaluable contribution to chapters 6 and 7 of this book. Dr. Crockett has dedicated his life to engraving young minds with the foundational truths concerning our nation's politics, with a focus on the American presidency—providing hope for America and the world.

CONTENTS

SECTION ONE

ALL ROADS LEAD TO JERUSALEM

MY JERUSALEM

Jerusalem is the only place on earth that is called the city of God. Benjamin Disraeli, prime minister to the United Kingdom under Queen Victoria, once said, "The view of Jerusalem is the history of the world—it is more, it is the history of earth and of heaven."

My personal encounter with Jerusalem began as an affair of the heart—this City of God connected heaven and earth within my soul. Once I stepped foot on its sacred soil, it became my Jerusalem.

Jerusalem, the center of the universe.
Jerusalem, the City of Gold.
Jerusalem, the undivided capital of the Covenant nation of Israel.
Jerusalem, the place that the God of Abraham, Isaac,
and Jacob calls home.
Jerusalem, the experience that forever changed my life.

From the moment I first walked the ancient cobblestone streets of that Holy City, I sensed a divine presence there—a type of supernatural peace known nowhere else. I have traveled the world, but only Jerusalem has felt like home.

Jerusalem is where Abraham, the father of all who believe, placed his beloved son, Isaac, on the altar of sacrifice at Mount Moriah, reflecting his absolute faith in God Almighty!

Jerusalem is the city King David conquered over three thousand years ago, making it the eternal capital of Israel!

Jerusalem is where Jeremiah and Isaiah penned the principles of righteousness that became the moral foundations of civilization.

Jerusalem is where a rabbi named Jesus of Nazareth established the covenants of my faith that are chiseled in the depths of my soul.

Jerusalem is where Messiah will rule the earth for one thousand years of perfect peace in the world to come.

Jerusalem is where God Almighty, the King of the universe, will establish His Eternal Throne.

Jerusalem is the city that holds my heart.

When I first prayed at the Western Wall, I stood next to a rabbi who bowed his head at every mention of God's Holy Name. I knew the Lord was listening to his prayer and to mine. At that very moment, I heard the Lord speak to my heart to bring Christians and Jews together in an atmosphere of unconditional love and mutual respect. It was a seemingly impossible task were it not for the help of the Almighty.

I entered Jerusalem a pilgrim . . . and walked out of its gates a Zionist. I believe all that the Holy Scriptures say of Jerusalem and have dedicated my life to sharing these truths with the world.

All of Zion rejoiced as Jerusalem celebrated its Jubilee, and we pray that God's continued favor will be its cherished hope for tomorrow. Yes, this holy place has forever changed my life.

Jerusalem is everlasting, for it is the "port city on the shore of eternity."[1]

CHAPTER 1

ISRAEL— SEVENTY YEARS OF MIRACLES

Great is the LORD, and most worthy of praise, in the city of our God, his holy mountain. Beautiful in its loftiness, the joy of the whole earth . . . Mount Zion, the city of the Great King. (Psalm 48:1–2 NIV)

Ancient charts show Jerusalem as the center of the world, and for the Jewish, Christian, and Islamic faiths, this mapping certainly holds true. Historian Simon Montefiore exquisitely describes this unique city: "Jerusalem is the house of the one God, the capital of two peoples, the temple of three religions and she is the only city to exist twice—in heaven and on earth: the peerless grace of the terrestrial is as nothing to the glories of the celestial."[1]

The Midrash,[2] an ancient commentary on Hebrew Scriptures, states:

The Land of Israel is the center of the world—Jerusalem is the center of the Land—the Holy Temple is the center of Jerusalem—the Holy of Holies is the center of the Holy Temple—the Holy Ark is the center of the Holy of Holies and the Foundation Stone from which the world was established is before the Holy Ark.[3]

Jerusalem is one of the oldest cities in the world, dating back to the fourth century BCE. It is not only an ancient city; *it is a consecrated city*—it is the city of God. Jerusalem has been the spiritual epicenter of the Jewish people since 1010 BCE, when King David danced into the city before the Ark of the Covenant and established it as the capital of the Jewish nation (2 Samuel 6:14–15).

Teddy Kollek, former mayor of Jerusalem, beautifully described this city's connection to the Jewish people:

For three thousand years, Jerusalem has been the center of Jewish hope and longing. No other city has played such a dominant role in the history, culture, religion and consciousness of a people as has Jerusalem in the life of Jewry and Judaism. Throughout centuries of exile, Jerusalem remained alive in the hearts of Jews everywhere as the focal point of Jewish history, the symbol of ancient glory, spiritual fulfillment and modern renewal. This heart and soul of the Jewish people engenders the thought that if you want one simple word to symbolize all of Jewish history, that word would be "Jerusalem."[4]

The sacred Scriptures not only laid the foundation of God's hallowed city—they also foretold its future. Jerusalem is where the

Final Throne will be established, for God declares, *"This is my resting place for ever and ever; here I will sit enthroned, for I have desired it"* (Psalm 132:14 NIV).

During its long history, Jerusalem has been destroyed twice, besieged twenty-three times, attacked fifty-two times, and captured and recaptured forty-four times.[5] But no matter its travailing history, God has future plans for Jerusalem.

> *Again the word of the LORD of hosts came, saying, "Thus says the LORD of hosts: 'I am zealous for Zion with great zeal; with great fervor I am zealous for her.' Thus says the LORD: 'I will return to Zion, and dwell in the midst of Jerusalem. Jerusalem shall be called the City of Truth, the Mountain of the LORD of hosts, The Holy Mountain.'" (Zechariah 8:1–3)*

For more than three thousand years, Israel has been a target for conquest and Jerusalem the reward; and its future is no different. However, another, more important reality holds true—there is a God in heaven who declares, *"I am jealous for Jerusalem and for Zion"* (Zechariah 1:14).

Remember this truth: Jerusalem is the Holy City of the past, present, and future. I have written books surrounding Jerusalem through the years, motivated by biblical prophecy and the city's prominence in world news, and today is no different—Jerusalem is still at the forefront of global events.

The kingdoms of this earth want Israel as their prize—the Kings of the North covet its warm-water ports for its global navy, the Kings of the East are bent on world domination, the Kings of the South seek to control all of God's Covenant Land, and the King of the West aspires to establish his apocalyptic throne there. But there is a King in heaven who protects Jerusalem day and night. And there is room for only one throne—the Eternal Throne of the Living God—the One True God of Abraham, Isaac, and Jacob, and He will share the glory of Jerusalem with no one!

Abrahamic covenant . . . land grant . . . Israel . . . Jerusalem . . . blessing . . . prophecy . . . Gog and Magog . . . Armageddon. Most of us are familiar with the words, but how do they connect, and why are they important to America, to the nations of the world, and to us personally?

My prayer is that the pages of this book will help the reader understand the importance of Israel, Jerusalem, and the Jewish people in the economy of God. There is no doubt that all roads in the future of the world lead to Jerusalem.

The covenant God made with Abraham, Isaac, and Jacob centuries ago exploded on the front pages of every newspaper in the mid-twentieth century on May 14, 1948, as Prime Minister Ben-Gurion announced the State of Israel's rebirth, and Israel still lives today and will do so forevermore!

Shout it from the housetops—"Israel lives . . . Israel lives . . . Israel lives!"

THE PEOPLE OF ISRAEL LIVE

The year 2018 (5778 on the Jewish calendar) marks the seventieth birthday of Israel. The rebirth of modern Israel is one of the greatest miracles of the last century. In fact, the survival of the Jewish people as a culture, still anchored to the same Holy Scriptures, the same language, the same traditions, and the same land for more than three thousand years, might be one of the greatest miracles of all time.[6]

Despite all the tragedies and abuses the Jewish people have suffered, the descendants of Abraham are living and prospering in the land that God promised them in the book of Genesis. Israel's history over the last seventy years has been a continuous demonstration of the Lord's protection and blessing.

The miracle of Israel is perfectly summed up in the Hebrew phrase *Am Yisrael Chai*, which means "the people of Israel live!" Israel and the Jewish people have experienced the adversity of defamation, persecution, dispersal, systematic annihilation, and crushing wars—and they have not only supernaturally survived—they have thrived!

In my opinion, it is symbolically significant that Israel's seventieth anniversary takes place in a year ending in the number 18. The Hebrew word *chai* means life and also represents the number 18. Certain numbers have always held special meaning in Jewish tradition, so we can look at 2018 as symbolizing a *year of life*.

Just seventy years after starting with nothing and with almost no help, Israel is one of the most successful nations on earth. They have built cities out of swamps and transformed the desert into farmland. They have become a global leader in the technological and medical fields. Israel today is healthy, joyful, prosperous, and generous.

The hand of the Almighty has been on the Hebrew nation since day one, and God has used her to bless the nations as He promised Abraham. My hope is that Israel's amazing account will inspire and motivate you to take your place as one of the pivotal players in the greatest human story ever to unfold on the stage of modern time.

EXILE AND RESTORATION

Israel is the only nation in the history of the world that was created by a sovereign act of God. But that didn't happen in 1948. It took place over four thousand years before (2100 BCE), when God spoke to Abraham and made an everlasting covenant with him and his descendants.

The God of Abraham, Isaac, and Jacob very clearly included both the Jewish people and the land of Israel in His covenant.

> *I will make you very fruitful; I will make nations of you, and kings will come from you. I will establish my covenant as an everlasting covenant between me and you and your descendants after you for the generations to come, to be your God and the God of your descendants after you. The whole land of Canaan, where you now reside as a foreigner, I will give as an everlasting possession to you and your descendants after you; and I will be their God. (Genesis 17:6–8 NIV)*

When the Lord used the word *everlasting* to describe His covenant with Israel, He meant it—it stands *forever!* God's land covenant with Abraham and his descendants is mentioned throughout the Bible. This foundational truth is very important for Christians to understand. The God we serve does not break covenant. The Bible says, *"The LORD your God, He is God, the faithful God who keeps covenant and mercy for a thousand generations" (Deuteronomy 7:9).* That's one hundred thousand years when you consider that a generation according to Genesis 15:16 is technically a hundred years. The meaning of this phrase is, "I am the Lord that keeps covenant longer than forever."

> *O seed of Abraham His servant, you children of Jacob, His chosen ones! He is the LORD our God; His judgments are in all the earth. He remembers His covenant forever, the word which He commanded, for a thousand generations, the covenant which He made with Abraham, and His oath to Isaac, and confirmed it to Jacob for a statute, to Israel as an everlasting covenant, saying, "To you I will give the land of Canaan as the allotment of your inheritance." (Psalms 105:6–11)*

When God gave Abraham, and his descendants, through Isaac, the title deed to the land of Israel, it was never revoked. But through the centuries that followed, the Jewish people were driven from their land and scattered among the nations of the world in what is called the *diaspora*, referring to the Jewish people living outside of the land of Israel.

Yet despite the fact that many of the Jews were forced into exile through the centuries by the Assyrians in 722 BCE, the Babylonians in 587 BCE and the Romans in the year 70 CE, they always maintained a presence in their historic homeland. Even though the Jewish people were not always in political control of the land and were not always the majority of the land's population, they have lived in Israel continuously from the time of Joshua's conquest more than 3,500 years ago (1500 BCE) until the present day.[7]

During thousands of years of exile and suffering, the chosen people never lost the hope of returning home. And they clung to God's many promises given to the Hebrew prophets that one day the children of Israel would be restored to Zion and reclaim their inheritance.

The Jewish people base their right to the land of Israel on biblical and historical facts:

- First and foremost, God promised the land to the patriarch Abraham through an irrevocable covenant recorded in Genesis 12:1–3; 15:18.
- Second, the Jewish people settled and developed the land as described by the prophet Jeremiah (Jeremiah 24:6; 42:10).
- Finally, the international community granted political sovereignty to the Jewish people through the Balfour Declaration in 1917; the United Nations partition resolution of 1947; and Israel's recognition as a sovereign ation on May 14, 1948, fulfilling the prophecy recorded in Isaiah 66:8, 22.

The appointed time for the rebirth of Israel had come at last. As promised throughout Scripture, God's mighty hand began to gather the exiles back to their Promised Land:

Remember, I pray, the word that You commanded Your servant Moses, saying, "If you are unfaithful, I will scatter you among the nations; but if you return to Me, and keep My commandments and do them, though some of you were cast out to the farthest part of the heavens, yet I will gather them from there, and bring them to the place which I have chosen as a dwelling for My name." (Nehemiah 1:8–9)

The LORD builds up Jerusalem; He gathers together the outcasts of Israel. He heals the brokenhearted and binds up their wounds. (Psalms 147:2–3)

"Therefore behold, the days are coming," says the LORD, "that it shall no more be said, 'The LORD lives who brought the children of Israel from the land of Egypt,' but, 'The LORD lives who brought up the children of Israel from the land from the north and from all the lands where He had driven them.' For I will bring them back into their land which I gave to their fathers." (Jeremiah 16:14–15)

Thus says the Lord GOD: "When I have gathered the house of Israel from the peoples among whom they are scattered, and am hallowed in them in the sight of the Gentiles, then they will dwell in their own land which I gave to My servant Jacob. And they will dwell safely there, build houses, and plant vineyards; yes, they will dwell securely, when I execute judgments on all those around them who despise them. Then they shall know that I am the LORD their God." (Ezekiel 28:25–26)

INDEPENDENCE (1948)

After thirty years of promises from the British and other world leaders, in 1947 the Jewish people finally received formal approval from the United Nations General Assembly for the re-creation of an independent Jewish state in the land of Israel. According to the UN's partition plan, the Jews would receive a tiny fraction of the land originally set aside for them by previous agreements.

UN Resolution 181 passed on November 29, 1947. Hesitant yet desperate Jewish leaders accepted the offer of these disjointed scraps of land, and as the news spread, overjoyed Jewish families danced in the streets. However, irate Arab leaders rejected the partition plan and instigated months of attacks against their Jewish neighbors while preparations for statehood went forward.

On May 14, 1948, David Ben-Gurion proclaimed Israel's official independence. Eleven minutes later, President Harry Truman of the United States was the first world leader to officially recognize the newborn state of Israel. In that historic moment, God miraculously restored the land of Israel to His people and the ancient prophecy was fulfilled: *"Who has ever heard of such things? Who has ever seen things like this? Can a country be born in a day or a nation be brought forth in a moment? Yet no sooner is Zion in labor than she gives birth to her children"* (Isaiah 66:8 NIV).

However, the celebration was short-lived. The next day, five Arab armies attacked Israel. Short on manpower, resources, and with almost no international assistance, Israel inexplicably survived and even gained ground. But independence came at a great cost. Israel lost 6,373 people in the war, nearly 1 percent of its entire population.[8]

After more than a year of fighting, the Arab nations made armistice agreements with Israel and withdrew. For the first time in nearly two thousand years, since the 70 CE diaspora, the Jewish people could return to their God-given national home.

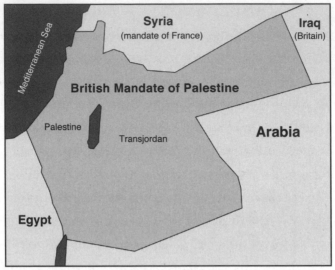

Map of British Mandate (1917)

Map of UN Partition (1947)

BUILDING A NATION (1949 TO 1967)

Israel grew quickly as Jewish immigrants flooded back to their homeland from around the world. Jews who had suffered in post–World War II refugee camps were finally allowed to leave Europe. The survivors of the Holocaust brought a wealth of skills and knowledge to the reborn state, but very little else.

At the same time, the surrounding Arab nations were so enraged by Israel's existence that they began harshly persecuting and evicting their Jewish citizens. More than 850,000 Jewish refugees from the Middle East and North Africa were forced to flee the communities where they had lived for nearly 2,600 years. These families lost all they owned, their homes, their possessions, their ancestral heritage, and their religious artifacts—everything had to be left behind.[9]

Some of the Jewish refugees went to North America or Europe, but it was Israel that opened its doors to welcome them home. Those that immigrated to the Promised Land were bound together by their divine destiny and desire to pioneer a barren land, and they were unified by the resurrection of the ancient Hebrew language that had been modernized by Eliezer Ben-Yehuda during the late nineteenth century.

The Jewish people formed collaborative farming communities known as *kibbutzim*, where they worked together to transform the arid land into green fields. An Israeli pioneer invented the world's first drip irrigation system and revolutionized not only Israel's agricultural industry but also transformed how farmers all over the world irrigated their crops.

Much of the country was desert, and Israel faced a severe shortage of water for drinking, agriculture, and industry. Finding a way to get a reliable source of water to all of its cities and farms was critical. In 1964, the government completed a massive project to transport water from the Sea of Galilee in the north to the center of the country and the southern communities in the Negev.

Through the Lord's blessings, and with hard work, determination, and ingenuity, Israel flourished and grew stronger. Once again, the Jewish people participated in the fulfillment of biblical prophecy: *"The wilderness and the wasteland shall be glad for them, and the desert shall rejoice and blossom as the rose" (Isaiah 35:1).* Yet peace remained elusive, as its Arab neighbors continued to brazenly threaten Israel with annihilation.

THE SIX DAY WAR (1967)

Increasing terrorist attacks along their borders plagued Israelis for years. Arab leaders spoke openly of their desire to wipe Israel off the map and to massacre every Jewish man, woman, and child. Syria threatened Israel's water supply from the Jordan River, leading to a military confrontation with Israel in April of 1967. The Syrians then called on their ally Egypt to attack Israel, and in May Egyptian troops expelled UN forces stationed in the Sinai Desert and closed off Israel's access to shipping routes. Israel's allies in Europe and the United States refused to intervene and warned Israel not to start a war, even though the Jewish state faced an invasion of nearly half a million Arab troops positioned along every border.

Yet, by June 1, it was clear that if Israel did nothing, the Arab armies on its borders would wipe them out. Lebanon, Jordan, and Iraq joined Syria and Egypt in preparations to fight Israel. The Jewish people spent anxious weeks in preparation for the slaughter they knew was forthcoming.

Then, in the early morning of June 5, Israel's air force launched a surprise attack on Egypt's airfield and destroyed airplanes parked on the ground. Israel continued to fight and win astonishing victories over its enemy's armies for five more days. But it was the battle for Jerusalem that became the pivotal moment that defined modern Israeli history.

Israel had lost the eastern half of Jerusalem during the 1948 war for independence. The Old City, where Jews had lived continuously, even under foreign rule since the Romans sacked the city in 70 CE, was captured by Jordan. All Jews were forced out of their homes, and none were allowed to visit the Temple Mount or the Western Wall. The holiest site in the world for the Jewish people was taken from them, and for more than nineteen years, they mourned their profound loss.

Initially, Israel had no intention of fighting against Jordan to recapture eastern Jerusalem. But when King Hussein ignored Israel's pleas to stay out of the war, Israeli paratroopers stormed into the Old City on June 7. Within four hours, Israel had retaken control of the Temple Mount, and the world witnessed young Israel Defense Force (IDF) soldiers weep as they touched the Western Wall for the first time in their lives.

Brigadier General Shlomo Goren, who later became the Chief Rabbi of Israel, sounded the *shofar* and led his troops in prayer. There at the Western Wall, Israel's soldiers jubilantly rededicated Jerusalem to the Lord and mournfully remembered the lives they'd lost to liberate the Holy City. IDF Commander Motta Gur issued these words to his troops:

> For some two thousand years the Temple Mount was forbidden to the Jews. Until you came—you, the paratroopers— and returned it to the bosom of the nation. The Western Wall, for which every heart beats, is ours once again. Many Jews have taken their lives into their hands throughout our long history, in order to reach Jerusalem and live here. Endless words of longing have expressed the deep yearning for Jerusalem that beats within the Jewish heart. You have been given the great privilege of completing the circle,

of returning to the nation its capital and its holy center. Jerusalem is yours forever.[10]

By the end of the Six Day War, Israel had captured enough land to triple its size. Most of it they would eventually and willingly exchange for peace agreements, but Jerusalem was too precious to give up or divide. After years of separation, the Jewish people again had access to their holiest sites. Under Israeli authority, Jerusalem was made safe for people of all faiths to live in and freely worship according to their own traditions.

The land of Israel gained during the Six Day War included the Sinai Peninsula, the Golan Heights in the north, the Gaza Strip, and the ancient biblical heartland of Judea and Samaria. This miraculous victory transformed the way the world saw Israel, and the way Israelis saw themselves. No longer was the Jewish state seen as weak, and Israel's enemies were not only humiliated—they were furious.

This stunning victory came at a steep price. Israel lost 777 soldiers, and 2,586 more were wounded in the battle. This number may seem small, but proportionate to Israel's total population it is on par with the number of casualties the United States faced during eight years of the Vietnam War.[11]

THREE NO'S

Although Israel had decisively won the Six Day War, almost immediately the Israeli government offered to give up the vast majority of its newly acquired territory in exchange for peace.

On June 19, 1967, Israel offered to return the Sinai Peninsula to Egypt and the Golan Heights to Syria. Despite the immense economic benefits and strategic military value of controlling these territories, Israel was willing to sacrifice this prized land if the Arabs would agree to accept Israel's right to exist. However, the Arab leaders were in no mood to negotiate. Stung by their shaming defeat and outraged by the suggestion that Jews had a right to live *anywhere* in the land, they immediately rejected Israel's offer of a permanent peace treaty.

Consequently, at the Arab League's Khartoum Conference in Sudan, the league adopted an official position against Israel that included the infamous Three No's:

NO Peace
NO Recognition
NO Negotiation

For twelve years, the Three No's prevented all peace efforts, and to this day, they are still major obstacles to establishing peace between Israel and many of its neighbors.[12]

LAND FOR PEACE

The outcome of the Six Day War not only angered the Arabs, the United Nations also viewed Israel's control of its new territories with disapproval. Since the beginning of time, nations have recognized the right of the victors in war to retain control of territory justly won in battle. Nevertheless, the United Nations decided that this was no longer valid, and on November 22, 1967, the Security Council passed Resolution 242.

This resolution became the foundation for all future efforts to influence peace between Israel and the Arabs. It called on Israel to trade land it had won in the 1967 war for peace agreements, and it called on the Arab states to recognize Israel's right to exist.

Israel has consistently shown its willingness to trade land for peace; in stark contrast, Arab-Palestinian rejection has consistently undermined efforts to end the conflict. The Palestinian leadership has yet to truly accept Israel's existence as a nation.

Even during negotiations, the Palestinians continuously seek to find a way to destroy Israel. For example, Palestinians claim that Arabs who left the fledgling state of Israel in 1948—and all of their descendants—have a "right" to return to the land of Israel (which they refer to as Palestine). Such would end the Jewish character of the Jewish state. In addition, as you'll read later, even when Israel made dramatic and painful offers of peace, or unilaterally sought to disengage from the Palestinians, violence and obstinacy are all the Israelis got in return.

Until the Palestinians accept that Israel has a right to exist as the Jewish state, no international pronouncement will serve to advance an end to the conflict.

YOM KIPPUR WAR (1973)

It was Saturday, October 6, 1973, in Israel. The country was quiet and focused on observing the Day of Atonement, the holiest day in Judaism. Suddenly the solemn and sacred atmosphere was shattered.

Catching the IDF unaware while many soldiers observed Yom Kippur, Egypt and Syria attacked Israel simultaneously on two fronts. Less than 500 Israeli soldiers faced an overwhelming force of 600,000 Egyptians in the south, while in the north, 180 Israeli tanks defended the country against 1,400 Syrian tanks. US president Richard Nixon, motivated by fears of an Arab victory backed by the Soviet Union, authorized a massive emergency airlift of weapons to Israel on October 12.

Though vastly outnumbered, Israel shocked the world by surviving the initial attacks and rallying to push the invaders back across the borders. Eighteen days after Egypt and Syria first attacked Israel, the Arab leaders agreed to a cease-fire rather than suffer further losses. Israel won the Yom Kippur War, but 2,688 Israeli soldiers sacrificed their lives to protect the Jewish homeland. It was an agonizing price to pay.

Angered and stunned by yet another miraculous Israeli victory, the Arab world realized that conventional warfare against Israel was not working. They changed their strategy, and sought to isolate Israel from sympathetic foreign governments by declaring an oil embargo against the West. The oil crisis lasted from October 1973 until March 1974.

The embargo worked, and nations began altering their policies toward Israel. This model of economic and diplomatic warfare became the basis for the anti-Israel BDS (Boycott, Divestment, and Sanctions) movement around the world.

Foreign affair attitudes grew increasingly hostile and irrational toward Israel after the Yom Kippur War. Then, in November of 1975, the United Nations General Assembly took it one step too far and declared that Zionism was a form of racism. It labeled the Israeli government as the *racist occupier and oppressor* of the Palestinian people.[13]

Israel was accused of being akin to the apartheid regime in South Africa, and this smear campaign did lasting damage to Israel's international reputation. The UN finally revoked this hateful and undeserved resolution (UNGA 3379) in 1991; nevertheless, Israel is still repeatedly singled out by the United Nations for more condemnation than any other country.

PEACE WITH EGYPT (1979)

Israel's first peace treaty with an Arab state began with Egyptian president Anwar Sadat's visit to Jerusalem in 1977. Sadat shocked and enraged the Arab world by standing in the Knesset and declaring that he sought peace between Egypt and Israel. Israel's prime minister, Menachem Begin, received this pronouncement in good faith and began making difficult, often unpopular moves to achieve peace.

The Camp David Accords took place as a series of meetings in the United States during the Carter presidency in the fall of 1978. The administration sought worldwide support for the negotiations and asked religious leaders to pray for success. Finally, a peace treaty between Egypt and Israel was signed on March 26, 1979.[14]

The concessions Israel made for peace were painful. Menachem Begin agreed to return 91 percent of the territory it had won in the Six Day War to Egypt, and willingly gave up the strategic and economic benefits of the Sinai Peninsula. But peace with Egypt was the first step in achieving the peace and security Israel's people had sought for decades.

Menachem Begin and Anwar Sadat were awarded the Nobel Peace Prize in 1978 for their courage in participating in the Camp David Accords. Unfortunately, the Arab League rejected Sadat's actions. Just two years after making peace with Israel, members of the Egyptian Islamic Jihad would assassinate Sadat.[15]

A *fatwa*, which is a religious ruling authorized by an Islamic ruler, sanctioned Sadat's murder. This fatwa was directed by Omar Abdel-Rahman, known in the United States as the "Blind Sheikh." Rahman was sentenced in 1995 to life in prison by a US court for being part of "an organization whose aim was to wage jihad, or holy war, of terror against the United States."[16]

OPERATION BABYLON (1981)

Israel watched Saddam Hussein's attempts to acquire nuclear weapons with alarm for many years while the world looked the other way. France helped Iraq build research facilities, and resisted Israel's urgent warnings that Saddam Hussein intended to use nuclear weapons to perpetrate a nuclear holocaust against Israel. Pleas for help to the Italians also fell on deaf ears.

America's defense secretary, Caspar Weinberger, and secretary of state, Alexander Haig, agreed with the Israeli assessment of the Iraqi nuclear program's goal of destroying Israel, but the United States refused to act.[17] Despite estimates that Iraq was only five to ten years away from acquiring nuclear weapons, and some reports saying that Saddam could have the bomb within a year, world leaders would not take the threat seriously.

Israel did not have the luxury of hoping for the best. Past experience had proven that when an Arab dictator declared he intended to wipe Israel off the map, it was not an empty threat. History had also confirmed that Israel could not rely on any of its allies, even the United States, to intervene on its behalf when it came time for war.

After Israeli intelligence confirmed Iraq would complete the bomb within a year, Prime Minister Begin ordered a covert strike on the Osirak reactor. On June 7, 1981, fourteen F-15s and F-16s flew at low altitude over enemy airspace and launched a surprise attack on the nuclear facility. It was over in less than two minutes.[18] Immediately, a firestorm of criticism erupted around the globe. The United States was furious, and voted for a United Nations Security Council resolution condemning Israel for the attack.

While watching the news coverage at home, I grew extremely frustrated with the worldwide outrage over Israel's strike on the Iraqi nuclear plant. I was so irritated that I decided to do something revolutionary by planning the first Night to Honor Israel. To my surprise, the local Jewish community was skeptical of my offer of support—they believed I had a hidden agenda.

A gesture of unconditional love and support had never been extended before, but thanks to the courage of a righteous orthodox rabbi, the Jewish community agreed to the event. Despite death threats and harsh opposition from many bigots, I went forward and hosted the Night to Honor Israel with the backing of my family, our church, and my newfound friend, Rabbi Aryeh Scheinberg.

On the appointed night of September 10, 1981, the crowd of Christians and Jews that gathered at the Lila Cockrell Theater in downtown San Antonio experienced a divine sense of brotherhood. To demonstrate our support, the Christians in the room raised $10,000 and presented the gift to Israel's Hadassah Hospital. As Rabbi Scheinberg gave the final benediction, the director of security quietly informed me that they had just received a bomb threat to the building.

No bomb went off that night in San Antonio—instead, a new movement exploded within our hearts. Since that historic night, Rabbi Scheinberg and I, along with the help of thousands of Christians and Jews in cities around the country, have held hundreds of Night to Honor Israel events for over thirty-eight years. It is my great privilege to report that through our united efforts, Christians United for Israel is now hosting over thirty pro-Israel events every month throughout our great nation in churches, on college campuses, and within local communities.

FIRST LEBANON WAR (1982)

Lebanon has long been a safe harbor for terrorist groups such as the Palestine Liberation Organization (PLO) and Hezbollah. The PLO was created in 1964 during the Arab League Summit in Cairo, Egypt, with the alleged purpose of the "liberation of Palestine." In reality, its main objective was the destruction of the nation of Israel through acts of terror.

In 1978, PLO terrorists penetrated the northern border of Israel and murdered thirty-nine innocent victims, thirteen of which were children. After this attack and others like them, Israeli forces crossed into southern Lebanon, pushing the terrorists back from the border, but to no avail—the terror war continued.

Even after the United States helped broker a cease-fire agreement in 1981, the PLO repeatedly violated the truce and continued to build their forces and increase their arsenal while killing Israelis along the way. During the eleven-month "cease-fire" period, Israel endured 270 PLO terror attacks that killed twenty-nine Israelis and injured more than three hundred people.[19]

In June 1982, the IDF moved into Lebanon to drive out the Palestinian terrorists through "Operation Peace for Galilee." Secretary of State Henry Kissinger under President Ronald Reagan defended the Israeli operation: "No sovereign state can tolerate indefinitely the buildup along its borders of a military force dedicated to its destruction and implementing its objectives by periodic shellings and raids."[20]

The war in Lebanon was fought on two fronts—on the ground and in the media. Despite a series of attempted cease-fires by the Israelis, the PLO orchestrated assaults that generated required responses from the IDF. Unfortunately, the world press chose to accept the PLO's spin and blamed Israel—rather than the provocateurs—for the violence.

For the first time since Israel's rebirth as a nation, there was a civil debate on the war, and as a result of the extreme internal dispute, Israel pulled most of its troops out of Lebanon in 1985. Despite Israel's voluntary withdrawal, its civilians continued to suffer terror attacks along the Lebanese border.[21]

During the clashes between Israel and the PLO in the early '80s, Hezbollah (the party of god) gained strength and took root in southern Lebanon with the financial and military backing of Iran. Hezbollah later published an "open letter" identifying the United

States as one of Islam's principal enemies and called for the "obliteration" of Israel.

OPERATION MOSES (1984)

Israel's Knesset passed an extraordinary law in 1950 that essentially defined the nation's fundamental purpose: "Every Jew has the right to immigrate to this country . . ." This Law of Return established that all Jews everywhere are entitled to Israeli citizenship. After the rebirth of the nation of Israel, the two thousand years of wandering was officially over.

In 1975, Israel's Chief Rabbinate recognized the Ethiopian Jewish community's status as Jews, which entitled them to the Law of Return, giving them the right to immigrate to Israel. For three thousand years, these displaced Jews had been faithful to the Torah and Jewish customs handed down to them by their ancestors. After Israel became a state, they desperately wanted to join their Jewish brothers and sisters in the Holy Land.

There was a problem, however. Ethiopia forbade the Jews to leave. Unwilling to accept their government's decision, thousands of Ethiopian Jews secretly traveled to the Sudanese border and waited for transport to Israel. The journey was dangerous, and many died along the way. Reports reached Israel that thousands of Ethiopian Jews were dying, and Israel decided to mount a rescue mission.

On November 21, 1984, the Mossad, Israel's national intelligence agency, collaborated with the CIA and the Sudanese National Intelligence and Security Service to covertly smuggle nearly eight thousand Ethiopian Jews out of Sudan. Over seven weeks, cargo planes made more than thirty secret flights to pick up the refugees while Israel clandestinely paid Sudanese officials to look the other way.[22]

Operation Moses gave thousands of Ethiopian Jews the hope of a new life in Israel and fulfilled three thousand years of longing to be reunited with their spiritual homeland. Today, after two more rescue operations in 1991 and again in 2010, there are over 140,000 Ethiopian Jews living and thriving in Israel, fulfilling the words of the Lord through the prophet Zechariah:

Thus says the LORD of hosts: "Behold, I will save My people from the land of the east and from the land of the west; I will bring them back, and they shall dwell in the midst of Jerusalem. They shall be My people and I will be their God, in truth and righteousness." (Zechariah 8:7–8)

FIRST PALESTINIAN INTIFADA (1987)

A four-year period of violence and terrorism broke out in December 1987 after deliberate misinformation was spread in Gaza that Israel had killed four Palestinians in retaliation for the stabbing death of an Israeli. Huge riots soon broke out among the Palestinians, and each additional death added fuel to the fire. In the eyes of the international community, as in times past, Israel was seen as the guilty party and was harshly condemned for using necessary force in an attempt to quell the terrorism.

Enemy propaganda continued to circulate that Israel was murdering Palestinians. The UN investigated and determined the stories were false, but the damage had been done. The *intifada* (Arabic for violent uprising) continued to grow, and the IDF reported hundreds of attacks, including bombings and shootings. What was reported in the world press as spontaneous mob violence was soon revealed to have been orchestrated and encouraged by the PLO, led by Yasser Arafat.

To make matters worse, at the height of the intifada, King Hussein of Jordan decided to sever "administrative and legal" ties with the West Bank (Judea and Samaria). This created an instant refugee problem with over one million Palestinian Arabs losing their Jordanian citizenship overnight. King Hussein explained his decision as one of deference to Yasser Arafat and his desire for national autonomy.[23] Arafat did not care about the welfare of his own people. He did not care how many suffered in the death camps that he helped create—he only cared about making the world believe it was Israel's fault.

Meanwhile, the intifada became its own worst enemy. Many of the victims were themselves Palestinian targeted by their own people who accused them of collaborating with Israel. The murder rate grew, and the Palestinian leadership could not put out the fire they had started. Arafat was losing control, and a more extreme ideological organization was emerging.

One such militant group to emerge was Hamas. It was backed by the Egyptian Muslim Brotherhood and was not interested in a secular nationalist movement. Hamas's intent was to create an Islamist society of religious extremists engaged in a *jihad* (Arabic for holy war) against the Jews.

OSLO ACCORDS (1993)

Israel's success in trading land for peace with Egypt led them to believe they could accomplish the same thing with the Palestinians. Yasser Arafat had announced a plan for a two-state solution in 1988, and in 1993, Israel began secret negotiations with the PLO.

Israel and the Palestinian leaders worked on a plan to divide the West Bank, an area known to Jews and Christians by its biblical name of Judea and Samaria. In the years since 1967, Jewish pioneers had built towns in Judea and Samaria, and Israel's leaders wanted most of them to become part of the nation in any final peace accord. Under this plan, the united city of Jerusalem would also remain in Israel. After eight months of peace talks, Israel and the Palestinian leadership reached an agreement.

Israeli prime minister Shimon Peres and PLO chairman Yasser Arafat signed the Oslo Accord in September 1993. Arafat recognized Israel's right to exist and renounced terrorism, and Peres agreed to recognize the PLO as the leader of the Palestinian government. Under these terms, they pledged to continue seeking a solution for the conflict.

The success of the accords encouraged Jordan to negotiate its own separate peace treaty with Israel. As a result, a final peace treaty was signed and a cooperative relationship was formed between Jordan and Israel in October 1994.

A second round of talks between Israel and the Palestinians, known as Oslo II, took place in 1995. The two parties agreed to a temporary system of government for the Palestinian Authority (PA) that still gave Israel security control over strategic areas. The agreement was supposed to expire in 1999, but the peace process stalled and the temporary arrangement has hung in limbo for almost twenty years.

Although Yasser Arafat told Israel and the United States that he had renounced violence and recognized Israel's right to exist peacefully, he told Arab audiences that these negotiations were just a mechanism to buy time and gain a better position from which to launch future attacks. During the period after the Oslo Accords between September 1993 and September 2000, terrorists killed nearly three hundred Israelis.[24] Trust between Israel and the Palestinians broke down, and peace remained out of reach once again.

BECOMING A GLOBAL POWERHOUSE (1990S)

Despite decades of war and terrorism, by the 1990s Israel had become a global powerhouse of innovation. As a tiny nation dependent on making the most out of every resource, Israel, by necessity, developed a philosophy of creativity and collaboration.

Israel's government changed its economic policies in the 1980s to provide funding and incentives for startup companies and inventors. Government investment in the private sector led to a boom in high-tech innovation. By providing the venture capital for inventors but allowing private individuals the freedom to manage their work unhindered, Israel unleashed a powerful growth engine.

During the '90s, Israel also experienced a huge wave of Russian immigration as Jews fled the former USSR after the fall of the Iron Curtain. The Israeli government invested in programs to provide the skilled engineers and scientists from Russia with the resources they needed to become entrepreneurs in Israel. These programs eventually expanded and included Israelis of all backgrounds. Israel's high-tech industry produced several inventions during this period that would change the way the whole world functioned.

A group of three young computer programmers created the world's first commercial firewall software in 1993. Their virus protection technology soon grew into one of the world's leading cybersecurity companies. Another invention that came out of Israel in 1998, the PillCam, revolutionized the way doctors diagnosed patients. Considered common today, this ingestible camera gave doctors a video recording of the intestinal tract.

Because Israel was compelled to develop its own infrastructure so quickly, it was and is uniquely equipped to aid developing countries with innovations in agriculture, water management, education, medicine, and other areas of need. In addition, as Israel's economy grew, the Jewish state began looking for ways to reach out to the rest of the world with humanitarian aid.

In 1994, Israel provided medical aid for Rwandan refugees. Since 1995, Israeli doctors, through Save a Child's Heart, have provided free, lifesaving heart operations to over 4,500 children from around the world. Half of these patients are from the Palestinian Authority,

Iraq, Jordan, and other Arab nations. In 1998, Israel gave medical aid to flood victims in Central America and aided Turkish earthquake victims in 1999. Israel became the world's first responder in many major disasters. The promise of Genesis 12:3 stands.

CAMP DAVID SUMMIT (2000)

Having successfully brokered the Oslo Accords, US president Bill Clinton was eager to try again for an Israeli-Palestinian peace agreement before the end of his last term in office. Israeli prime minister Ehud Barak and PLO chairman Yasser Arafat accepted Clinton's invitation to a summit at Camp David in July 2000.

Barak offered Arafat 91 percent of Judea and Samaria (the West Bank) and 100 percent of the Gaza Strip for a Palestinian state. He even offered the Palestinians sovereignty over the Arab neighborhoods in Jerusalem, a plan that would divide the very heart of Israel and cause great emotional pain to the Jewish people. Arafat refused the offer, and gave no terms of his own that he would be willing to accept. The two-week summit ended without a deal.

SECOND PALESTINIAN
INTIFADA (2000)

After the 1967 war, Israel immediately granted control of the Temple Mount to the Arab Muslim religious authorities in Jordan and restricted their own access to the area. This action prohibited the Jewish people from praying at the Temple Mount, which is Judaism's holiest site since King Solomon built it in 957 BCE. The heartbreaking gesture by the Israeli government was extended to avoid a religious war over access to two Islamic sites on the Temple Mount: the Al-Aqsa Mosque and the Dome of the Rock, which were established in the seventh century CE. This status quo has been in effect for over fifty years.

I cannot overemphasize all the sacrifices Israel has made in exchange for the mere possibility of living in peace with its Arab Muslim neighbors. The sacredness of the Temple Mount in Judaism is based on Genesis 22:2 and 2 Chronicles 3:1. It is where Abraham prepared to offer his son Isaac to God (2054 BCE). King David later purchased this biblical threshing floor for fifty shekels in 1000 BCE (2 Samuel 24:18–25), and it is the location of Solomon's Temple (967 BCE).[25] One day it will be the home of the final temple during the Millennium.

In September 2000, Ariel Sharon visited the Temple Mount in Jerusalem after receiving permission and assurance from the head of the Palestinian Preventive Security Organization, who said, "If Mr. Sharon refrains from entering the mosques on Temple Mount, there will not be any problem."

Nevertheless, even with official Palestinian consent, Sharon's visit was used as a pretext by the PA to spark violent riots among the Palestinians. Yasser Arafat instigated the riots and planned the intifada in advance. In fact, there were reports that the violence had begun before Sharon entered the Temple Mount. In November, the US sent a committee to Israel to investigate the root of the uprising, and in April 2001, the Mitchell Report concluded that the intifada had *not* been caused by Sharon's visit to the Temple Mount.[26]

This intifada was more deadly than the first due to the radical increase of suicide bombings. No one was safe. Over one thousand Israelis were murdered over the next six years through various acts of terror. This compelled Israel to build a security barrier in 2002, through Jerusalem and parts of Judea and Samaria, to protect innocent civilians from sniper fire and suicide bombers.

In spite of the security barrier's obvious necessity, pro-Palestinian propagandists managed to convince many in the media and the international community that the fence was a burden to ordinary

Palestinians. Anti-Israel activists oversimplified the issue and labeled the life-saving security barrier an "apartheid wall."[27]

The United States tried to broker a peace agreement that would stop the unrelenting terror. At the beginning of this intifada, in December 2000, Prime Minister Ehud Barak accepted a proposal from President Clinton that was even more generous to the Palestinians than what had been offered at Camp David five months earlier. Once again, Arafat said no.

After Arafat's refusal to make peace, the United States, the European Union, Russia, and the United Nations formed a mediating body called the "Quartet." In 2002, without consulting Israel, the Quartet created the "Road Map to Peace" and laid out a process based on the land for peace scheme.[28] The Road Map to Peace failed, but Israel's security fence succeeded. In 2002, there were forty-seven suicide bombings; by 2006, this number dramatically dropped to three.

WITHDRAWAL FROM GAZA (2005)

From its rebirth Israel has held true to the fundamental goal to live in harmony with its Arab neighbors. Establishing peace is not only part of the foundation of Jewish tradition; it is also a "declared policy of the State of Israel," and it has come at a great price.[29]

In an attempt to ease tensions with the Palestinians, Prime Minister Ariel Sharon initiated a Disengagement Plan in 2005, which called for Israel's unilateral withdrawal from the Gaza Strip and northern Samaria. The plan's dual purpose was to increase Israel's security and create yet another opportunity for peace with the Palestinians. Sharon believed that in order for this peace initiative to work, it required the great sacrifice of the over nine thousand people who lived in the twenty-five settlements located in Gaza

These brave families who had worked hard for generations to

establish a good and prosperous life abandoned their homes and livelihoods at the mandate of the Israeli government. Israeli ambassador to the United States, Daniel Ayalon, called the Disengagement Plan a "test for the Palestinian leadership."[30]

Hamas met Israel's sacrificial gesture of faith and goodwill in the peace process with the immediate takeover of Gaza. Hamas had no interest in a peace agreement, and used its new political power and strategic position on Israel's border to begin launching daily rocket attacks into Israeli cities. This hardened many Israelis on the idea of exchanging land for peace.

Hamas's unrestrained domination of the Gaza Strip has haunted Israelis and Gazans ever since. Their unrelenting pursuit of evil has led to tremendous suffering on both sides of the border. Hamas terrorists divert humanitarian resources away from the Gazan people to buy weapons, build bunkers, and dig tunnels for their continued and escalated war with Israel. Needless to say, the Palestinians failed the "test case for peace."

SECOND LEBANON WAR (2006)

On July 12, 2006, Hezbollah crossed the Lebanese-Israeli border and ambushed an IDF patrol. They killed eight soldiers and kidnapped two others. In the ensuing conflict, Israel bombed known Hezbollah strongholds while the terrorists launched rockets at Israel's northern population centers. For nearly five weeks, Hezbollah launched more than one hundred rockets per day into Israel. Anxious Israeli families slept in their bomb shelters.

To make this onslaught of terror even more difficult to engage, the IDF faced a cowardly enemy who purposely hid among the civilian population in Lebanon. The terrorists stored their weapons in private homes and fired their rockets from neighborhoods filled with women and children. Knowing that Israel values all human life, Hezbollah used the Arab people as human shields. This barbaric tactic became their signature.[31]

Israel was under intense international pressure and criticism for the unavoidable civilian deaths. By divine arrangement, Christians United for Israel had formed in February of that year. Over 3,600 CUFI members descended on Washington, DC, for our first summit at the exact time this war broke out. We were able to meet with members of Congress and urge them to support Israel against the tidal wave of international condemnation. It was a time when Israel desperately needed friends, and by the grace of God, we were ready to speak out during Israel's hour of need.

The war ended with a cease-fire on August 11, 2006. Israel withdrew without destroying Hezbollah; nonetheless, the IDF was able to severely cripple their operations in Lebanon. Sadly, the Second Lebanon War took the lives of 164 Israelis.

Two years later, Hezbollah released the bodies of the two kidnapped IDF soldiers captured at the start of the war in a prisoner exchange for five known terrorists, one of which was Samir Kuntar. Kuntar was convicted of viciously murdering four Israelis, including a father and his four-year-old daughter.[32] After his release from prison, Kuntar received Syria's highest medal and was honored by Iranian president Mahmoud Ahmadinejad while Israel grieved the loss of their fallen soldiers.[33] Kuntar later played an operational role, with the assistance of Iran and Syria, in "building up Hezbollah's terrorist infrastructure in the Golan Heights."[34]

OPERATION CAST LEAD (2008)

After three years of sustained rocket fire from Gaza, Israel's citizens had had enough. The IDF entered Gaza on December 27, 2008.

Hindered by Gaza's dense population and the fact that Hamas terrorists hid among the civilians, the IDF faced a huge challenge.

Hamas launched many of its rockets from schools, hospitals, and buildings owned by the United Nations. When Israel retaliated, the biased international media focused on stories about Israel bombing schools instead of blaming the terrorists for using human shields— once again, the propaganda war focused on vilifying the Jewish people.

To save as many innocent lives as possible, Israel voluntarily gave up the strategic advantage of surprise. The IDF sent voicemail messages and fliers in Arabic to thousands of Gazan residents before sending in an air strike. This gave civilians time to evacuate, but also warned the terrorists to escape. During the operation, Israel lost nine soldiers.[35]

Still, a new day had dawned for the pro-Israel movement— during the three weeks of fighting, CUFI staff and lay leadership organized multiple events around the country to draw attention to Israel's extraordinary efforts to save innocent lives. While Israel was being hammered in the media, Christians United for Israel was able to rally support in American communities and on college campuses.

HIGH-TECH ISRAEL

Fueled by the lucrative startup boom in previous years, Israel's high-tech industry took off in the first decade of the new century. The successful entrepreneurs of the 1990s became venture capitalists themselves and began investing in the next generation of promising ideas. Foreign investment in Israeli startups also increased as industry leaders around the world recognized the value of Israel's scientific, medical, and high-tech advancements.

Flash drive technology was invented in Israel, and after its release in 2000, this new data storage system was quickly adopted by every nation in the world. One of the most popular navigation smartphone apps, Waze, was developed in Israel in 2008. Millions of people in major cities all around the world now use this app to track the flow of traffic and find the best route to their destination. Google, which has operated a research and development (R&D) center in Israel since the mid-2000s, purchased Waze for $1.1 billion and helped spur global interest in Israeli startup companies.

Google's partnership with Israel has been profitable. Its six-hundred-employee research center in Tel Aviv created Google's "autocomplete" search engine feature. Another tech giant, Microsoft, operates R&D centers in Haifa and Herzliya, where computer scientists developed motion-sensing cameras and facial-recognition software.

The medical and technological advancements coming out of Israel are remarkable. They are at the forefront of major health breakthroughs such as discovering a compound that disables cancer cells, developing the world's first bone implant, and creating an artificial cornea. Israel is literally inventing ways to allow paraplegics to walk, give sight to the blind, create water out of thin air, and cure the worst diseases known to mankind.

Israel also played a vital role in humanitarian aid for natural disasters in the 2000s. The devastating 2004 tsunami that hit Indonesia was recorded as the sixth-deadliest natural disaster in history. Israel was one of the first three countries to send a team of medical and logistical personnel to assist in the recovery efforts, along with sixty tons of emergency supplies.

When Hurricane Katrina hit New Orleans in 2005, Israel's first responders brought eighty tons of critically needed goods and equipment donated by Israeli companies. Three days after a massive earthquake leveled Port-au-Prince, Haiti, in January 2010, the IDF established a fully functional field hospital in the devastated city, providing the swiftest and most critical care available.

Among the countless acts of unconditional assistance, Israel, in

2013, came to the aid of the Philippines after the Category 5 Super Typhoon Haiyan killed more than 6,300 people. Israel dispatched doctors and IDF members to Mexico in 2017 after a 7.1 magnitude earthquake killed over 300 people and injured over 6,000 more. In 2018, a team of Israeli ophthalmologists traveled to Papua New Guinea and restored eyesight to over 80 visually impaired people. Then most recently, the humanitarian organization IsraAID sent a team to Guatemala to distribute relief after a volcanic eruption killed 62.

Israel is blessing the nations of the world!

OPERATION
MY BROTHER'S KEEPER (2014)

In June 2014, three teenage Jewish boys disappeared while waiting at a bus/hitchhiking station near the city of Hebron. Authorities soon determined they had been kidnapped, and for eighteen agonizing days Israel's soldiers, police, and security services launched a massive search for the victims. The mission created to find the Hamas terrorists responsible for the abductions was named "My Brother's Keeper."

Israeli civilians also helped in the mission through a group of volunteer searchers familiar with the terrain. They eventually found the boys' bodies hidden under a pile of rocks fifteen miles from where they were abducted.

It was quickly determined that the missing teens had been murdered almost immediately after their capture. Israel's national heartbreak was shared by millions of Christians and Jews in the US who had prayed for the safe return of Gilad, Eyal, and Naftali as if the boys were their own family.

Eventually Israel learned that Hamas had been behind the kidnapping and murders and had funded the three terrorists responsible. One of the terrorists was captured and imprisoned, while the other two were killed during a firefight with the IDF. The kidnapping shook Israeli society and awoke Israel to the growing threat of Hamas's influence in Judea and Samaria.[36]

OPERATION
PROTECTIVE EDGE (2014)

For eight years, Israelis along the border with Gaza endured daily rocket fire from Hamas. In the summer of 2014, while Israel was searching for the three kidnapped teenagers, the rocket attacks suddenly escalated. For weeks, Israel's government sought to negotiate a cease-fire without success. Then on July 7, Hamas fired over one hundred rockets into Israeli neighborhoods in one day. This situation was intolerable—Israel had to act.

In response to the massive terrorist escalation in rocket fire, the IDF launched Operation Protective Edge on July 8, 2014, with a ground incursion of Gaza. Sending in soldiers to fight in the cramped streets and booby-trapped buildings of the Gaza Strip was not an easy decision. It put the IDF in extreme danger, but it also minimized the risk of civilian casualties.

However, as Israel entered Gaza, they discovered an even more chilling threat. Hamas had been secretly building a network of underground tunnels beneath the border with Israel since the end of 2009. Hamas had diverted hundreds of millions of dollars and supplies, intended as foreign aid for the war-torn Gazan population, toward the building of their terror tunnels.[37] I have personally witnessed eighteen-wheeler after eighteen-wheeler stacked with humanitarian aid cross from Israel into Gaza.

Israel has helped facilitate the transfer of goods provided by the United Nations and others into the Gaza Strip. These trucks are filled with electrical appliances, iPhones, computers, cement, steel rebar, mattresses, washer/dryers, and even toys, supposedly intended to rebuild day cares and schools and improve the lives of everyday Gazans. Instead, what Hamas didn't sell on the black market was used to build the tunnels and supply their military installations.[38] In the first year alone, over 26,298 truckloads of humanitarian aid crossed the Gazan border, comprising nearly 600,000 tons of goods, and these massive deliveries continue to this day.[39]

The terrorists intended to use these tunnels to infiltrate Israel's towns and kidnap and murder Israeli citizens. Several times during the war, Hamas sent groups of terrorists into Israel through these secret passages, sometimes disguised in IDF uniforms. Thankfully, none of their planned massacres succeeded, but the discovery of this new threat alarmed Israel. The tunnels had to be destroyed.

Meanwhile, around the world, anti-Semitism surged during Operation Protective Edge. Massive anti-Israel rallies were held in several Western countries. The pressure on Israel to withdraw from Gaza before their mission was complete grew intense.

Israel desperately needed a friend, and Christians United for Israel became one of the leading voices speaking up for Israel's right to protect itself. CUFI placed multiple full-page ads in national newspapers exposing Hamas's stated vow to destroy the Jewish state. Later that summer, CUFI organized an emergency pastors' solidarity mission with the expressed purpose of demonstrating unconditional Christian support for Israel's morally justified acts of self-defense.

Finally, Hamas accepted a cease-fire agreement. Israel had successfully destroyed the tunnels beneath the border and dealt a crippling blow to the terrorist infrastructure in Gaza. Yet Israel paid the price with the deaths of sixty-four soldiers and three civilians during the operation.[40]

Israel's humanitarian actions during the war were finally recognized. An independent assessment of NATO's military leaders exonerated and praised Israel, stating in their 2015 report that the IDF had conducted itself by the highest possible moral standards.

THE IRAN DEAL (2015)

The tragic miscarriage of American foreign policy known as the Iran deal, or more formally as the Joint Comprehensive Plan of Action (JCPOA), has gone down in history as one of the worst mistakes of modern times. Its consequences have not been fully revealed, but already we can see how this bad deal jeopardized Israel's and America's security, as well as the security of the entire free world.

Shortly after coming to office, President Obama decided to pursue a nuclear deal with Iran that he believed would be a historic achievement and end decades of hostility between Iran and the West. Details are still being revealed showing just how much Obama was willing to put America's and Israel's safety at risk to get a deal inked on paper, but even before those details began to come to light, it was obviously a fatally flawed agreement.

After years of negotiating with Iran to set aside its nuclear program for a short period in exchange for lifting decades of crippling international financial sanctions against the Iranian government, President Obama and the leaders of China, France, Germany, Russia, the United Kingdom, and other members of the European Union reached an agreement with Iran in 2015.[41]

This epically bad deal essentially gave Iran *not one, but two* paths to a nuclear bomb, which the Iranian government has always made clear they intend to use first against Israel and then against the infidels, the United States, in the West.[42]

On May 8, 2018, President Trump announced he would not renew the Iran sanction waivers, effectively withdrawing the United States from the disastrous nuclear agreement with Tehran. It is hardly surprising that the president chose not to continue this agreement, which he called "the worst deal ever." The Joint Comprehensive Plan of Action (JCPOA) had a number of significant flaws, such as a weak inspection and verification regime, an automatic sunset provision, and failure to restrict Iran's growing ballistic missile program.[43]

STABBING INTIFADA (2015)

On Rosh Hashanah, in September 2015, a wave of violence emanating from Jerusalem began to spread across the country. This hostility was fueled by the hateful and deceitful rhetoric of the Palestinian Authority. Believing the lie spread by Palestinian media that Israel was threatening the Muslim holy sites on the Temple Mount, Palestinian men, women, and even children began terrorizing Israelis in the streets and in their homes. These assaults, which have lasted for more than two and half years, became known as the "Stabbing Intifada" because of the frequency of knife attacks.

In the first several months, hundreds were injured in the riots and terror outbreaks. Jewish civilians were attacked in their cars, at bus stops, near holy sites, and even in their own homes. Twenty-seven Israelis were murdered before the end of 2015. Over the next few years, that number grew to include over sixty victims brutally killed and over nine hundred more wounded. Along with the stabbings, many victims were shot, rammed with a vehicle, firebombed, or beaten with large stones.

One of the victims was Taylor Force, a young American citizen on a study-abroad trip in Israel. Taylor, who had served his country in Iraq and Afghanistan, was stabbed and killed by a Palestinian terrorist near Tel Aviv on March 8, 2016. The twenty-eight-year-old's tragic murder led to the Taylor Force Act in the United States, a piece of legislation designed to cut off the flow of American tax dollars to the PA until they stopped all payments to terrorists.

It has been customary for many years for the Palestinian Authority to reward terrorists or their families with a lifelong pension worth more than most Palestinians could hope to earn in their lifetime. This financial incentive to commit terror was funded by international foreign aid, to the tune of $350 million a year. When Americans discovered their tax dollars were being used to reward terrorism, they were outraged.

Christians United for Israel members sent over one million emails to Congress, insisting that they pass the Taylor Force Act and end the PA's "pay-to-slay" policy. Thankfully, the law was passed and signed as part of an omnibus bill by President Trump in the spring of 2018.

SURROUNDED BY VIOLENCE

Iran has been firmly entrenched on Israel's northern border since 2011, when the Islamic Republic's military began operating in Syria in support of President Bashar al-Assad's regime during its Syrian Civil War. On the morning of February 10, 2018, Iran invaded Israeli airspace by sending an unmanned drone, equipped with explosives, across Israel's border.

Iran's presence in Syria was already considered dangerous to Israel's security, and the drone invasion was seen as a flagrant attack by Iran's government on Israel's sovereignty. Iran had crossed a clear red line—by any definition, it was an act of war.

Immediately after the drone entered Israel's airspace, the IDF shot it out of the sky. In response to the drone invasion, eight Israeli fighter jets were sent into Syria and destroyed the Iranian command post that had launched it. Tensions escalated as Israel mobilized a massive counterattack against both Syrian and Iranian forces. Israel made it clear that they would not tolerate attacks on its sovereignty or its right to self-defense.[44]

Iran, its terrorist army, Hezbollah, and their Syrian allies continue to pose a dangerous threat to Israel's northern border. This invasion of Israeli airspace proved that Iran is eager to provoke war with Israel. Only five months after February's attack, Syria infiltrated Israeli air space on July 10 with an unmanned aerial vehicle, which traveled 6.2 miles over the Sea of Galilee. Within minutes, the IDF intercepted the drone with a Patriot missile. In response, Israel's air force attacked three military positions in Syria.[45] Sadly, it will not be long before Iran tries to violate Israel's sovereignty once again.

MARCH OF RETURN

In the west, along Israel's border with Gaza, another serious threat emerged in March 2018. Hamas announced that it would sponsor a massive "March of Return" toward the security fence in protest of Israel's upcoming seventieth anniversary. A long-standing goal of Palestinian leaders has been to force Israel to accept the "return" of millions of Palestinians descended from those who fled the 1948 war. This "return" would mean the end of Israel as a Jewish state.[46]

It is important to reiterate that Israel withdrew totally from the Gaza Strip in 2006, and Hamas has had complete control since 2007. This "March of Return" was not a protest against Israeli occupation. It was not a protest against a disputed border, because the current border between Gaza and Israel follows the same line that has existed since 1949. Bottom line, these riots were not a protest at all—they were a sustained act of choreographed mass terrorism.

Remaining true to their threat, beginning on the morning of Passover, March 30, 2018, tens of thousands of Palestinians began rioting along the Gaza-Israel security fence in an attempt to provoke a violent response from the IDF soldiers opposite them. This premeditated hostility was methodically organized and scheduled to increase daily for over six weeks up to May 14, Israel's Independence Day. The Palestinians refer to this event as the *Nakba* (Arabic for catastrophe); it was also the day the US had scheduled their embassy dedication ceremony in Jerusalem.

What was publicized as a "spontaneous show of peaceful protest" was not. I was there—it was orchestrated to a tee. Hamas furthermore emboldened the Palestinians to be as confrontational and violent as possible in the two months of mass protests at the Gaza border. They offered a reward of $3,000 to the family of any Palestinian killed during the riots, and $500 for anyone seriously wounded by the IDF.[47] These "peaceful protesters" burned thousands of tires along the border to obscure the IDF's vision as they continued to try to sabotage and penetrate Israel's security fence and invade the Jewish state.

The Palestinian Authority, Hamas, and the Islamic Jihad acknowledged that many of the casualties resulting from the "March of Return" riots were in fact members of their radical terror groups. Moreover, in early June of 2018, the Palestinian ambassador to France disclosed that the Hamas demonstrations were "fully financed" by Tehran.[48] Could it be that these riots were paid for with our tax dollars? God only knows!

Israel cannot and will not allow its border to be breached by even a single terrorist, much less thousands of hostile combatants. It might seem that the "March of Return" was a futile act, but in fact, it was designed to be a clever propaganda weapon to inflict massive political damage on Israel. Shamefully, the liberal anti-Israel media and the biased United Nations supported this intended farce by publicizing the Palestinian Authority's staged photos and video footage and inaccurate casualty reports.

Israel is currently surrounded on almost every side by violence and threats of a much larger regional war. Behind the scenes, Iran's invisible hand is pulling the strings of its puppets Hamas and Hezbollah, the Syrian government, and smaller terrorist groups like Palestinian Islamic Jihad to squeeze Israel in a vice.

Eventually, Israel will be forced to defend itself in a major confrontation with Iran and its proxies. We can expect the United Nations and the international media to condemn Israel for any defensive action, because they continually ignore the acts of aggression that force Israel to respond. What most matters though is that Israel is morally and legally justified in defending its sovereignty, the security of its borders, and the safety of its people.

JERUSALEM JUBILEE (2017)

Israel recently celebrated Jerusalem's Jubilee, the fiftieth anniversary of the reunification and restoration of Jerusalem as Israel's undivided capital. Both the Bible and history specify that 2017 would have prophetic significance. Remember this truth: God does everything at an appointed time, especially when it comes to Israel.

The importance of the Jubilee Year comes from Leviticus 25:10–11:

Consecrate the fiftieth year and proclaim liberty throughout the land to all its inhabitants. It shall be a jubilee for you; each of you is to return to your family property and to your own clan. The fiftieth year shall be a jubilee for you; do not sow and do not reap what grows of itself or harvest the untended vines. (NIV)

From this passage, we know God measures time in modules of fifty years, and at the end of each module, He declares a Year of Jubilee. However, God's prophetic clock only runs when the Jewish people are in the Promised Land of Israel.

This prophetic clock last stopped when the Roman army under General Titus conquered Jerusalem in 70 CE, destroying the Second Temple. According to the historian Josephus, over one million Jews were slaughtered in the siege and hundreds of thousands more were taken as slaves to Rome or dispersed among the nations of the world.

The clock began ticking again in 1917, with the creation of the Balfour Declaration. This British pronouncement stated that the Jewish people could return and rebuild their national home on a small piece of land representing a portion of the total real estate given to them by God in the book of Genesis.

When you add 50 to 1917, you reach the year 1967, when in just six days Israel miraculously defeated five Arab armies who were armed to the teeth by Russia. The astonishing victory of the Six Day War more than doubled the size of Israel's land mass. But more importantly, Jerusalem was reunited with the nation of Israel for the first time since 70 CE, when it was besieged by Rome. The Six Day War was a war of miracles—and a Year of Jubilee.

Finally, from 1967 add fifty years and you come to 2017. I believed with all my heart that this Jubilee Year would be monumental for Israel and the Jewish people.

In the spring of 2017, I had the honor of meeting with President Trump and Vice President Pence in the White House, and of course, Jerusalem was on the agenda. We discussed the importance of moving the US embassy to Jerusalem, something the last three presidents had failed to do, despite the law Congress had passed mandating the move over twenty years ago.

God's prophetic clock hovered on the edge of striking fifty as the appointed time drew near. And on December 6, President Donald Trump stunned the world and all the foreign policy experts by publicly announcing that the United States of America recognized Jerusalem as the official capital of Israel. Furthermore, President Trump announced that his state department would immediately begin preparations to move the US embassy from Tel Aviv to

Jerusalem. Jerusalem's Jubilee Year ended with another miraculous event for the Jewish people.

AM YISRAEL CHAI

After nearly two thousand years of exile and longing, in 1948, Israel was reborn as a modern independent nation, and the last seven decades have been miraculous. Despite all the wars, all the terrorism, and all the sacrifice, Israel has thrived. The people of Israel are alive and well. The desert has bloomed. The barren places are fruitful again. And Israel, as assured by the Almighty, is blessing the nations of the world through its innovations, as promised in Genesis 18:18.

Israel's awe-inspiring story throughout the last 3,500 years has indeed been miraculous. After God's eternal covenant with Abraham, Israel has overcome a relentless barrage of attacks, constant struggles and sacrifices, and heartbreaking tragedies. This is not a revelation to those of us who believe what the Word of God says. Our God keeps His covenants for a thousand generations. The world may be mystified at Israel's perseverance and triumph, but we are not.

The miracle of Israel at seventy is that such a tiny nation surrounded by a massive sea of enemies has so quickly become one of the brightest torches of freedom, generosity, courage, and blessing in the world. While the rest of the Middle East has been a dark place of torment for thousands of Christians and other religious minorities, the Jewish state has been a place of refuge, safety, and prosperity. In Israel, women, as well as ethnic and religious minorities, are free to pursue their dreams, worship as they choose, and participate in every level of society.

This Covenant nation, restored by destitute refugees and Holocaust survivors, bequeathed a legacy of resilience, optimism, and faith to its over 6.5 million modern descendants. With this legacy, the Jewish people have embraced peace instead of war, love instead of hate, and life instead of death.

Through the foundation of their faith, Israelites have found the divine grace to show compassion to all of humanity. Not only do the people of Israel live—they are an example to the rest of the world of how we can live under the blessings and hope of God.

The God of Abraham, Isaac, and Jacob is unfolding Israel's prophetic destiny before our eyes, and Christians everywhere should proudly stand with His chosen people as He fulfills His mighty plan. As the Lord's Covenant nation celebrates seventy years of miracles, we unite with one voice and declare, *"Am Yisrael Chai—the people of Israel live!"*

However, it is imperative that today's Christians understand how pivotal a role Israel and the Jewish people play in God's holy plan for mankind. Therefore, it is my continued mission in life to educate the world with the truth of God's Word, and warn believers not to allow history to repeat itself. We must not permit the war against the Jews to continue.

CHAPTER 2

THE WAR AGAINST THE JEWS

Look, the people of the children of Israel are more and mightier than we; come, let us deal shrewdly with them, lest they multiply, and it happen, in the event of war, that they also join our enemies and fight against us, and so go up out of the land. (Exodus 1:9–10)

There is no denial—the world has been at war with the Jewish people ever since God gave them His Torah on Mount Sinai.

Most Christians do not understand their Hebraic roots, and even more are unaware of the atrocities that were committed against the Jewish people in the name of Christ. King Solomon declared, *"The mind of the prudent acquires knowledge, and the ear of the wise seeks knowledge" (Proverbs 18:15 NASB)*. With this in mind, allow me to take you on a short journey of the endless war against the Jews.

Both biblical accounts and secular history give multiple examples of failed attempts to eradicate the Hebrew nation. For centuries, the

Jewish people have suffered defamation, persecution, dispersal, and systematic annihilation.

This all-consuming hatred has not been a consequence of their enemy's aims of achieving a political ideal, or a necessity to acquire vast resources, or even the objective to confiscate territory. The unrivaled animosity exists simply because they are Jews. This one-of-a-kind bigotry has been branded anti-Judaism or anti-Semitism.

ANTI-SEMITISM

Father Edward H. Flannery wrote in his book *The Anguish of the Jews*, "The sin of antisemitism contains many sins, but in the end it is a denial of Christian faith, a failure of Christian hope, and a malady of Christian love."[1] Bottom line: no one has to hate Jews in order to love Jesus.[2]

Anti-Semitism is an ancient and sustained crisis of civilization. It is one of the most malicious forms of racism in human history—it is a despicable fear, hatred, and contempt of the Jewish people without cause. This loathing for God's Chosen has remained so widespread since ancient times that recently the International Holocaust Remembrance Alliance—an intergovernmental group composed of thirty-one nations—adopted the definition of anti-Semitism as "'a certain perception of Jews, which may be expressed as hatred toward Jews that can also target the state of Israel."[3] Early anti-Semitism was first termed *anti-Judaism* and was defined as the opposition to the Jewish faith and those who practiced it. At the core, they are one in the same.

When Jacob and his sons first entered Egypt to reunite with Joseph, they were honored guests, but this hospitality was short-lived. The book of Exodus records various examples of Gentile phobia and scorn toward the Jewish people. One such example was

Thutmos III, the pharaoh of the Exodus. He singled out the Jewish people for fear they would overtake his reigning government, a myth that would live through the centuries:

Now there arose a new king over Egypt, who did not know Joseph. And he said to his people, "Look, the people of the children of Israel are more and mightier than we; come, let us deal shrewdly with them, lest they multiply, and it happen, in the event of war, that they also join our enemies and fight against us, and so go up out of the land." (Exodus 1:8–10)

After the exodus from Egypt (1446 BCE), Joshua led the Israelites to victory in battles throughout Canaan. Following Joshua's death, Israel was ruled by a series of judges until the prophet Samuel appointed Saul and later David as kings of Israel. David conquered the Jebusites and made Jerusalem the capital of Israel (1010 BCE). After King David's death, his son Solomon built and dedicated the First Temple in the Holy City (960–953 BCE).

Following the reign of King Solomon there was a breaking away of the Northern Kingdom of Israel (ten tribes) from the Southern Kingdom of Judah (two tribes). Eventually the Northern Kingdom of Israel was destroyed by the Assyrians, bringing about the deportation of ten of the twelve tribes throughout the Assyrian Empire (722 BCE).

A little over 130 years later, King Nebuchadnezzar conquered the Kingdom of Judah, resulting in the destruction of the First Temple and the exile of the Jews to Babylon (586 BCE). I will expand on this dispersion, or scattering of the Jews (diaspora), in a later chapter dealing with the capture and displacement of the prophet Daniel.

HAMAN'S FINAL SOLUTION

Throughout their time in exile, the Jewish people experienced indoctrination, torture, and death, but they remained faithful to the Torah. In time, the Babylonians were defeated by King Cyrus the Great of Persia in the fourth century BCE. Eventually King Xerxes, son of Darius, became the leader of the Persian Empire, which encompassed over 127 nations, to include the vast majority of displaced Jews. While a certain number of Jews were allowed to return to Jerusalem after the Edict of Cyrus to rebuild the temple, most remained in their displaced lands.

Esther and her cousin Mordecai lived in Shushan, a robust cultural, political, and religious center within the empire. The book of Esther records a deliberate incident of anti-Judaism, which began when King Xerxes appointed Haman, the Agagite, as his prime minister (475 BCE).

Haman was a descendant of Agag, king of the Amalekites, who were the first enemies Israel encountered after crossing the Red Sea en route to the Promised Land. Haman demanded that the whole of the kingdom pay him homage. However, there was one who would not—Mordecai, the leader of the Jewish people. Mordecai refused to bow before Haman lest he offend the Lord.

Haman was incensed with Mordecai's defiance but was not satisfied with punishing one man; he instead devised a plan to eradicate the entire Hebrew population from the Persian Empire. Professor Rabbi Martin Lockshin proposes that "on the political level, Haman may have been the first to articulate the 'dual loyalty' argument, arguing that the Jews' allegiance to their own laws [the Torah] causes them to be disloyal to the laws of the state."[4]

Haman approached King Xerxes with his lethally deceptive and enticing offer:

There is a certain people [the Jews] scattered and dispersed among the people in all the provinces of your kingdom; their laws [Torah laws] are different from all other people's, and they do not keep the king's laws [dual loyalty]. Therefore it is not fitting for the king to let them remain. If it pleases the king, let a decree be written that they be destroyed, and I will pay ten thousand talents of silver into the hands of those who do the work, to bring it [the wealth of the Jews] into the king's treasuries. (Esther 3:8–9)

Mordecai's nemesis proposed to increase the king's coffers by nearly two-thirds with the spoils he expected to seize from the Jews through his deceitful plot. Haman is often referred to as the first "persecutor of the Jews" because of his attempt to exterminate the seed of Abraham. But the Lord remained faithful to His promise as recorded in Genesis 12 and totally destroyed Haman and his family instead.

THE GREEKS AND THE ROMANS

The Persian Empire, which included Judea, was conquered by Alexander the Great in 331 BCE. After Alexander's premature death, the Greek Empire was divided among his four generals. One of the kings descending from this dispersion of power was Antiochus IV Epiphanes. This ruler was notorious for his cruelty against the Jews of Judea and Samaria.

The Greeks wasted no time in introducing repulsive pagan practices into the established customs of the Jewish people. They attempted to "de-Judaize" observant Jews by forcing them to worship other gods; however, the majority of the Jews refused to denounce their faith. As a result, Antiochus ordered the plunder of Jewish property and the slaughter of the dissenters. Ultimately, it was the desecration of the Holy Temple that drove the Jews to revolt.[5]

When the practice of the Mosaic law was outlawed, the Jewish citizenry became outraged and joined forces with a priestly family known as the Maccabees. The successful rebellion against Antiochus IV brought an end to Jewish oppression and allowed for the reconsecration of the defiled temple of Jerusalem (167–160 BCE).

The supernatural victory of the Maccabean Revolt brought with it a resurgence of national pride. This sense of liberation produced a wave of Jewish writings declaring the "glories of Israel and envisioned her ultimate triumph over all nations under the scepter of her Messiah."[6]

However, this newfound independence ended when the Roman general Pompey captured the city of Jerusalem from the Greeks in 63 BCE. Rome embraced the Greek disdain for the Jewish people, and as a result of Pompey's conquest, twelve thousand Jews were slaughtered and many more were exiled.

The Romans were proud of their gods and were absolutely intolerant of any religion that would undermine their own. On the other hand, the Jewish people knew that the God of Abraham, Isaac, and Jacob was a jealous God who forbid any form of idol worship. Once again, the Jewish people stayed true to their faith.

The Greeks and the Romans, like other societies before them, incessantly targeted the Jewish people because they would not adapt to their cultures or polytheistic religions. The Jews of the diaspora considered Jerusalem to be their Holy City and Jehovah God to be their *only* God. But the refusal to embrace their Gentile ruler's demands prompted great resentment for the Jews and was viewed as a direct rebellion against the established government—Haman's lie of "dual loyalty" lived on.

What the Gentile nations failed to understand was that the Jewish people were set apart *to* God—*by* God. From the time Moses led the Israelites out of Egypt through the moment Joshua led them into the Promised Land, they were cast into a "religious and social solidarity." Edward Flannery describes this cohesion perfectly:

> From the heights of Sinai, the voice of Yahweh had thundered forth the tenet of unity: "I, the Lord, am your God . . . you shall have no other gods besides me" (Exodus 20:2–3); and Israel's election was made no less plain: "I, the Lord, am sacred, I, who have set you apart from the other nations to be my own" (Lev. 20:26).[7]

THE PHARISEES, THE SADDUCEES, THE ESSENES, AND THE ZEALOTS

A short history of the four sects of Judaism will help to understand both the religious and political integration of Jewish life during the Roman rule of first-century Jerusalem.

The Pharisees are known as the "spiritual fathers" of modern Judaism. They believed in the Torah or Written Law. They also believed in the Oral Law that God gave Moses at Sinai. This oral tradition was written down approximately three centuries later within the Talmud. The Pharisees considered the Torah and Talmud to be codependent, yet held that nothing superseded the authority of the written Word. They also believed that God gave Moses the interpretation and application of His laws.

The Pharisees supported the concept of the resurrection of the dead, the existence of an afterlife, and God's punishment of the wicked and His reward of the righteous in the world to come. They also believed in a Messiah who would usher in an age of world peace. The Pharisees continued to observe the principles of Judaism even after the destruction of the temple, including individual prayer and corporate gatherings in synagogues.

On the other end of the spectrum we have the "elitist" Sadducees, who wanted to uphold the priestly class. This sect of Judaism was freely tolerant of the integration of Hellenism into their everyday lives.

Hellenism was a "body of humanistic and classical ideals associated with ancient Greece." These Greek principles included the study of reason and the arts, the pursuit of secular knowledge and civic obligation, the development of the mind and body, and polytheism (the worship of many gods). In their purest forms, Hellenism and Judaism were opposing forces—the first believed in the holiness of the beauty while the other believed in the beauty of holiness.

The Sadducees believed in the sacrificial rites of Judaism but rejected the idea of the Oral Law, insisting on a literal interpretation of the Written Law. Consequently, the Sadducees did not believe in an afterlife and primarily focused on partaking in rituals associated with the temple. Shortly, after the destruction of the Second Temple, the Sadducees and their writings disappeared.

While the Sadducees led the good life and sought power in high places, the Pharisees believed that it was God's will for them to remain loyal to His Oral and Written Law. Enter the Essenes, who removed themselves from the struggle between the two opposed groups and retreated to their desert community. They believed in a stricter interpretation of the law and abstained from temple worship in Jerusalem. The Essenes were known for voluntarily living in poverty and devoted much of their time to studying the Torah.

At the beginning of the Christian era (Common Era), a fourth Jewish faction rose among the Jewish people called the Zealots. Where the Essenes avoided confrontation, the Zealots welcomed it. These anti-Roman revolutionaries held the basic conviction that political and religious liberty from Rome was essential and should be achieved by any means possible.

Jerusalem had long been Hellenized by the Greeks, and now the Romanization of some within the Jewish community eventually brought with it a corruption that had previously flared under Antiochus IV Epiphanes. However, not all Jewish people supported the Herodian position. The Pharisees, led by Rabbi Yochanan ben Zakkai, were deeply opposed to the contamination of the Jewish religion, but they also opposed the Zealots' insurgence. Inadvertently, Rome created a "class divide" within the Jewish religion, and a Zealot uprising would later set off what history calls the Great Revolt (66–70 CE).

Jewish historian Josephus records the devastating defeat of the Jewish Revolt of Jerusalem by the Roman General Titus. The destruction of Jewish lives was relentless. Titus's ruthless and bloody assault ended with the destruction of the Second Temple and the slaughter of over one million Jews.[8]

The Jewish people were sent into exile as captives, slaves, and refugees, with nearly one hundred thousand taken to Rome to build the Coliseum. As foreigners and outcasts in the nations of their scattering, they were exposed to discriminatory laws, exorbitant taxes, humiliation, and active persecution, even more so after the rise of Christianity.

However, even through the centuries of exile, the hope for redemption of the land of Israel remained a central point of the Jewish faith and the people's beloved national identity.[9]

THE CHURCH FATHERS AND JUDAISM

By now, the majority of the Jews of Jerusalem were dispersed throughout the ancient world, and their unwavering devotion to their faith became an offense to the nations to which they migrated. For the most part, the Jews were tolerated; however, the advent of

Christianity within the Roman Empire caused anti-Semitism to expand its ugly borders.

Initially, believers in Christ as Redeemer were recognized as just another Jewish sect, since Jesus and the disciples were Jewish and preached a form of Judaism. For a time both existed in some semblance of harmony. However, because of the mandate given in the Great Commission, the apostles evangelized all people with the gospel through their travels in Europe and the Middle East. Soon, the body of Christ exponentially multiplied to include non-Jews.

With the conversion of the emperors, beginning with Constantine, an idolatrous form of Christianity eventually became the recognized religion of the Roman Empire and the official successor to Judaism. Constantine's acceptance of Christ was motivated by political purposes and was, at best, a blend of paganism and a Hellenistic type of Christianity.

In an attempt to solve various doctrinal controversies facing the newly formed Roman Church, Constantine called for the Council of Nicaea (325 CE). This ecumenical gathering was the first empire-wide council of church leaders, which resulted in the creation and adoption of the Nicene Creed. By its end, the council also successfully accomplished its goal to separate Christianity from Judaism.[10]

Several new doctrines were recognized by the Council of Nicaea that contributed to the church's formal disconnect with the Jewish roots of the newly established Christian doctrine and practices. In Constantine's own words, the objective was simple: "Let us have nothing in common with the detestable Jewish crowd."[11]

From this point forward, Christians were prohibited from following the Torah and observing the Sabbath and the Jewish feasts. With a stroke of the pen, the Council formally substituted the observance of the God-ordained Passover Feast with the celebration of Easter, adapted from the pagan feast of Ishtar:

We also send you the good news of the settlement concerning the holy pasch [Passover], namely that in answer to your prayers this question also has been resolved. All the brethren in the East who have hitherto followed the Jewish practice will henceforth observe the custom of the Romans and of yourselves and of all of us who from ancient times have kept Easter [Ishtar] together with you.[12]

However, observant Jews continued to adhere to the Torah, which was the law of God. They refused to participate in pagan ritual practices and continued to faithfully observe the feasts of the Lord. In addition, the Jewish people declined to accept Jesus as Lord in obedience to the mandate of God to Moses declaring, *"Hear, O Israel: The LORD our God, the LORD is one!" (Deuteronomy 6:4).* These actions were collectively viewed as a deliberate defiance against Rome's rulers and their newly adopted "Christian" faith, which at this time embraced idols, remnants of pagan ritual worship, and in many cases, sustained polytheism.

Many early church fathers were trained in the principles of logic and rational thought through the teachings of Greek philosophers such as Socrates, Plato, and Aristotle. Since Judaism and Christianity were both rooted in the Old Testament, church leaders, like Ignatius, Origen, Martyr, Marcion, and others, thought it reasonable to affirm the newly found Christian doctrine by claiming it *superseded* Judaism. For example, Ignatius, bishop of Antioch (98–117 CE), stated in his Epistle to the Magnesians, "For if we are still practicing Judaism, we admit that we have not received God's favor. . . . It is wrong to talk about Jesus Christ and live like Jews. For Christianity did not believe in Judaism, but Judaism in Christianity."[13]

This doctrine of Supersessionism is very much alive in the modern church today. It argues that the Jews are no longer deemed to be God's chosen people and are "replaced" by the Church as a result of their rejection of Christ. This type of incessant denunciation of the Jewish people within the church's leadership contributed to the sustained animosity demonstrated against them.

Hatred for the Jews within the Christian movement grew exponentially as additional church leaders like Justin Martyr ruthlessly vilified them. In his document *Dialogue with Trypho*, dated approximately 160 CE, Martyr stated:

> The custom of circumcising the flesh, handed down from Abraham, was given to you as a distinguishing mark, to set you off from other nations and from us Christians. The purpose of this was that you and only you might suffer the afflictions that are now justly yours; that only your land be desolate, and your cities ruined by fire; that the fruits of your land be eaten by strangers before your very eyes; that not one of you be permitted to enter your city of Jerusalem. Your circumcision of the flesh is the only mark by which you can certainly be distinguished from other men. . . . As I stated before, it was by reason of your sins and the sins of your fathers that, among other precepts, God imposed upon you the observance of the Sabbath as a mark.[14]

John Chrysostom (349–407 CE), referred to in history as the "Golden Mouth," at times praised the Jews for being God's Chosen, but he more often cursed and maligned them, calling them "wretched and miserable," "good-for-nothing," and much worse after they refused to convert to Christianity. An example of his anti-Jewish vile is as follows:

> Jews are the most worthless of men—they are lecherous, greedy, rapacious—they are perfidious murderers of

Christians, they worship the devil, their religion is a sickness. . . . The Jews are the odious assassins of Christ and for killing god there is no expiation, no indulgence, no pardon. Christians may never cease vengeance. The Jews must live in servitude forever. It is incumbent on all Christians to hate the Jews.[15]

Chrysostom's warped theology was a continued form of anti-Jewish Supersessionism, which was the precursor to modern replacement theology.[16] His spiteful rhetoric was intended to discourage Christians from observing the Jewish feasts and customs and to prevent them from becoming "sick with a Judaizing disease."[17] Sadly, Chrysostom's anti-Semitic rants, and those of other church leaders before him, were used to validate sustained hatred and violence against the Jews.

Throughout the third century, discrimination against the Jewish people continued to significantly increase, due in part to the persistent denunciation by church fathers such as Saint Augustine (354–430 CE), a contemporary of Chrysostom.

In his autobiographical work titled *Confessions*, Augustine wrote, "How hateful to me are the enemies of your Scripture! How I wish that you would slay them [the Jews] with your two-edged sword, so that there should be none to oppose your word! Gladly would I have them die to themselves and live to you!"[18]

By the fourth century, Jews were officially ostracized from the societies they had lived in for generations; they were forbidden to marry Christians or even eat together with them. The Jews in Italy were confronted with forced conversion. The Jews of Carthage (modern-day Tunisia) were expelled, and complete Jewish communities in Europe were destroyed. Jews were banned from Jerusalem, and the Roman emperor Honorius called for the confiscation of all the gold and silver from the synagogues in the Holy City.

The next four hundred years (the fifth through the eighth centuries) were marked by additional malicious milestones in the sustained war against the Jews. There was the creation and ratification of the Theodosian Code, which was a compilation of laws of the Roman Empire. In it, the Jewish people were prohibited from holding important financial positions as well as judicial and executive offices. They were also prevented from testifying against a Christian in court.

In addition, the ban against building new synagogues was reestablished. The Jewish people were forbidden from reciting the psalms while burying their dead, and in Spain, Jews were hanged or burned at the stake by the thousands for refusing to convert.[19]

As time progressed, Jews were not allowed to join trade guilds. Jewish craftsmen such as goldsmiths, silversmiths, diamond cutters, and glass blowers began to fade away. Jewish people were excluded from owning land, holding office, and banned from becoming doctors or lawyers. Over the course of time, Muslim caliphs, medieval bishops, and, finally, Nazi organizers mandated the use of an identifying badge to mark the Jews.

Over the centuries, Jewish people were disgraced by having to wear "distinguishing garments" such as an emblem (yellow star), an insignia (Juden), or some other form of atypical clothing that set them apart from Christians. In Canon 26 of the Third Lateran Council of 1179, Jews were forbidden to be plaintiffs or witnesses against Christians in court and were also prohibited from withholding an inheritance from their descendants who had converted to Christianity.

Within this time period, Pope Urban II of Rome decreed for the Christians of Europe to take up the cross and sword and liberate the Holy Land from the Muslims.[20] This call to action began what is now known as the first of eight Crusades (1095–1291 CE). These violent campaigns increased the ranking of European Christians within the region, giving them a major standing in the contest for land in the Middle East.

As a consequence of Rome's vicious campaign, sanctioned mobs of murderous vigilantes marched under the sign of the cross, sweeping through Jewish communities looting, raping, and massacring tens of thousands of Jews on the road to Jerusalem.[21] Fundamentally, the seed of Abraham, the Chosen, the cherished, the Covenant people of God were slaughtered beneath the cross of Christ.

Evil lies about the Jews continued to surface, such as the capricious tales of "blood libel." On Passover 1144, a Christian boy disappeared in Norwich, England. Immediately, the local citizens alleged that the Jews had murdered the young man in order to use his blood for ritual practices such as the making of matzo at Passover.[22]

It may be hard to believe, but radical Muslim communities teach this same treacherous lie to their children even to this day. They also maintain that the Jewish people are the enemy of Allah and that Islam must continue to engage in a religious war against the Jews. Ultimately, this radical Islamic rhetoric teaches that killing Jews is a holy obligation.[23]

After my first trip to Israel in 1978, I began a two-year study of the historical relationship between Jews and Christians. I became deeply disturbed to learn that one of the great perpetrators of Jewish hatred was Martin Luther, the founder of Protestantism. This was not taught in any doctrinal seminars I had ever attended.

After the Catholic Reformation of the sixteenth century, Luther became despondent that the Jews would not convert to his liberating form of Christianity. As a consequence of Luther's unrestrained anger, he authored a vile pamphlet entitled *On the Jews and Their Lies.*

In it he asserted that Jews were the Christ killers and demanded their torture and death. Luther stated that the Jews should have their tongues cut out through the back of their heads, their synagogues burned to the ground, and their children sold into slavery.

> Set fire to their synagogues or schools and to bury and cover with dirt whatever will not burn, so that no man will ever again see a stone or cinder of them. This is to be done in honor of our Lord and of Christendom, so that God might see that we are Christians.[24]

The Nazis would reprint Luther's inflammatory pamphlet in 1935, which later helped spawn the evils of Hitler's Final Solution. Some historians believe that the slanderous attacks from church leaders such as Chrysostom and Luther marked the critical transition of "anti-Judaism" (the Christian hatred toward the Jewish religion) and "anti-Semitism" (the world's abhorrence toward the Jews as a racial group).[25]

John Calvin (1509–1564) was a French theologian and spiritual statesman who was a contemporary of Martin Luther. He is recognized as the most influential ecclesiastical leader within the second generation of the Protestant Reformation. But like others before him, his twisted views of the Jewish people continued to fuel the flame of hatred:

> I have had much conversation with many Jews: I have never seen either a drop of piety or a grain of truth or ingenuousness—nay, I have never found common sense in any Jew.[26]

> Their [the Jews] rotten and unbending stiffneckedness deserves that they be oppressed unendingly and without measure or end and that they die in their misery without the pity of anyone.[27]

There was no end in sight of the virulent spread of anti-Semitism within and without the church.

THE CRUSADES, THE POGROMS AND THE GHETTOS

The crusaders were allegedly created to "liberate" Jerusalem from the infidels. However, during the First Crusade in 1095, Jewish communities were attacked on the road to Jerusalem under the idea that "Why fight Christ's enemies abroad when they are living among us?" Consequently, nearly 5,000 Jews were murdered in cities throughout Germany alone during the first of these vicious campaigns. In 1124, the entire Jewish quarter of Kiev, Russia, was destroyed, and in Morocco 100,000 Jews were massacred in Fez, along with another 120,000 in Marrakesh by angry mobs.

The continued carnage of the Jewish people during the Crusades induced the birth of the *pogrom*. The word *pogrom* means "to destroy, to wreak havoc, or to demolish violently," and specifically refers to the outbreaks of anti-Jewish violence by non-Jews. The first recorded pogrom arose against the Jews in 1241 in Frankfurt, Germany, after a debate over interfaith marriages between Jews and Christians. This assault, where 180 Jews were killed and 24 were forced to be baptized, is known as the "Slaughter of the Jews" or *Judenschlacht*. On Easter Sunday in 1389, the Jewish quarter in Prague, Poland, was burned and nearly 1,500 Jews were massacred.[28]

Increasingly, Jews were subjected to political, economic, and social discrimination. By the thirteenth century, Jewish people were systematically removed from their homes and required to live in designated communities, which eventually became known as the "Jewish Ghetto." The term *ghetto* originated in 1516 from the name of the Jewish quarter in Venice, Italy, where Jews were forced to live.[29] By the sixteenth and seventeenth centuries, Jewish ghettos were created in Frankfurt, Rome, Prague, and other cities throughout Europe.

The Jews were blamed for everything. Even the bubonic plague of the Dark Ages, which killed an estimated one-third of Europe's population, fueled further anti-Jewish hatred. The Jews were accused of poisoning wells, leading to the spread of the "Black Death," as this devastating disease was called. For this and other false allegations related to the plague, nearly one hundred thousand Jews were burned alive in Germany and Austria alone.[30]

By the 1800s, pogroms became commonplace as waves of anti-Jewish riots moved through Russia. During this time, more than two hundred anti-Jewish events occurred in Kiev and Odessa, Russia, as well as in Warsaw, Poland. The *New York Times* described the first Kishinev pogrom of Easter of 1903 with these words:

> The anti-Jewish riots in Kishinev, Bessarabia [modern-day Moldavia] are worse than the censor will permit to publish. There was a well laid-out plan for the general massacre of Jews on the day following the Russian Easter. The mob was led by priests, and the general cry, "Kill the Jews," was taken up all over the city. The Jews were taken wholly unaware and were slaughtered like sheep. The dead number 120 and the injured about 500. The scenes of horror attending this massacre are beyond description. Babes were literally torn to pieces by the frenzied and bloodthirsty mob. The local police made no attempt to check the reign of terror. At sunset the streets were piled with corpses and wounded. Those who could make their escape fled in terror, and the city is now practically deserted of Jews.[31]

Pogroms became so prevalent and strongly associated with the persecution of Jewish people that in subsequent years historian

John Klier stated, "By the twentieth century, the word 'pogrom' had become a generic term in English for all forms of collective violence directed against Jews."[32]

The church's *desecration* of the Jewish people is among the ever-present arguments over its contribution to the eventual attempt of the *extermination* of the whole Jewish race during the Holocaust.

The term *anti-Semitism* was first conceived by Wilhelm Marr in his work *Victory of Judaism over Germanism*.[33] He believed the Jews should be barred from citizenship because of their conspiracy to rule the state—the spirit of Haman lives!

In the same vein, *The Protocols of the Elders of Zion* was published in 1905 by Russian writer and mystic Sergei Nilus. I want to emphasize that this document was completely fictitious and promoted, without substantiated proof, the perpetual myth that the Jews had devised a "secret plan to rule the world by manipulating the economy, controlling the media, and sponsoring various religious conflicts."[34]

These writings were seen as the "most notorious and widely distributed antisemitic publication of modern times."[35] *The Protocols* greatly contributed to the exponential rise in anti-Semitism and Jewish hatred. This anathema for God's people was additionally fueled by the development of Social Darwinism and other so-called scientific philosophies based on the bogus concepts of racial inferiority and superiority.

POST-WORLD WAR I GERMANY

Germany was humiliated by its defeat in World War I, and more so after the Treaty of Versailles. This accord obligated the German people to give up territory and pay reparations to countries whose lands it had damaged during the war. Enter Adolf Hitler.

Hitler was a charismatic leader, and it was inevitable for the German people to fall in hypnotic obedience to his demagogic authority. He reminded the German masses of the "blood libel" lies, the supposed root cause of the bubonic plague and other such fabrications. In addition, Hitler quoted the works of Chrysostom and Luther to promote fear within the people that the Jews would in due course contaminate their "superior Aryan race."

The German people were desparate for any political and social revolution that would promise a return of their glory days of European dominance while restoring Germany's lost dignity. This outcry for supremacy permitted Nazism to explode as a political movement that endorsed racially anti-Semitic philosophies as articulated by Adolf Hitler in his book *Mein Kampf* (translated *My Struggle*).

The demand for the resurgence of German national pride, coupled with Jewish hatred, culminated in Hitler's meteoric rise to power in 1933. His National socialist regime promoted the methodical exclusion of Jews from society from its inception. The Jewish people were relentlessly demonized and accused of being the driving force behind international Marxism and what Joseph Goebbels called "immoral Capitalism."

Hitler was quoted as saying, "If the Jews didn't exist, we would have to invent them." The hatred of the Jewish people was the foundation of Hitler's unifying power.[36] He predicted that if left unchallenged, the Jews would eventually drag their beloved Deutschland into another world war. Goebbels and his Nazi propagandists convinced the German citizenry that the Jews were the root cause of every social, religious, and economic problem they faced.

Widespread anti-Semitic indoctrination saturated German society, resulting in the mass hatred of the Jewish people. Laws were ratified excluding Jews from state and civil service. The Bavarian Ministry of the Interior denied Jewish students entrance to schools and universities. Jewish doctors were forbidden from treating non-Jewish patients, and they were denied reimbursement of services from public or state-supported health insurance funds, leaving them virtually bankrupt.

By 1934, Jewish lawyers and notaries were prohibited from participating in legal matters. Licensing credentials were revoked from Jewish tax advisors, Jewish actors were no longer allowed to perform on stage or screen, and Jewish butchers "could no longer slaughter animals according to ritual purity requirements, effectively preventing them [observant Jews] from obeying Jewish dietary laws."[37]

The question now arose—who was considered a Jew? Hitler believed he was the sole authority on racial policy and he had the final say about what the law stated. Therefore, on September 15, 1935, the Nuremberg Laws were swiftly ratified. These anti-Semitic statutes marked a major step in clarifying Hitler's "ethnic purity" mandate and consequently removed all Jewish influences from Aryan society. Their said purpose was to protect "German blood and honor" by regulating the "the problems of marriage between 'Aryans' and 'non-Aryans.'"[38]

Additional Nazi decrees were issued after the Nuremberg Laws that incrementally repealed a Jewish citizen's political, legal, religious, and civil rights. Ultimately, these decrees divested the Jewish people of their rights as human beings. They were deliberately designed to provide the legitimate path for the systematic discrimination, persecution, and subsequent extermination of the Jewish people in Germany and throughout their occupied territory.

The Reichstag, Germany's parliament, sponsored the philosophy of "racial hygiene" as a tool to build an Aryan "master race." In order to accomplish their diabolical plan, it was essential to establish "racial cleansing," which demanded the forced sterilization of the Jewish people and others deemed undesirable by the State. The integration of bogus medical science, unethical doctors, and inhuman medical agendas would further the purpose of the führer's National Socialism aim of racial integrity—a fundamental model within the Nazi doctrine.

By 1938, Jews could not legally change their personal names or the names of their businesses. The Order for the Disclosure of Jewish Assets required Jews to report all property in excess of five thousand Reichmarks. And the Decree on the Confiscation of Jewish Property directed the transfer of assets from Jews to non-Jewish Germans.

Finally, the Reich Ministry of the Interior canceled all German passports held by Jews, with the stipulation that the passport could only be revalidated after the letter J was stamped on it. Violation of any of these decrees resulted in strict fines, incarceration, or deportation to labor camps.[39]

THE NIGHT OF BROKEN GLASS

On November 7, 1938, the seventeen-year-old son of Jewish parents learned that German police had confiscated his family's life possessions and had forcibly deported them to Poland. Living with an uncle in Paris, the young man became hopelessly distraught over his family's plight, and in retaliation he attempted to assassinate the German ambassador to France. However, his plan failed, and instead he fatally wounded an embassy undersecretary who died two days later.

Joseph Goebbels, Hitler's chief of propaganda, immediately labeled the attack a conspiracy by "International Jewry." He announced to the German people that the deliberate act was a direct assault on the führer. This ill-fated incident was all Goebbels needed to instigate retaliation against the Jewish people throughout Germany, Austria, and other newly acquired Nazi territories.

This sanctioned revenge against the Jewish people produced the infamous *Kristallnacht* or the "Night of the Broken Glass" of November 9 and 10, 1938. Within forty-eight hours, the Nazis burned down 200 synagogues, destroyed hundreds of Jewish homes, vandalized Jewish day schools, sacked and looted 7,500 Jewish shops, and murdered nearly 100 Jews throughout Germany and Austria. In the wake of this terrible injustice, some thirty thousand Jewish men were arrested and sent to Dachau, Buchenwald, and Sachsen-hausen—all established Nazi concentration camps.

Prior to Kristallnacht, the oppressive Nazi policies of anti-Jewish boycotts, staged book burnings, and sanctioned anti-Jewish legislation had been painfully hostile; however, after this two-day onslaught, conditions for German and Austrian Jews instantly grew far worse.

Within days of Kristallnacht, the Nazis issued a decree forcing all Jews to transfer their businesses to Aryan hands. Jewish students were expelled from all German schools, and the government levied a collective one billion Reichmarks ($400 million) "penalty" against German Jews for the destruction of property during the reprehensible Night of the Broken Glass.[40]

A few months later, Hitler delivered his infamous speech to the Reichstag in celebration of the sixth anniversary of his ascent to power. Now führer and Reich Chancellor, Hitler made a self-proclaimed prophecy regarding the future of the Jewish people.

> Today I will once more be a prophet: If the international Jewish financiers in and outside Europe should succeed in plunging the nations once more into a world war, then the result will not be the Bolshevization of the earth, and thus the victory of Jewry, but the annihilation of the Jewish race in Europe![41]

Germany was brainwashed into believing they had a widespread "Jewish problem." Prior to his speech, Hitler's Third Reich took part in ongoing negotiations with the Intergovernmental Committee on

Refugees regarding the complete emigration of Jews from Germany.

There was a glitch, however; the potential recipient nations did not want the Jews without their wealth, and the Reich was not willing to allow them to leave with any of their possessions, which they believed rightfully belonged to Germany.[42] There was no solution in sight; the gates of escape were quickly closing.

PERSONA NON GRATA

After Hitler's Reichstag speech, the Jewish people were persona non grata (unacceptable) throughout Europe. A classic example of their rejection among the nations is the voyage of the *St. Louis*. After Kristallnacht, many Jews who could sought asylum in other countries, especially America. Some Jews had by this time willingly emigrated from Europe, but others now considered relocating to the West as a path to personal survival.

On May 13, 1939, 937 Jewish passengers boarded a German transatlantic liner named the *St. Louis* in Hamburg en route to Havana. For most of the passengers, this voyage was the last hope to escape the horrors of Nazism. They took great pains to meet the strict immigration laws, which now involved increased levies, overpriced visas, and often mandatory sponsorship. The passengers of the *St. Louis* had secured travel vouchers and required visas; however, their visas were invalid by the time they arrived to the shores of Cuba.

The Cuban people were not happy with increased migration to their country. They believed that immigrants were the direct cause for a lack of jobs, which negatively affected their failing economy. In response to their protests, Cuban president Federico Laredo Brú refused to allow the *St. Louis* to dock in port.

This denial was a perfect opportunity for the Nazis to justify their anti-Jewish goals and policies of forced emigration. Once again, propaganda mastermind Joseph Goebbels decided to use the *St. Louis* as part of a bigger plan. Goebbels sent his SS agents to Havana to provoke Jewish hatred using the same lies and distortions that had been so successful throughout Europe. He painted the passengers of this doomed voyage as "undesirables" too dangerous for the Cuban good.

The plight of the *St. Louis* gained international attention, and even though some countries sent the Cuban government telegrams of protest, no nation was willing to offer the Jews asylum. On June 2, the ship was forced to leave Cuban waters after only allowing 29 of the 937 passengers admittance to their country (28 had valid visas, and one passenger who had tried to commit suicide was evacuated to a hospital).

In desperation, international Jewish groups looked for a country willing to accept the refugees, yet no government granted safe harbor to the *St. Louis*.

While negotiations with other nations continued, the *St. Louis* sailed around Cuba, eventually reaching the coastline of Miami in anticipation that the United States would receive the refugees. However, the US Coast Guard prevented them from coming closer. In response to this travesty, a Virginia resident wrote,

[The] press reported that the ship came close enough to Miami for the refugees to see the lights of the city. . . . The U.S. Coast Guard, under instructions from Washington, followed the ship . . . to prevent any people landing on our shores. . . . When this horrible tragedy was being enacted right at our doors, our government . . . made no effort to relieve the desperate situation of these people, but on the contrary gave orders that they be kept out of the country. . . . The failure to take any steps whatsoever to assist these distressed, persecuted Jews in their hour of extremity was one of the most disgraceful things which has happened in American history and leaves a stain and brand of shame upon the record of our nation.[43]

The captain had no choice but to return the *St. Louis* and its "banned cargo" to Europe. However, because of God's intervention and extraordinary negotiations, the American Jewish Joint Distribution Committee (JDC) was able to find several countries in Europe that would accept the refugees.

Thirty-six emotionally charged days after departing Germany, the ship was allowed to dock at Antwerp, Belgium, on June 17 with 907 passengers (one had died en route); 181 went to Holland, 224 to France, 288 to Great Britain, and 214 to Belgium.[44] America accepted none. Of the original 937 passengers who boarded the *St. Louis*, approximately 594 survived after the war and 343 did not.[45]

However, the damage was done. Goebbels had successfully spun the plight of the *St. Louis* into a worldwide propaganda bonanza, claiming it validated that Jews were universally detested, distrusted, and unwanted.

WORLD WAR II

The years between the first and second world wars were a time of international volatility. After World War I, President Woodrow Wilson founded the League of Nations in 1920, a global organization intended to regulate future conflicts between nations and preserve world peace. However, the League soon proved to be ineffective. Before long, international turmoil developed between world powers once again.

The financial devastation of America's Great Depression in 1929 plunged the world into a deep recession. When Hitler skyrocketed to power in 1933, he used this worldwide economic decline and the German people's deep resentment of the Treaty of Versailles to declare that his country needed to expand its "living space." As a result, in 1936 Hitler remilitarized the Rhineland, which was a direct violation of the Versailles Treaty.[46]

During this same period, Italy's prime minister, Benito Mussolini, elected to follow Hitler's example by conquering territory he thought rightfully belonged to Italy. The Italians had already colonized portions of Africa, believing this annexation would provide more job opportunities for unemployed Italians as well as acquire more mineral resources to drive back the effects of the world economic depression.[47]

These and other flagrant violations by Hitler and Mussolini confirmed the incompetence of the League of Nations, which did nothing to stop their aggression. Nazi Germany's goal of expansion through the methodical conquering and colonization of Europe and Mussolini's desire to re-create the Roman Empire by overtaking parts of the Mediterranean and Africa brought both nations into alliance—there was nothing to stop these dictators an their agendas.

To add to this volatile coalition we insert Japan. The Japanese deeply resented America's refusal to recognize its racial equality clause in the covenants of the League of Nations. This rejection, along with the League's failure to flex its authority, led to Japan's alienation from the West.

As a means to resolve growing economic problems, Japan declared war on China in 1937. America demonstrated its opposition to Japan's onslaught by imposing trade embargoes and economic sanctions. Japan imported over 90 percent of its fuel, and the US oil embargo was the last straw. The world became ripe for war.

In late August of 1939, Hitler reached an agreement of non-intervention with Joseph Stalin of the Soviet Union known as the

Hitler-Stalin Pact.[48] One week later, on September 1, Hitler invaded Poland. In response to the invasion, France and Great Britain declared war on Germany two days later. By the summer of 1940, Italy had allied with Germany.

The Nazis continued to advance through Europe and the Mediterranean and, as was Hitler's intent all along, targeted the Soviet Union. The Soviet Union kept Germany out of Moscow with a major offensive and as a result became a key player within the Allied powers (countries opposed to Germany).

America had avoided participation in the war in Europe, but when Japan attacked Pearl Harbor on December 7, 1941, we declared war on them the next day. By December 11, Germany and Italy declared war on America. Once the lines were drawn, the combatants were defined as the Axis and Allied powers. The Axis nations included Nazi Germany, fascist Italy, and imperial Japan. The Allied nations were composed of the constitutional monarchy of Great Britain, the communist states of the Soviet Union, and the democratic United States of America.

By its conclusion, World War II had engaged nearly every major nation on earth. For 2,190 consecutive days, more than 32,400 people were killed every twenty-four hours, making it the most destructive conflict in human history.

However, few in the world knew that Hitler was also conducting his *secret war against the Jews* within the confines of his conquered territory. By the end of the war, the Nazis would be directly responsible for murdering two-thirds of the Jewish population of Europe.[49]

THE HOLOCAUST—
HITLER'S FINAL SOLUTION

From 1938 to 1942, the Jewish people of Europe suffered great humiliation, persecution, torture, displacement, and the loss of all their possessions, including their rights as German citizens and, in due course, as human beings. They underwent forced relocations into cramped and disease-infested ghettos and experienced compulsory deportations to concentration camps.

Throughout Hitler's reign, there were several contributing factors that ultimately influenced the evolution of Nazi racial anti-Semitism into Jewish genocide. Among the major influences were:

1. Hitler's never-ending lies depicting the Jews as an inferior race.
2. The incessant portrayal of the Jewish people as "communist subversives, as war profiteers and hoarders."
3. The false Nazi propaganda of the Jewish goal to gain world dominance at the expense of German Aryans.
4. Violent pogroms such as Kristallnacht.
5. The Nuremberg Laws.
6. The massive complications arising from the overcrowded, disease-infested Jewish ghettos and concentration camps.
7. Hitler's demand for a solution to the Jewish problem.[50]

In January of 1942, Reinhard Heydrich was delegated by Hitler to conceive a comprehensive plan for the Final Solution. Heydrich, who was second in command of the SS or *Schutzstaffel* (German for "Protective Echelon"), convened the Wannsee Conference in Berlin. He gathered fifteen top Nazi bureaucrats to coordinate a systematic plan to exterminate the entire Jewish population of Europe, which was projected to be approximately eleven million people.[51]

Every Jewish man, woman, and child in Europe and North Africa was tagged for annihilation, and eventually six million (including two million children) were murdered by the Nazis between 1942 and 1945. This supreme act of genocide is called the Holocaust.

To implement their grisly plan, the Nazis transported Jews to "purpose-built extermination camps" in occupied Poland. Once there, the Jewish captives were systematically murdered in gas chambers. By the time the war was over, a total of six killing centers and thousands of concentration camps existed in Germany and Nazi-controlled territory.[52]

It is impossible to sufficiently present the horrors of the Holocaust within this book; however, countless volumes have been written on the atrocities committed against the Jewish people, including first-hand accounts.

Christians must know the truth about what happened to God's chosen people. It is important to understand the cautious response of our Jewish friends when we extend our hand of friendship—a gesture they haven't seen in the past. I highly recommend you read as many reliable resources as possible to further educate yourself of the atrocities that were committed against the Jewish people in the name of Jesus Christ.[53]

We ask, how could this happen? How could human beings murder over six million people in cold blood and the world stand idly by? How could the world's Christians ignore this? How is it that those who shared God's Torah with us, who brought forth the patriarchs, who gave us the apostles and, most importantly, our Redeemer, could be so despised? Why were we silent?

The church as a whole was silent in defense of the Jewish people, but it was not silent in condemning them. Holocaust historian Raul Hilberg described how anti-Semitism within the church presented the perfect atmosphere for Hitler's Final Solution of the Jewish problem:

The missionaries of Christianity had said in effect: You have no right to live among us as Jews. The secular rulers who followed had proclaimed: You have no right to live among us. The German Nazis at last decreed: You have no right to live.[54]

Many have asked, "Why didn't America do more to intervene with the evil of the Holocaust?" The Allied nations ranked victory over their enemies above anything else. The humanitarian concern of saving the Jews from Hitler's Final Solution was not a top priority. In combination with anti-Semitic sentiments and domestic concerns, including unemployment and national security, there was little to no attention paid to the plight of European Jews.

Even though history records the actions of Jewish organizations and a few righteous Gentiles throughout the world who bravely confronted the evils of anti-Semitism, most were apathetic and silent. At best, America was guilty of indifference.

Elie Wiesel, survivor of the Final Solution and my friend, provided an answer to the question *why*:

The opposite of love is not hate, it's indifference. The opposite of beauty is not ugliness, it's indifference. The opposite of faith is not heresy, it's indifference. And the opposite of life is not death, but indifference between life and death.[55]

Elie also shared a painful truth: "What hurts the victim most is not the cruelty of the oppressor but the silence of the bystander."[56] And it was our sin of silence that God Almighty heard the loudest.

CHAPTER 3

THE SIN OF SILENCE

Silence in the face of evil is itself evil: God will not hold us guiltless. Not to speak is to speak. Not to act is to act. (Dietrich Bonhoeffer)

Anti-Semitism is very much alive and thriving. The mechanism by which this evil hatred displays its ugly talons is modernized, but the overall message is the same: dehumanize and demonize the Jewish people at every opportunity through all means possible.

One of the most prominent anti-Semitic propaganda movements to advance in the last twenty-plus years in North America and Western Europe has been the organized efforts to deny the existence or diminish the consequences of the Holocaust—the mass slaughter of six million Jews. Kenneth Marcus, in a blog post titled "The Horror of Holocaust Denial," defined this deliberately orchestrated repudiation perfectly: "Holocaust denial is not just an ordinary form of ignorance but rather a modern cloak for the return of old-fashioned anti-Semitism."[1]

The primary premise of this evil distortion of truth is that if *no one* (non-Jews) actually witnessed the Holocaust, and if *no one* truly heard about it—then it really didn't happen. Those who advocate this deceit claim that the Jews were, and continue to be, conniving perpetrators of lies and exaggerations to gain sympathy with the world for their personal benefit. The Holocaust deniers attack four basic realities surrounding this heinous event. I will challenge each of their false assertions by presenting the truth about:

1. The existence of the extermination camps
2. The capacity of the gas chambers
3. The actual number of Jewish victims
4. The massive extent of the Nazis' crimes against humanity[2]

THE TRUTH ABOUT THE DEATH CAMPS

The Holocaust was the "systematic, bureaucratic, state-sponsored persecution and murder of six million Jews by the Nazi regime and its collaborators."[3] The personal declaration of major Nazi players to eradicate all the Jewish people from Europe confirmed that their repugnant goal was part of their ultimate agenda. I quoted Adolf Hitler in the last chapter, but his statement bears repeating. In the führer's speech to the German parliament on January 30, 1939, he avowed the following:

> Today I will once more be a prophet: If the international Jewish financiers in and outside Europe should succeed in plunging the nations once more into a world war, then the result will not be the Bolshevization of the earth, and thus the victory of Jewry, but the annihilation of the Jewish race in Europe![4]

On December 12, 1941, one day after Germany declared war on America, Hitler called a meeting of the Reich Chancellery. It was here that he reaffirmed the imminent annihilation of the Jewish race to the top-ranking officers of the Nazi Party. Hans Frank, governor general of occupied Poland, and Joseph Goebbels, the Reich's minister of propaganda, documented the details of the secretive meeting. An excerpt of Goebbels's notes reads as follows:

[Regarding the Jewish question, the führer] warned the Jews that if they were to cause another world war, it would lead to their own destruction [referring to the Reichstag speech of 1939]. Those were not empty words. Now the world war has come. The destruction of the Jews must be its necessary consequence. This question is to be regarded without sentimentalism. We are not here to have sympathy with the Jews, but rather with our German people. If the German people have sacrificed 160,000 dead in the eastern campaign, so the authors of this bloody conflict will have to pay for it with their lives.[5]

The chancellery meeting was a defining moment in the Nazi government's true intent for the Jewish people. This covert gathering played a major part in the comprehensive transition from propaganda, terrorization, and assaults against the Jewish people to the premeditated and calculated genocide of six million Jews. The Wannsee Conference of January 1942, which I mentioned in chapter 2, was the turning point for the presentation of the "Final Solution to the Jewish problem." This conference included the final plans for the killing camps.

By November of 1943, the rumors of the Final Solution became more widespread. Julius Streicher, anti-Semitic propagandist and father of the German Socialist Party, wrote in his Nazi newspaper,

> It is really the truth that the Jews, so to speak, have disappeared from Europe and that the Jewish reservoir of the East, from which the Jewish plague has for centuries beset the peoples of Europe, has ceased to exist. However, the Fuehrer of the German people at the beginning of the war prophesied what has now come to pass.[6]

THE TRUTH ABOUT
THE GAS CHAMBERS

The Nazis were masters of efficiency, keeping thorough records and detailed files. The number of deported Jews, the location to where they were transported, the names and tattoo numbers of concentration camp prisoners, and so on. They were also resourceful in everything they did. The ovens were in operation twenty-four hours a day, seven days a week—so much so, that witnesses said the doors melted off their hinges. The Nazis instructed their Jewish workers, or *Sonderkommandos*, to "burn the corpses, stoke the fires, drain body fat, and to periodically turn over the 'mountain of burning corpses' for even combustion and a peak fire-temperature."[7] These unwilling slaves "were well aware that they, too, would meet exactly the same fate."

With classic Nazi proficiency, all the remains of the dead were "recycled." Human hair was used for stuffing pillows and mattresses, and the human ash from the crematoriums was applied as fertilizer. The Nazis were "cost-conscious" as well; they made surviving Jews pay for as many items and services as possible.

When a Jewish person was killed and cremated in the camps, his or her relatives would receive a postcard informing them that their loved one had died of a heart attack or some other natural cause. In addition, the card notified the family members that if they would "kindly send 3 ½ [German] Marks," the Nazi government would in turn send them the ashes of their loved one.[8] The Nazis also developed various extermination procedures so as to be as practical as possible when it came to carrying out the "Final Solution."

Adolf Eichmann, who led the Gestapo Department for Jewish Affairs, was charged with implementing Nazi policies concerning the extermination of the Jews in all the sixteen German-occupied countries. As he rose through the ranks, Eichmann became one of the key logistical officials in charge of deporting and transporting the Jews throughout Europe to the death camps. It was said he kept the "trains rolling."[9]

On one occasion, Eichmann observed the Nazis lead Jewish men, women, and children at gunpoint to the outskirts of a small town. Once they reached a designated area, they were then taken en masse to the edge of a freshly dug ditch and forced to disrobe. As they were ordered to kneel, the German soldiers shot them in the back of the head. The dead fell into the mammoth grave, and the workers immediately covered the bodies with mounds of dirt.

Eichmann described the gruesome scene after the war at the Trial of the Major War Criminals before the International Military Tribunal in Nuremberg: "The execution ditch had been covered over with dirt, but blood was gushing out of the ground 'like a geyser' due to pressure from the bodily gasses of the deceased."[10]

When his superior, Heinrich Himmler, later witnessed a similar scene, he almost fainted. Himmler, along with Heydrich and Eichmann, were Hitler's most loyal henchmen charged with carrying out the Final Solution. It was Himmler who established the first concentration camp in Dachau, Germany. He also led the SS (Hitler's elite force) and the Gestapo (secret police). After Himmler viewed the bloody massacre, he wanted to spare his men the trauma of the horrible aftermath, so he ordered Eichmann to develop and implement a more "humane method" to accomplish their grisly task. Himmler was not concerned for the Jewish victims but for the perpetrators. It was at this time that the Nazis focused their efforts on gassing the Jews en masse.

To some degree, death by carbon monoxide gas was already in use within the Nazi "Euthanasia Program." Mobile gas vans were first used to streamline the existing operations for executing the elderly, the deformed, and the mentally impaired. Now it was time to expand their eradication program to include the building of gas chambers and crematoriums within the death camps as a better way to rid the world of the "sub-human vermin."

Rudolf Höss, the barbarous commandant of Auschwitz, was the poster child for both evil and proficiency. He, like so many other Nazi leaders, was a classic study in contradiction. Höss was described as a "mild-mannered, happily married Catholic who enjoyed normal family life with his five children," yet he represented humanity's utmost decline into the abyss of evil. Höss was the designer and administrator of the gas chambers and is referred to as "history's greatest mass murderer" and the "architect of Auschwitz"— the largest of the killing centers.[11]

Höss analyzed the extermination procedures at other killing camps and "perfected" the process so he could more efficiently gas as many as two thousand Jews at one time within the death chambers. He believed that the most effective way to gas the prisoners was by using a cyanide gas called "Zyklon B" instead of the carbon monoxide gas, which was previously used. Höss is recorded as stating,

The gassing was carried out in the detention cells of Block 11. Protected by a gas mask, I watched the killing myself. In the crowded cells, death came instantaneously the moment the Zyklon B was thrown in. A short, almost smothered cry and it was all over. . . . I must even admit that this gassing set my mind at rest, for the mass extermination of the Jews was to start soon, and at that time neither Eichmann nor I was certain as to how these mass killings were to be carried out. It would be by gas, but we did not know which gas and how it was to be used. Now we had the gas, and we had established a procedure.[12]

At full capacity, the gas chambers at Auschwitz gassed and cremated ten thousand to twelve thousand Jews per day. These numbers only reflect murders by gassing; death also came by disease, torture, starvation, shooting, and severe bludgeoning. Auschwitz was a place of suffering, torment, and slaughter—it was a living hell.

Survivors testified at Höss's trial that they remembered him "counting corpses with the cool dedication of a trained bookkeeper."[13] Höss confessed before his execution how he repeatedly felt "weak-kneed at having to push hundreds of screaming, pleading children into the gas chambers":

I did, however, always feel ashamed of this weakness of mine after I talked to Adolf Eichmann. He explained to me that it was especially the children who have to be killed first, because where was the logic in killing a generation of older people and leaving alive a generation of young people who can be possible avengers of their parents and can constitute a new biological cell for the reemerging of this people.[14]

Höss was found guilty for the murder of 2.5 million Jews and was hanged next to the main crematorium at Auschwitz.

Another high-ranking Nazi party official was Hans Frank, who was also Hitler's personal legal advisor, among his many other duties. As acting Bavarian minister of justice, Frank played a major role in revolutionizing the "New Order" of the Nazi state legal system. During his time in office, Frank kept a meticulous diary, which later was used to convict him and other Nazi criminals during the Nuremberg trials.

Frank's journal was composed of thirty-eight volumes in which he provided detailed descriptions of the daily, minute-by-minute brutalities that took place within the death camps. I have included one such despicable entry in Frank's diary not to *offend* but to *educate* with the *truth* of what happened within the death camps. The following is one of Frank's daily entries that depict the calculated mass herding, dehumanizing, and massacre of Jews in the gas chambers of Auschwitz:

> The mass extermination of the Jews in Auschwitz occurred as follows. The Jews selected to be killed were led, men and women separately, as calmly as possible to the crematoria. In the undressing room, Sonderkommando prisoners [Jewish *slave* labor used to assist the Nazis] spoke to the Jews in their native tongue, telling them that they were only going to be bathed and deloused, that they should keep their clothes items together, and above all to remember where they left them, so that they could find them quickly after the delousing. . . . After undressing, the Jews entered the gas chamber, furnished with showerheads and water pipes to give the impression of a bathhouse.
>
> The women and children entered first, then the men, of whom there were always fewer. . . . [The Jews] were calmed by the Sonderkommando prisoners . . . as well as one of the SS guards [who] always remained in the gas chamber until the last moment. Next the door was quickly closed and bolted,

and the awaiting disinfectors immediately threw in the gas [pellets] through an opening in the ceiling down special pipes to the floor. This instantly caused the gas to dissipate.

Through a viewer in the door you could see that those nearest to the inlet pipes fell dead immediately. The remainder started to stagger, shout and gasp for air. The shouting, however, soon turned into wheezing, and, after a few minutes, everyone was down. After 20 minutes at most, no one was moving. Depending on the weather, whether it was humid or dry, hot or cold, and depending on the quality of the gas, which was not always the same, finally, depending on the transport, whether many were healthy or old, or sick, or whether there were many children, the gas became effective within five to ten minutes.

Loss of consciousness occurred just after a few minutes, depending on the distance from the inlet shafts. Those shouting, the elderly, the weak and the children died faster than the healthy and young. Within half an hour after the gas was thrown in, the door was opened and the ventilators were turned on. The extraction of the bodies commenced immediately. They showed no signs of physical change, contraction or discoloration. Only after they had been lying for several hours did post-mortem lividity appear. Bodies being soiled with feces was also rare. No physical injuries were ever identified. . . .

The Sonderkommando pulled gold teeth out of the corpses, and the women had their hair cut off. Next the bodies were transported up in lifts to the already burning furnaces. Depending on the size of the bodies, up to three corpses could be fitted into one furnace chamber. Likewise, the cremation time depended on the type of corpse, but on

average it lasted 20 minutes. As I mentioned earlier, crematoria I and II together were able to burn around 2,000
corpses within 24 hours. The burning of larger numbers of
corpses was not possible without causing damage.

Crematoria III and IV were supposed to be able to burn
1,500 corpses within 24 hours, but I do not know whether
that figure was ever reached. During the burning, the cinders and ashes constantly fell through the grids. They were
also constantly taken away or first pulverized. The ashes and
crushed cinders were transported in trucks to the Vistula,
and there they were thrown into the water with spades to
immediately flow away and disperse.[15]

Just another day . . . just another entry.

However, amidst the monstrous atrocities of the Holocaust,
there was another Hand keeping meticulous records in the chronicles of heaven. It was a Jewish hand. Every tear was counted, every
lash of the whip recorded, and every death mourned.

Sometime soon there will come the Judgment Day, when God
Almighty will settle the accounts of every act of Jewish hatred in the
history of the world. The gates of hell will be fully opened, and there
all anti-Semites who have not repented of their sin of hatred toward
the Jewish people will be incarcerated for eternity (Deuteronomy
7:15; 30:7; 1 John 2:9–11; 3:15; 4:20; Romans 2:5–11).

THE TRUTH ABOUT THE NUMBERS

It is important to remember that by war's end, the Nazis and their
butchery encompassed the majority of the European continent.
Most of us who know anything about the Holocaust refer to only
a few of the twenty-three camps that existed throughout Nazi-
occupied territory. However, what few people know is that within

the twenty-three larger camps, to include the familiar names such as Auschwitz, Buchenwald, Dachau, and Treblinka, were sub-camps that were connected to them.[16]

Current research has determined that the Nazis actually established about 42,500 camps and ghettos between 1933 and 1945. These sites included 30,000 slave labor camps, 1,150 Jewish ghettos, 980 concentration camps, 1,000 POW camps, 500 brothels filled with sex slaves, and thousands of other camps used for euthanizing the mentally disabled, sick, and elderly, as well as the infamous death camps that slaughter the masses.[17]

We have already noted that the Jews of Europe were the primary victims of the Nazis. In 1933, 9.5 million Jews lived in the countries that would eventually be occupied by Germany during the war. By 1945, two out of every three European Jews had been murdered.[18]

I could present substantiated number after substantiated number in this chapter, but I ask, what's in a number?

Can you determine the value of people—and of their souls—with a number? Can you tell what they looked like or what they studied in college? Can you know whom they married or how many children they had? Can you determine what they did for a living or what their gifts and talents were? Can you conclude their pastimes, dreams, and aspirations? Can a number in a German log or on a Jewish arm reveal the significance of a human being?

Absolutely not!

Every one of the statistical figures mentioned in history books was God's creation, filled with a hope and a future. Each one was like you and me—someone with a life story, living every day to the fullest, anticipating the hug of a loved one after arriving home from a long day's work—*except they were Jewish.*

They were productive members of their communities where their ancestors had lived for generations—*except they were Jewish.*

They were mothers, fathers, shopkeepers, doctors, rabbis, lawyers, students, craftsmen, bakers, poets, musicians, and professors; they were everyday people—*except they were Jewish.*

Two million of them were young children naïve about the evils of this world. They were like our children and grandchildren—full of innocence, filled with spontaneous laughter and joy—and some were yet unborn. Every one of them was known to God; He called them by name, *and they were Jewish.*

No matter how alike or diverse the victims were. No matter the horrors of torture, starvation, pestilence, and disease they experienced. No matter the name of the camp or the length of their imprisonment—the observant Jewish people remained faithful to the Lord by obeying His commandments.

If there was a Hanukkah candle to light, they lit it; if there was a prayer to recite, they recited it; if there was a psalm to sing, they sang it; if there was a Sabbath to welcome, they welcomed it; and if there was a Passover to observe, they observed it. Through whatever means they had, they remained true to the God of Abraham, Isaac, and Jacob.

> *My son, keep my words,*
> *And treasure my commands within you.*
> *Keep my commands and live,*
> *And my law as the apple of your eye.*
> *Bind them on your fingers;*
> *Write them on the tablet of your heart.*
> *(Proverbs 7:1–3)*

Even though the Nazis kept fastidious records of deportations, internments, and gassings, no master list of those who perished in the Holocaust exists.

As the end of the war neared, the Nazis kept fewer tallies and destroyed many of their existing records in order to have more time to achieve as much of the Final Solution as possible and still hide the evidence that this diabolical plan had ever happened. For example, it was estimated that during this period, as many as twenty thousand Jewish people a day were being murdered in one way or another at Auschwitz alone.

Most who espouse Holocaust denial advocate that the death of nearly two-thirds of all the Jews of Europe was merely a result of collateral damage owed to the ravages of war—not so! In spite of the whitewash of some German journal accounts, several reputable estimates of the total number of Jewish deaths have been made through the years. These recognized calculations were drawn using the existing Nazi records as well as criteria gathered in the comparison of before and after World War II population surveys.

Trained historian Dr. Wilhelm Höttl initially cited the total number of Jewish people who died at the hand of the Nazis. Höttl served in the SS and testified at the Nuremberg trials of a conversation he had with Adolf Eichmann on the subject of numbers:

Eichmann confided to [Höttl] in August 1944 that some four million Jews had been killed in the "various extermination camps," and another two million had been killed in other ways, mostly in shootings by Einsatzgruppen forces in the course of the military campaign in Russia.[19]

Since then, there have been other notable scientific calculations to include those by Raul Hilberg, who determined there were a total of 5.1 million Jews killed in the Holocaust.[20] And those of Lucy Dawidowicz, who used pre-war birth and death records to come up with the more detailed figure of 5,933,900 deaths.[21] And also

German scholar Wolfgang Benz, who calculated a range of 5.3 to 6.2 million total Jewish victims.[22]

After Germany's surrender in May of 1945, Adolf Eichmann was arrested but later escaped and achieved asylum in Argentina under the assumed name of Ricardo Klement. In 1960, the Israeli Mossad captured him and took him to Jerusalem, where he was put on trial as a Nazi war offender and charged with crimes against humanity, specifically the Jewish people.

Over one hundred witnesses testified against him during the trial. When Eichmann spoke in his defense, he did not deny the existence of the Final Solution, dispute its horrors, or debate the vastness of its numbers—he merely said he was obeying orders.

Two of the most appalling statements Eichmann made throughout the trials were: "I regret nothing"[23] and "I will leap into my grave laughing because the feeling that I have five million human beings on my conscience [is] for me a source of extraordinary satisfaction."[24] Eichmann was found guilty on all counts by the Jewish court, sentenced to death, and hanged;[25] and, I can assure you that he is not currently laughing in the flames of hell.

In 2015, former SS officer Oskar Gröning, known as the "Accountant of Auschwitz," was sentenced to four years after being tried and convicted of being complicit in the murder of three hundred thousand Auschwitz inmates. In his testimony, Gröning felt it was important to speak out in light of the mounting propaganda surrounding the Holocaust denial movement; his message to the deniers was clear and direct:

> I want to tell those deniers I have seen the gas chambers, I have seen the crematoria, I have seen the burning pits—and I want you to believe me that these atrocities happened. I was there.[26]

Ironically, his lawyers appealed the sentence, arguing that Gröning's "fundamental right to life and physical safety was being violated." However, the German court denied the appeal, ruling in December of 2017 that Gröning "was part of the 'machinery of death,' helping the camp function and collecting money stolen from the victims to help the Nazi cause, and thus could be convicted of accessory to the murders committed there."[27] The ninety-six-year-old Gröning died in March of 2018 before serving his sentence.

Noted author and documentary film director of *Auschwitz: The Nazis and the "Final Solution"* Laurence Rees said the following about Gröning's trial and conviction: "It was too little too late." In June of 2017, seventy-two years after World War II ended, the German media reported that twenty-eight prosecutions against alleged war criminals and concentration camp guards were in progress. However, the defendants were over ninety years old; they had all led full lives—too little too late.

A calculation you might find troubling: there were nearly ten thousand Nazis who worked at Auschwitz,[28] and unlike their victims, seven thousand of them survived the war. Of the seven thousand, fewer than eight hundred were put on trial. Of those tried, less than eighty were prosecuted.[29]

THE TRUTH ABOUT THE CARNAGE

As the war was ending in the early fall of 1945, Allied troops swept throughout Europe with a chain of successful military incursions against the Nazis. It was then that they discovered the horrible truth of Hitler's Final Solution. The Allies found camp after camp packed with thousands of concentration prisoners—most of whom were the walking dead. What the Allies didn't see were the millions who had mercilessly died before the liberation of the death camps.

Most of the survivors had experienced years of untold cruelty and suffering, including the loss of all their family members. The prisoners were nothing more than human skeletons infested with fleas, lice, and rodent bites. All were suffering from the ravages of disease, infection, and extreme starvation. Even though the Allies were eyewitnesses, no one could wholly grasp the full extent of the Nazi horrors against the Jewish people.

One of the first Nazi camps to be liberated by American troops was Ohrdruf, a sub-camp of Buchenwald. On April 12, Generals George Patton, Omar Bradley, and Dwight Eisenhower entered the gates of the camp and found, among many other atrocities, 3,200 naked, emaciated corpses in shallow graves, sheds holding stacks of dead bodies ready for cremation, and more victims partly incinerated on Nazi constructed pyres.[30]

General Patton became physically ill and was so enraged by what he saw that he demanded that local German citizens take an immediate tour of the camp and witness what they had allowed to happen. Patton ordered over two thousand residents of the town of Weimar to view firsthand the carnage of the site. Weimar was famous for its classic poets Goethe and Schiller and its beloved composers Johann Sebastian Bach, Richard Strauss, and Franz Liszt. Now its citizens were touring a nearby death camp where thousands had been massacred. Weimer's inhabitants were horrified yet claimed they were "unaware" of what was taking place, even though they lived barely four miles away.

General Bradley later commented as they walked through the camp that "the smell of death overwhelmed us." It was reported that General Dwight D. Eisenhower, the supreme commander of the Allied Forces in Europe, "turned white at the scene inside the gates, but insisted on seeing the entire camp." Eisenhower commented, "We are told that the American soldier does not know what he was fighting for; now, at least he will know what he is fighting against."[31]

Eisenhower gave the order that all American units in the area were to tour the camp. He felt it was imperative to have as many witnesses as possible of the insidious carnage the Jewish internees had suffered. Eisenhower immediately sent a message to his leadership in Washington, DC, regarding his tour of the Nazi camp:

> The things I saw beggar description. . . . The visual evidence and the verbal testimony of starvation, cruelty and bestiality were so overpowering. . . . I made the visit deliberately, in order to be in a position to give first-hand evidence of these things if ever, in the future, there develops a tendency to charge these allegations merely to "propaganda."[32]

Apparently General Eisenhower sensed, even then, that the inhumane brutalities against the Jewish people might one day be challenged or denied.

Even though hundreds of thousands of Jews died in the ghettos, through pogroms, on death marches, and in concentration camps, nearly one-half of the six million who died in the Holocaust were exterminated within the six designated killing camps located in Nazi-occupied Poland. The camps were named Auschwitz-Birkenau, Treblinka, Belzec, Sobibór, Chełmno, and Majdanek.

In order to get the truth to the world about what the Nazis had done to the Jewish people, Eisenhower called on President Truman. He asked the president to send a congressional delegation along with members of the American press to personally witness the carnage. You must remember that there was a time in America when the media represented and reported the straightforward facts about history and current events versus today's mass liberal media, who merely broadcast their personal sociopolitical version and opinion of what they perceive to be true.

Truman granted Eisenhower's plea, and within a short time, a congressional delegation accompanied by top journalists and experienced photographers came to tour the concentration camps. Once there, no one could believe what they saw.

Leading journalist Edward R. Murrow, who had become a legend on American radio during World War II, was among them. Murrow prided himself in taking the news to the world as it happened. It was said that when Murrow reported on the bombing of London it was as if he "burned the city of London in our houses and we felt the flames that burned it."[33]

In a legendary broadcast on April 15, 1945, Edward R. Murrow gave the American radio audience a heart-wrenching yet factual description of Buchenwald. Buchenwald was one of the largest forced labor concentration camps within the old borders of Germany. The main camp had 174 sub-camps, where prisoners were worked, poisoned, and starved to death, used in horrific medical experiments, and shot or hung. The dead were either buried in mass graves or burned in crematoriums. Survivors and liberators alike testified of seeing skins of prisoners that were used to cover books, make lampshades, or simply taken as souvenirs.[34]

As many as 238,980 prisoners walked through Buchenwald's gates between 1937 and 1945, and of those at least 43,045 were murdered in one way or another; the balance were transported to the killing camps.[35]

The following are excerpts of what Murrow described to America that day:

Permit me to tell you what you would have seen and heard had you been with me. . . . There surged around me an evil-smelling stink. Men and boys reached out to touch me. They were in rags and the remnants of uniforms. Death had already marked many of them, but they were smiling with their eyes. . . .

When I entered [the barracks], men crowded around, tried to lift me to their shoulders. They were too weak. Many of them could not get out of bed. I was told that this building had once stabled 80 horses. There were 1,200 men in it, five to a bunk. The stink was beyond all description. When I reached the center of the barracks, a man came up and said, "You remember me, I am Petr Zenkl, one time mayor of Prague." I remembered him, but did not recognize him. . . .

As I walked down to the end of the barracks, there was applause from the men too weak to get out of bed. It sounded like the hand-clapping of babies, they were so weak. . . . As we walked out into the courtyard—a man fell dead. Two others . . . were crawling toward the latrine. I saw it, but will not describe it.

In another part of the camp they showed me the children, hundreds of them. Some were only six. One rolled up his sleeve, showed me his number. It was tattooed on his arm B-6030, it was. The others showed me their numbers. They will carry them till they die. . . . I could see their ribs through their thin shirts. . . . The children clung to my hands and stared.

We crossed to the courtyard. Men kept coming up to me to speak to me and touch me, professors from Poland, doctors from Vienna, men from all of Europe. Men from the countries that made America.

We went to the hospital; it was full. The doctor told me that two hundred had died the day before. I asked the cause of death. He shrugged and said: "Tuberculosis, starvation, fatigue, and there are many who have no desire to live. It is very difficult." . . .

We proceeded to the small courtyard. . . . There were two rows of bodies stacked up like cordwood. They were thin and very white. Some of the bodies were terribly bruised, though there seemed to be little flesh to bruise. Some had been shot through the head, but they bled but little. All except two were naked. I tried to count them as best I could, and arrived at the conclusion that all that was mortal of more than five hundred men and boys lay there in two neat piles. . . .

Murder had been done at Buchenwald. God alone knows how many men and boys have died there. . . . I was told that there were more than twenty thousand in the camp. There had been as many as sixty thousand. Where are they now?

As I left the camp, a Frenchman who used to work for Havas [news agency] in Paris came up to me and said, "You will write something about this, perhaps?" And he added, "To write about this, you must have been here at least two years, and after that—you don't want to write anymore."

I pray you to believe what I have said about Buchenwald. I have reported what I saw and heard, but only part of it. For most of it, I have no words. Dead men are plentiful in war, but the living dead, more than twenty thousand of them in one camp. . . . If I have offended you by this rather mild account of Buchenwald, I'm not in the least sorry.[36]

Media reports such as Murrow's, along with eyewitness testimonies from prominent delegations, in addition to thousands of photographs by expert and amateur photographers, as well as actual newsreel clips of the atrocities shown in theaters around the globe contributed to a stark awakening. Finally, an otherwise clueless (or indifferent) world acknowledged the horrible reality of what was done to the European Jewish people in an attempt to eradicate all 11 million from the face of the earth.

THE RIGHTEOUS GENTILES

Most of us have read or quoted Edmund Burke's statement, "The only thing necessary for the triumph of evil is for good men to do nothing." This profound truth resonated within the horrors of the Holocaust. It has been said that had more people taken a stand for righteousness, many of the atrocities committed against the Jewish people and other innocent victims could have been avoided, and millions would have been saved. Jesus Christ will judge the nations of the world for the sin of silence as recorded in Matthew:

> *Then He will also say to those on the left hand, "Depart from me . . . for I was hungry and you gave Me no food; I was thirsty and you gave Me no drink; I was a stranger and you did not take Me in, naked and you did not clothe Me, sick and in prison and you did not visit Me." Then they also will answer Him, saying, "Lord, when did we see You hungry or thirsty or a stranger or naked or sick or in prison, and did not minister to You?" Then He will answer them, saying, "Assuredly, I say to you, inasmuch as you did not do it to one of the least of these, you did not do it to Me." And these will go away into everlasting punishment, but the righteous into eternal life. (25:42–46)*

Erwin Lutzer tells the following story from an eyewitness in Germany during the Holocaust:

I lived in Germany during the Nazi Holocaust. I considered myself a Christian. We heard stories of what was happening to Jews, but we tried to distance ourselves from it because what could we do to stop it. A railroad track ran behind our small church and each Sunday morning we could hear the whistle in the distance, and then the wheels coming over the tracks. We became disturbed when we heard the cries coming from the train as it passed by. We realized that it was carrying Jews like cattle in the cars. Week after week the whistle would blow. We dreaded to hear the sound of those wheels because we knew that we would hear the cries of the Jews in route to a death camp. Their screams tormented us. We knew the time the train was coming, and when we heard the whistle blow, we began singing hymns. By the time the train came past our church, we were singing at the top of our voices. If we heard the screams, we sang more loudly and soon we heard them no more. . . . Although years have passed, I still hear the train whistle in my sleep. God forgive me, forgive all of us who called ourselves Christians and yet did nothing to intervene.[37]

Those of us that saw the movie *Schindler's List* remember the emotional closing scene where Oskar Schindler tearfully cries out, "Maybe I could have saved one more—just one more!" All of humanity must ask the question of themselves, "If my Jewish friends and neighbors were threatened, would I risk my life and the lives of my loves ones in order to come to their rescue?" This is the question exceptional men and women answered during the Holocaust—and their answer was yes!

"Righteous Gentiles" is a name given to non-Jews who chose to take great risks to help and in most cases save thousands of Jewish lives from the devastation of the Final Solution. The survivors identified hundreds of these honorable men and women, but hundreds more go unrecognized except by the Righteous Judge of Heaven. Allow me to share a few compelling stories of these brave rescuers.

Adelaide Hautval

A devout Protestant, Dr. Adelaide Hautval lived in southern France during World War II. Hautval was captured by German police in the spring of 1942 and transported to prison when she attempted to cross into occupied Paris after the Nazis denied her permission to attend her mother's funeral.

By that summer, Jewish captives wearing the yellow Star of David began to arrive at the prison. It became evident shortly after their arrival that the Jewish prisoners were being treated much more severely than the other inmates. Dr. Hautval courageously objected to their inhumane treatment, and the guards punished her by sentencing her to the same fate as the Jewish women. This did not influence the doctor's convictions—in response to her captor's pronouncement, Adelaide "pinned a piece of yellow paper to her clothing that read, 'Friend of the Jews.'"[38]

By early 1943, Dr. Hautval had been relocated to the Birkenau death camp, where she shared a barracks with five hundred Jewish women. This caring doctor was soon nicknamed "the saint" because of her kindness toward her fellow Jewish inmates. With no medical resources at her disposal, she secretly treated and isolated those who were infected with contagious diseases. Dr. Hautval not only protected the healthier prisoners from illness, she also did not report the sick as she was instructed to—sparing hundreds from an instant death sentence.

Dr. Hautval was later transferred to Auschwitz I camp, where medical experiments were performed by the likes of Drs. Eduard

Wirths, Wladislaw Dering, and of course, Josef Mengele. While at Auschwitz, she refused to participate in any medical experiments and boldly declared, "No person was entitled to claim the life or determine the fate of another."[39] Miraculously, she was not killed for insubordination and was sent back to Birkenau and later to Ravensbrück, where she survived until freed by the liberators.

The Jewish survivors Dr. Hautval came in contact with remembered her compassion, encouragement, and determined dignity. Many quoted her as saying, "Here [Auschwitz] we are all under a sentence of death. Let us behave like human beings as long as we are alive." She later provided eyewitness testimony against the doctors at Auschwitz at a hearing held in London and was described as "one of the most impressive and courageous women ever to testify before a court in Great Britain—a woman of strong character and an extraordinary personality."[40] Dr. Hautval proved to be a true friend to the Jews.

Roddie Edmonds

American master sergeant Roddie Edmonds of Knoxville, Tennessee, was credited with saving the lives of two hundred Jewish soldiers at a German prisoner of war camp. The righteous actions that Edmonds took personified the united stand the American people took against the Nazis once they came in contact with the carnage of the Holocaust.

Edmonds was taken prisoner and sent to Stalag IX-A by the Germans during the Battle of the Bulge. In January 1945, the German commandant of the camp announced that all Jewish prisoners of war were to report in front of their barracks the following morning. It was presumed by Edmonds and others that the Jewish soldiers were going to be transported to a Nazi extermination camp for execution.

Edmonds, the highest-ranking soldier in the camp, instead ordered all Jews and non-Jews to report in formation. Shocked by the over 1,270 inmates before him, the German camp commander shouted at Edmonds, "They cannot all be Jews!"

Edmonds firmly responded, "We are all Jews here."[41]

When threatened at gunpoint by the camp commander, Edmonds gave his name, rank, and serial number and declared to the commandant and all present, "If you shoot me, you will have to shoot all of us, and after the war you will be tried for war crimes."[42] Shockingly, after Edmond's bold statement, the commandant walked away.

When testifying of the incident, a Jewish prisoner at the camp stated, "Although 70 years have passed, I can still hear the words he [Edmonds] said to the German camp commander." Another Jewish soldier who was captured with Edmonds recalled, "There was no question in my mind, or that of Master Sgt. Edmonds, that the Germans were removing the Jewish prisoners from the general prisoner population at great risk to their survival. Master Sgt. Edmonds, at the risk of his immediate death, defied the Germans with the unexpected consequences that the Jewish prisoners were saved."[43]

There are only five Americans who are recognized as the Righteous Gentiles Among the Nations at Yad Vashem, Israel's Holocaust memorial, and Master Sergeant Roddie Edmonds is one of them.

The Sleizen Family

Leah Berzak and her eldest daughter, twelve-year-old Renia, escaped the disease-infested Jewish ghetto of Baranovichi after the Nazis slaughtered Leah's husband, their three young children, and her mother. Seeking refuge, Leah and Renia hid in the frozen fields surrounding the city and begged the local farmers for help, but they were turned away time after time.

In desperation, Leah and her daughter managed to evade the Nazi guards and slip unnoticed into the outskirts of town to the farm of their Christian friends. Leah pleaded with the Sleizen family for shelter. Although the Sleizens knew the severe penalty for hiding Jews was immediate deportation and execution, they decided to do what was right in the sight of God.

Initially, Leah and Renia were hidden in the family barn. Eventually, the Sleizens dug a rectangular ditch under the floor of their home. The family set a rug and sofa over the grave-like pit to conceal its opening. The hiding place was just long enough to accommodate Leah's height and wide enough to cradle both mother and daughter as they lay side by side. This dark, cold, and damp sepulcher became their place of refuge.

Every morning at 3:00 a.m., Mrs. Sleizen would free Leah and Renia from their blackened tomb, feed them, and give them a brief opportunity to stretch their cramped bodies and relieve themselves. Day after day, the mother and daughter lay there. When Renia cried in claustrophobic agony, Leah would lovingly touch her frightened daughter and say, "Soon the war will be over. We will be free and everything is going to be fine. Jehovah God will see to it my darling, Renia . . . . He will see to it!"

To give her daughter peace, Leah would recite the Sh'ma. The Sh'ma is the most sacred prayer in Judaism derived from Deuteronomy 6:4–9; 11:13–21; and Numbers 15:37–41: "Hear, Oh Israel, the Lord our God, the Lord is One. Praised be His Name. His glorious Kingdom is forever and forever."[44] It is said many Jewish people recited this prayer on their way to their deaths during the Holocaust.

The Sleizen farm was often subject to searches by SS soldiers. When the troopers approached the farmhouse hunting for Jews, the Sleizens would quickly signal Leah and Renia by having their young children sit on the sofa and sing special songs until their stalkers left—it was only then that all could breathe a sigh of relief.

Finally, after 840 days—twenty-eight long months—mother and daughter were freed from their hiding place and given Christian birth certificates and passports that the Sleizen family obtained for them. Because of the help of their brave friends, Leah and Renia managed to walk through the Italian Alps and eventually came to a place called Palestine. How do I know the details of Leah and Renia's story? Renia became the mother of one of our dearest friends, and my wife, Diana, and I had the honor of hearing her tell the personal account of her survival of the Holocaust.

Hitler did not extinguish this noble Jewish line; he could not, for it was redeemed by the Hand of God through the actions of Righteous Gentiles.

The Danes

How did nearly all of the Jews of Denmark survive the Holocaust? The answer is simple: Denmark was the only occupied country in Europe that stood for righteousness in defiance of the Nazis. Even though most Europeans did not actively participate in the Final Solution, they did little or nothing to prevent it. Professor of history and expert of the Holocaust Peter Longerich concluded that the success of the Holocaust was "dependent to a considerable extent, on the practical cooperation and support of an occupied country or territory."[45]

But not Denmark.

After the Nazi occupation, the Danes were covertly informed of the SS plans to deport the Jews of Denmark to the death damps. Instead of yielding to the horrific Nazi policies, the Danish government took action to protect their Jewish citizens. The Danes took a bold stand and believed that an attack on the Jews of Denmark was an attack on the whole nation. The extermination of a people—of an entire race—requires cooperation. Denmark refused to collaborate with the Nazis; therefore, the implementation of the Final Solution within their country became unachievable.

When the Nazis came, the Jews immediately left their homes and sought refuge in farmhouses, homes, and churches—and they were all welcomed. Next, the Danish government formulated a national effort to secretly transport all Jews to safety into the neutral country of Sweden. Because of the cooperation of the entire Danish citizenry, over 90 percent of the nation's Jews were able to clandestinely gather on the coast. Within a few days, fishermen succeeded in ferrying seven thousand Danish Jews across the Baltic Sea to their safe haven.[46]

Government officials from both parties did not shy away from their position, declaring,

> The Danish Jews are an integral part of the people, and therefore all the people are deeply affected by the measures taken, which are seen as a violation of the Danish sense of justice.[47]

These and other honorable rescuers add to the list of witnesses against the lie that the Holocaust never occurred. The actions of these Righteous Gentiles attest that inherent goodness, moral conviction, self-sacrifice, and bold action can prevail even under unspeakable situations.

LEST WE FORGET

Diana and I have visited the Dachau concentration camp twice. The first time we walked the grounds alone, and the second time we had over two hundred of our ministry partners with us.

The camp is located in the city of Dachau, which is a short drive outside of Munich in the beautiful upper Bavarian countryside. It was the first Nazi concentration camp that opened shortly after Hitler became chancellor in 1933. In its early stages, Dachau only held political prisoners, but it later evolved into a death camp where thousands upon thousands of Jews were killed through slave labor, starvation, disease, despicable medical experiments, mass gassing, or by other merciless forms of execution.

I had preached in West Berlin at the US military chapel and later ministered to the people of East Berlin, behind the Iron Curtain, in the spring of 1984. After my assignment, Diana and I traveled to Munich because I felt I had a responsibility to see at least one of the many camps before returning home. We rented a car and followed the directions to Dachau, but we somehow missed a turn.

I remember stopping along the way to ask several local business owners and residents if they could tell us where the camp was located, but as if we were transported back in time, no one would acknowledge the camp's existence. We finally found our way there.

Diana and I walked into an antechamber that led to an iron gate reading *Arbeit Macht Frei*, which ironically means "Work Makes Freedom." The gate opened to a large courtyard where the prisoners stood for hours several times a day while the captors methodically counted their captives—lest they escape their place of torture. I tried to absorb all that once happened there, but it was overwhelming, to say the least.

As we stood in the square, I had a sudden flashback of a story told to me by one of our many friends who had survived Dachau.

Sandor "Shoney" Alex Braun had been incarcerated along with his father and brother at Auschwitz, then one of the sub-camps, and finally Dachau. While in the sub-camp, the father observed a birthday. His sons could think of no better way to honor their beloved father than to give him their day's bread rations—the only thing of value they possessed.

Reluctantly, their father took the bread and slowly ate it with tears streaming down his face at the sacrificial gesture of his precious sons. Shoney's father, who had eaten more food that day than he had in months (three pieces of stale bread), fell fast asleep on the hard, wooden bunk, and missed morning roll call. Shoney then recounted what occurred at dawn that fateful day:

One prisoner was missing. After several recounts . . . one prisoner was still missing. So the Kapos [prisoners assigned to supervise prisoners] went to the barrack to look for him. And they found the missing man sleeping in a corner. My father. They dragged him from his collar to the SS guard. . . . And the SS guard turned to the assembly, to us, said, "As I understand, the Jewish dog has here two sons. I want them to step out and come near him. Witness his punishment."

So we had to step out . . . and we were standing near him [their father]. Then he [the SS guard] turned to the rest of them. He said, "This dirty Jewish dog kept Germany from victory ten minutes, because that's how long it took to find him." Then he gave a swift kick to my father, which signaled the Kapos to start the punishment.

They rushed toward him . . . kicking and beating him from all directions . . . whipping him. We fell on our knees. And we turned to the SS and said, "Please, stop. Beat us. Please don't do that." The beating was even more severe.

They were beating him until he collapsed; my father was silent, except for his lips were moving . . . he tried to say something. I came closer, and I noticed that he was reciting the declaration of faith of the Jewish people, Sh'ma. The Sh'ma: "Sh'ma Yisrael, Adonai Elohenu, Adonai Echad— Hear, O Israel, the Lord our God, the Lord is One." Then he was very silent.

Diana and I continued our gloomy journey. We entered the cramped barracks where over one thousand prisoners had been shoved into filthy bunks for a few hours' sleep each night before enduring eighteen hours or more of slave labor the next day.

We walked through the museums that held instruments of torture as well as those used in brutal medical experiments that were devised by Josef Mengele, the mastermind behind the medical experiments on twins. It was Mengele, the "Angel of Death," who harvested "specimens" from every train delivery at Auschwitz.

As the human freight was unloaded from the trains, they were told to disrobe and wait for their fate. They stood before Mengele who, by the flick of his hand, determined who would go directly to the gas chambers, the slave labor camps, or the medical quarters. It was said that those who went directly to the gas chambers had a better fate compared to those who endured the torturous death of Mengele's so-called medical research.

These death-inducing experiments were a wicked distortion of the medical profession, but more importantly, they were an insult to God and His creation. They were performed on the Jewish people because the Nazis believed them to be sub-human and therefore disposable. Mengele was not the only physician to take part in these malicious events, but sadly, like Mengele, many of the doctors escaped criminal prosecution.

Diana and I walked beyond the barracks and came to the door of the gas chamber where thousands had stood before us. The multitudes who were selected to go to the gas chambers had been told that they were about to receive a much-needed shower, but instead, within minutes of the door shutting behind them, they gasped their last torturous breaths. We could still smell the stench of death and see their claw marks on the walls—it was heart-wrenching.

After the gas chamber, Diana and I walked into the crematoria. By this point, we could hardly draw air into our lungs for the anguish that gripped our throats. There we saw leather cots leading into the ovens. I will always remember that the stretchers had the impressions of human bodies left on them from the thousands they had fed into the blazing inferno. Tall smokestacks jutted out of the building. In the days before the liberation of Dachau, these chimneys spewed the ashes of the dead twenty-four hours a day—seven days a week.

The origins of the word *Holocaust* comes from the Greek *holos* ("entire") and *kostos* ("burnt"). Together, "totally burnt" refers to the sacrifice of an animal, which was utterly burnt on an altar. In Hebrew, the term *shoah* (sho-Ah), which is found in the Bible several times (Psalms, Isaiah, Jeremiah, Lamentation, Ezekiel, Daniel, Micah, Zephaniah), signifies complete and utter destruction.

I remember thinking, *Oh my God, will we ever know the number of Your beloved who were sacrificed on the altar of hate?* We walked in silence as we read the accounts within the museum. Tears poured from our eyes—there was no stopping their flow. By the end of our tour we held each other in an effort to console. I remember that day as if it were yesterday.

I knew then that I had to bring others to see what we saw. My first objective was to show reverence to the thousands who had died at Dachau pledging that there would be more witnesses to the existence of this hideous place. Second, I wanted to somehow bring a degree of comfort and consolation to the relatives of the deceased who were sent to their deaths elsewhere within the chain of concentration camps.

My thoughts went to the words of the prophet Ezekiel, who wrote, *"Then I came to the captives . . . and I sat where they sat, and remained there astonished among them seven days" (Ezekiel 3:15).*

I expressed to Diana my desire to return to Dachau for a "Lest We Forget" memorial service to remember the Jewish people who died in the Holocaust. A few months later, we brought over two hundred witnesses who could later testify to their children and grandchildren that Dachau was a real place that housed, tortured, and killed thousands of prisoners, the majority of them Jewish.

Our group toured the repulsive camp where God's Covenant people had suffered and died. We did what Ezekiel did and stood where they stood. We lined up in formation on the camp's courtyard as thousands had stood before us. Each one of us wore a black armband with a yellow Star of David to symbolize the fact that those imprisoned at Dachau and at other camps within Nazi-occupied territories had committed no crime or broken no law—they were there simply because they were Jewish.

Our time in Germany was short; we were there less than thirty-six hours, for our mission there was complete. We walked out of Dachau and left for our final destination: the State of Israel. Rabbi Israel Ba'al Shem Tov taught that "forgetfulness leads to exile, but in remembrance lies the key to redemption."[48] We were there to remember—*lest we forget* what happened to our Jewish brethren at the hand of pure hatred.

Soon after arriving in Israel, we gathered for the Night to Honor Israel forest that our ministry established years before. While there, we planted two hundred trees in honor of the millions who died in the camps, wrapping the black armbands we had worn at Dachau around each trunk.

It was our way of symbolizing that the memory of those who had succumbed to the evil of the Holocaust would now forever be attached to the land of Israel. No longer would they be identified with a place of death; their sacred memory lives on in a place of life—for *Am Yisrael Chai*—the people of Israel live!

FOUR KINDS OF PEOPLE

Despite the twisted reasoning used by Holocaust deniers to veil their attacks upon the memories of the survivors, or their blatant disregard of the liberators' eyewitness accounts, or their flagrant refusal to acknowledge the confessions of the agents of death who committed the crimes, Holocaust denial is still deeply rooted in anti-Semitism, and it has remained the language of hate.

Soon there will be no one left to tell the personal stories of their horrifying encounters with the evils of the Holocaust. Elie Wiesel said it well: "For the dead and for the living—we must bear witness."

In order not to repeat the mistakes of the past, it is crucial to remember that this catastrophic event involved four kinds of individuals: the mobs of torturous perpetrators, the millions of innocent victims, the few who righteously intervened, and far too many apathetic bystanders. These diverse groups of people are still present in the world today; the question we must ask ourselves is: *Which are we?*

Even after the attempted annihilation of God's chosen people during World War II, a miracle was about to take place . . . the rebirth of the Jewish nation.

CHAPTER 4

BATTLE FOR JERUSALEM

Jerusalem has been our capital for 3,000 years and it's going to be our capital for eternity. (Naphtali Bennett)

Many of the greatest civilizations of the last three thousand years have sought to rule Jerusalem, yet only one people were given the divine right to claim the Holy City as its eternal inheritance—the Jews. And because God's Chosen have refused to relinquish this claim, they have paid a terrible price in blood and suffering.

Historic Christian anti-Judaism and European anti-Semitism produced massive horrors such as the Great Inquisition, the Russian pogroms, and Hitler's Final Solution. However, in the Middle East, the struggle for control of the Holy Land, especially Jerusalem, has also been stained with Jewish blood for centuries.

Even in the first century CE, after the Romans destroyed Jerusalem, massacred over one million of its inhabitants, and sent hundreds of thousands more into exile, there was still a remnant of the Jewish people who never left their biblical homeland.

The Jewish people who were dispersed among the nations were for centuries considered outcasts and were continuously confronted with bigotry and hatred in their host countries. Many began to realize that the only way to escape deep-rooted anti-Semitism and its deadly consequences was to regain their national independence. In essence, the Lord was calling His people home.

HERZL'S JEWISH STATE

After nearly two millennia in exile, in the late nineteenth and early twentieth centuries, a new movement for Jewish sovereignty began to gain worldwide traction. In 1896, Theodor Herzl's Zionist pamphlet, *The Jewish State*, laid out a vision that would eventually culminate in the rebirth of the State of Israel. Herzl believed he had an answer to the Jewish Question:

> We are a people—one people. . . . We want to lay the foundation stone, for the house which will become the refuge of the Jewish nation. Zionism is the return to Judaism even before the return to the land of Israel.[1]

The ideal of Zionism, the belief that the Jewish people had a right to national independence and sovereignty as natives of their ancestral homeland, began to flourish. Jewish immigrants started to flood into what was then Palestine and purchase land from wealthy Arab landholders at exorbitant costs. The land had been mostly barren and sparsely populated for centuries, and to most it seemed worthless, except to the Jews, who dreamed of coming home.

Palestine began to prosper as Jewish exiles cultivated the land, eliminated disease-infested swamps, and brought a higher standard of living and more economic opportunity to the area.[2] A beautiful thing was taking place: the Arab population grew and flourished alongside their Jewish neighbors, and for a time the two groups coexisted peacefully.

The Balfour Declaration of 1917 initially supported political Zionism. During World War I, Britain and the Allied powers defeated the Ottoman Turks and divided its Middle Eastern empire into territories set aside for future states. The British promised Palestine to the Jewish people and assumed responsibility for guarding it through the process of Jewish statehood. This temporary stewardship was entrusted to Britain by the League of Nations and was called the Mandate for Palestine.[3]

In 1919, an agreement between Zionist leader Chaim Weizmann and the Arab leader, Emir Faisal, was accepted.[4] The terms allowed for the idea of a Jewish state in the land, which also protected the rights of local Arabs. However, by 1920, just as the mandate period began, the hope for peace started to break down. There was a struggle for power between two prominent Palestinian Arab families, which soon led to an outbreak of anti-Jewish violence.

A CENTURY OF TERROR BEGINS

Nearly a century ago, Palestinian leader Haj Amin al-Husseini began recruiting suicide squads to attack local Jews in protest against the international agreement to create a Jewish state.[5] Terrorism soon became the preferred political tool of extreme Palestinian Arab nationalists and set in motion an era of violence and hatred toward the Jewish people.

By 1921, the British had partitioned the land set aside for a Jewish national home under the mandate into two prospective states. The partition gave 77 percent of the land to an Arab state called Transjordan and 23 percent to the Jewish people.[6] However, the Arab riots of the 1920s and 1930s prompted Britain in 1937 to once again partition the land, with 80 percent going to an Arab state and 20 percent to a Jewish state. Palestinian Arab leaders once again refused to accept this larger partition, and neither plan materialized.[7] Please note that any and all land offered to the Jewish people throughout history has been vigorously protested by their Arab neighbors.

The bloody Arab uprisings convinced the British that any promise to the Jews was not worth the trouble. In addition, Zionism was also very unpopular with the officers assigned to administrate Britain's mandate power in Palestine.[8] In defiance of their *own* government's obligation to protect Jewish inhabitants, some British officers went so far as to encourage the Palestinian Arabs to use terrorism against the Jews in hopes the violence would cause Britain to entirely abandon entirely the idea of a Jewish state.[9]

Jews were not allowed to own weapons or defend themselves against Arab extremist aggression, and those who did were arrested and sent to prison. Tragically, during the British Mandate period, terrorists murdered hundreds of Jews.

Empowered and aided by the British overseers, Haj Amin al-Husseini later became the mufti of Jerusalem. As mufti (a Muslim legal expert who makes rulings on religious matters), he was given authority over the Muslim holy places and therefore wielded tremendous political and religious influence. From his position of power, he continued to incite resentment and violence against the Jewish people.

Fearing that Zionism was gaining international financial backing, al-Husseini started a rumor of a Jewish plot to seize control of the Muslim holy sites, which successfully instigated riots.[10] The propaganda tactic worked, prompting British authorities to uproot Jewish families from their ancestral homes in Hebron and Gaza. The British also severely restricted Jewish immigration to Palestine and once again drastically reduced the size of the land intended for a Jewish state. However, none of these extreme actions satisfied Arab leaders.

ARABS REJECT
ISRAEL'S RIGHT TO EXIST

During World War II, al-Husseini went to Germany and met with Hitler because the führer's hatred for the Jews and plans for their annihilation appealed to him.[11] As a result, the mufti collaborated with the Nazi regime to recruit tens of thousands of Muslims for the *Schutzstaffel*—better known as the SS.

In the aftermath of World War II, al-Husseini was forced to flee prosecution for war crimes and lived abroad for the rest of his life. However, his legacy of terrorism and propaganda were used as a highly effective political tool against the Jewish state and became the prototype for future anti-Israel despots such as Yasser Arafat (PLO), Mohammed Badie (Muslim Brotherhood), Hassan Nasrallah (Hezbollah), Osama bin Laden (al-Qaeda), Abu Bakr al-Baghdadi (ISIS), and Ismail Haniyeh (Hamas).

Weary of the problem posed by Arab rejectionism, and trying to work within the shadow of the horrors committed against the Jews during the Holocaust, Britain handed over responsibility of Palestine's future to the newly formed United Nations. On November 29, 1947, the United Nations voted in favor of Resolution 181 and adopted a partition plan for Palestine that divided the land west of the Jordan River into two states roughly equal in size but distinctly unequal in value.

The disjointed pieces of land reserved for the Jewish people consisted of mostly arid desert without defensible borders and excluded Jerusalem, which was designated an international city. Jewish leaders, desperate to build a national home and provide a refuge for the displaced Jews who had survived the Holocaust, accepted the plan.

Arab leaders had previously established that they would not accept *any* plan that included a Jewish state, and almost immediately made good on their threat to launch large-scale attacks on Jewish communities. Consequently, hundreds of Jews were killed in riots and other terror attacks between November 29, 1947, and Israel's independence on May 14, 1948.[12]

The day after the declaration, the British departed and the Palestinian Arabs were joined by five Middle East armies—Egypt, Syria, Transjordan, Lebanon, and Iraq—to launch a war of annihilation against the newly reborn State. Israel's existence as a Jewish state in the middle of what had once been an Islamic empire was entirely unacceptable for Arab leaders. They successfully conjured up rabid anti-Semitic fervor among their people as they called for a *jihad* or a "holy war."

The international community stood back and quietly watched without giving much hope to the fledgling state.[13] To the world's astonishment, Israel miraculously prevailed. To avoid further disgrace and loss of territory, the Arab states signed an armistice agreement with Israel in 1949. But their insatiable goal of destroying Israel remained. The next seventy years would be marked by multiple attempts to wipe Israel off the map.

THE MIZRAHI JEWS

In retaliation for their humiliating defeat, Muslim countries in the Middle East and North Africa began harshly persecuting their native Jewish communities. These inhabitants known as Mizrahi Jews had existed in many of these countries for more than 2,500 years.[14]

By 1948, nearly one million Mizrahi Jews lived in Algeria, Egypt, Iran, Iraq, Libya, Lebanon, Morocco, Syria, Tunisia, Turkey, and Yemen. They had thriving businesses, well-established schools, and religious centers, and spoke Arabic just like their Muslim neighbors. Yet soon after Israel was established as a nation, they were treated as the enemy.

During the next few decades, nearly 850,000 Mizrahi Jews were forcibly removed from their homes, had their wealth and possessions confiscated, and were expelled from the Middle Eastern countries they had inhabited for centuries. Some immigrated to America and others went to Europe, but many went to the land that God had promised Abraham centuries before

The reborn Jewish state welcomed these refugees, gave them citizenship, and provided as much government assistance as possible to help them start new lives. Today, over half of Israel's population descends from the Mizrahi Jewish refugees.

THE EVOLUTION OF
ANTI-SEMITIC TERRORISM

The Arab extremists, bent on destroying Israel, learned the power of terrorism during the British Mandate period. Terrorism was not only an effective political tool against the Jewish state, which weakened it internally; it also produced external pressure from the international community.

The generational goal to eradicate Israel fueled the rise of several Islamic extremist factions. Fundamental to each of these terrorist groups was an anti-Semitic interpretation of Islamic theology that left no room for acceptance of the State of Israel, the Jewish people, and consequently, the possibility of peace.

Muslim Brotherhood

One of the first extremist groups to form was the Muslim Brotherhood. It was initially founded in 1928 as a political and social effort to bring back Islamic Sharia law (Islamic religious law)

and reinstitute an Islamic Sunni caliphate (Islamic State) in the Middle East.

However, the Brotherhood soon embraced violent anti-Semitism as part of its ideology. During 1938 and 1939, the Brotherhood repeatedly attacked and threatened Egyptian Jews. Its leaders admired Hitler's plan to eliminate the Jews and passed out Arabic translations of Hitler's *Mein Kampf* and the Russian *Protocols of the Elders of Zion.*[15]

During the 1950s and 1960s, the radical Islamic scholar Sayyid Qutb officially branded the Jews as nefarious agents of Satan who planned to destroy Islam and corrupt society's morals. He relied on the false doctrines of the *Protocols of the Elders of Zion* to "prove" his accusations, leaving no room for the possibility of the existence of "a good Jew." Qutb's solution for the Jewish "threat" was the same as all other anti-Semites since Haman: total extermination.[16]

The Muslim Brotherhood laid the ideological foundations for the rise of both Sunni and Shia Islamist extremist groups. The Brotherhood declared that it is incumbent on all Muslims to wage *jihad* over the entire world to "liberate" non-Muslim lands from the infidels.[17] The radical extremist theology and political goals of these groups rapidly evolved from the desire to win back lands that had once been under Islamic rule to conquering and dominating the entire world under Sharia law. This remains their objective to this day.

By the 1960s, the Muslim Brotherhood had exported its anti-Semitic ideology and fanatical devotion to jihad across the globe. All radical Muslims were encouraged to become "martyrs" for the cause, which spawned the phenomenon of suicide attacks.

Nearly every major radical Islamist terrorist group of the last fifty years can trace its ideological roots back to the Muslim Brotherhood and the teachings of Sayyid Qutb. In the West, the

Brotherhood founded "nonviolent" Islamic institutions that preach the same hateful radical ideology while funneling money from their so-called charities to fund terrorist organizations around the globe.[18]

Palestinian Terrorism

Today, anti-Zionists assert that any terrorist actions against Israel and her citizens stem from the aftermath of the 1967 Six Day War, when Israel defended itself against enemy armies. The outcome of the war resulted in Israel winning control of the Gaza Strip, Judea, and Samaria. Israel's detractors unjustifiably call this event "the occupation" of the Palestinian land and people by the Israeli army.

This deceitful label cannot be further from the truth. The Palestine Liberation Organization (PLO) was founded in 1964. Gaza was under the control of Egypt and Jordan, who also controlled Judea and Samaria. So when the PLO began attacking Israelis in 1964, what "occupation" were they fighting? Obviously, the answer is that the Palestinian leadership has considered the entire State of Israel illegitimate, even though a Jewish remnant has remained in the land for more than three thousand years.[19]

The Palestine Liberation Organization

Created by the Arab League, the PLO was led by Yasser Arafat and his Palestinian nationalist party, Fatah. Arafat was a terrorist, a cold-blooded killer who had more Jewish blood on his hands than any man in the twentieth century other than Adolf Hitler.

The PLO's national charter declared its intent to overthrow the State of Israel, calling Zionism an "illegal" and "colonialist" movement.[20] The charter further stated that the entire region designated as the British Mandate for Palestine in 1920, which includes all of modern Israel and Jordan, belongs entirely to the Palestinian Arabs.

It further declared that only Jews who were living in the land prior to 1917 had a right to remain. The charter also designated every present and future child descending from a Palestinian Arab living in the land prior to 1947 should be considered a Palestinian refugee, regardless of that person's citizenship status in any other country. Finally, the PLO's charter stated that violence was the only way to liberate Palestine from the Zionist presence.[21]

During the 1960s and '70s, the PLO operated out of Jordan and Lebanon while they attacked Israel at home and Jews around the world. Hundreds of Israelis were murdered in numerous terror attacks. An affiliate of the PLO, Black September, became notorious for launching several major terror attacks against Jews in the early 1970s.

In May of 1972, this PLO splinter group hijacked a Belgian airliner in Vienna bound for Tel Aviv. Four terrorists held 90 passengers hostage and forced the pilot to land in Israel while they demanded the release of 315 Palestinian terrorists from Israel's prisons. After disabling the plane, IDF commandos disguised as maintenance workers boarded the airliner and subdued the terrorists, but not before one of the passengers was fatally wounded.[22]

Later that year, Black September operatives broke into the apartments of Israeli athletes at the Munich Olympics, killed two in the initial scuffle, and took nine more hostages. German authorities attempted to rescue the hostages but failed, and all nine Israeli hostages were murdered.[23]

Another infamous Palestinian terror attack took place in 1976. Two members of the PLO faction known as the Popular Front for the Liberation of Palestine and two German terrorists sympathizers hijacked a flight from Paris and forced the plane to land at Entebbe Airport in Uganda.

Once they landed, the terrorists held 105 Jewish passengers hostage and released the non-Jews. For a week, Israel's government negotiated with the terrorists while the IDF planned a daring rescue mission. In just under an hour after arriving at Entebbe, the hostages were rescued. Israel lost three people that day—two hostages and the leader of the mission, Yoni Netanyahu.[24] Yoni's brother Benjamin would go on to become the prime minister of Israel and serve in that leadership capacity longer than anyone in Israel's history.

In 1978, members of the PLO out of Lebanon hijacked an Israeli bus full of civilians and killed thirty-four hostages. In response, the IDF crossed the Lebanese border to push the terrorists farther north. The ensuing conflict dragged on for four years while PLO terrorists hiding in Lebanon conducted hundreds of attacks on Israelis. Israel could no longer tolerate the buildup of a massive PLO army in Lebanon, and on June 6, 1982, launched a full-scale war known as Operation Peace for Galilee to root out Yasser Arafat and his terrorists thugs from southern Lebanon.[25]

A NEW ERA OF HOLY WAR

In 1979, the radical Shia Muslim leader Ayatollah Khomeini overthrew the shah of Iran and his secular government, instituting an Islamic revolution. Inspired by the writings of Sayyid Qutb and the ideology of the Muslim Brotherhood, Khomeini reinterpreted Shia theology and transformed the historically peaceful religious minority sect into one committed to violent *jihad*.[26]

What Qutb had done for extremist Sunni Muslims, Khomeini did for the Shiite Muslims, thereby furthering the war against the Jews.[27] Iran's radicalized government during the 1980s made *jihad* its primary focus against Israel, Jews, and their allies worldwide.

Hezbollah

Seeing an opportunity to export his Islamic revolution's theology of holy war against the Jews, Khomeini sent his Iranian Revolutionary

Guard Corps (IRGC) into southern Lebanon to establish and train a new terrorist group called Hezbollah. While Israel fought to up-root the PLO from Lebanon in 1982, *Hezbollah* (Arabic for "Party of God") was created as a proxy of the Iranian government and given the mandate to destroy Israel.[28]

When Israel withdrew from Lebanon, Hezbollah remained and grew stronger, until it became a dominant political and military force in the country, effectively placing the Lebanese government under the thumb of Iran.[29] In collaboration with Iran, Hezbollah has become one of the deadliest terror organizations in the world. Motivated by the twisted theology that blames every social and po-litical problem on the Jews, Hezbollah has spread its anti-Semitic terror throughout the world.

During the 1990s, Hezbollah sent its operatives to Argentina, where they bombed the Israeli embassy in Buenos Aires. Two years later, they bombed a Jewish community center in the same city. In 2012, Hezbollah bombed an Israeli tour bus in Bulgaria.[30] Hezbollah's leader, Hassan Nasrallah, has made it clear he considers all Jews anywhere in the world to be targets for extermination.

Nasrallah was quoted in Lebanon's *Daily Star* as saying, "If they [Jews] all gather in Israel, it will save us the trouble of going after them worldwide."[31] Iran's government and its proxy, Hez-bollah, have made no secret of their desire to complete Hitler's work of eradicating the Jewish people from the face of the earth.

Think of it—Iran, recognized as an international sponsor of terror, was on the verge of bankruptcy as a result of world economic sanctions. Yet, astonishingly, in July of 2015, the United Nations Security Council adopted the "Iran Deal," which lifted the sanc-tions, releasing over $100 billion in frozen assets into the Iranian coffers. In addition, the sunset clause stated that the restrictions on Iran's uranium enrichment and plutonium reprocessing would expire in ten to fifteen years, allowing Iran to expand its nuclear program.[32] As bad as this was, the situation got worse.

In the fall of 2016, President Obama authorized the government to shell out an additional $1.7 billion under the guise of paying back a deposit ($400 million) plus interest ($1.3 billion) that we supposedly "owed" due to a failed arms deal made with the shah of Iran in 1979. To add insult to injury, this "payback" was not wired back to bank but was sent to Iran in various world currencies via US military cargo planes.[33]

One can only assume that the intended purpose of this clandestine transport of cash was for nefarious transactions. This calculated "reimbursement" was a deliberate act of betrayal to Israel, America's only friend in the Middle East. As a result, Iran has funded a massive buildup of missiles inside Lebanon under Hezbollah's control with our tax dollars.

IDF sources estimate that Hezbollah currently has an arsenal of 130,000 to 150,000 short-, medium-, and long-range missiles and rockets. During the entire Second Lebanon War, Hezbollah fired approximately 4,000 rockets into Israel. However, it is projected that during the next war, they will fire as many as 1,500 to 2,000 missiles into Israel *every day*. In addition, Hezbollah has amassed a trained fighting force of approximately fifty thousand soldiers, with another ten thousand fighters in southern Syria ready to join the fight.[34]

Sadly, the lethal goal of wiping Israel off the map is not letting up. Iran recently hosted the 2018 International Hourglass Festival (also known as the Holocaust Festival), celebrating its plans to destroy Israel within twenty-five years.[35] It seems ironic that the Iranian regime both denies and glorifies the history of the Holocaust, all the while seeking to perpetrate a new one.

In June of 2018, Iran's supreme leader, Ayatollah Ali Khamenei, once again threatened to annihilate Israel on social media, the latest propaganda tool. "Our stance against Israel is the same stance we have always taken. #Israel is a malignant cancerous tumor . . . that has to be removed and eradicated: it is possible and it will happen."[36]

The significance of the ayatollah's statements was not lost on Israel's prime minister, Benjamin Netanyahu, who responded to the threat by declaring, "Ayatollah Khamenei, the ruler of Iran, declared his intention to destroy the State of Israel. Yesterday he explained how he would do this—with the unrestricted enrichment of uranium in order to produce an arsenal of nuclear bombs. We are not surprised. We will not allow Iran to obtain nuclear weapons."[37]

Time is running out.

PROJECT AMAD EXPOSED

On April 30, 2018, Netanyahu revealed to the world on international television the existence of Iran's secret nuclear weapons program. These explosive revelations confirmed what we long believed, but now know without a doubt: Iran's unrelenting pursuit of nuclear weapons continues to threaten the security of the entire world through Project Amad. To substantiate the allegations, the prime minister presented a half ton of files containing one hundred thousand Iranian secret documents obtained by Israel's intelligence agencies.[38]

Dubbed by Israel's intelligence officers as the "Atomic Archive," these Iranian files contain stunning details of the scope and intent of Iran's nuclear weapons development program. Contrary to the claims Iran made to the International Atomic Energy Agency (IAEA) report, upon which the 2015 Iran Deal was based, we now know the following:

- Iran had a covert nuclear weapons development program known as Project Amad.
- Iran funded and directed scientists to work extensively on technology specifically designed for constructing a nuclear bomb.

Iran's blatant lies to the IAEA completely undermined and rendered useless the Iran Deal signed by President Obama. Furthermore, the secret files Israel obtained also revealed that Iran's nuclear weapons research continues.

These documents, which proved Iran lied to the IAEA and continues to lie to the world by denying it ever conducted a nuclear weapons program, leave no doubt that the Iran Deal was fatally flawed from the start.

AL-QAEDA

The era of the Islamic fundamentalist revival and resurgence of calls for holy war against the Jews, which produced Iran's Islamic Revolution and generated Hezbollah, also birthed al-Qaeda in the 1980s. Osama bin Laden, perpetrator of 9/11, was likewise motivated by the anti-Semitic writings of Sayyid Qutb and embraced his theology of *jihad* as a major tenet of faith.[39]

Surprisingly, or perhaps not, both al-Qaeda and Osama bin Laden's successors have found a sympathetic partner and safe haven in the Republic of Iran, despite their different interpretations of Islamic theology. Their common bond is, unsurprisingly, their hatred of Jews and Israel's strongest ally, America.

ISIS

Out of al-Qaeda was born a radical and barbaric splinter group now known as the Islamic State in Iraq and Syria (ISIS).[40] In 2014,

President Obama infamously dismissed ISIS as the "JV team." However, the world soon learned how naïve his assumption was and witnessed a surge in mass-casualty terrorism at the hands of ISIS fanatics. Their victims included Jews, Christians, and Muslims alike.

ISIS's goal of creating an Islamic caliphate in the Middle East appears to have been weakened by recent losses in Syria and Iraq, helped in part by President Trump's military mission to eradicate ISIS in Syria. However, ISIS has been extraordinarily successful at exporting its anti-Semitic and anti-Western theology over the internet to a new generation of homegrown terrorists across the globe.

With their dreams of a caliphate slipping away, ISIS has turned its attention to Israel. Israel's intelligence experts are carefully watching the growth of ISIS in the Sinai Desert along Israel's western border with Egypt and the attempt by ISIS operatives to challenge Hamas for supremacy in Gaza.

HAMAS

Hamas, an Arabic acronym for the Islamic Resistance Movement, was created by the Muslim Brotherhood in the 1980s. Hamas was originally labeled as a "social welfare" organization for the benefit of Palestinians in Gaza.[41] However, this radical group quickly mutated into a terrorist organization dedicated to attacking Israel and brutally enforcing strict Islamic law on the Palestinians under its influence.

Hamas gained power due to the frustration of some Palestinian extremists with Yasser Arafat's political doublespeak. Arafat often engaged in "diplomatic" talks with Israel in which he promised to restrain the PLO and Fatah party's support for terrorism. But in reality, Arafat was only posturing for sympathy from the United Nations and never renounced terrorism. But his mere pretense of compromise with Israel enraged Islamist radicals. Thus, Hamas recruited an even more extreme brand of terrorist than the PLO and dedicated itself to the complete destruction of Israel with no room for negotiation.[42]

In an attempt to garner goodwill from the Palestinians, while also relieving the IDF's burden of overseeing the Gaza Strip, Israel unilaterally withdrew from Gaza in 2006. Hamas, however, took advantage of the power vacuum created by Israel's absence and easily won the 2007 elections. It is from here where nine thousand Jewish families left their homes and livelihoods to give peace a chance. Instead, Gaza has become a launching pad for rockets into Israel.

This political loss forced the Fatah-led Palestinian Authority government out of Gaza. The results were immediately disastrous. Hamas murdered Palestinians suspected of sympathizing or collaborating with Israel or its political rivals, and they began launching a constant barrage of missiles into Israel.[43]

Hamas's charter, like that of Hezbollah, specifically dedicates itself to the total annihilation of the Jewish state. Like Hezbollah, Hamas intentionally targets Israeli civilians and uses its own civilian population as human shields. One of the worst crimes against humanity perpetrated by these two terrorist organizations is their practice of deliberately hiding their weapons in civilian areas. This attempt to force Israel to kill innocent men, women, and children in order to defend itself from the terrorists is a calculated maneuver.[44]

The purpose of such an evil strategy is obvious: they want to inflame worldwide hatred against Israel and thereby force Israel to either commit national suicide by standing down, or suffer extreme worldwide political and economic retaliation for its actions of self-defense. This despicable plan has worked exceptionally well in helping Israel's enemies falsely portray the Jewish nation as a "cold-hearted monster," when it is Hamas and Hezbollah who are guilty of war crimes under international law. This is a classic illustration where truth becomes a lie and lies have become truth.

Since May of 2018, terrorists in the Gaza Strip have launched hundreds of helium balloons and kites bearing flammable materials into Israeli territory, starting over 250 fires. The "terror kites," some of which are decorated with swastikas, are fitted with a long string to which a Molotov cocktail, a pouch of burning fuel, or an improvised explosive device, are attached, causing them to explode upon impact.

Nearly 4,300 acres, or 7 square miles, of agricultural fields, forest, and grasslands, which is more than half of Israel's nature reserves, have been burned because of these destructive kites, causing 2.5 million dollars' worth of damage.[45] The IDF has declared, "It's not a game—it's a war."[46]

In the middle of July 2018, shortly after the start of the kite onslaught, Gaza terrorists fired over two hundred rockets at Israeli border towns. This massive rocket barrage is the most serious outbreak of fighting since Operation Protective Edge in 2014. In response, the IDF bombed dozens of Hamas posts in the Gaza Strip including two terror tunnels, a Hamas headquarters post, and a high-rise building that served as a Hamas urban warfare training facility.[47] Prime Minister Netanyahu said of the incursion, "Our policy is clear—if anyone attacks us, we will deal them a forceful counterattack. I hope that they [Hamas] got the message. If not, they will in the future."[48]

Israel cannot tolerate this devastation much longer. The Gaza Strip is a ticking time bomb that could explode into a full-fledged war for Israel at any moment.

Remember this truth: Hamas has no interest in a Palestinian state alongside Israel, regardless of whatever concessions Israelis are willing to make on borders or within the city of Jerusalem. Hamas wants it all, and it won't stop until it achieves its goal!

Additionally, Hamas's ceaseless fight for control of the Palestinians in Judea and Samaria (West Bank), and its growing popularity there, threaten to unseat Fatah as the ruling party of the Palestinian Authority. The sustained incitement to terrorism and the extreme anti-Semitic rhetoric coming from the PLO, Hamas, and now ISIS have inspired a new breed of terrorism. Whereas previous terror attacks were usually planned and carried out by organized terror cells, deadly "lone wolf" attacks have become commonplace since 2015.

Lone Wolf

The lone wolf terrorists are often young Palestinian men and women who spontaneously attack Jews with whatever weapon is at their disposal. The PLO encourages these attacks by providing pensions and salaries to the murderers and their families.

In early 2018, the United States passed a law, the Taylor Force Act, restricting American foreign aid to the Palestinian Authority until it ends their "pay to slay" reward system. However, in defiance, the Palestinian Authority announced in 2018 that it was increasing the budget for this terrorist incentive from $347 million to $403 million.[49]

Clearly, this "unholy" war against the Jews over the last century and the emphasis on violent *jihad* in the last forty years are far from over. Although the various radical Islamic terror groups are in competition with each other, they are united in their intense hatred of Israel and the Jewish people. The spirit of Hitler lives within their theology, their political discourse, their youth brainwashing programs, and their culture of death worship.

Looming above it all is the shadow of Iran's ambition for a nuclear holocaust that threatens to spark a third world war. Iran invests billions of dollars in funding its own military, Hezbollah in Syria, and Hamas in Gaza. Its total objective is the destabilization of the entire Middle East and the rebuilding of the Persian Empire.

Iran's subversive acts mark its obsession with anti-Semitism, which leads people to value death more than life. This warped philosophy produces suffering for millions of innocent Arabs, Christians, and Muslims alike, who become collateral damage in the ongoing war against the Jews.

THE RESURGENCE OF JEWISH HATRED

It is clear that Jewish hatred did not originate or end with Adolf Hitler. As I have detailed, God's Chosen have been persecuted since ancient times, and this unrivaled animosity lives on worldwide.

Jewish bigotry in America never advanced to the lethal level of Nazi-led Germany, but it was widespread nonetheless. Anti-Semitism has never truly disappeared from society; however, the terrors of the Holocaust significantly suppressed its public expression for a season.

As time has elapsed, recollections have become dim, and the survivors have passed on, the global condemnation of the Jewish State of Israel and its people has intensified. Anti-Semitism was, and in some cases, is still very prevalent in social, religious, political, and educational circles, as well as within some so-called influential progressive movements.

The advent of social media has caused anti-Semitic propaganda and threats against Jews to soar. The internet provides the "facelessness" that anti-Jewish extremists thrive on, sadly allowing them the opportunity to influence millions with their false rhetoric.

In recent years, there has been a deeply concerning upsurge of anti-Semitism around the world, including in the United States. Some of the settings may have changed, but the hateful rhetoric remains the same—accusing the Jewish people of long-standing claims ranging from dual loyalty to using their influence to control the world because they have a "disproportionate amount of political and economic power."

The manifestations of Jewish hatred are becoming increasingly blatant as we witness an increase of violent anti-Semitic incidents throughout the world. We see it with the reemergence of replacement theology within the church, within places of higher learning, and through apartheid accusations and the BDS movement (Boycott, Divestment, and Sanctions).

Malcolm Hoenlein, a close friend who leads the Conference of Presidents of Major American Jewish Organizations, believes that for several years it was accepted for Americans to say that they were *anti-Israel*; however, "today it is accepted to say I am *anti-Jewish*." This, Hoenlein believes, is partly due to the anti-Israel BDS, which provides a "cover for anti-Semitism."[50]

College campus students and tenured professors have become more comfortable with not only criticizing Israel but also attacking Jewish students for simply being Jewish or because they support the ideals of the Jewish state. Furthermore, increasingly non-Jewish students are being spat upon for supporting their Jewish friends on campuses throughout America and the world.

Why have America's college campuses become a hotbed for anti-Semitism? Because the enemy knows the future belongs to the next generation. Here, hatred for Israel is disguised as a deserved punishment for the false accusation that the Jewish nation is an "aggressor" against the "oppressed" Palestinians. This deceptive portrayal of being an "apartheid regime"—one that discriminates on the grounds of race—has caused severe damage to the way the world views Israel.

A report released in early 2018 showed a dramatic 57 percent increase in anti-Semitic incidents in America compared to 2016.[51] For the second year in a row, the number of incidents on college campuses nearly doubled. Moreover, for the first time in at least seven years, an anti-Semitic incident was recorded in every state of the Union. Militant Muslim extremism has skyrocketed worldwide, and so has widespread hatred for the Jewish people. These numbers are deeply troubling.

You may tag a sophisticated label on anti-Semitism, but it is still sin, and as sin, it damns the soul. This Jewish hatred is once again spreading like a contagious virus. It is a cancer growing on the soul of America and the world. Anti-Semitism is not just a Jewish problem—it's the world's problem. I fully agree with Malcolm Hoenlein that fighting anti-Semitism starts with the Jewish community, but as he says:

> . . . it doesn't end with it. This is not our problem. It's society's problem. It's Christianity's problem. It's everybody's problem, when there's hatred against Jews. We're the victims; we're not the cause of it. It's not because we did something wrong. It's because of who we are and our values.[52]

THE BLESSING OF BLESSING ISRAEL

How does our Christian walk intersect with Israel? I have said that it is not possible for Christians to love Jesus Christ and hate the Jewish people living across the street. The thousands of years of Jewish hatred that is imbedded in our world culture has caused many Christians to have anti-Semitic leanings or, at best, to be indifferent toward the Jewish people.

I was guilty of indifference—I knew that the nation of Israel was important in Bible prophecy, but I did not connect my personal involvement with the Jewish people as being a vital part of God's plan for all believers until I visited Israel.

I made my first journey to the Holy Land over forty years ago, and as I mentioned earlier, I went there a tourist and returned home a Zionist.

I stood at the Sea of Galilee where Jesus miraculously fed the multitudes and healed the sick. I prayed at the Western Wall where the prophets Ezra and Nehemiah sought the face of God, and I walked the cobblestoned streets of the Old City where my Redeemer carried His cross to Calvary—I had found my spiritual home.

I left Israel with a longing to discover the history of the Promised Land, and during my years of study, I unearthed the Jewish roots of my Christian faith. Sadly, I also came face-to-face with the virulent religious hatred that birthed the Crusades, the Spanish Inquisition, and the harvest of hatred that produced the Holocaust.

But most importantly, I realized God's boundless love for the Jewish people, for His Covenant Land, and for the city of Jerusalem. Jesus Christ was and always will be Jewish. When He spoke to the Samaritan woman, He identified Himself with the Jewish people. Jesus told the Samaritan woman, *"You worship what you do not know; we [Jesus and the Jewish people] know what we worship, for salvation is of the Jews"* (John 4:22).

Gentiles owe their salvation to the Jewish people. God promises to bless those who bless Israel and His people. Paul wrote, *"For if the Gentiles have been partakers of their [the Jews'] spiritual things, their [the Gentiles'] duty is also to minister to them in material things"* (Romans 15:27). Repeatedly Scripture chronicles the principle of God blessing those who bless the Jewish people.

Jacob and Laban

This Bible principle is illustrated with the story of Jacob and Laban. Jacob, one of the patriarchs, worked for a Syrian by the name of Laban. Laban changed Jacob's wages ten times, each time to his loss. Jacob became disillusioned and informed Laban he was leaving.

Laban responded remorsefully, saying, *"Please stay, if I have found favor in your eyes, for I have learned by experience that the LORD has blessed me for your sake" (Genesis 30:27).*

Laban was one Gentile who recognized that the blessings of God followed the Jewish people.

Joseph and Pharaoh

The blessing continues in the story of Joseph and Pharaoh. Joseph saved the Gentile world from starvation through his divine power to interpret dreams. Pharaoh blessed Joseph by making him the prime minister of the nation and by giving to his family the rich farmlands of Goshen, which were the best in Egypt. Pharaoh treated Joseph and the Jewish people as an extension of his own family.

In accordance with Joseph's interpretation of Pharaoh's dream, the seven years of abundance began, and Joseph erected large storehouses all over the country, gathering the surplus of grain that had flooded the markets. The seven years of plenty passed and the years of famine began; now the entire country found itself dependent upon the provisions stored away under the wise administration of Joseph.

During the time of lack, the people sold their land and livestock to Pharaoh in exchange for food. Through the genius of Joseph, the stored food not only provided nourishment for the masses but also purchased vast amounts of real estate outside of Egypt, thereby enlarging Pharaoh's kingdom. The Gentile king blessed the Jewish people, and God saw to it that he was blessed beyond measure.

The Centurion's Servant

Why was Jesus Christ willing to go to the house of the centurion in Capernaum and heal his sick servant? The Roman centurion deserved the blessing of God, for he had demonstrated his love for the Jews by building a synagogue in Israel (Luke 7:5).

When you display practical acts of love to bless the Jewish people and the State of Israel, God will bless you.

Cornelius of Caesarea

Why did God the Father select the house of Cornelius in Caesarea to be the first Gentile house in Israel to receive the gospel? The answer is given repeatedly in the book of Acts, which says: *"a devout man [Cornelius] and one who feared God with all his household, who gave alms generously to the people, and prayed to God always" (Acts 10:2).* Who were the *people* to whom Cornelius gave these alms? They were the Jewish people who lived around him.

Acts 10:4 states, *"Your prayers and your alms have come up for a memorial before God."* Acts 10:31 reads, *"Your alms are remembered in the sight of God."*

The point is made three times in the same chapter: a righteous Gentile who demonstrated his unconditional love for the Jewish people in a practical manner was divinely selected by heaven to be the first house to receive the gospel of salvation and the first to receive the outpouring of the Holy Spirit.

These combined scriptures verify that prosperity (Genesis 12:3; Psalm 122:6), divine healing (Luke 7:1–5), and the outpouring of the Holy Spirit (Acts 10) came first to the Gentiles who blessed the Jewish people and the nation of Israel in a practical manner.

The Bible also teaches that love is not what you say—love is what you do (1 John 3:18). It has been said that "a bell is not a bell until you ring it . . . and love is not love until you give it away."[53]

It is imperative that we express our love and support for Israel and the Jewish people through practical acts of kindness and prayer.

Pray for Jerusalem

Remember this truth: when it comes to prophecy and the End of Days, it's all about Jerusalem. In Psalm 122:6, King David commands all people to *"pray for the peace of Jerusalem: 'May they prosper who love you.'"* Righteousness and peace are destined to spring forth from Jerusalem to all the nations of the earth; therefore, it befits all people to pray for this Holy City. It is the only city God mandates us to pray for in Scripture.

Daniel prayed three times each day toward the city of Jerusalem while he was in Babylon. Even though these prayers were outlawed by the Persian Empire, he chose to continue to pray and endure the consequence of the lions' den. The Lord protected Daniel for his courage and obedience, and intervened on his behalf so he could continue to pray for the City of God.

The scriptural principle of personal prosperity is tied to blessing Israel and praying for the city of Jerusalem. This prosperity is not purely associated with material blessings but also includes the Lord's spiritual blessings, favor, and protection.

The principle of blessing the Jewish people is as applicable today as it was in biblical times, and it will be relevant in the days to come, especially as Jerusalem becomes the pawn for those who desire to bring destruction to the Jewish state.

The Watchmen

The future of Jerusalem is the centerpiece of God's blueprint for eternity. Make no mistake: God will remove, reclaim, restore, reorder, renovate, redouble, redistribute, recommit, and redeem until the Holy City has become the crowning gem of all the cities on earth.

Biblical watchmen were stationed on city walls (2 Samuel 18:25; 2 Kings 9:18; Psalms 127:1; Isaiah 62:6), on watch towers (2 Kings 9:17; 17:9; 18:8), or on hilltops (Jeremiah 31:6). It was their duty to alert the king of an imminent hostile action against the city (2 Samuel 18:24–27; 2 Kings 9:17–20).[54] The past atrocities committed against the Jewish people and the city of Jerusalem attest to the reality that the church, as a whole, has failed to accomplish the mandate God set before us as watchmen over Israel.

I have set watchmen on your walls, O Jerusalem; they shall never hold their peace day or night. You who make mention of the LORD, do not keep silent, and give Him no rest till He establishes and till He makes Jerusalem a praise in the earth. (Isaiah 62:6–7)

Watchmen should not remain silent or passive when Jerusalem is threatened—we must take action! God has appointed His people as guardians and, as such, we should never allow Jerusalem to be threatened in any way—whether by missile attacks, political propaganda, or as a "bargaining chip in achieving peace."[55]

The Jews are God's Covenant people, and Jerusalem is His everlasting city. Jehovah God never intended the heart of Israel to be divided, and He declares that any individual, group, race, or nation that attempts to end Jewish control of Israel or Jerusalem is in direct opposition to His known will (Joel 3).

God's will for His people is for them to shine forth as a bright light to the Gentiles. The Almighty loves the Jewish people; He delights in them and rejoices over them—they are the apple of

God's eye. God alone dictates Jerusalem's future, and He will pro-tect His Holy City at all costs. Jerusalem's future is not to be dic-tated by the Vatican, "The Quartet" (United Nations, United States, European Union, and Russia), nor Iran, Hamas, Hezbollah, or any radical extremist terrorist groups!

This time we must accept our role as watchmen on the walls of Jerusalem and sound the alarm with our united voices—God Almighty has entrusted our generation with this crucial assignment, and we must not fail.

The world is still grappling with the age-old conflict between two half brothers—one, the father of the Jewish nation, and the other, the father of the Arab nations. The outcome of this struggle will affect every person on earth. Results from any future negotia-tion for peace or the lack of it will be noticed at the gas pump, the grocery store, and with banking institutions worldwide. If you think the battle for Jerusalem won't affect you—think again!

Please note that the battle for control over the Promised Land, and specifically Jerusalem, is not merely political or economic. This is foremost a spiritual struggle, and the repercussions of the strife between these ancient foes will continue to reverberate across the globe until Messiah comes.

I want you to understand God's plan for His Holy City, because with every passing sunset, we move one day closer to the hour when Jerusalem will take center stage in world events. As the conflict rages and world leaders strive to find a peaceful solution to the problems in the Middle East, the significance of Jerusalem will only increase.

This Time

The nation of Israel was rebirthed out of its passion for survival. The Israelites must never be without a country again. From out of the concentration camps and crematoriums of Europe echoes the cry, "Never again!" Let our united voices of unconditional love and steadfast support be heard in the courts of heaven until the End of Days when Jerusalem becomes the praise of all the earth.

Our generation is headed for a perfect storm, and in order not to repeat the mistakes of the past, we must learn from this simple mandate: "Thou shalt not be a victim, thou shalt not be a perpetrator but, above all, thou shalt not be a bystander."[56]

This time in world history Christians must not stand idly by.

This time righteous people must take a stand against evil.

This time we must circle the wagons and fight the battle against Jewish hatred.

This time Christians and Jews must unite and win the war against anti-Semitism.

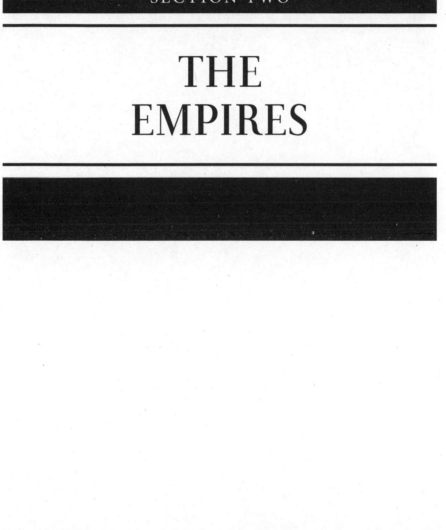

SECTION TWO

THE
EMPIRES

CHAPTER 5

THE BIRTH OF
THE EMPIRES

This agglomeration which was called and which still calls itself the Holy Roman Empire was neither holy, nor Roman, nor an empire. (Voltaire)

An empire is a political concept in which one state dominates over another state, or a series of states. An emperor or monarch commonly rules over an empire. On the simplest level, the control of the "core state" over the "peripheral state or states" is accomplished through military occupation or other formal political intervention, but it can also include economic, cultural, religious, and ideological influence.[1]

Since the beginning of time, it has been man's desire to rule over others. Conquerors have taken lands by force, by treaties, and, at times, by persuasion. Those who lived in these seized domains would either give their allegiance to the new leaders or face death. History is cluttered with kingdoms that rose and fell from power, which are now forgotten and consigned to obscure and dusty corners of empty libraries.

The desire to amass an empire, with all of its inherent wealth and power, has never escaped man's prideful nature. However, as civilization has evolved, so too have the mechanisms of gaining and holding power. In today's world, at least in the familiar cultural confines of Western civilization, most men seeking an empire attempt to do so through business agreements and mergers rather than by bloody battles.

The notion of emperors and empires is outdated in most parts of the world. And in some cases, individual freedom and democratic forms of government have replaced violent conquests and authoritarian rule. It is important to remember that democracies that are governments ruled by the people are relatively new concepts when placed in the scope of human history. Yet what goes around comes around, and in some places of the world, the means of attaining power by force is once again gaining ground.

America is an oddity in world history. Since our independence, the idea of being conquered and subjugated to a ruler is foreign to us. As a nation, we have never known an emperor or a king. We were birthed from a revolution against tyranny and have remained intact even after a devastating Civil War. Additionally, since the end of World War II, we have managed to quell any further full-scale worldwide conflicts. This is mainly due to political pandering, intimidating arms races, and dubious diplomacy. However, because we can play "the game" so well, we have been lulled into a false sense of security, and that bubble is about to burst. The Fourth Reich is coming.

THE EVIL EMPIRE TO COME

When we hear the word *empire*, we automatically think of some of the largest, most powerful, and highly influential kingdoms that have crossed the world stage of history. The top five empires that come to mind are the Persian, Roman, Arab (Caliphate), Mongol, and British. However, few of us would consider Germany as one of the most dominant empires ever to exist.

The German word *reich* means empire or kingdom, and it has been used to describe three historical periods during which Germany aspired to dominate Europe and expand its power across the world. These Reichs were precursors to the future Fourth Reich, which will force the citizens of the world to live under the political, religious, and financial dictatorship of one man: the Antichrist.

The Antichrist will make his entrance on the world stage promising peace, but instead will initiate the most massive, vicious, global bloodbath the world has even known. World War I and II, both products of the imperial ambitions of the Second and Third Reich, will pale in comparison to the coming death and destruction foretold by prophets accompanying the Fourth Reich.

The day is quickly coming when billions of people will enthusiastically choose to surrender their freedom and even their souls to a satanic empire. The Antichrist will force every person on planet Earth to take his mark on their right hand or forehead. Refusal to do so will result in decapitation. After three and a half years, his primary target will be the Jewish people. As we have learned, this will not be the first time man has attempted to eradicate God's Chosen. The pages of history are filled with stories of emperors and empires who shared a common hatred for the Jews, but where are they now?

Pharaoh's horsemen and chariots chased the Jews through the Red Sea, and God turned them into fish food (Exodus 15:19).

Where is the Babylonian Empire? Gone.

Where is the Medo-Persian Empire? Gone.

Where is the Greek Empire? Gone.

Where is the Roman Empire? Gone.

Where are the goose-stepping barbarians who followed Adolf Hitler? Gone. Buried in the boneyard of ancient history to be forgotten forever.

Where is Israel? Israel lives!

In every age and culture where the Jewish people have settled, they were treated as unwanted and undesirable enemies. I have already written about the long, sordid history of anti-Semitism and its murderous consequences.

The fact of the matter is, Satan's obsession with eradicating the Jewish people began in the Garden of Eden. However, God Almighty made a provision for all humankind when He promised that the seed of the woman (Jesus) would bruise the head of the serpent (Satan) (Genesis 3:15). This war against the Jews will continue in the Fourth Reich until Satan is ultimately defeated and thrown into the eternal lake of fire.

The Fourth Reich, which the Antichrist will rule, will be earth's last empire until the glorious return of the Messiah, who will establish an Eternal Kingdom on the new earth in the New Jerusalem.

THE GERMAN EMPIRES

I feel it is important to give a brief account of the German Reichs, and the times and events surrounding them, in order for you to have a better understanding of the background that led to the infamous Third Reich and why these empires are the precursor for the coming Fourth Reich.

The following pages will briefly cover the birth of the First Reich (962–1806), the Second Reich (1871–1918), and the infamous Third Reich of Hitler (1933–1945).

This is not a mere history lesson. Many people are unaware of the deep-rooted anti-Semitic foundations these empires were built upon. Satan, from the gates of Genesis, has sown seeds of hatred, prejudice, jealousy, and lust for power that led ordinary people to commit grotesque acts of evil without even a prick of conscience. However, the Word of God has warned us,

> *Now the Spirit expressly says that in latter times some will depart from the faith, giving heed to deceiving spirits and doctrines of demons, speaking lies in hypocrisy, having their own conscience seared with a hot iron. (1 Timothy 4:1–2)*

FROM THE ROMAN EMPIRE TO THE HOLY ROMAN EMPIRE

The Roman Empire, founded by Julius Caesar and his successors, ruled a powerful kingdom on three continents for five hundred years. However, the empire began to crumble during the reign of Constantine, who initiated a split between the eastern and western portions of the kingdom. This led to the abandonment and disintegration of the Western Roman Empire in Europe.[2]

Remember, it was Emperor Constantine who forcibly separated Christianity from its Jewish origins. He then merged Christianity with paganism to institute a form of state-sponsored religion. It seems fair to point out that Constantine left behind an empire that would be forcibly ripped apart by internal and external forces. A classic example of "you reap what you sow."

As Roman power weakened in Europe, the Germanic tribes asserted dominance over the region. In the year 410 CE, German Visigoth warriors sacked Rome, which by then was the capital city of only the western half of the former glorious Roman Empire. This invasion sent shock waves throughout Europe.

By 476 CE, the Western Roman Empire's ruler, Romulus Augustulus, was forced to surrender to the German chieftain Odoacer. Thus the Roman Empire in the west died, while its stronger and wealthier eastern half, the Byzantine Empire, continued to dominate the Middle East until it finally fell to the Ottoman Turks during the fifteenth century.[3]

Between the fall of the Western Roman Empire and the establishment of the Holy Roman Empire (First Reich), central Europe contained hundreds of small kingdoms ruled by tribal chieftains, warlords, and minor kings. It was also within this period that the Roman Catholic Church split into the Orthodox Church in the east and the Roman Catholic Church in the west.

The Roman Catholic Church remained a powerful religious and political institution, as the conquering Germanic tribes chose to convert to Catholicism.[4] Eventually, the Western Roman Catholic Church would provide the key to unifying the independent tribes and kingdoms into one empire.

THE FIRST REICH—
THE HOLY ROMAN EMPIRE (962–1806)

The Holy Roman Empire, or First Reich, was established in 962 CE. It was centered in Germany and soon stretched across central Europe, including present-day northern Italy, Austria, the Czech Republic, Switzerland, the Netherlands, Belgium, Slovenia, parts of eastern France, and western Poland.[5] This empire began with the crowning of Otto the Great and lasted for more than eight hundred years.

Otto was the strongest of the warring Germanic kings, squashing several rebellions, which helped to protect the Roman Catholic Church and its territories. These successful campaigns won the support of Pope John XII, who crowned the German king as the head of a new Roman Empire, anointing him as emperor.

There had been several previous attempts to establish a new Roman Empire since Pope Leo III crowned the Frankish conqueror

Charlemagne in the year 800 CE. However, until Otto I succeeded in the unification and subjugation of the many different regions of central Europe under his rule, the new Roman Empire had not truly existed.[6]

The link between Otto's empire and the ancient Roman Empire was established through the medieval concept of *translatio imperii*. This model was rooted in the Catholic philosopher Saint Augustine's theological division of world history into seven ages, with the final age being the reign of Christ on earth.[7]

Catholic writers during the fourth and fifth centuries built on Augustine's theory and began viewing four of the ages as a succession of world empires: Babylon, Persia, Greece, and Rome—the four kingdoms of Daniel's vision. In order to define the transition of power between the ages of history from one empire to the next, these medieval writers created the idea of *translatio imperii*, which literally means "translation of empire."[8]

Following this line of logic, Otto's establishment of the Roman Empire represented the sixth world empire that would exist until the second coming of Christ, which was compatible with Augustine's philosophy. In this way, during the Middle Ages it was generally believed that Otto was the natural successor to the empire of Charlemagne, who had been the successor of the original Roman Empire.

Yet this assumption of self-grandeur did not occur suddenly. Otto I aspired to be the emperor of only Germany and Italy, with the blessing of the pope to give him added legitimacy. However, it was his son, Otto II, who added "Roman" to his title of emperor. It was his way of competing with the Byzantine emperor, who had ambitions of reacquiring control of southern Italy.[9]

By the reign of Emperor Conrad II (1027–1039)—the name of the kingdom became commonly known as the Roman Empire (referring to Germany). In the first few centuries of the Golden Era, the German emperor was the most powerful political and religious figure in Europe. He was regarded as the guardian of the church, and his office had supreme authority over the pope. He had the power to appoint or unseat the pope in Rome as he desired.

The emperor's supremacy was eventually challenged when Pope Gregory VII (1073–1085) asserted his independence from the emperor of the Roman Empire, Henry IV (1056–1105). This struggle between the political and religious authorities prompted megalomaniac Emperor Frederick I (1157), also known as "Red Beard," to rename his empire "the Holy Roman Empire."[10] His ambition for power was limitless, and he considered himself second only to God. Red Beard's intended goal was to rule over Italy and the Pope.

Because of this sustained contention, the Holy Roman Empire not only lost territory in Italy but also the guaranteed support of the Catholic Church. By the thirteenth century, the German kingdom (aka Holy Roman Empire) had rivals in France and Italy for imperial power in Europe. In one of the great ironies of history, the Holy Roman Empire "was neither holy, nor Roman, nor an empire," as noted by eighteenth-century French philosopher Voltaire.[11]

Yet the name remained, and so did the idea that Germany should be the guardian of Christendom.

The Guardian of Christianity

Germany's self-appointed guardianship would eventually become the foundation to its cultural and ethnical convictions of superiority and natural right of rulership over Europe. Every empire in history has believed in its own superiority, and Germany was no different.

By the early sixteenth century, competing forces were pulling the Holy Roman Empire apart both politically and religiously. Not only was the empire in crisis, but so was the Catholic Church. The lines of succession had become unclear, and multiple contenders fought each other for the titles of emperor and pope. Like previous empires in history, the First Reich looked around for a scapegoat to take the blame for their internal woes and decided that the Jews were responsible.

The historical treatment of Jews in Europe had been growing successively worse over the centuries. The divergence of power between the emperors and the popes, and its subsequent effect on the supremacy of papal authority over every Christian kingdom in Europe, resulted in an expansion of religious law and a hardening of church doctrine. This stringent policy gradually emphasized corporal punishment for sin and apostasy, and the Jews were the natural target.[12] Heresy, which any observant Jew was guilty of by the standards of medieval Christian theology, became a crime punishable by torture, imprisonment, or death.

By the late tenth century, Jewish communities in Europe began to suffer increased violent attacks from their Christian neighbors who viewed them with suspicion and resentment. Earlier popes made some occasional statements against the forced conversion of Jews to Christianity. However, others insisted the Jews at least deserved protection from physical harm. Nevertheless, this fleeting attitude of tolerance disappeared as the church grew more powerful and the empire's grip on its territories grew more precarious. In competition for supreme authority over Europe's citizens, the church and the empire both exploited the latent anti-Jewish feelings of medieval Christians to their own advantage.

By the twelfth century, European Jews were routinely accused of blood libel and their religious books burned as dangerous heretical teachings; they were forced out of many occupations and segregated into ghettos. The period of the Crusades produced extreme feelings of hatred for religious outsiders, which included the Jews, and precipitated several shocking massacres, especially in Germany's Rhineland.[13]

In previous chapters, I have well documented the persecution of the Jews by the church during this time. It is worth repeating that edicts such as requiring Jews to wear identifying clothing later inspired Hitler when he formed the Third Reich. This forced practice of identification and selective ostracism also foreshadows the prophesy of the coming Fourth Reich, which will require those left behind to either take the mark of the Beast or be killed.

Although by the thirteenth century the Holy Roman Empire no longer enjoyed the status of being the pope's chosen kingdom in Europe, it still upheld church law to give legitimacy to its claim as the guardian of Christendom. Convinced by his advisors that the Jewish religion was a threat to not only Christianity but also the stability of his empire, Holy Roman emperor Maximilian I ordered all Jewish books other than the Hebrew Bible to be gathered and burned in 1509.[14] Increasingly, Jews were treated as dangerous intruders in Germany and a threat to both the church and the empire.

The tensions between Pope Leo X and the Holy Roman Emperor Charles V were exacerbated by Martin Luther's rebellion against the Catholic Church in 1517 that precipitated the Protestant Reformation.[15] Luther's challenge to papal authority led to a crackdown on perceived heretics everywhere, especially against the Jews.

The Holy Roman Empire feared losing its authority because of Luther's teachings and decided to help eradicate the "heretic Jews" by forcibly expelling them from parts of their empire. This practice spread across Europe during the Middle Ages, resulting in the banishment of entire Jewish communities.

In 1670, Holy Roman emperor Leopold I issued an order that all Jews had to leave Austria by August 1. This was the second time Jewish citizens of Austria had been banished by the empire—the first expulsion took place in 1421 and lasted over two hundred years.[16]

Sadly, as I mentioned earlier, Luther himself later contributed to the poisonous atmosphere of anti-Semitism growing in Germany and throughout Europe by publishing his scathing epistles against the Jews. Germany's population would eventually split into nearly equal portions of Catholics and Protestants by the time Hitler came to power. Both religious camps shared the same animosity toward the Jews, thanks in part to Luther and his venomous hatred that spread through Europe like wildfire.

As time went on, the Holy Roman Empire was gradually forced to concede much of its centralized authority to the princes and rulers of its local territories. During its final two hundred years, the empire existed more on paper and in the imaginations of its people than in reality.

Nonetheless, up until the very end of the Holy Roman Empire, Jewish communities were subjected to cruel and bigoted treatment. In 1802, just four years before the empire dissolved, a Jewish delegation pleaded with Emperor Francis II (1792–1806) to grant them the rights of German citizens and abolish their many restrictions, including the discriminatory poll tax that German Jews had to pay in order to enter any town or province. Their request was denied.[17]

Weakened by internal feuds and the political impact of the French Revolution, the Holy Roman Empire finally dissolved in 1806 when the emperor abdicated the throne in order to avoid being overthrown by Napoleon Bonaparte's triumphant march across Europe.[18]

BETWEEN THE REICHS

Napoleon fancied himself the successor of the ancient Roman Empire, just as the Holy Roman Empire had believed it inherited that mantle through *translatio imperii*. At first, it seemed that

Napoleon Bonaparte might be a different kind of emperor, one who was willing to give the Jews of Europe the rights of citizenship and who promised to allow the Jews to return to their homeland after his attempt to conquer Palestine, but those hopes were soon dashed.[19]

Napoleon's "Infamous Decree," published two years after he unseated the Holy Roman Empire, imposed economic restrictions on eastern European Jews and limited their freedom of movement across the continent. Napoleon's short-lived reign was the catalyst for major social upheaval in Europe that actually strengthened the perceived conflict between Jews who remained loyal to the Torah and their righteous traditions, verus those who assimilated to the new idea of modern nationalism.

Another important effect of Napoleon's conquest of Europe was the change in the balance of power between the Roman Catholic Church and the kingdoms of Europe.[20] Prior to the conquest, the pope had enjoyed supremacy over the kings and queens of Europe since the thirteenth century. Heads of state had acted as enforcers of the church and relied upon papal support to retain control.

However, after Napoleon rose to power, he oversaw a movement to secularize much of the national government and placed himself above the authority of the pope. Napoleon's example changed how future European rulers viewed the relationship between church and state.

After Napoleon's defeat at Waterloo by the British Alliance in 1815, Pope Pius VII (1800–1823) tried to reassert his authority, but the Catholic Church never regained the same level of political power it had enjoyed during the days of the Holy Roman Empire. Napoleon Bonaparte may have successfully ended the First Reich, but it had already left an indelible mark on the culture of Germany. For sixty-five years, Germany's imperial ambitions would lie dormant, but would once again rise as the Second Reich.

North German Confederation

During the six and a half decades after Napoleon's defeat, the disjointed German states attempted to regroup under new leadership but struggled to come to a lasting agreement. Initially, thirty-nine German states struck a bargain for a mutual defense pact, but once again, the lust for ultimate power led to a war between rival German leaders and resulted in victory by the Prussian state.

In 1866, the ambitious Prussian prime minister Otto von Bismarck established the North German Confederation and succeeded in unifying twenty-two of the thirty-nine German states under his authority.[21] This laid the foundation for the rise of the Second Reich. The confederation united the twenty-two states under a single judicial and legal code, and placed economic authority in the hands of the federal government. The individual states would retain control of their religious and educational affairs.

France declared war against the North German Confederation in 1870 because it feared the Prussians' ambition of German unification would shift the balance of power in Europe. However, France's declaration backfired and caused the remaining seventeen German states to affirm their loyalty to Prussian king William I.

It was during this Franco-Prussian War that the bitter seeds of World War I were sown by the rivalry of France and Austria against Germany. At the end of the war, Germany decided to humiliate their defeated enemies by imposing a debt of 5 billion francs. This was a foreshadowing of their own future humiliation via the Treaty of Versailles after Germany's defeat in World War I, which ultimately led to World War II.[22]

German Emancipation of the Jews

In 1812, Prussia had passed a law allowing its Jewish residents to claim all the rights, privileges, and responsibilities of Prussian citizens. When Prussia became the dominant member of the North German Confederation, this citizenship was extended to all Jews within the confederation. Then after German unification in 1871, all German Jews were declared legal citizens for the first time in Germany's history.

This law, however, did not remove the deep anti-Semitic root that had been planted centuries earlier. Even though the German government could see the advantage of securing the loyalty of the Jewish people by giving them citizenship, their fellow German countrymen deeply resented this change in the social tradition.[23]

THE SECOND REICH (1871–1918)

The Second Reich was formed in January 1871 when Prussian king William I was declared emperor of the united German states. The new German Empire, called the *Deutsches Kaiserreich*, retained most of the North German Confederation's constitutional provisions, and annexed the conquered French province of Alsace-Lorraine into their empire against the will of its French population.[24]

At this time, Chancellor Otto von Bismarck led the German Empire into a direct confrontation with the Catholic Church that further ingrained the idea in German culture of their government's inherent authority over church doctrine. Bismarck strongly objected to the 1870 ruling of the First Vatican Council that conferred infallibility upon the office of the pope, so he led the German Catholic people to split off and form their own Old Catholic Church.[25] He did this more for political reasons than for any strong religious conviction.

Bismarck secularized marriage for the first time, removed Roman Catholic officials from government, and seized control of education from the church. In hindsight, these moves were the beginning of a trend toward preparing German citizens to replace the authority of the church with a combined religious and political loyalty to the state.

A key philosophical foundation of Bismarck's approach to government authority was his belief that he needed to give the German people a "common enemy" in order to unify them and maintain control. This philosophy still remains the preferred way for dictators and despots to distract their people from internal problems and hold on to power.

Throughout his time as chancellor, Bismarck chose various "enemies" to unite the German people. First with foreign wars, then by fighting the Roman Catholic Church, and later by targeting the socialist politics of Karl Marx.[26]

In several ways, Otto von Bismarck paved the way for Adolf Hitler's ascension to power. Bismarck laid the groundwork for instituting the German state's national government. He gave the chancellorship supreme authority and effectively overturned centuries of local German political autonomy. Following Bismarck's model, Hitler recognized that the best way to secure control of the German people was to present a common enemy. Both men were ruthless, calculating, and determined to elevate the power of the state over the church.

German Nationalism

During the Second Reich, the growing nationalism of the German people demanded that the empire seek to expand. Bismarck had built his career out of provoking conflict with neighboring states in order to keep the German people unified under his leadership. However, in the later years of his rule, he found himself having to play an increasingly complicated game of substituting one fake enemy for another as he instigated minor conflicts along all of Germany's borders to appease factions within the empire.[27]

Chancellor Bismarck governed for nearly twenty years, but failed to create a system of government that could survive once he was no longer holding the reins. When the original kaiser (emperor), William I, died and his son, the crown prince, died shortly afterward, the German Empire was left in the hands of a young emperor, William II, who had no loyalty to Bismarck. Asserting his constitutional authority, Emperor William II forced Bismarck to resign in 1890, which began the demise of the Second Reich.[28]

However, the young emperor was unprepared to deal with the challenges Germany faced as it entered the twentieth century. Bismarck's two decades of cultivating war with France as a means to solidify the German people's nationalism resulted in a mutual animosity between the two countries. In addition, Germany found itself increasingly isolated from foreign allies who had been alienated by Bismarck's policies of hostility.

Emperor Willam II made a catastrophic miscalculation by not acknowledging the limits to Germany's power. While Bismarck had been wise enough to try to restrain the German people's appetite for imperial expansion, the new kaiser foolishly believed the conquest for new territory was his and Germany's supreme mandate.

By 1914, William II had gained popular support for a confrontation against France and Russia, setting in motion a military build-up that he was powerless to stop.[29] That June, World War I began, and it became a self-perpetuating calamity. It evolved into one of the deadliest conflicts in human history, with more than 16 million people losing their lives, including nearly 1.8 million Germans. Germany had expected the war to be over in six months; instead, it lasted four years.

In order to end the war and sign a peace agreement with the Allied powers, Germany was required to transition its government to a constitutional monarchy. However, faced with an internal revolt, Emperor William II abdicated his throne.

As a result, the German party of the Socialist Democrats, combined with the established military leadership to form a new democratic republic.[30] This effectively ended the Second Reich, and introduced the disastrous period between 1918 and 1933 known as the Weimar Republic.

THE WEIMAR REPUBLIC (1918–1933)

The aftermath of World War I created feelings of humiliation, shame, frustration, and resentment among the German people, and it was the Weimar Republic that took the blame for it. In reality, those most responsible for the war and the accompanying economic disasters handed their fiasco over to this newly formed democracy, a type of government that had not previously existed in Germany. To make matters worse, the very essence of democracy found in the Weimar Bill of Right and free elections, which was now available to all German citizens including the Jewish people, had a devastating side effect. The repercussions of the war produced an aggressive increase in anti-Semitic sentiment among Germans who strongly resented their Jewish neighbors being given increased freedoms while they felt theirs had been stripped away.[31]

German Jews had bravely fought alongside their Christian counterparts during World War I. However, anti-Semitic propaganda was spewing a different tale. The Jews were portrayed as slackers who avoided fighting on the front lines. During the post–World War I revolution of 1918–1919, angry mobs in Munich and Berlin viciously attacked Jewish citizens.

Long before Hitler rose to power, the German people were already venting their frustrations and anger over losing the war by blaming the Jews. The evil propaganda espoused by both the state and the church that had circulated in Germany for centuries had successfully persuaded average German citizens that all their problems could be rationally attributed to the Jews.

A DICHOTOMY OF MORALITY

By the late nineteenth century, Germany was one of the most cultured and educated countries in Europe. It published the most books, had the highest literacy rate, and housed some of the most prestigious institutions of higher education in the civilized world. This is the era into which Adolf Hitler was born.

During his reign, Hitler's top ten advisors were learned economists, lawyers, and philosophers. Others were recognized ambassadors and experts on world affairs. Another was a specialist in designing mass transportation and infrastructure. They had strong family units, enjoyed the arts, and were passionate about their beliefs. One could easily conclude that Hitler's inner circle was, at the very least, the best Germany had to offer.

However, during this same time, the state had elevated its power and prestige over the church. The so-called "guardians of Christianity" had morphed into something incredibly evil. Even though nearly 98 percent of the German population considered themselves Christians, it was becoming increasingly obvious that neither culture, education, nor religion guaranteed the making of a God-honoring society.

Christianity had eroded throughout Europe, and as the Third Reich rose to power, any religion that worshipped anyone above Hitler was unacceptable. The Nazis had their own brand of "religion"; it was the highest form of self-adulation since Lucifer fell from the Third Heaven.

Their ultimate goal was to oppose traditional Christian values and replace them with a "reformed religion" that would fully incorporate Nazi principles. Instruction of conventional Christian doctrines in schools was first made optional, then altogether replaced with mandatory teachings about Nazi philosophies. Eventually, the crucifix was replaced with photos of Adolf Hitler as the Nazi regime became the new state religion of the Third Reich.

Hitler surrounded himself with an elite gang of fanatical yes-men. The führer's neurotic leadership, coupled with the men's obsessive commitment to his warped ideology, generated political, economic, and social institutions of legitimized terror, leading to the imminent annihilation of the Jewish people. These same highly intelligent and educated men, who were later found to be "normal" after receiving psychological exams during the Nuremberg trials, were participants in the most indescribable atrocities ever known to man against the Jewish people. Unbelievably, most claimed they were simply following orders and that their actions were warranted, while few regretted what they had done.

Yet, on the surface, everything seemed copasetic—everything appeared to be in excellent order. These men went to church and sang the hymns, worshipped baby Jesus, heard the homilies, and kissed the toe of the Virgin Mary. Then these monsters left their places of worship, and with cold-blooded deliberation commanded Mary's descendants into the gas chambers and flung their dead bodies into the ovens.

These "guardians of Christianity" were actually sent by hell itself to destroy God's Chosen.

THE RISE OF THE THIRD REICH (1933–1945)

The impact of the previous two Reichs had perfectly positioned the German people to accept and follow Adolf Hitler's satanic cult called Nazism:

- The Holy Roman Empire established a mythology of grandeur among the German people that enabled centuries of their leaders to exploit the inherent national German pride in their superiority and right to safeguard the "Christian" culture of Europe.
- The struggle between the emperors of the First and Second Reichs and the Catholic Church had gradually established a tradition that placed the people's ultimate loyalty in the hands of the state over the church, even in matters of deciding religious doctrine.
- The anti-Semitic policies pursued by the Holy Roman Empire and the Catholic Church and the Protestant Reformation, coupled with the propaganda taught during the Middle Ages, were later resurrected and used to remind German Christians that "the Jews have always been our enemy" and a threat to the stability of the nation.

By the time the Nazis came on the scene as a political force in the 1920s, Germany was split almost evenly between Catholics and Protestants. While Catholics had their own issues with anti-Semitic theology, Martin Luther's legacy had trained Protestants to hate and despise the Jews just as much.

A strong element of economic jealousy was also prevalent within German anti-Semitism. After World War I, the ascent of the National Socialist German Workers' Party (the Nazis) reinvigorated the old beliefs that Jews were unfairly profiting off their Christian neighbors.

Adolf Hitler was a product of his own time. He understood that his fellow countrymen were disillusioned with the status quo, and more than anything, Hitler desired Germany to regain world supremacy as it had during the First and Second Reichs. Undoubtedly, he was an admirer of Chancellor Bismarck, who was considered a hero to the German nationalists and honored as the founder of the Second Reich.

Hitler was also fully convinced that the Jewish people were evil and were the perpetrators of all the failures his country had endured. It was not difficult for him to persuade the German people that the Jews were their enemies and worthy of the worst possible abuse.

The time was ripe for the birth of the Third Reich.

THE BLITZKRIEG OF A DEMONIC DICTATORSHIP

The following is a timeline of Hitler's meteoric rise to power and the numerous "decrees" he put into motion within days of winning his election in 1933. It is important to note that Hitler became both chancellor and führer of Germany in less than two years— taking total control of his evil empire. I have included this graphic representation to demonstrate how quickly the geopolitical climate of the world can change, ushering forth the Antichrist and his Fourth Reich.

THE BLITZKRIEG OF DICTATORSHIP

1889

Adolf Hitler born

1914–1918

- Hitler serves in World War I
- Promoted to corporal

1919–1920

Hitler joins German Workers' Party—renamed
National Socialist German Workers' Party—Nazi

1921

Hitler Becomes Nazi Party Leader
- Party grows to 70,000 members
- Storm troopers (brownshirts) formed

1923–1925

- Hitler is imprisoned for leading a failed revolution against Weimar Republic
- Writes *Mein Kampf*

1925–1929

Hitler is released and reestablishes and reorganizes the Nazi Party

October 1929–January 29, 1933

The World Economic Crisis
- Begins the demise of the Weimar Republic democratic system
- One-third of labor force is unemployed

October 1929–January 29, 1933 (cont.)

- Article 48 of Constitution invoked to govern by "decree"
- German government now ruled by a presidential dictatorship
- Nazis and Communists deliberately create disorder and chaos in the streets
- Nazis deliberately and systematically intensify German anti-Semitism

January 30, 1933

- **Adolf Hitler appointed chancellor**
- Nazi Party gains a third of the seats in the Reichstag (parliament)
- Death of Weimar Republic

February 1, 1933

"Decree for the Protection of the German People"
- Prohibits public assembly or publications by parties not sanctioned by government
- Rounds up Communists and Social Democrats, thereby crippling anti-government campaigns

February 8, 1933

Hitler approves rearmament and rebuilding of military forces

February 20, 1933

Hermann Göring secures financial backing from twenty leading German industrialists and financiers to rebuild and maintain economy

February 27, 1933

The Reichstag Fire
- Set by a mentally unstable 25-year-old male. Hitler uses it to blame Communists.

February 28, 1933

"Decree of the Reich President for the Protection of the People and State" (aka "Reichstag Fire Decree")
This decree, which was never lifted during the twelve years of the Reich, *immediately*:
- Suspends free speech and freedom of the press
- Restricts right to public assembly and free association
- Suspends right to private postal correspondence and telephone communication
- Authorizes house searches and confiscation of property
- Allows imprisonment without trial
- Authorizes SA/SS to take over state police forces
- Provides the foundation for future injustices and atrocities against Jews

March 5, 1933

Joseph Goebbels Appointed Propaganda Chief
- Takes control of all forms of media outlets (film, radio, newspapers), fueling fear and distrust of Jews

Heinrich Himmler Appointed Head of SS
- The *Schutzstaffel* (or SS) is the "Protective Echelon" of the Nazi Party
- **Himmler opens the first concentration camp**
  - Social Democratic and Communist opponents are sent to the camp along with "intellectual elites" aka Jewish college professors who opposes the Nazi Party
  - "Führer Principle" is propagated—Hitler has all the solutions—whatever he says is right. Anyone questioning the führer commits treason and is either sent to the concentration camp or executed

March 23, 1933

"Law to Remove the Distress of the People and the State"
- Also known as the "Enabling Act"
- The chancellor is authorized to prepare laws
- The cabinet (handpicked by the chancellor) enacts the laws
- The official government paper, headed by Goebbels, publishes the decrees of the Reich
- The SS enforces the laws

April 7, 1933

"Law for the Restoration of the Professional Civil Service"
- Immediately disqualifies all non-Aryans for civil service jobs. The law primarily targets:
  - Jews
  - individuals married to Jews
  - someone with one Jewish grandparent
- Allows the government to force anyone into retirement (Jewish sympathizers)
- Directly and immediately impacts faculty in schools and universities

May 2, 1933

Communist Workers' Party Union Abolished
- All assets are seized
- Union is replaced by German Labor Front

July 14, 1933

"Law for the Prevention of Offspring with Hereditary Diseases"
- Compulsory sterilization for those the government deemed dangerous as sources of:
  - disease
  - racial pollution
  - criminal tendencies
  - genetically inferiority or impurity
  - incapacity to change due to bloodline

July 14, 1933 (cont.)

- Hitler combines his anti-Semitism with broader plans to purify the Aryan race

July 20, 1933

The Reich Concordat
- The Reich is officially recognized by the Vatican as the Third Reich (Holy Romany Empire)
- The Nazi Party is declared the only legitimate political party in Germany—solidifying Hitler's dictatorship

December 1, 1933

"Law to Ensure the Unity of Party and State"
- Hitler states, "The National Socialist German Labor Party [Nazi Party] is the bearer of the concept of the German State and is inseparable from the state."

1934

The Führer Principle
- "Hitler is Germany and Germany is Hitler. Whatever he does is necessary. Whatever he does is successful. Clearly the führer has divine blessing." (Rudolf Hess)

June 30–July 2, 1934

"Operation Hummingbird"
- The elimination of the SA's (brownshirts) leadership through executions and targeted assassinations makes the SS the only paramilitary force with Heinrich Himmler, SS Commandant:
  - believes race purity can be achieved by eliminating "biological corruption"
  - declares SS officers have to be free of Jews in their genealogy from 1750 forward
  - maintains the right to approve or reject proposed marriages of members

September 10–16, 1935

Nuremberg Rally
- Establishes clear racial criterion for German citizens
- Bans intermarriage/sexual relations between German Jews and Aryan Germans

September 17, 1935

Systematic State Seizure of Jewish Property
- Confiscates all property and assets
- Restricts buying and selling of said property
- Expels families from Germany—penniless

November 9–10, 1938

Kristallnacht
- Nazis declare it was part of an international Jewish conspiracy
- Goebbels recommends "spontaneous" outbreak against Jews—countrywide campaign ensues
- 100 dead; 7,000 Jewish businesses and 267 synagogues destroyed

January 30, 1939

Hitler's Prophecy
"Today I will once more be a prophet: If the international Jewish financiers in and outside Europe should succeed in plunging the nations once more into a world war, then the result will not be the Bolshevization of the earth, and thus the victory of Jewry, but the annihilation of the Jewish race in Europe!" (Adolf Hitler)

September 1, 1939

- Germany invades Poland
- War in the European theatre begins

January 20, 1942

The Wannsee Conference and the "Final Solution to the Jewish Question"

- Himmler establishes special unit of the SS: *Einsatzkommandos*—mobile killing units
  - mission: exterminate Jews, Polish intellectuals, Romanis, homosexuals, Communists, and NKVD (Russian police)
  - ultimate goal: to murder more than 11 million Jews, including those in England, Ireland, Finland, Portugal, Spain, and Switzerland
- Himmler, now the authority over the Jewish Question, enlists Reinhard Heydrich and other specialists in the systematic deportation and killing of Jews on a massive scale

April 30, 1945

Adolf Hitler commits suicide

May 8, 1945

Victory in Europe is declared

**World War II—Cost of Human Life
in the European Theater Alone**

- Over 6 million Jews systematically murdered in ghettos and concentration camps
- 22 million soldiers killed
- Over 49.8 million civilians are murdered

CHAPTER 6

THE EVOLUTION OF AMERICAN LEADERSHIP

"I urge, then, first of all, that petitions, prayers, intercession and thanksgiving be made for all people—for kings and all those in authority, that we may live peaceful and quiet lives in all godliness and holiness." (1 Timothy 2:1–2 NIV)

Many Americans are unaware of our country's deep roots regarding democracy and the fundamental way our government functions. We started as colonies under the watchful tyrannical eye of the British Empire. Our resources, livelihoods, and basic religious freedoms were under attack . . . so we rebelled against one of the largest military forces ever assembled.

There had never been a revolution such as ours—we were the first independent, foreign-recognized nation and the first European colonial entity to break from its mother country. However, were we destined to become our own empire or a true democracy by the people and for the people?

THE AMERICAN EMPIRE

While Americans do not typically think of the United States as an empire, the idea of an "empire of liberty" goes back to Thomas Jefferson. And while it was hardly a global power at its birth, the United States grew in influence to become the dominant world power after World War II, and the only truly global power after the Soviet Union broke apart in 1991. Thus, any analysis of empires past, present, and future has to come to terms with the American story.

Leadership in the United States runs along two tracks: moral leadership that is based on the founding principles of the American republic, and political leadership that is situated in a constitutional system and alternately empowered or constrained by a cycle of partisan eras.

In this chapter we will explore these two types of leadership and then trace their development through American history up to the present day. That story will help clarify the nature of America's current struggles and leadership crisis—a crisis that cannot help but have an impact on global politics.

Moral Leadership: America's Genetic Code

Americans celebrate the birth of the United States every July 4, marking the unanimous adoption of the Declaration of Independence. This document contains several foundational principles that are part of the DNA of the American republic. The document, however, did not spring out of nothing. Underappreciated by Americans is the fact that the colonists wrestled with the principles and processes of liberty for over 150 years before John Hancock affixed his famous signature to the Declaration of Independence.

Americans were governed by such documents as the Mayflower Compact (1620) and the Massachusetts Body of Liberties (1641) long before 1776, and most of the ideas that lay at the foundation of democracy, self-government, and majority rule arose in church debates in the 1600s before they became political debates in the 1700s.

The Founders of the American republic established their system of government on what Michael Novak called the "two wings" of common sense and religious faith. The commonsense reasoning of such thinkers as Aristotle, Cicero, John Locke, and Baron de Montesquieu was baptized, in a sense, by a biblical worldview that was partly Protestant, but even more so Hebraic.[1]

Many Americans saw the United States as an "American Israel," with George Washington standing in the place of Moses. The dynamic collision of these different but complementary perspectives caused most of the Founders to understand and agree with a very simple set of precepts.

First, liberty is the goal or objective of the American republic. Second, liberty cannot exist without virtue. Liberty *needs* virtue to thrive and succeed. Third, virtue is impossible without religion. Therefore, because liberty requires religion, the American experiment can only succeed in a healthy religious environment.[2]

We can see evidence of this perspective in the Declaration of Independence itself. In that document, Thomas Jefferson famously referred to the "Laws of Nature and of Nature's God"—language that borrows explicitly from the natural law tradition of Cicero and Thomas Aquinas. Jefferson also declared the existence of several self-evident truths: "that all men are created equal, that they are endowed by their Creator with certain unalienable Rights, that among these are Life, Liberty, and the pursuit of Happiness."

To call a truth "self-evident" is to say that it is basic and fundamental. There are no truths more fundamental than these truths, and they are knowable by human beings with the unaided power of reason. There is in the very structure of the created order of the universe—given by God—a set of objective moral principles or universal truths by which we can evaluate and judge human laws, politics, and customs.

Human nature itself is fixed and unchanging, and the existence of a fixed human nature means there are fixed and permanent natural rights that come from a source higher than the state, putting constraints on the state. These fixed moral principles guide government power and provide for limited constitutional government, which in turn protects life, liberty, and property.

These objective moral principles inform us that all human beings are created equal. We are not, of course, equal in every area of life. We are obviously not equal when it comes to economic condition, talents and skills, intelligence, moral virtue, and character qualities. But we *are* all equally human. No one is more human than anyone else.

That means we are all equal under the law. And because of that innate equality of all human beings, we all have the same natural rights to life, liberty, and the pursuit of happiness. Positive rights are given by the government, and therefore the government can take them away. But natural rights—what Jefferson called unalienable rights—are given by God, and government cannot legitimately take them away.

Jefferson and the Constitution

Jefferson argued that securing these rights is the very reason we have government, an assertion that connects the Declaration of Independence to the Constitution. The central reason why the Framers of the Constitution separated the powers and functions of government into separate bodies of officials was to prevent any single individual or group of individuals from accumulating all powers into their hands, leading to tyranny.[3]

Thus, embedded into the very structure of the American constitutional order is a concern to protect the rights and liberties guaranteed by the Declaration of Independence. The Constitution itself replaced the Articles of Confederation, which proved inadequate to securing "the blessings of liberty to ourselves and our posterity."

Just in case anyone was in any doubt about these principles of liberty, the first task of the First Congress was to draft and ratify a Bill of Rights. This document, comprising the first ten amendments to the Constitution, further reinforces basic and fundamental principles of liberty. Most important, the First Amendment guarantees the free exercise of religion, a fact that provides more evidence of the central place of religion in the thinking of the Framers. We also enjoy freedom of speech, freedom of the press, the right to bear arms, and various rights of the accused—all designed to protect citizens from the unjust, coercive, and intrusive power of the state.

These are the fundamental principles embedded into the genetic code of what it means to be an American. It is a genetic code supported by both the philosophy and religious worldview of the architects of the American political system. The great French commentator Alexis de Tocqueville understood the important role religion played in supporting and sustaining liberty, arguing in the 1830s that the common Judeo-Christian morality taught by all religious sects in America helped regulate and constrain its politics. He no doubt had in mind some of the more radical and destructive schemes of his own nation's French Revolution. This is why Tocqueville called religion "the first of their [America's] political institutions."[4]

America is strong when it understands and embraces these foundational principles—and its strength is endangered when it forgets them. America is now in a revival of paganism and secularism; the more secular we become, the more godless we become. It's time for a revolution of righteousness to sweep America.

The Place of the Presidency

In many nations, the focal point for moral leadership may be found in a monarch. Whether king, queen, kaiser, czar, or emperor, these individuals, even as mere figureheads, embody a nation's identity and values. They represent the nation on the world stage. Dictators, führers, ayatollahs, and "Dear Leaders" (Kim Jong-Un) do the same for tyrannies.

Although the United States is not a monarchy, that does not mean it has no need for political leadership. In fact, the Framers of the constitutional system understood the need for leadership, and carefully constructed the federal political institutions to provide for it. Leadership is not a quality often found in Congress, but that is hardly the fault of national legislators.

Congress is not designed to provide national leadership. It is a plural institution designed to implement policies that reflect the popular will of the people. It is structured to make deliberation about the merits of policy more likely through its large, two-chambered and frequent elections (every two years for the House of Representatives). Action and efficiency are not qualities Congress possesses.

Nor do we find national leadership in the federal court system—an institution composed of a small group of highly educated experts who have job security so that they can protect individual rights and liberties by accurately interpreting and applying the law in cases and controversies.[5]

Instead, the focal point for national leadership is the presidency.

Its function, in the words of Alexander Hamilton, is to concern itself with "the execution of the laws and the employment of the common strength."[6] In some ways the president is a type of clerk to Congress, for the Constitution charges him to "take care that the laws be faithfully executed." But the president is also a leader—an independent constitutional officer designed to clarify and set goals and respond to crises, whether they be of an economic, a national security, or a natural disaster variety.

The very fact that the presidency is composed of one individual makes the office "the bulwark of the national security," and enables the president to act swiftly and decisively, with "vigor and expedition."[7] The unitary nature of the office also allows citizens and voters to hold the individual accountable for his actions—to be able to give credit or lay blame for the president's conduct of his office.

However, it would be a mistake to assume that all presidents are created equal, with equal opportunities to accomplish their objectives. Presidential greatness surveys that rank presidents from one to forty-five feed this mistaken perspective. In fact, most presidents have only a marginal ability to control their own success or failure. Larger forces are already in place whenever a new president takes office, and the most important thing a president can do is have a strategic sense of what he can accomplish within his term.

What is the nature of these larger historical constraints? American political history can be divided into a series of political eras that tend to favor one party over the other. We can think of the advantaged party in an era as the "governing party" and the disadvantaged party as the "opposition party." For example, the Democratic Party during the Jacksonian era enjoyed a natural advantage over the Whig Party. That does not mean that the Whigs never won elections, only that the natural advantage lay with the Democrats.

Similarly, the Democratic Party during the New Deal era enjoyed a natural advantage over the Republican Party. The principal advantage enjoyed by the governing parties in these eras is that they retained the power to define what the political debate was about—which issues dominated and how we talk about them. The core ideology of the governing party becomes the dominant governing philosophy of the nation for that era.

We can see American history, then, as a cycle of partisan "regimes." One party takes control in a redefining election, becomes the major player for several decades, loses office a couple of times, but always comes back to power. Then the party becomes weak and vulnerable, and less able to adapt to changing issues and circumstances. It eventually loses power to the opposition party in some sort of crisis that delegitimizes its leadership, and the opposition party takes control in another redefining election . . . and the cycle begins all over again.[8]

The important question for any president, given this cyclical understanding of American history, is where in the cycle he takes office. The presidents with the greatest abilities to truly lead and reshape politics in America in a genuinely transformational way are those who come at the beginning of the cycle. These are the epoch-making regime founders who come to power opposed to the previous regime when that regime is weak and vulnerable and collapsing, usually due to some trigger event that causes a crisis of legitimacy.

Constitutionally, then, all presidents are leaders. Historically, all presidents must adjust their leadership goals to account for their placement in the partisan era of their time. In *all* cases, presidents, as the embodiment of America on the world stage, represent the basic foundational principles of the American republic—those self-evident truths Jefferson wrote about. To the extent that presidents and their parties faithfully adhere to those transcendent truths, the nation thrives. When the presidents and their parties stray from these principles, the nation is endangered. It is to that story that we turn next.

PRESIDENTIAL LEADERSHIP FROM THE FOUNDING TO THE CIVIL WAR

We can trace the two-party competition that marks American political history back to the founding era, where the first battle was fought over the ratification of the Constitution. Federalists supported ratification, while Anti-Federalists opposed it. Federalists won the initial dispute, but the argument splashed over into the administration of George Washington.

George Washington, America's first president, was perfectly fitted for the job. Washington had chaired the Constitutional Convention, and when the Framers were debating the structure and powers of the presidency, they had their eye on the man at the front of the room—the man everyone knew would first inhabit the office. Washington understood that everything he did as president would set a precedent for future presidents, from how to conduct foreign policy to how to employ the veto.

Washington was both a national founder (an architect of the American republic) and a regime founder (of the Federalist era). In the great debate between his secretary of the treasury, Alexander Hamilton, and his secretary of state, Thomas Jefferson, Washington sided with Hamilton. Hamilton and Jefferson became the leaders of America's first political parties, the Federalists and the Democratic-Republicans.

These parties separated in disputes over the power of the federal government, whether there should be a national bank, and whether the United States should favor France or Great Britain in foreign policy. Washington claimed for the presidency powerful administrative and foreign policy authority, and his economic policies helped put the young nation on a much firmer financial foundation.

Despite Washington's success, the two parties of the 1790s hated each other and saw each other as borderline treasonous. Jefferson's Democratic-Republicans saw the Federalists as undemocratic, commerce-loving monarchists who betrayed the accomplishment of the revolution, while John Adams's Federalists saw the Jeffersonians as godless, French-loving, agrarian radicals.

Neither party had any sense that the other group represented a legitimate presence in American politics. Jefferson's victory over Adams in 1800 sent the Federalists into a death spiral from which they never recovered, leaving Jefferson's party as the only significant force in American politics—a period known somewhat inaccurately as the "Era of Good Feelings."[9]

Thomas Jefferson was the chief architect of this new era, which saw three straight two-term presidencies, all from Virginia. Unquestionably, Jefferson's most significant accomplishment was the acquisition of the Louisiana Territory from France, an act that immediately doubled the size of the nation and extended its reach to the Pacific.

Jefferson's successors asserted themselves on the international stage by declaring the hemisphere off-limits to European meddling in the Monroe Doctrine and made the first significant attempt to manage the slavery issue with the Missouri Compromise. Jefferson's party was so dominant that when James Monroe ran for reelection in 1820, he faced no opposition, winning every electoral vote but one.

Political ambition and competition do not rest, however. Just as the Jeffersonian system reached its zenith, the presidential nomination process broke down. In a four-way split in 1824, Andrew Jackson won more electoral votes than anyone else. He failed to win a majority, however, and the House of Representatives selected John Quincy Adams to be president. Jackson spent the next four years castigating Adams as corrupt, and the Jeffersonian system collapsed as Jackson won the presidency in 1828.

Andrew Jackson's presidency witnessed a resurgence of party competition, with Jackson serving as the founder of the new Democratic Party, and the various factions opposed to Jackson coalescing under the banner of the Whig Party. Both parties evolved out of different factions of Jefferson's Democratic-Republicans. They stood for different policy choices and philosophies of governance, and both believed they were faithful defenders of the Constitution, as well as of the basic principles of American government articulated in the Declaration of Independence.[10]

Jackson's Democrats clearly dominated the era, however, which is named after him. The president launched a successful assault on the Second Bank of the United States, a symbol of elite power against the masses, by vetoing its 1832 attempt to be rechartered. Jackson also sought to secure western expansion, and part of that project included the removal of the Cherokee Nation from the state of Georgia in the "Trail of Tears," an event that violated the natural rights principles of the American republic.

Jackson enforced his policy by flagrantly ignoring a Supreme Court decision mandating a return of Cherokee lands, an act that undermined separation of powers.[11] Every policy decision by Jackson's followers, from the destruction of the Second Bank to the acquisition of Texas, prompted counterefforts by Whig leaders.

The Great American Original Sin

Had the political battle been limited to economic policy and western expansion, the party system could have regulated the typical conflict that marks such disputes. Instead, slavery—the great American original sin—took center stage. Slavery was part of American politics from the beginning, of course, but in the early years of the republic, it was seen by all sides as an unfortunate institution.

People like Washington, Jefferson, and Madison—all slave owners—knew the institution was unjust and corrupt, but they were unsure how to deal with it. In fact, a famous quote by Jefferson summed up their dilemma: "But, as it is, we have the wolf by the ear, and we can neither hold him, nor safely let him go. Justice is in one scale, and self-preservation in the other." The geographic phenomenon of slavery centered in Southern states created tensions with the acquisition of new states, leading to famous conciliations like the Missouri Compromise and the Compromise of 1850.

But the Indian Removal Act of 1830 placed the Democratic Party on treacherous ground where "unalienable rights" were concerned, and the annexation of Texas—begun by Whig-in-name-only John Tyler and completed by Jackson's protégé, James K. Polk—pushed the nation toward a crisis of "self-evident truths."

The self-evident truths Jefferson wrote about have their own power, and their inherent logic gave rise to the abolitionist movement. Unfortunately, the two political parties were not capable of regulating the discourse about slavery. Anti-slavery elements rightly argued that slavery was oppressive and despotic—a violation of the principles of the Declaration of Independence. No one likes being called immoral, so Southern Democrats began to make arguments that slavery was not just an unfortunate institution; it was actually a positive good, both for the slave master and for the slave.

People like John C. Calhoun made the argument that white Europeans and African slaves were not equal, physically, morally, or intellectually. In fact, Calhoun explicitly rejected Jefferson's argument that all men are created equal, saying, "There is not a word of truth in it."[12] Others called it "a self-evident lie."[13]

A party that was descended from Jefferson explicitly rejected his most important political insight, arguing, in effect, that all men are *not* created equal, and thus do *not* have natural rights to life, liberty, and the pursuit of happiness. This argument constituted a rejection of the objective moral principles and universal truths the nation was founded upon.

The Whig Party—also descended from Jefferson—proved not much better. Although not a pro-slavery party, the Whigs wanted the issue of slavery kept off the political scene just as much as Democrats did, because they knew how unsettling the issue was. But as events moved forward, with the Fugitive Slave Act (enforced by Whig president Millard Fillmore) and the Kansas-Nebraska Act (pushed by Democratic president Franklin Pierce), those who opposed slavery bolted from their respective parties. Democrats survived as a party because of their regional strength in the South, but the Whigs self-destructed and disappeared.

The new Republican Party arose to replace the Whigs as the second major party in American politics, founded as an anti-slavery party, pledging not to get rid of slavery in the South but to prevent it from spreading into new territories and states. It was a party founded on Jefferson's original argument that all men are created equal—this notion, again, that there are self-evident truths and objective and universal principles, right for all and known to all at all times, in all places and cultures.

These ideas, part of America's DNA, are also part of the genetic code of the Republican Party, which came into existence as an attempt to reclaim these ideas for the nation at a time when both political parties had forsaken them.

We can see this in the way Abraham Lincoln, one of the founders of the Republican Party, talked about this basic dispute. Lincoln explicitly invoked Jefferson's language from the Declaration, that all men are created equal. And although Lincoln was hardly a racial progressive the way we might think of the concept today, he understood that slavery is despotism. It was one man governing another without his consent—an explicit rejection of the principles of our founding documents.[14]

The first time the Republican Party ran a presidential candidate was 1856, and the party platform could not have been clearer. The platform resolved that "the maintenance of the principles promulgated in the Declaration of Independence, and embodied in the Federal Constitution is essential to the preservation of our Republican institutions, and that the Federal Constitution, the rights of the States, and the union of the States, must and shall be preserved." The platform repeated the self-evident truths that all men have unalienable rights to life, liberty, and the pursuit of happiness. The party opposed both slavery and polygamy as barbaric institutions.[15]

However, a Supreme Court stacked by Jacksonians declared in the 1857 *Dred Scott* case that slaves were "beings of an inferior order, and altogether unfit to associate with the white race."[16] Slaves had no rights, despite the clear understanding of the Declaration that some things are *never* right if they violate natural rights.

Alexander Stephens, who became the vice president of the Confederacy, rejected Jefferson's language as "fundamentally wrong." He said the cornerstone of the Confederacy was the "great truth, that the negro is not equal to the white man; that slavery . . . is his natural and normal condition."

In fact, according to Stephens, African slaves were unequal because the Creator made them that way, and the true natural law was the subjugation of one race by another.[17] This was the position defended by the final Jacksonian presidents: Franklin Pierce and James Buchanan, whose lack of moral leadership encouraged the secession crisis and consequently ended the era of Democratic Party dominance.

The pro-slavery argument worked like a cancer, metastasizing in a threat to national union. This disease infected the American constitutional order and attacked the most basic principles of the Declaration of Independence. The Republican Party was a party established to reclaim the political and moral fact that there are some universal principles that are right for everyone, because we are all equally human. The argument against slavery was also an argument for an entrepreneurial society where people were economically independent, socially mobile, and free from class conflict and the agitation of rich versus poor.

THE PROGRESSIVE THREAT TO AMERICA

The end of the Civil War allowed the Republican Party to achieve its core objectives in exceptionally swift fashion. The party retained its basic economic vision, as well as its focus on civil rights, natural rights, and transcendent moral truths. Lincoln's Republican successors often blur together in a collage of unknown bearded presidents: Ulysses Grant, Rutherford B. Hayes, James Garfield, Chester Arthur, and Benjamin Harrison.

Operating in Lincoln's shadow, these men sought for and achieved the first civil service reform. They fought for sound monetary and fiscal policy, working for balanced budgets and a strong economy. The party continued to fight to secure the rights of freed slaves against the terrorism of the Ku Klux Klan. It fought for voting rights for women, low taxes, and a strong commercial republic. Under William McKinley, the United States became an international power with its victory in the Spanish-American War. Theodore

Roosevelt continued to expand America's global influence, inserting himself into international affairs and building the Panama Canal.

By the turn of the century, another threat arose to the basic principles of the American republic: the rise of the Progressive movement. Just as pro-slavery elites rejected the self-evident truths of the Declaration, and in turn endangered the integrity of the constitutional order, so the Progressives launched their own attack on these fundamental principles.

Progressives believed that the central defect of the American constitutional order was the "separation of powers" system, which gets in the way of an activist government that seeks to expand its scope of power and control in an effort to regulate ever larger portions of our lives. And because separation of powers is linked to the self-evident truths of the Declaration, Progressives also rejected the natural rights understanding of that document. Regrettably, they sought to put in place instead a "living" Constitution that could grow and adapt to allow political leaders to do anything they wanted to do.

This new virus infected both parties. Woodrow Wilson claimed the Progressive mantle for the Democratic Party, and it was fully embraced by the time of Franklin Roosevelt. But there were also progressive Republicans, most notably Theodore Roosevelt. He began his presidency operating as a more traditional Republican, albeit with his own unique style. But as he moved forward in his career, especially when he ran for a third term in 1912 by attacking the more traditional constitutionalist Republican president William Howard Taft, Roosevelt fully embraced the Progressive critique of the American founding.

Progressives believed that human nature was not fixed. There were no permanent "laws of nature and nature's God." They rejected the natural rights tradition, arguing instead that rights come from the state, and the state can revise those rights to account for modern problems. Roosevelt himself once said that the rights articulated in the Declaration were merely "sentimental attachments."

Individual rights, private property, and limited government were outmoded notions. In their place, Progressives sought to install centralized planning, regulation, and redistribution. All of these notions constituted a direct assault on the founding principles of our nation. The very notion of a fixed and unchanging human nature means there are natural rights that come from a source higher than the state, putting constraints on the state. If human nature is not fixed but is malleable, then neither are natural rights fixed—and there is nothing higher than the state constraining them.[18]

Woodrow Wilson was an opposition president—one of only two Democratic Party presidents elected to office in the long Republican era that stretched from Lincoln to Herbert Hoover. He was consequential, however, in establishing many Progressive policies and institutions that laid the foundation for the later New Deal. Wilson fully accepted the Progressive criticism of separation of powers, reinterpreting the role of the president to be a popular leader capable of moving Congress and public opinion in his desired direction as an agent of rapid change.

Wilson adhered to a Darwinian understanding of politics, with government (and the Constitution) as a living and adapting phenomenon. There should be no limits on this change, so Wilson advocated discarding or ignoring the first two paragraphs of the Declaration of Independence, rejecting the natural rights understanding of the American republic and empowering a growing administrative state to manage national life.[19] Wilson demonstrated what a national leader can do if he articulates a different understanding of human nature and political philosophy.

Wilson's insertion of the United States into World War I continued the expansion of American global influence begun by McKinley and Roosevelt. Wilson overreached, however, failing to recognize the reluctance of many Americans to embrace his League of Nations and the diminishing of national sovereignty that would come with entrance into that organization.

In fact, because of the excesses of Wilson's presidency, Progressives did not find an easy home in the Republican Party. Republicans Warren G. Harding and Calvin Coolidge represented a conservative rejection of progressivism, and a restoration of a more traditional understanding of the constitutional order. In fact, Calvin Coolidge understood the conservative-progressive debate better than we give him credit for. He understood that the basic principles of the Declaration are final and unchanging.

Coolidge stated, "If all men are created equal, that is final. If they are endowed with inalienable rights, that is final. If governments derive their just powers from the consent of the governed, that is final. No advance, no progress can be made beyond these propositions."[20] This sense that some things are permanent and unchanging is the very antithesis of progressivism.

THE GREAT DEPRESSION

The Great Depression brought the long Republican era that began with Abraham Lincoln to an end. When one party dominates American economic policy for seven decades, it gets the blame for the nation's greatest economic crisis.

While Woodrow Wilson failed to make a reality out of the Progressive vision, Franklin Roosevelt used the Great Depression to fulfill Wilson's dream. The New Deal represented a transformation of the role of the federal government in American life.

Roosevelt was shrewd enough to realize that Americans would not tolerate an open rejection of the principles of the Declaration of Independence, so he simply amplified the concept of rights. In addition to freedom of speech and freedom of religion, Roosevelt added freedom from want and freedom from fear—two goals that cannot help but infuse greater power in the state.

We have a right to life, but now we also have a right to a comfortable living. We have rights to liberty and the pursuit of happiness, but now we also have rights to a job, a decent home, medical care, a good education, and the protection from the economic fears of old age, sickness, accident, and unemployment. We have, in short, the right to a risk-free life, secured by the power of an enlightened administration. And that enlightened administration would be concentrated in a newly expanded and empowered White House that centralized control in the Oval Office.[21]

Thus, Roosevelt inaugurated a new era of Democratic Party dominance: the New Deal era. He was not particularly successful in pulling the nation out of the economic catastrophe, but American involvement in World War II made the nation a true military and economic world power. In the greatest conflict in world history, Roosevelt stands on equal footing with some of the most significant world leaders of the century—men like Hitler, Stalin, Tojo, de Gaulle, and Churchill.

He holds the record for the longest presidency in American history, winning four straight elections, and the combination of his administration with that of Harry Truman gave the Democratic Party twenty years of control over the executive branch. Most of this period was marked by strong Democratic Party majorities in both houses of Congress, and Roosevelt and Truman together appointed all nine justices on the Supreme Court. The destruction of the Axis powers and the subsequent fall of the British Empire made the United States the most powerful country in the world, with a monopoly (briefly) on nuclear weapons.

For twenty years after World War II, American politics traveled along two tracks. In the area of domestic policy, the programmatic liberal New Deal paradigm reigned supreme. Conservative Republicans tried to figure out how to rescind the New Deal, but after two decades of Roosevelt and Truman, they were not a strong enough faction to determine the direction of national policy.

Even Republican president Dwight Eisenhower accepted the New Deal as a fact of life and sought not to get rid of it but to manage it more efficiently, making the New Deal a bipartisan endeavor. When John F. Kennedy and Lyndon Johnson restored Democrats to the White House, they pushed the New Deal agenda more aggressively. Johnson pledged to end poverty and racial injustice—with all the government programs that necessarily come with such a promise. As the role of government got bigger and bigger, the place for freedom and liberty got smaller and smaller.

In the area of foreign policy, the United States entered nearly forty-five years of a Cold War with the Soviet Union, in a duel of superpowers that flared hot in places like Korea and Vietnam, but avoided nuclear annihilation. Because Eisenhower embraced the basic precepts of American global leadership—containment of communism and the spread of freedom and democracy—there was a rough bipartisan consensus in many areas of foreign policy.

What separated Truman, Eisenhower, and Kennedy were questions of emphasis and tactics, not national strategy. Soviet leaders like Stalin, Khrushchev, and Brezhnev tested American leaders, but the rough foreign policy consensus held until Vietnam blew it apart.

The cultural war had begun!

CHAPTER 7

THE CONSERVATIVE RESURGENCE

When you open your heart to patriotism, there is no room for prejudice. The Bible tells us, "How good and pleasant it is when God's people live together in unity." (President Donald Trump)[1]

The assassination of President John F. Kennedy brought Lyndon Baines Johnson to power in the early '60s and had a Pandora's box effect. Lyndon Johnson's excesses—the combination of the costly, ill-advised Vietnam War and his New Deal on steroids, aka the Great Society—nearly drove the Democrats off the national stage. Then Richard Nixon proved unwilling to pursue conservative leadership, opting instead to govern essentially as a moderate Democrat, until his own personal demons caught up with him in the Watergate scandal.

This collapse of moral leadership put the nearly defunct New Deal on life support during the 1970s, as Gerald Ford was forced to basically tread water. It was Jimmy Carter's great misfortune to inherit an exhausted administration, and with his own foreign policy debacles, he helped set the stage for a genuine conservative resurgence.

THE CULTURAL WAR BEGINS

As early as 1964, Ronald Reagan warned of the growing power of the central government and cautioned that natural rights were now seen more as a privilege of the state—a perversion of the Framers' original design. Barry Goldwater's campaign for president that year articulated a staunch conservative political philosophy that marked a direct frontal assault on the New Deal system.

Goldwater lost badly to Lyndon Johnson, but in the process he pushed the Republican Party to become a more consistently conservative force in American politics, centered on more traditional notions of liberty and limited constitutional government.[2]

The contemporary conservative political movement got its greatest push from the turmoil of the 1960s. The period between Johnson's landslide election in 1964 and his departure in 1969 witnessed what appeared to be a collapse of the social order. Urban riots sparked by racial tensions exploded each summer in American cities, capped by the assassination of Martin Luther King Jr.

Student unrest at "Johnson's War" in Vietnam led to campus violence, street protests, and the burning of draft cards and American flags. Liberation was a dominant theme, especially with the new hedonism and *Playboy* philosophy of the sexual revolution. Traditional social mores fell under attack as the political philosophy of the Progressive elites and academics from earlier decades became the popular philosophy of the masses.

CONSERVATIVES Believe . . .	PROGRESSIVES Believe . . .
that there is a transcendent moral order that sets moral standards, and by which we can evaluate and judge human institutions and politics. They believe nature is fixed and normative, which is why things like slavery, abortion, drug use, and sexual perversion are not wrong at one point in time and right in another—they are always wrong.	that nature is plastic, changing, and adaptable, which is why we cannot speak of natural rights that are right always and everywhere. Some things that were once considered perverted may become normalized.
that history can teach us something and that tradition contains the wisdom of the past.	that history is something we can escape from as we move into a more utopian future.
that people have different social roles and responsibilities, and that there are differences between men and women, and between parents and children.	that distinctions between men and women are arbitrary and oppressive and should be abolished, and that men and women are exactly alike.
that progress is dubious at best—not that we cannot do some things better, but that we cannot merge heaven and earth.	that we can engage in experiments in living to discover better ways of ordering society.
that equality in our human nature and natural rights allows us to pursue liberty.	that equality requires limitations on liberty as we seek to bring everyone to the same economic level.[3]

Where the Framers of the American republic envisioned a system of ordered liberty channeled by moral virtue, the architects of the protest movements of the 1960s understood true liberty to be freedom from any old-fashioned moral constraints.[4]

The list of hot-button issues is familiar to anyone who has paid attention in the past few decades. Abortion, drugs, school prayer, pornography, gay rights, racial and gender quotas, sexual experimentation, skyrocketing out-of-wedlock births, fatherless families, situational ethics, moral relativism—Conservatives could rightly believe that society was experiencing a disintegration of traditional values.

Some scholars see this period as the beginning of a "culture war" based on competing religious perspectives. Traditional Protestants, Catholics, and Jews became united in their commitment to a transcendent authority against progressive Protestants, Catholics, and Jews, as well as against secularists, who adapted their faith to modern sentiments. The result was a cultural realignment that set the stage for the rise of Ronald Reagan.[5]

This cultural realignment brought into the open the central conflict between Conservatives and Progressives.

Dredd Scott *Decision and* Roe v. Wade—
The Battles for Equality

There is, in fact, continuity between the contemporary culture war and the earlier crisis of self-evident truths of the 1850s in the linkage between slavery and abortion. The central question in the infamous *Dred Scott* Supreme Court decision in 1857 was whether the slave was primarily and essentially a human person, and thus entitled to the personal liberty guaranteed by the Constitution.

The central question in the *Roe v. Wade* decision in 1973 was whether the fetus is a person within the meaning of the Fourteenth Amendment. The Supreme Court's position in *Dred Scott* was that the slave was not a person within the meaning of the Fifth Amendment, arguing that blacks, whether slave or free, were "beings of an inferior order . . . and so far inferior that they had no rights which the white man was bound to respect."

The Supreme Court's position in *Roe* was that the unborn are not persons within the meaning of the Fourteenth Amendment's due process clause, arguing that "we need not resolve the difficult question of when life begins," while at the same time apparently resolving that question by asserting that the unborn are merely "potential life" and "prenatal life"—two concepts that are mutually exclusive.

Dred Scott declared slavery legal and constitutional; *Roe* declared abortion legal and constitutional. The first said blacks may be human, but they were not persons in a constitutional sense; the second said the unborn may be human, but they are not persons in the constitutional sense. In both cases, blacks and the unborn do not merit legal protection.[6]

Broadening the scope beyond Supreme Court jurisprudence, proponents of slavery said slaves were the property of their owners; proponents of abortion rights say the unborn are the property of their owners. One said the right to property trumped the right to *liberty*; the other says the right to personal liberty trumps the right to *life*.

Alternatively, the right to personal liberty for one person (slave owner or pregnant woman) supersedes the right to personal liberty for another (slave or unborn). One defended slavery using the argument that abolitionists should not impose their morality on the rest of the nation; the other defends abortion using the argument that those who support the right to life of the unborn should not impose their morality on the rest of the nation.

Finally, one led to the perverse conclusion that slaves were partially persons in *some* circumstances (they could be held responsible for their actions under the law) but not in others (they were also re-garded as property and as extensions of their masters' will); the other led to the perverse conclusion that the unborn ought to be protected in *some* circumstances (we have laws that punish the killing of the fetus in an unlawful way, such as assault or drunk driving), but not in others (it is permissible to destroy the fetus if you are the mother).

Put simply, one side in both debates is "pro-choice," and the other is "pro-life" and "pro-liberty." In both cases, the "pro-choice" side rejects the natural rights perspective of the Declaration of Independence, leading to a similar rejection of the limited govern-ment understanding of the American Constitution.

THE REAGAN REVOLUTION

Ronald Reagan's inauguration as president in January 1981 rein-serted these themes into the national dialogue. The realignment of American politics that followed made the Republican Party a conser-vative party, because the party attempted to conserve the permanent truths about human nature, natural rights, and limited constitutional government.

Reagan pursued this agenda in three major areas. First, in the area of economic policy, Reagan sought to cut taxes in order to starve "big government" of the funding necessary to sustain it. This would reduce the footprint of the federal government in American life and expand the scope of personal liberty.

Though less successful in reversing the growth of government, Reagan did succeed in slashing income tax rates that had exceeded 90 percent at the height of the New Deal era to less than half that level. The basic argument has hovered around that lower level ever since, for no serious Democratic Party presidential candidate advocates returning to income tax rates in excess of 90 percent.

Second, in the area of foreign policy, Reagan sought not a truce with expansionist communism but victory over it. The principal objective behind Reagan's military buildup and programs like the Strategic Defense Initiative was to end the Cold War on American terms. Reagan understood that the totalitarian impulse of the Soviet Union represented a clear assault on the central moral principles of the American constitutional system, against permanent and eternal truths.

Reagan had the moral vision to call the Soviet Union the "focus of evil in the modern world"[7] and to call for the tearing down of the Berlin Wall, the stark symbol of the Soviet threat. In this campaign Reagan was joined by British prime minister Margaret Thatcher and Catholic pope John Paul II. Less than a year after Reagan left office, the Berlin Wall fell. Two years later, the Soviet Union broke apart.

Finally, in the area of social policy, Reagan sought a return to traditional virtues that supported the family and fought against the erosion of the culture. Pro-life, pro-family, anti-pornography, "just say no" to drugs, resistance to the increasing dependency of American citizens on the state—these too were part of Reagan's agenda. This was his most difficult task, for presidents have much less power to move culture in their desired direction than they do to implement tax policy and foreign policy.

Some of these items required changes on the Supreme Court, and progressive forces fought successfully to kill the nomination of Robert Bork, a man who would have provided the necessary fifth vote to overturn *Roe v. Wade* in 1992. University academics had already succeeded even before Reagan came to office in corrupting the standard moral language. They favored and taught "subjective" truth and "values" as opposed to simple truth and virtues. This indoctrination of the young minds with terms such as *values clarification* and *lifestyle choices* created a wider chasm between Progressives and Conservatives.

With the rise of postmodernism, any attempt to make the case for Jefferson's "laws of nature" and "self-evident truths" would be branded as oppressive, patriarchal, and culturally insensitive—a perspective embraced by the elite news media and popular culture. Reagan's efforts injected a strong rhetorical opposition to the progressive Left, but the battle continues.[8]

THE DECLINE OF POWER—
POST-REAGAN PRESIDENCIES

The Reagan era is not exempt from the normal pattern of political cycles. Reagan was clearly the founder of a conservative era that transformed the way Americans think about politics. His immediate successor, George H. W. Bush, inherited the burden of following in Reagan's footsteps, trying to serve as a type of third Reagan term the same way Madison, Van Buren, Grant, and Truman followed their founders.

Bush attempted to follow the path laid out for him by Reagan, to varying degrees of success. He demonstrated in the Persian Gulf War that the post–Cold War American military was unmatched by any other military in the world. But Bush also reversed his "no new taxes" campaign pledge, earning the wrath of conservative purists. The entrance of independent candidate Ross Perot in the 1992 presidential race split the Republican Party and gave the presidency to Bill Clinton.

Clinton was a classic opposition president. With the end of the Cold War, a draft-dodging child of the 1960s took advantage of the lack of a significant national security threat to win the presidency. He attempted to govern as a progressive president, with his signature domestic agenda centered on universal government-run health care.

Clinton did not recognize that he was president in an era in which Reagan conservatism and suspicion of government programs was still resilient. In 1994, Republicans took control of both houses of Congress for the first time in forty years, prompting Clinton to move toward the center, declaring that the era of big government was over and pledging to balance the budget.

He also signed welfare reform and the Defense of Marriage Act, which defined marriage as a relationship between a man and a woman. Clinton's own immoral sexual indulgences, however, cost him greatly in his second term, leading to only the second impeachment trial of a president in American history.

Clinton's own quibbling over the meaning of the word *is* exemplified the classic moral relativism and postmodern abuse of language that Conservatives fought against. The fact that Clinton retained very strong public approval ratings during this period testifies to the durability of the more lax code of ethics inherited from the 1960s.

George W. Bush restored the Reagan agenda after the close election of 2000. He succeeded in cutting income taxes twice, in a direct extension of the Reagan revolution. He also attempted to further a social conservative agenda with his Supreme Court appointments, staunch support of marriage, and resistance to federal funding of embryonic stem cell research. He welcomed religious groups into the White House and encouraged their unique activities in American public life.

Most consequentially, the terrorist attacks of September 11, 2001, transformed the Republican national security posture from an out-of-date Cold War setting to a global contender in the war on terror. Bush succeeded in toppling the Taliban regime in Afghanistan and Saddam Hussein in Iraq, but as the American body count rose, the two wars became increasingly unpopular. The double shot of war and financial crisis in 2008 gave the presidency to another opposition president, Barack Obama.

BARACK OBAMA—
THE SOCIALIST AGENDA PRESIDENT

Obama represented a distinct threat to the vitality of the aging Reagan era. He clearly wanted to be the founder of his own progressive regime. His agenda was staunchly liberal, with health-care reform representing the summit of leftist dreams for decades. He ran a campaign on "change we can believe in." He rescinded the "don't ask, don't tell" policy on homosexuals serving in the military and ceased to enforce the Defense of Marriage Act.

Obama was always supportive of abortion on demand, dismissing the question of the moral status of the unborn as "above my pay grade."[9] He launched a campaign against religious freedom through the mechanism of the Affordable Care Act and his eventual open support of gay marriage. In almost every way, Obama's social agenda represented an attempt to repudiate the Reagan stance and win the culture war.

He arguably accomplished this project, at least in part, in the campaign to redefine marriage, a pre-political institution that has been understood as a conjugal relationship between a man and a woman—part of the "laws of nature and of nature's God"—for millennia. Obama had the full weight of the cultural elite on his side, aided by a Supreme Court—though staffed with a majority of Republican appointees—that overturned the Defense of Marriage Act in 2013 and legalized gay marriage in 2015. Obama continued his campaign to transform the culture with his imposition of transgender rights late in his second term.

In the area of economic policy, Obama proved willing to increase spending to almost unthinkable levels, working vigorously to expand the scope of federal action in American life. But he proved incapable of truly reversing Reagan in the area of income taxes, promising tax cuts for almost all Americans—except for the top 1 percent. The focus on the top 1 percent marked a return to a class-based politics that placed inequality at the center of Democratic Party discourse, making it possible for a socialist candidate, Vermont senator Bernie Sanders, to mount a serious threat to the presidential nomination of the Democratic Party in 2016.

In the area of foreign policy, Obama retained a variety of Bush-era security policies but chose to confront the war on terror through drone aircraft, drastically reducing our military presence in the campaign against Islamic extremism. During this time, the radical Islamic terrorist organization ISIS rose from the ashes in Iraq, seizing territory and surreptitiously using social media as a recruiting tool to gain foot soldiers.

While Obama referred to them as "a JV team,"[10] these terrorists were prepared to commit vile attacks throughout Europe and the United States. Their goal was not only to wipe Israel "off the map," but to remove all who opposed them.

Yet Obama worked to diminish American influence in the world, choosing to "lead from behind" and often focused on America's faults in his public rhetoric, unwilling to draw clear distinctions between good and evil, virtue and vice. Despite his efforts to destroy America and its values, the Republican Party, led by an energized Tea Party movement, captured control of the House of Representatives in 2010 and the Senate in 2014.

Lacking control of the legislature, Obama proceeded to enact as much of his anti-American agenda as he could through executive power. From selective enforcement or nonenforcement of federal statutes, to the use of unilateral foreign policy power in forging a nuclear deal with Iran, which never would have been allowed to see the light of day if it had required a treaty ratification fight in the Senate, Obama found a way. All of which brings us to our current leadership crisis.

DONALD J. TRUMP—
MAKING AMERICA GREAT AGAIN

President Trump has inherited an exceptionally dangerous leadership challenge. He has to restore the Reagan revolution to renewed vigor and dominance while also adjusting it to changing times as he also attempts to turn back the resurgent progressive forces who believe that Obama's agenda represented the future of the nation.

Trump has to articulate the virtues of a conservative economic agenda, including limited government and federalism, while trying to tame a seemingly intractable national debt. Trump has to restore America's global leadership at a time when the growing threats to national security seem to multiply daily with a military force armed with aging weapons systems and a population suspicious of foreign engagements.

Trump has to make a compelling case for conservative views on social issues. Most important of these is the issue of religious freedom in the face of an aggressive and predatory "marriage equality" movement. He must confront the spread of social radicalism on our college campuses, which now requires universities to supply safe spaces for "marginalized groups" or suffer economic ramifications under civil discrimination suits.

Trump has to do all of this in a period that has witnessed increasing political polarization, as the Republican Party has become increasingly and more uniformly conservative and the Democratic Party increasingly and more uniformly liberal. Such polarization—the highest it has been since the Civil War—makes it difficult to push a legislative agenda through a narrowly divided Congress, as each side sees the other as a dangerous threat to the republic. Progressive forces are entrenched in the elite news media, higher education, and popular culture in opposition to the central principles of the Reagan era.[11]

Thus, Trump is presented with two leadership problems: how to be successful as a conservative political leader late in the Reagan era and how to be successful as a moral leader in an age that no longer recognizes the "laws of nature and nature's God." The genetic code of the republic is also the genetic code of the Republican Party.

Trump's Accomplishments

At the time of this writing, during Donald Trump's first term as president, it would be useful to briefly survey the political landscape and see what Trump has been able to accomplish given his constrained circumstances.

In the area of economic policy, Trump followed in the footsteps of Reagan by signing into law a $1.5 trillion tax cut, lowering the income tax rates for individuals while also reducing the corporate tax rate from 35 percent to 21 percent.[12] This tax cut legislation also eliminated the individual mandate of the Affordable Care Act (Obamacare).

While the Republican-led Congress could not agree on a specific legislative package to replace Obamacare, the end of the individual mandate guts the law of its primary fiscal lifeline. With this one move, Trump succeeded both in restoring Reagan-era tax policy to prominence while also attacking and undermining the accomplishments of the president who most threatened the vitality of the Reagan era.

The Trump administration has also made significant progress in cutting regulations. Trump used the Congressional Review Act fourteen times to end Obama-era regulations. Federal agencies have shifted their focus from writing regulations to cutting them. This reduction of the footprint of the federal government in American life expands the scope of personal liberty following eight years of movement in the opposite direction under President Obama.

The result of these moves has led to a healthy economy and continued growth. Many corporations publicly announced major bonuses for employees after passage of the tax cut. The stock market hit historic highs, job growth increased steadily month to month, wages rose, and the unemployment rate sank to 4.0 percent in June of 2018, the lowest level since December 2000.[13]

In the area of social policy, clearly the most important development was Trump's nomination and appointment of Neil Gorsuch to the United States Supreme Court. Trump received a major assist in this area from the Republican-controlled Senate.

The unexpected death of conservative icon Antonin Scalia early in 2016 gave Obama the opportunity to shift the basic balance of power on the Supreme Court decisively in a liberal direction with his nomination of circuit court of appeals judge Merrick Garland. However, Senate majority leader Mitch McConnell refused to hold hearings on the nomination, effectively killing the nomination when Trump won the presidency. The consequences of this blocking tactic are incalculable. Garland represented a fifth and decisive liberal voice on the Court, potentially shifting the Court to the left for a generation. Instead, Gorsuch's appointment solidified the conservative bloc.

And now, as of this writing President Trump has another historic opportunity to strengthen this bloc after nominating Judge Brett Kavanaugh to replace Justice Anthony Kennedy, who recently announced his resignation from the high Court. With two liberal justices over the age of eighty, the chances of Trump getting at least one more future nomination in this term is high. The impact of these appointments on everything from abortion to free speech rights to religious liberty is beyond huge. The Trump Supreme Court will control the legal destiny of America for the next forty years.

Trump's accomplishments in judicial nominations are not limited to the Supreme Court. Most judicial matters never get to the

Supreme Court and are instead settled at lower levels of the federal judiciary. With the cooperation of Republicans in the Senate, Trump has nominated and appointed federal judges at a record pace, helping shape the future trajectory of the judicial branch for years to come.

In addition to using executive power to reinstate pro-life policies, Trump followed the examples of Reagan and George W. Bush by speaking live via video feed to the 2018 March for Life. He has consistently supported the Second Amendment, speaking at the National Rifle Association's annual conference in 2017 and 2018. Federal agencies have begun reversing Obama-era policies and supporting religious liberty and conscience protections.[14] The administration has even slowed down and reversed efforts to advance the gender identity campaign.

In the area of foreign policy and national security, the president has much greater leeway to act at his own discretion. Trump has been more noticeably and openly critical of the United Nations since taking office. He has pushed NATO members to increase their defense spending. He revoked the Iran nuclear deal.

Trump withdrew the United States from the Trans-Pacific Partnership on trade and began the process of renegotiating the North American Free Trade Agreement. He imposed tariffs on steel and aluminum and began several trade actions targeting China. Most recently, Trump withdrew the US from the United Nations Human Rights Council over bias against Israel and its ineptness to prevent abuse by "the world's most inhumane regimes."[15]

Between 2006 and 2016, the United Nations Human Rights Council passed sixty-seven resolutions condemning human rights violations around the world to include the massacre of half a million people in Syria, the genocide in Darfur, and the execution of lesbian, gay, and bisexual people in Iran. In that same decade, the Human Rights Council passed sixty-eight resolutions condemning

Israel for fighting for its life against murderous terror organizations. This flagrant injustice reflects the appalling discrimination of the UN when it comes to Israel.[16]

Trump also took an aggressive stance against ISIS, targeting its strongholds in Syria, Iraq, and Afghanistan, and the terrorist entity has lost most of the territory it once controlled. He has demonstrated a much firmer hand against the use of chemical weapons in Syria and leveled sanctions against Russia for its use of chemical weapons against two citizens in Great Britain. He has made national security concerns a central feature of the administration's immigration policy.

Trump has taken a much more aggressive stance against North Korea, officially designating the rogue nation a state sponsor of terrorism. At the same time, he expressed a willingness to hold a summit with North Korean leader Kim Jong-Un. This face-to-face meeting, something never before done in American foreign policy, occurred in June of 2018. Kim Jong-Un began making overtures of peace to South Korea, talking about formally ending the Korean War and eliminating all nuclear weapons from the Korean peninsula. One month later, President Trump also participated in the Helsinki Summit with Vladimir Putin of Russia for a two-hour, one-on-one meeting. The results of the behind-closed-door encounter have yet to unfold.

Finally, Trump visited Israel in May 2017, the fiftieth anniversary of the Six Day War and Israel's reunification with Jerusalem. In December of that year, he officially recognized Jerusalem as the capital of Israel and ordered the State Department to begin the process of moving the American embassy from Tel Aviv to Jerusalem. On May 14, 2018, the United States embassy was officially opened in Jerusalem, despite a United Nations Security Council resolution condemning the move. I had the honor of participating in the opening ceremony of the US embassy in Jerusalem by offering the benediction prayer. It will be a day etched in my mind forever!

In all of these areas, Trump has worked to advance the basic principles and commitments established at the dawn of the Reagan era, at the same time working vigorously to reverse and cancel the progressive gains of the Obama presidency. He still faces significant headwinds as he goes into a midterm election year, where presidents typically lose ground in Congress. Events in the next twelve to eighteen months will set the stage for the 2020 presidential election, pitting Trump against what is likely to be the most progressive Democratic Party candidate since George McGovern in 1972.

WHAT IS OUR FUTURE?

Reagan succeeded in recalibrating the public debate over these time-less values, but he did not succeed in defeating the many forces conceived in the Progressive movement and birthed in the 1960s. For Trump to succeed, he will have to reset the political clock of the Reagan era for another generation and clearly articulate the historic understanding of the universal and absolute truths of the American founding.

If President Trump fails, we will more than likely enter a new progressive era—a prospect that does not bode well for liberty, limited government, and self-evident truths. It will produce a liberal dictatorship that will attack religious freedom and traditional marriage and will advance the slaughter of the unborn and embrace social revolution where tyranny and anarchy in the streets of America overwhelm the police forces.

"Equal justice under the law" will be a mere slogan chiseled over the doors of the Supreme Court building, not a fact of life any longer in these United States.

Make way for the New World Order!

CHAPTER 8

THE NEW
WORLD ORDER

The führer gave expression to his unshakable conviction that the Reich will be the master of all Europe. We shall yet have to engage in many fights, but these will undoubtedly lead to most wonderful victories. From there on the way to world domination is practically certain. Whoever dominates Europe will thereby assume the leadership of the world. (Joseph Goebbels, Reich Minister of Propaganda, May 8, 1943)

A "New World Order" (NWO) is any period of history that demonstrates a dramatic change in world thought, causing a shift of balance of power among the geopolitical actors on the world stage. Since the post–Cold War era, the NWO has been redefined as an organization of power in which nations tend to cooperate through treaties as opposed to entering into war.

The New World Order is not an original phenomenon. It began

in the book of Genesis and was intended to cast the authority of God Almighty out of the earth and away from the humanity that He created.

ONE LANGUAGE, ONE WORLD ORDER, ONE RELIGION

Shortly after creation, the Lord commanded mankind to move throughout the world and cultivate it:

> *Then God blessed them, and God said to them, "Be fruitful and multiply; fill the earth and subdue it; have dominion over the fish of the sea, over the birds of the air, and over every living thing that moves on the earth." (Genesis 1:28)*

After generations of wickedness and corruption, the Lord used a flood to destroy humanity, saving only Noah and his family:[1]

> *So the LORD said, "I will destroy man whom I have created from the face of the earth, both man and beast, creeping thing and birds of the air, for I am sorry that I have made them." But Noah found grace in the eyes of the LORD. (Genesis 6:7–8)*

After the Great Flood, Noah and his sons, Shem, Ham and Japheth, began to repopulate the earth. A pivotal incident occurred, resulting in Noah pronouncing a curse on one of his sons and blessing the remaining two. Ham found his father drunk and quickly revealed his disgraceful state to his brothers. However, when Shem and Japheth heard of their father's nakedness, they entered his tent backward and respectfully covered his shame (Genesis 9:18–24). When Noah heard of Ham's lack of respect, he he spoke a curse over him:

Cursed be Canaan [Ham's descendants];
A servant of servants
He shall be to his brethren [Shem and Japheth]. (Genesis 9:25)

In contrast, Noah rewarded Shem and Japheth with his spoken blessing:

Blessed be the LORD,
The God of Shem,
And may Canaan [Ham's descendants through Canaan] be his
  servant.
May God enlarge Japheth [Gentiles],
And may he dwell in the tents of Shem [Abraham];
And may Canaan be his servant. (Genesis 9:26–27)

Why is this event significant? Abraham and the Jewish people are direct descendants of Shem—they are the righteous line. The Gentiles descended from Japheth's line—we are the branches that were grafted into the root according to the book of Romans (11:17, 19). Ham's sons were Cush, Mizraim, Put, and Canaan. His descendants, which included the Jebusites and other Canaanite people, represented the ungodly and rebellious line, who were later conquered by Israel (Joshua 24:11).

Cush had a son named Nimrod, who was known as *"a mighty hunter before the LORD" (Genesis 10:9)*. Nimrod's name in Hebrew means "revolt," and it exemplifies the rebellion he instituted against God's authority. In reality, he "hunted" men and brought them under subjugation to his evil goals. The Bible also references Nimrod in 1 Chronicles 1:10 and Micah 5:6.

It has been said that the purpose of life is life's purpose. And in order to be blessed by God and accomplish our divine destiny, our purpose should always align with that of our Creator. However, Nimrod had ambitions outside of God's purpose—he became the first personal kingdom builder.

Nimrod built four cities in Shinar: Babel, Erech, Accad, and Calneh (Genesis 10:10). In Assyria, he built Nineveh, Rehoboth Ir, Callah, and Resen (Genesis 10:11–12). His obsession with power birthed secular humanism, from which arose a tyrannical form of dictatorial government.

This "man of revolt" designed a tower in the city of Babel with his father that would defy God and introduce the Prince of Darkness as the new leader of the world through a counterfeit religion. Nimrod's defiance of God's mandates began with the attempt to construct a stronghold that would reach the heavens, allowing man to stay in one place, keeping one world language—and thus retaining and gaining more and more power (Genesis 10:8–12; 11:1–4; 1 Chronicles 1:10; Micah 5:6).

Josephus, the Jewish historian, said the following of Nimrod and his diabolical purpose:

He [Nimrod] also gradually changed the government into tyranny, seeing no other way of turning men from the fear of God, but to bring them into a constant dependence on his power. He also said he would be revenged on God, if he should have a mind to drown the world again; for that he would build a tower too high for the waters to be able to reach and that he would avenge himself on God for destroying their forefathers![2]

This tower was an example of man's sinful pride—the same pride that cast Lucifer out of the Third Heaven. It was located in Babel on the plain of Shinar; a city that later became Babylon.

When the Almighty visited Babel and its tower, He confused the language of the people and scattered them throughout the world:

But the LORD came down to see the city and the tower which the sons of men had built. And the LORD said, "Indeed the people are one and they all have one language, and this is what they begin to do; now nothing that they propose to do will be withheld from them. Come, let Us go down and there confuse their language, that they may not understand one another's speech." So the LORD scattered them abroad from there over the face of all the earth, and they ceased building the city. Therefore its name is called Babel, because there the LORD confused the language of all the earth. (Genesis 11:5–9)

Nonetheless, Nimrod's wicked aspirations allowed for the evolution of the first New World Order. This form of government enabled the creation of a one world religion outside of God's perfect plan of redemption for humanity. Nimrod's defiant deed would eventually birth the initial appearance of the church of Satan.

Tradition says that Nimrod wanted to maintain his authority over the people after the destruction of the Tower of Babel (Genesis 11). To accomplish this goal, following his father's death, he married Semiramis—his mother. Semiramis is recorded in history as the most important queen of Assyria, who conquered much of Asia Minor, Libya, and Ethiopia. She later restored ancient Babylon and built several palaces in Persia.

Semiramis is depicted in Babylonian mythology as the mother and wife of Nimrod and the mother of Tammuz; she is also known as Ishtar or Isis.[3] Nimrod became the self-declared king of Babylon and Semiramis the first queen, and together they commanded the worship of the masses, initiating Ba'al worship. Sadly, many willingly submitted.

Satan used these rabid occultists to divert their followers from the worship of the One True God of heaven, the God of Abraham. To do this, the evil one needed a bogus religion that included human sacrifices to pagan idols, so a "holy day" was created in honor of the sun god (Ba'al), which we know as Sunday, opposing God's sacred day of worship—the Sabbath. Satan is the Great Imitator!

However, Nimrod would not continue his evil reign for much longer. One day Abraham's grandson Esau (from Shem's lineage) encountered Nimrod in the wilderness while they were both hunting. Nimrod had great jealousy toward Esau because he was related to Abraham, the father of many nations. Nimrod was indeed one of the first anti-Semites.

The young Esau, knowing of this hatred, hid in the brush, ambushed the aged Nimrod, and cut off his head.[4] Nimrod's followers were grief-stricken and lost without their religious cult leader, so they went into hiding for fear that they would experience the same lot.

Mother-Child Cult

Historian and Bible scholar Alexander Hislop states,

> The Tower of Babel was actually the worship of Satan in the form of fire, the sun and the serpent. However, Satan worship could not be done openly because of the many who still believed in the true God of Noah. So a mystery religion began at Babel where Satan could be worshipped in secret.[5]

However, Semiramis demanded more than secret worship of Nimrod's counterfeit religion, so this demonic queen consoled the people by conjuring up a mesmerizing tale. She claimed that the child she was pregnant with was actually Nimrod reembodied and she named him Tammuz, which means "the son who rises."

Semiramis continued her far-fetched fable by saying that Tammuz would go into the forest during the winter solstice and place a gift on a tree to honor Nimrod. Thus, Nimrod became known as Ba'al, meaning "lord," and was worshipped by the Babylonians as the sun god. This was the time of year when the sun was thought to be "reborn," so December 25 was celebrated as Ba'al's birthday.[6] The prophet Jeremiah described rituals of this heathen practice very vividly:

> *Do not learn the way of the Gentiles;*
> *Do not be dismayed at the signs of heaven,*
> *For the Gentiles are dismayed at them.*
> *For the customs of the peoples are futile;*
> *For one cuts a tree from the forest,*
> *The work of the hands of the workman, with the ax.*
> *They decorate it with silver and gold;*
> *They fasten it with nails and hammers*
> *So that it will not topple. (Jeremiah 10:1–4)*

Semiramis brazenly announced that her son was both "god, the father, and god, the son" and should be worshipped along with her, his mother. This practice established the Mother-Child Cult, which would later be duplicated in the *unholy triune* of Satan, the Antichrist, and the False Prophet.

The Mother-Child Cult, composed of Nimrod, Semiramis, and Tammuz, was derived from Ba'al worship, which originated in Babylon. The Babylonian Empire became the seat of pagan worship until the Medes and the Persians conquered it in 539 BCE. Most of the pagan priests associated with Ba'al worship relocated to

Pergamos, which is why Christ referred to this city as the throne of Satan in His letter to its citizens:

> *I know your works, and where you dwell, where Satan's throne is. And you hold fast to My name, and did not deny My faith even in the days in which Antipas was My faithful martyr, who was killed among you, where Satan dwells. (Revelation 2:13)*

After Pergamos, the pagan priests migrated to Rome and Alexandria, where they set up the sun worship under its emperors.[7] Socrates Scholasticus, the author of *Historia Ecclesiastica* (*Church History*), documents the history of ancient Christianity during the years 305 to 439, recording this shift:

> For although almost all churches throughout the world celebrate the sacred mysteries [of the Lord's Supper] on the Sabbath of every week, yet the Christians of Alexandria and at Rome, on account of some ancient tradition, have ceased to do this.[8]

The Mother-Child Cult established several pagan practices. In the spring they observed the Feast of Ishtar (another name for Semiramis). This was a celebration of life marked by the giving of brightly colored eggs as the sign of fertility. This feast later evolved into the celebration of Easter—a substitute for the Lord's Feast of the Passover—through the Council of Nicaea in 325 CE, which was covered earlier in chapter 2, "The War Against the Jews."

Nimrod/Ba'al's birthday and the Feast of Ishtar are but a few of the pagan imageries that Satan inspired this false religion to craft that would contaminate and distort what God had put into place since the beginning of the ages. Remember, Lucifer was lovingly and perfectly created by the Great I AM. God Almighty had a divine assignment for this anointed cherub, but instead, Lucifer chose a path that would lead him to be branded as an agent of death and destruction, who is now known as Satan. Since the time of his fall until now, the Adversary has attempted to foil God's plan of redemption by destroying the chosen line from which our Messiah comes.

Satan was laying the foundation for every future evil empire of the world designed to deceive God's creation, preventing them from knowing His Son as their Redeemer and thereby inheriting eternal life. Satan is the father of lies.

THE ILLUMINATI

Another notable appearance of a New World Order came out of European history. It was a secret order called the Illuminati, or the "enlightened ones." Most people today think of the Illuminati as a fantasy. Others believe it is a fictional narrative created by paranoid conspiracy theorists.

However, the Illuminati actually came into existence through an eighteenth-century German professor named Adam Weishaupt. Professor Weishaupt felt his new society would offer "freedom 'from all religious prejudices; cultivate the social virtues; and animate them by a great and speedy prospect of universal happiness.'"[9]

To achieve this new order, Weishaupt intended to create "a state of liberty and moral equality, freed from the obstacles which subordination, rank, and riches, continually throw in our way."[10] In other words, a professor from Bavaria desired a New World Order devoid of God that promoted Universalism, as opposed to national patriotism, and left the definition of "social virtues" up to the founders of the order.

The inaugural meeting occurred on the night of May 1, 1776, in a dark forest near Ingolstadt, Bavaria. There were only five men who participated in this first clandestine meeting, and they established the guidelines that were to govern the order. Any future candidates for membership needed to be men of well-established social connections and wealth, and required the original five's consent. The Illuminati would soon include Bavarian aristocracy and wealthy financers.

Barons to bankers, such as Adolph von Knigge and Mayer Amschel Rothschild, were initiated into the order.[11] Each were given symbolic secret names, and there were thirteen degrees of initiation, divided into three classes. Ironically, Professor Weishaupt did not seem to keep to his own ideals of "freedom from the obstacles of subordination, rank, and riches." The Illuminati was an atheistic league that defended secular humanism, suicide, and human sacrifice through abortion.

It seems appropriate that the followers of the *"angel of light"* *(2 Corinthians 11:14)* thought of themselves as the source of light or the "enlightened ones." However, the true purpose of the Illuminati was to kick God, the Light of the World, out of society.

"The Order of the Illuminati grew from five members to thousands in just a few years, but then, after Karl Theodor became ruler of Bavaria, secret societies were made punishable by death, and there the order ended."[12] However, many believe that it did not actually end but went deeper underground, just like the secret worshippers of Ba'al.

THE LEAGUE OF NATIONS
AND THE RISE OF HITLER

Following World War I, "the war to end all wars," man's relentless pursuit to have a one world government continued. President Woodrow Wilson called for and organized the League of Nations. The League of Nations was an intergovernmental organization founded on January 10, 1920, as a result of the Paris Peace Conference.[13] Its purpose was to oversee the governments of the world in an effort to avoid another catastrophe like World War I.

Originally, sixty-three nations participated in the League, but America was not one of them. The majority of our leaders wanted to avoid involvement in Europe's disputes in an effort to circumvent ensnarement in another global war. Germany was not allowed to join the League until 1926 due to the Treaty of Versailles. However, the League's worst fears became reality when in 1933 a demonized madman raised his hand and took the supreme oath of office in Germany. His name was Adolf Hitler, and just a few months after he became chancellor, Germany withdrew from the League of Nations.

Hitler's agenda was to conquer Europe and become the savior of Germany and the ruler of the world. This failed artist and an inconspicuous corporal of the German Army thought of himself as God, and the Third Reich was to be his empire that would last a thousand years. He swore to the citizens of Germany that he would bring a new world order that would produce peace, prosperity, and global power.

The masses believed Hitler, yet there were those who could rightly discern Germany's future path of destruction.

During Hitler's rise, Lutheran pastor Dietrich Bonhoeffer stated, "Germany cannot have two masters. Either we will serve the God of the Bible or we will serve Herr Hitler . . . but we cannot serve both."[14] Bonhoeffer was arrested, and died in prison for having the courage to speak the truth against the monstrous regime. His words, however, were seared into the hearts of believers for generations to come when he said, "To see evil and not call it evil is evil. Not to speak is to speak. Not to act is to act. God will not hold us guiltless."[15]

This divine warning should be given to the lukewarm clergy of

America today. To embrace evil and applaud the ungodly is treason in the courts of heaven. To compromise the truth of God's Word in exchange for the applause of a godless generation is a betrayal of Jesus Christ equal to that of Judas Iscariot in the Garden of Gethsemane.

Instead of peace, prosperity, and power, Adolf Hitler and his satanic SS led the German people into the bowels of a living hell. His Third Reich would eventually evolve into an occultist, merciless, and godless empire that would catapult the nations of the globe into World War II. This false messiah transformed Europe into a battlefield turned red by rivers of human blood resulting in the death of nearly 78 million people in the European theater alone.

COMMUNISM

The Communists, under the leadership of Joseph Stalin, pledged a New World Order—an atheistic, God-hating, empire. Understand that communism is an economic ideal, while atheism is a theological concept. These two models merged to form the Russian style of communism. Under Stalin's New World Order, thirty million of his own people were murdered in cold blood.

The old communist guard collapsed because of the bold leadership of former president Ronald Reagan, Prime Minister Margaret Thatcher, and Pope John Paul II. It was Ronald Reagan who challenged the Communists to "tear down this wall" in Berlin, and just twenty-four months later communism collapsed like a house of cards.

However, Russia's shadow government remained, and it is making a comeback as a superpower.

Dr. Peter Vincent Pry, chief of staff of the congressional Electromagnetic Pulse (EMP) Commission, stated that Russian dictator Vladimir Putin recently declared within his presidential address to the Federal Assembly that his country has developed nuclear superiority and war-winning capability against the entire world. Pry believes that Russia has achieved the holy grail of "escalation dominance." Escalation dominance means that a specific nation is able to prevail against the nations of world with superior nuclear capabilities in any crisis or conflict.

More importantly, *escalation dominance* is defined as being able to win a conflict without war through nuclear diplomacy, nuclear blackmail, and nuclear terror. This capability shapes the psychological geography of international relations and world order, not just during crises, but also in the daily lives of nations. This nuclear dominance overshadows every decision world leaders make, such as with NATO's (North Atlantic Treaty Organization) appeasement of Russian aggression in Crimea and Ukraine.

Included in Russia's arsenal of nuclear super weapons are the Sarmat missiles, dubbed as "Satan II" by NATO; Avangard warheads; and robot submarines described as "unmanned doomsday drones."[16]

The world just witnessed President Trump attend the G7 conference, hold a historical meeting with North Korea, and meet with Putin at the Helsinki Summit. I have no doubt that Moscow came to the negotiating table with the upper hand, embracing a position of nuclear superiority.

Please note that Putin's rhetoric is an act of nuclear blackmail demanding a New World Order where Russia becomes a major player in the *Final Game of Thrones*.

THE UNITED NATIONS

I believe that the United Nation's goal is to have a one world order, a one world bank, a one world constitution, a one world army, and a one world currency.

The European Union is ready to collaborate with the United Nations in building a more "cooperative world order." In a UN press release, Federica Mogherini, the European Union's high representative for foreign affairs and security policy, stated, "The European way is the United Nations way. . . . The European vision is the United Nations vision."[17] The press release further stated:

> Emphasizing that all European Union actions and initiatives were taken in full partnership with the United Nations, she noted that both organizations believed in the same principles and were built upon the same fundamental ideals. Both believed that security was not exclusively about military might, but also about diplomacy, development, economic growth and human rights. . . .
>
> "Confrontational approaches lead nowhere," [Mogherini] emphasized, declaring: "Between win-win and lose-lose, the European Union has picked sides. We stand on the side of dialogue and partnership. Where others see conflict, we look to cooperate." The bloc believed in a global order based on rules agreed together and respected by all.[18]

Can anyone say "seven-year peace treaty"?

ONE WORLD CURRENCY

For the record, another New World Order is coming soon. It will not be the socialist utopia that Professor Weishaupt of the Illuminati desired. Nor will it be the "workers unity" that the Marxist professors of the world's universities are clamoring for. It will not even be an era of peaceful cooperation, which the United Nations longs for. Instead, the coming New World Order will be the forerunner to a global economic crash, eventually leading to the greatest war humanity has ever seen.

Certain world-changing events must occur before the New World Order can come to power. The first has to do with money—remember: "It's the economy, stupid!" Bill Clinton's campaign used the then-prevailing American recession to successfully unseat President George H. W. Bush. And it will be the world's future economic depression that will lead to the destruction of the monetary system, ushering in a one world currency.

China, India, and Russia have already called for a one world currency. In 2009, at the G8 meeting, Russia's president presented a gold coin with the number 1 stamped in the middle of it, which he recommended to be the currency for the global economy.[19] At the recent G7 gathering early in the summer of 2018, the top global leaders conveyed their "unanimous concern and disappointment"[20] with the tariffs on steel and aluminum imports levied by Washington, inflicting mounted challenges with the world's top trade body.[21] It's all about the economy.

What will a one world currency mean for the US dollar, for America, and for your personal finances? It will lead to the death of the dollar as it is replaced as the reserve currency. America will no longer be permitted to print dollars ad infinitum to cover our debts. This will be a dark day for our nation.

Thirty years ago, in a 1988 Rothschild publication, the *Economist*, a bold prediction was made that a new world currency would be in circulation by 2018. The front cover even showed a phoenix rising from the flames of a pile of burning bank notes—dollars, pounds, and lira; all were ablaze.[22]

What would cause such a conflagration of the world's currency? Dr. Paul Craig Roberts, former editor of the *Wall Street Journal* and former US assistant secretary of the treasury for economic policy under Ronald Reagan, stated in a 2014 interview:

> The reason they want to hold the gold price down is they are afraid of its impact on the dollar. The reason why they had to suppress the gold price is they had to protect the dollar from quantitative easing (QE) because they were printing trillions and trillions of new dollars. This was worrying people around the world who hold dollars because the dollar was increasing, but not the goods and services in the American economy.
>
> So, when the gold price took off, the Fed said this endangers QE because if the dollar is declining in value relative to gold, it must also be declining in value relative to other currencies. Once the exchange rate starts collapsing, we lose control. So, we got to suppress gold. I don't know which side of the equation will play out first. I don't know if they will run out of gold to deliver to India and China or people will say this is a rigged scheme and we are just not participating anymore.[23]

Earlier I stated that China and Russia had been part of the world coalition calling for a one world currency. Why? Because they have become major players in the gold market.

According to the World Official Gold Holding chart, China is the world's largest gold producer and ranks sixth in the world, owning 1,842.6 tons. Russia is right behind China, ranking seventh in the world, owning 1,778.9 tons. Russia "doesn't need to import [gold] to add to its stockpile . . . as it has a billion-dollar gold mining industry."[24] Many financial experts believe these major players are underreporting their holdings,[25] which can only mean they are preparing for a major upheaval in the world's economy.

It is interesting to note that although the USA ranks number one, owning 8,133.5 tons of gold, it is *Germany* that ranks second in the world, with 3,373 tons. The third through fifth spots are all European: the International Monetary Fund (IMF), whose head-quarters are in Belgium, has 2,814 tons; Italy owns 2,451 tons; and France rounds out the top five with 2,453.9 tons.[26]

I can guarantee that the global economy will crash, and I can tell you when it will happen:

> *For the Lord Himself will descend from heaven with a shout, with the voice of an archangel, and with the trumpet of God. And the dead in Christ will rise first. Then we who are alive and remain shall be caught up together with them in the clouds to meet the Lord in the air. And thus we shall always be with the Lord. (1 Thessalonians 4:16–17)*

Saint Paul was describing the Rapture of the church in these verses, which will result in global economic chaos. The Pew Research Center reports that Christianity is the world's largest re-ligious group.[27] This means we are the majority. We work and pay the bulk of the taxes. When we are gone, the world's golden goose will have flown the coop. Where will the countries of the world get their loans? Who will sustain the United Nations? Who will fund the welfare system on which so many are dependent? Even George Soros could not fill that global financial vacuum.

The apostle John put his pen to parchment on the Isle of Patmos and wrote that there is coming a day at the end of time when the world will have a one world economy limited only to those who have the mark of the Beast—the Antichrist:

He [the Antichrist] causes all, both small and great, rich and poor, free and slave, to receive a mark on their right hand or on their foreheads, and that no one may buy or sell except one who has the mark or the name of the beast, or the number of his name. Here is wisdom. Let him who has understanding calculate the number of the beast, for it is the number of a man: His number is 666. (Revelation 13:16–18)

While there is a debate about what this mark may be, whether it is a literal "666" or perhaps a microchip, what we can be sure of is that the New World Order and the one world economy will be eagerly embraced by the nations of the world.

What are the consequences of taking that number? According to the Bible, it will cost you the loss of your soul. By taking the mark, you will have sworn allegiance to the Prince of Darkness. Receiving that number is not a fad . . . it is fatal.

And the smoke of their torment ascends forever and ever; and they have no rest day or night, who worship the beast and his image, and whoever receives the mark of his name. (Revelation 14:11)

THE LOSS OF INDIVIDUAL FREEDOM

Another major event marking the advent of the New World Order is the destruction of patriotism. To be a patriot is to love your country, defend your country, and give your life for your country if necessary to preserve freedom. Remember this truth: if we do not use our freedom to defend our freedom, we will lose our freedom.

America and the nations of the world are in the midst of a major identity crisis; we do not seem to know who we are, what we believe in, or what we are willing to defend as a nation or as individuals. We witness millionaire athletes refuse to stand and honor the flag— whose own freedoms were purchased with the blood and sacrifices of our military heroes—yet we still debate on whether it's right or wrong.

We see brainwashed anarchist students running in the streets of major cities of the world, led on by leftist professors from elite colleges and universities who have infected these young, pliable minds. They are protesting and pillaging without giving any thought to the danger and damage caused by their destructive actions. And yet they do not even know what they protest—and why! Christians are under attack, and Jewish hatred is sweeping like a wildfire throughout the nations of the world. We are on the brink of self-destruction!

Thank God for President Trump, who is working to secure our borders, strengthen our military, and renew our sense of purpose and patriotism in America. However, even with the best-intentioned world leaders of any nation, if believers do not recommit to God and family, do not rededicate to morality, honor, integrity, and the principles of righteousness as espoused in God's Word, then we are destined to repeat the mistakes of the Roman Empire and will collapse from within.

This must not happen . . . not on our watch! The Bible says, *"Blessed is a nation whose God is the LORD"* (Psalm 33:12), and *"Righteousness exalts a nation, but sin is a reproach to any people"* (Proverbs 14:34). These are God's mandates for all governments.

Jehovah God is the world's hope for tomorrow. Socialism is not our hope, communism is not our hope, and an atheistic New World Order is not our hope. Our hope is in the God of Abraham, Isaac, and Jacob, and there is no other.

If My people who are called by My name will humble them-selves, and pray and seek My face, and turn from their wicked ways, then I will hear from heaven, and will forgive their sin and heal their land. (2 Chronicles 7:14)

We are the Church triumphant. We have survived torture and torment at the hands of God-hating dictators. Yesterday, today, and forever, we have been and shall be victorious over death, hell, and the grave, over the world, the flesh, and the devil, over powers and principalities of darkness.

But take heed—the stage is being set for the Antichrist. He will come to power and rule the world as a ruthless dictator on the wings of a financial crisis just as Hitler did. And just as the German people were clamoring for a savior who would bring them back to European prominence, prestige, and power, so will the modern-day leaders seek a new Caesar. He will come as the prince of peace and prosperity, but in reality, he will be ruthless—those he does not kill, he will enslave.

Make no mistake: a New World Order will come to power. The Antichrist will rule the world. The enemies of Israel will break the seven-year treaty and invade the Holy Land. And Christ and His Church will return to triumph over the Beast and his hordes at Armageddon.

What should be our attitude concerning the future? Not one of doom and gloom. Jesus said, *"Now when these things begin to happen, look up and lift up your heads, because your redemption draws near"* *(Luke 21:28).* The King is coming. Look up; pray up; pack up. We are going up in the twinkling of an eye.

A final throne will be established, and its ruler will be Jesus Christ—the son of David, the son of Abraham, and the Son of

God. He will rule the world for a thousand years from the city of Jerusalem. Kings, queens, presidents, prime ministers, statesmen, and the rich and powerful of the world will line up in the streets of the Holy City to climb the Temple Mount and bow before the Carpenter's Son.

> . . . *that at the name of Jesus every knee should bow, of those in heaven, and of those on earth, and of those under the earth, and that every tongue should confess that Jesus Christ is Lord, to the glory of God the Father. (Philippians 2:10–11)*

The Word of God shall go forth from Jerusalem! The Lord will rule and reign over the earth in a theocracy with a rod of iron. That means He will not ask the ACLU what is acceptable. He will not ask the Supreme Court for a ruling. He will not ask the kings of the world or the government of ten for their consent.

He and He alone is the King of all kings and the Lord of all lords. The Son of King David will come to rule and reign. The King is coming with power and great glory. Lift up your heads and rejoice.

SECTION THREE

FROM AMALEK TO ARMAGEDDON

CHAPTER 9

FASCINATION WITH THE FUTURE

Never be afraid to trust an unknown future to a known God.
(Corrie ten Boom)

Mankind has always been fascinated with the future. People have long been captivated with horoscopes, futuristic movies, and science fiction books that attempt to predict the unknown. This mysterious attraction has led to an equally unconventional preoccupation with the "end of the world."

Questions like, "When will the end come?" "How will it come?" and "Who will survive it?" have prevailed throughout human history.[1] Yet, even with the meteoric rise of knowledge experienced by the human race, and the high-tech explosion available at everyone's fingertips, man has not accurately been able to forecast the future outside of the prophetic Word of God.

World history records a myriad of human obsessions with the End of Days; however, I will list only a few of these futile predictions.

THE ASSYRIANS

The Assyrians were a Semitic people who settled in the vast northern region of Mesopotamia as early as the twenty-fifth century BCE. They were conquered by various invading armies, and after centuries of wars, they finally secured their own sovereign state. Due to the relentless demands of combat, the Assyrians were inspired to produce unprecedented innovations of warfare.

Because of their proficiency in the sciences, they were the first to produce sophisticated iron weaponry. The Assyrian army became the largest in the Middle East, making them almost unconquerable in battle due to their invention of iron swords and lances, metal armor and chariots, and battering rams.[2]

Among their remarkable scientific and technological inventions were the mathematical division of the circle into 360 degrees, aqueducts, and the longitudinal and latitudinal measurements used in geographical navigation. They also developed sophisticated medical techniques that influenced the world, beginning with the Grecian Empire.

The Assyrians are accredited with many military, artistic, architectural, and astrological achievements, including the first recorded prediction of the lunar eclipse. Even though the Assyrians were notorious for their barbaric forms of torture, ironically they built a civilization that was astonishingly ahead of its time, which included an existential belief system. A classic example referring to their "End of Days" philosophy is a clay tablet discovered in Nineveh dating to 2,800 BCE displaying the following inscription:

> Our Earth is degenerate in these later days; there are signs that the world is speedily coming to an end; bribery and corruption are common; children no longer obey their parents;

every man wants to write a book and the end of the world is evidently approaching.[3]

As brilliant and innovative as the Assyrian civilization was, they were unable to effectively read the signs pointing to the end of the world.

THE MAYANS

The evolution of the New Age produced the so-called "end of the world" predications of the Mayan calendar. Among their many advanced accomplishments, the ancient Mayans invented a calendar of astonishing sophistication and accuracy. Several of the Mesoamerican nations, which include the regions of central Mexico, Belize, Costa Rica, El Salvador, Guatemala, and a portion of South America, including Colombia, adopted this shockingly precise calendar.

No matter how precise, the Mayan calendar misinterpreted the end of times. This miscalculation led to the "2012 phenomenon"—a series of eschatological beliefs that cataclysmic or transformative events would occur around December 12, 2012, which was the end of a 5,126-year-long cycle of the Mesoamerican Long Count calendar.[4] Thousands flocked to the pyramids of Mexico to learn more about this ancient prognostication of the end of the world.

It obviously did not happen.

THE MYTH OF Y2K

The modern era did not lag far behind with "end of the world" fascination and predictions, including the great Y2K scare of 1999. The world feared that the new millennium would bring with it the universal malfunction of computers. January 1, 2000, was predicted to introduce a modern-day apocalypse piloting the end of the world.

There was international chaos associated with this catastrophic expectation of a market crash and a massive world energy meltdown. Families around the globe scrambled to buy gas-powered generators, a year's supply of food, and constructed fallout shelters at exorbitant prices.

Additionally, computer programmers sold out of data-recovery software, while companies specializing in solutions to potential Y2K problems greatly profited in anticipation of the "end." The only phenomenon of this impending Y2K disaster was its global cost, which was estimated to be $200 to $600 billion.[5]

PORTRAIT OF HATRED

Apocalyptic scholars Natasha and Anthony O'Hear state that man for centuries has used the destruction of the world for various self-centered purposes "to numb people from real-world crises like poverty and war, to push political agendas, and to promote hatred of certain groups."[6] The "certain groups" they refer to are the Jewish people.

An example of this warped anti-Semitic agenda—within the arts—dates back to medieval times, when hate-filled themes were rampant in illustrations of the Apocalypse.[7] Yes, even the end time's prophetic scenes brought with them another path with which to funnel Jewish hatred. The O'Hears write,

> Jews featured heavily in apocalyptic depictions, as seen in some beautiful Anglo-Norman [the medieval ruling class in England] illuminated apocalypse manuscripts.[8]

It was also quite common for Christ and His followers to be portrayed as medieval knights, while the forces of Satan would be depicted as Jewish.[9] These false and relentless representations of the

Jewish people eventually led to the Edict of Expulsion ordered by King Edward I of England on July 18, 1290. This infamous decree expelled all Jews from England, allowing them to only take what they could carry. All other properties became the Crown's.[10]

No matter the source or purpose of various "end time" theories, the same questions still arise:

- Are we nearing the end of the world as we know it?
- Is the Apocalypse, with all of its horror and calamity, just before us?
- Will we know the season of its appearing?

The answer to these questions is *yes!* However, we must first study the Word of God, which reveals His truth concerning the End of Days.

CAN WE KNOW THE FUTURE?

The Bible is a book of profound mysteries and glorious unveilings. To the carnal mind, the Scriptures are foolish contradictions printed on paper, but to the student of the Word of God, it is the embodiment of precise logic and the manifestation of hope.

The Bible has been described as a house with many rooms; to the outsider looking in, it is unknown as to what makes up each room. However, for the one who holds the key to the house and has access to its interior, there is no secret to what each room contains.[11] As believers, we are given the access key to the revelation of Scripture, for Jesus declared, *"Most assuredly, I say to you, unless one is born again, he cannot see the kingdom of God" (John 3:3).*

Christians are eager to learn about healing, prosperity, and favor, but some are often intimidated by the study of biblical prophecy, even though we hold the key to the "prophecy room" and can know what lies within. Jesus considered prophecy important, saying, *"Do not think that I came to destroy the Law or the Prophets. I did not come to destroy but to fulfill"* (Matthew 5:17).

The Rabbi from Nazareth often spoke about coming events, and He rebuked those who did not recognize the importance of the signs that were occurring around them. In fact, He scolded those who surveyed the stars to foretell the weather but were blind to the prophetic indicators of the times that predicted the future. In Luke 12:56, Jesus said, *"Hypocrites! You can discern the face of the sky and of the earth, but how is it you do not discern this time?"*

It was no small thing to Jesus that the people of His generation remained ignorant to God's prophetic Word. And as believers in this generation, we too are mandated to study all Scripture as a guide for righteous living in preparation of Jesus's coming.

WHY STUDY BIBLICAL PROPHECY?

Approximately one-fourth of the Word of God was prophetic at the time it was written. The obvious conclusion any serious Bible student can make from this statistic is that if the Almighty devoted that much of His Word to the subject of prophecy, it certainly benefits every believer to study it. The knowledge of biblical prophecy produces the following important results.

The Bible's Authority

First and foremost, the study of the prophetic scriptures and their fulfillment attests to the *authority* of the Word of God. The detailed descriptions of coming events and their precise fulfillment validate that "Scripture is of divine origin, trustworthy, and to be studied with confidence."[12] All that man knows of God is recorded in His Word; without this assured foundation, we are nothing.

For I am God, and there is no other;
I am God, and there is none like Me,
Declaring the end from the beginning,
And from ancient times things that are not yet done,
Saying, "My counsel shall stand,
And I will do all My pleasure." (Isaiah 46:9–10)

God Almighty inspired the writers of His Holy Word through the communion of His Spirit with the spiritual nature and intellectual abilities of man. Remember this truth: *all* Scripture is written by God; it is *His* voice and *His* authority.

Knowing this first, that no prophecy of Scripture is of any private interpretation, for prophecy never came by the will of man, but holy men of God spoke as they were moved by the Holy Spirit. (2 Peter 1:20–21)

The Bible's Accuracy

Studying prophecy confirms the *accuracy* of God's Word. The Holy Scriptures are not merely man's account of historical events—they are a living, accurate, and authoritative message from God to His people. Christ acknowledged the Scriptures in His earthly ministry by referring to the Old Testament writings as those things "spoken to you by God."[13]

Saint Peter wrote,

We heard this voice which came from heaven when we were with Him on the holy mountain. And so we have the prophetic word confirmed, which you do well to heed as a light that shines in a dark place, until the day dawns and the morning star rises in your hearts. (2 Peter 1:18–19)

An eyewitness account is the highest standard of accuracy possible, but Peter declares that biblical prophecy is even more accurate than an eyewitness.

There are 353 prophetic scriptures in the Old Testament dealing with the birth, ministry, death, and resurrection of Jesus Christ. These accounts were recorded centuries before He came to earth, and every word has been fulfilled.[14] Man, with all of his knowledge and with the assistance of all the technology afforded him, cannot come close to this degree of accuracy—only God can.

The fulfillment of the following Old Testament prophecies concerning the life of Christ further testifies about the infallible precision of God's Word.

- His royal lineage: 2 Samuel 7:12–16; Psalms 89:3–4; 110:1; 132:11; Isaiah 9:6; Matthew 22:44; Mark 12:36; Luke 1:69–70; 20:42–44; John 7:42
- His virgin birth: Isaiah 7:14; Matthew 1:23
- His birth in Bethlehem: Micah 5:2; Matthew 2:6; John 7:42
- His return from Egypt: Hosea 11:1; Matthew 2:15
- His coming revealed by God's messenger: Isaiah 40:3–5; Malachi 3:1; 4:5; Matthew 3:3; 11:10–14; Mark 1:2–3; Luke 3:4–6; 7:27; John 1:23
- His anointing by the Holy Spirit: Psalm 45:7
- His ministry in Galilee: Isaiah 9:1–2; Matthew 4:15
- His use of parables: Psalm 78:1–2; Isaiah 6:9–10; Matthew 13:14–15
- His healing of the sick: Isaiah 53:4; Matthew 8:17
- His teachings and miracles rejected: Isaiah 53:3
- His triumphal entry into Jerusalem: Psalm 118:26; Isaiah 62:11; Zechariah 9:9; Matthew 21:5; John 12:14–15
- His betrayal by a friend: Psalm 41:9

- His being forsaken by His disciples: Psalm 31:11
- His being condemned with criminals: Isaiah 53:9, 12; Luke 22:37
- His garments being divided by lot: Psalm 22:18; John 19:24
- His being offered vinegar on the cross: Psalm 69:21; Matthew 27:34; John 19:29
- His side being pierced without His bones being broken: Exodus 12:46; Numbers 9:12; Psalm 22:14, 16; 34:20; Zechariah 12:10; John 19:36–37
- His dying words foretold: Psalm 21:1; 31:5; Matthew 27:46; Mark 15:34; Luke 23:46
- His resurrection: Job 19:23–27; Psalm 17:15

God's Wisdom

Studying prophecy reveals the *wisdom* of God. Only the Almighty, in His infinite capacity, can inspire the compiled writings of sixty-six books that were penned on three continents in three different languages—Hebrew, Aramaic, and Greek.

The Holy Scriptures were chronicled by approximately forty people of diverse education and backgrounds, including kings, shepherds, scientists, attorneys, an army general, fishermen, priests, and a physician, most of whom never met.[15]

> *Oh, the depth of the riches both of the wisdom and knowledge of God! How unsearchable are His judgments and unfathomable His ways! (Romans 11:33 NASB)*

The greatest harmony ever heard is within the symphony of the Word of God! This sacred masterpiece was written over a period of about 1,400 years, covering over 4,000 years of human history. There are 1,239 prophecies found in the Old Testament and 578 prophecies in the New Testament, for a total of 1,817, which comprise 8,352 verses.[16]

God revealed Himself to and through men with these sacred writings, which began with the prophet Moses and ended with John the Revelator. Yet, as inconceivable as it may seem, every word of the Scripture is orchestrated to harmonize with all other scriptures.

God's Power

The study of prophecy testifies to the *power* of God.

> *The LORD said to Moses, "Is the LORD's power limited? Now you shall see whether My word will come true for you or not." (Numbers 11:23 NASB)*

What was happening at this moment? Moses and the children of Israel were in the wilderness, and the Lord was about to punish them for their constant murmuring and unbelief. Moses, thinking in the natural, questioned God's ability to carry out His judgment (Numbers 11:21–22).

Moses's doubt challenged the power of the Divine (vv. 1–15). Had Moses forgotten that he had been not only a witness but also an instrument of the Almighty's work? God's matchless power had not waned from the time He had inflicted the plagues on Egypt, parted the Red Sea, and rained manna from heaven. The Great I AM had not become weak or weary—He remained the same, and His power was undiminished.

The study of prophecy and its fulfillment reveals that God's powerful hand will stretch as far as needed to achieve His divine plan. This is the same power that measures the depth of the seas and the heights of the heavens (Isaiah 40:12). Saint Paul desired that every believer would grasp the presence of God's power:

. . . the eyes of your understanding being enlightened; that you may know what is the hope of His calling, what are the riches of the glory of His inheritance in the saints, and what is the exceeding greatness of His power toward us who believe, according to the working of His mighty power which He worked in Christ when He raised Him from the dead and seated Him at His right hand in the heavenly places, far above all principality and power and might and dominion, and every name that is named, not only in this age but also in that which is to come. (Ephesians 1:18–21)

The greatest proof of God's power lies within His Word and its fulfillment, which includes our personal redemption from sin and conformity to Christ's resurrection. It is through the fulfillment of His Word that God responded to Moses's doubt. Remember this truth: God *is* power. His Word *is* power; therefore, when God speaks—it comes *to pass!*

God's Promises

Studying prophecy reaffirms God's fulfilled *promises.* Consider the rebirth of the nation of Israel (Isaiah 66:8). Every major prophet in the Old Testament prophesied that God would bring the Jewish people "out of their Gentile graves," which were the nations into which the Jewish people had been dispersed following various conquests.

Isaiah spoke of this phenomenon:

The Sovereign LORD declares—
he who gathers the exiles of Israel:
"I will gather still others to them
besides those already gathered." (Isaiah 56:8 NIV)

The Lord declared through the prophet Jeremiah about leading His Covenant people home:

"I will be found by you," declares the LORD, "and will bring you back from captivity. I will gather you from all the nations and places where I have banished you," declares the LORD, "and will bring you back to the place from which I carried you into exile." (Jeremiah 29:14 NIV)

Ezekiel prophesied concerning the restoration of the Jewish people into the land of Israel:

I will bring you from the nations and gather you from the countries where you have been scattered. (Ezekiel 20:34 NIV)

Amos foretold of the same ingathering:

And I will bring my people Israel back from exile.
"They will rebuild the ruined cities and live in them.
They will plant vineyards and drink their wine;
they will make gardens and eat their fruit." (Amos 9:14 NIV)

Jewish immigrants began returning to their homeland from around the world in the 1880s. This migration was known as the first *aliyah* (immigration to Israel). Theodore Herzl, motivated by Zionist ideology and Jewish persecution, inspired the second *aliyah*, from 1904 to 1914. By the beginning of World War I, the number of Jews living in the Promised Land was somewhere between eighty to ninety thousand.[17]

By May 14, 1948, when the United Nations officially recognized the State of Israel, over 800,000 Jews had fulfilled the prophecies of the ingathering. Currently, out of the 14.3 million Jewish people in the world, 43 percent of them reside in Israel; as of this writing, that equates to more than 6.4 million Jews.[18]

Only God could have foreseen this miraculous ingathering and rebirth over 2,500 years before it began, and only God had the power to make it happen!

God's Purposes

Studying prophecy makes known the *purposes* of God. God Almighty demonstrates beyond any doubt that He knows the end from the beginning and is orchestrating the events on earth to fulfill His perfect plan. The study of prophecy provides a better understanding of the current economic and political events in the world that will bring the Antichrist to power. Because of fulfilled and future fulfillment of prophecy, we can better comprehend:

- The global rush for a one-world currency (Revelation 13:17)
- The birth of a one-world religion (Revelation 13:12–16)
- The creation of a one-world government (Revelation 13:2, 7)
- The resurgence of Russia as a military superpower, which will lead a pan-Islamic army against Israel (Ezekiel 38:2, 5–7)
- The economic growth of China (Revelation 9; 16:12–19)
- The signs reflecting the season of Jesus's return to rule the earth from the Temple Mount in the city of Jerusalem (Matthew 24)

God's Peace

Studying prophecy produces *peace* in the heart of every believer. As we watch the daily news reports of North Korea and Iran preparing for nuclear proficiency; of ISIS, the Taliban, and the PLO creating turmoil and mayhem in the Middle East and the world; of Iran's backing of Hamas, Hezbollah, and the barbaric Syrian regime; and finally, of Russia coming into that region as a major player—it is no wonder we question the future!

When Jesus spoke of His approaching death and resurrection with His disciples, they naturally became troubled. Many today are also troubled due to the disturbing world conditions. We are asking the same questions the disciples most likely asked themselves: "What are we going to do? Who will watch over us? Who will defend us from our enemies?"

And just as Jesus spoke these words to the disciples, He reassures all believers, *"Let not your heart be troubled; you believe in God, believe also in Me" (John 14:1)*. Jesus, knowing the disciples were concerned about their future, calmed their fears with these prophetic words:

> *In My Father's house are many mansions; if it were not so, I would have told you. I go to prepare a place for you. And if I go and prepare a place for you, I will come again and receive you to Myself; that where I am, there you may be also. (John 14:2–3)*

Because they had already witnessed the fulfillment of Scripture through the life and ministry of Jesus, the disciples believed Him when He gave the prophetic promise of His return. Like the disciples and so many of God's people before them, we are also comforted by the fulfilled promises of prophetic scriptures, which confirm that every event on earth occurs by divine design:[19]

- Noah believed and his family was saved from destruction (Hebrews 11:7).
- Abraham believed and he became the father of all who believe (Hebrews 11:8–12).
- Joseph believed and he became the ruler of Egypt (Genesis 41:37–39).

- Moses believed and he led God's people to freedom (Hebrews 11:29).
- David believed and he defeated the giant and became king (1 Samuel 17:45–51; 16:1, 13; 2 Samuel 2).
- The Virgin Mary believed and she gave birth to the Son of God (Luke 1:38).
- Saint Paul believed and he wrote thirteen books of the New Testament (Acts 9:1–20).
- John believed and he received the book of Revelation (1 John 1:1–4; Revelation 1:1).

Blessed are those who have not seen and yet have believed. (John 20:29)

TIME LINE OF THE PROPHETS

In the next three chapters, we will explore some of the most notable men in biblical history who were shown the future by the Lord Almighty. Their revelations and the interpretation of those revelations were recorded in Scripture for coming generations.

- Abraham saw the Promised Land (Genesis 15).
- Daniel saw the dawn of eternity (Daniel 12).
- Ezekiel saw the judgment and salvation of God's people (Ezekiel 38–39).

To better understand God's message to His people, here is a timeline[20] of a few of the prophets and their prophecy, along with some of the major biblical events that occurred between the birth of Abraham and the birth of Jesus.

YEAR (BCE)	EVENT
2001	Birth of **Abraham**
722	Assyrians conquer Tribe of Israel—Northern Kingdom.
650	Birth of **Jeremiah**
628	Birth of **Daniel**
627	**Jeremiah** prophesies the Assyrian attack on Judah.
622	Birth of **Ezekiel**
612	The Babylonians destroy Nineveh and became the new world superpower.
608	Josiah, king of Judah, is killed in battle with Egyptians. • Jehoahaz becomes king but is taken to Egypt. • Jehoiakim becomes king. • The prophet **Jeremiah** is declared a traitor and imprisoned.
606	**Habakkuk** delivers a prophetic message to Jerusalem.
605	**Jeremiah** proclaims God's judgment on Judah as it's besieged by the Babylonians.
605	King Nebuchadnezzar of Babylon captures Jerusalem; exiles the best and brightest descendants of the king to Babylon, which includes **Daniel**, Hananiah (*Shadrach*), Mishael (*Mishach*), and Azariah (*Abed-Nego).*
604	**Daniel** interprets Nebuchadnezzar's dream (Daniel 2).

YEAR (BCE)	EVENT
598	Second Exile to Babylon (3,023 captives) • King Jehoiakim of Judah dies; Jehoiachin reigns.
597	Third Exile to Babylon (ten thousand captives) • King Jehoiachin and prophet **Ezekiel** deported. • The poorest are left in the land; Zedekiah begins his reign.
593	**Ezekiel** receives visions of heaven.
586	Babylonians plunder and destroy Jerusalem and the temple.
580	**Jeremiah** is freed from prison and is allowed to stay in Jerusalem.
570	**Daniel** interprets Nebuchadnezzar's vision of a tree (Daniel 4).
570	**Jeremiah** dies in Egypt
565	**Ezekiel** completes his book. There is no other recording of his life.
550	**Daniel** receives vision of four beasts (Daniel 7).
548	**Daniel** receives vision of the ram and the goat (Daniel 8).
539	**Daniel** interprets handwriting on the wall. (Daniel 5). • Belshazzar is murdered. • Cyrus the Great captures Babylon. • Persia becomes the new world superpower.
539	Medo-Persian Empire is established.

YEAR (BCE)	EVENT
536	**Daniel** is given the interpretation of the seventy-week prophecy. • King Cyrus enables the building of the Second temple.
537	**Daniel**'s Final Visions • Receives a vision of the Messiah (Daniel 10). • Is shown the future kings of Persia and Greece (Daniel 11:2–34) and the future leader of a world government during the end times tribulation (Daniel 11:35–12:13).
536	The prophet **Daniel** dies in captivity.
536	Exiles return to Jerusalem.
520	The prophet **Zechariah**, whose name means, "Yahweh Remembers," is brought to Jerusalem as a youth and begins his ministry.
519	**Zechariah** receives eight visions: 1. The Man among the Myrtle Trees (1:7–17) 2. The Four Horns and the Four Craftsmen (1:18–21) 3. The Surveyor with a Measuring Line (2:1–12) 4. Cleansing and Crowning of Joshua, the High Priest (chapter 3) 5. The Gold Lampstand and the Two Olive Trees (chapter 4) 6. The Flying Scroll (5:1–4) 7. The Woman in a Basket (5:5–11) 8. Four Chariots (6:1–8)

YEAR (BCE)	EVENT
485	Xerxes begins his reign as King of Persia.
480	Esther becomes Queen of Persia.
480–470	**Zechariah** receives vision of the redemption of Israel, the coming Messiah, and His Millennial reign.
445	Artaxerxes decrees rebuilding of Jerusalem (Nehemiah 2:1).
331	Alexander the Great Conquers Persia.
63	Roman general Pompey conquers Jerusalem.
6 CE	Birth of **Jesus Christ**

It is now time to look into the future as God reveals His eternal plan for all humanity through the prophets Abraham, Daniel, and Ezekiel.

CHAPTER 10

ABRAHAM'S VISION— THE PROMISE

I will make you a great nation. (Genesis 12:2)

E very serious student of eschatology has the privilege of drawing fresh water from the deep and refreshing wells of wisdom fashioned by respected biblical scholars such as Clarence Larkin, Arthur W. Pink, Myer Pearlman, J. Dwight Pentecost, and Derek Prince— and I am no exception. My purpose in this text is to condense and at times complement the vital works of these giants of Bible prophecy so that the reader can effectively use this knowledge to better understand the foreshadowing of things to come.

GOD'S PURPOSE

For the first two thousand years after creation, the earth was a spiritual wasteland; Jewish scholars refer to this season as "two thousand years of desolation." It was a time when God allowed the world to exist purely out of His goodness and mercy. This barrenness lasted until Abraham.

God used the first eleven chapters of the Bible to introduce the whole human race. Then in chapter 12, He chose one family, specifically the family of Abraham, to call into an everlasting covenant, which eventually brought forth the giving of the Torah on Mount Sinai to Moses. This life-transforming event was "like a spiritual sunrise after a night of almost endless blackness."[1]

The Almighty reveals His purpose for mankind through personal visitation, in His written Word, and also by dreams and visions to the few He calls His messengers. Ultimately, the Architect of the universe desires that good triumph and that evil be conquered. This is a theme that consistently runs through biblical prophecy, yet *how* God chooses to fulfill His purpose is often complex and inconsistent to human reasoning.

For example, there are times when we see good openly rewarded and evil openly punished. There are other times, however, when evil seems to prevail and goodness stands disgraced. No matter how hard this is to understand, we must trust that God's plans are not hindered. This one thing we know: we will not fully understand the ways of the Almighty until we are with Him in eternity. Until that time, God, in His infinite wisdom, chooses what and when to conceal or reveal to His children.

God's vision is perfect—ours is not! Man's vision has been likened to what a fly is able to see when it lands on an artist's painting—the broad scope of the entire picture is impaired because the fly can only see minute parts of the whole. Rabbi Hersh Goldwurm explains it this way: "Until we see the whole, we cannot understand the parts; when we see the whole—sometimes after generations, sometimes not until the End of Days—we will understand why each ingredient had to enter the picture when it did and as it did."[2]

THE COMMAND

At His chosen time, God Almighty allows His creation to look into the heavens and witness scenes that reveal future events. One such vision was given to Abram, as recorded in Genesis 15. Here, God made known to the *"father of all those who believe" (Romans 4:11)* the future of the Jewish people for thousands of years to come.

The prophetic use of dreams and visions is emphasized in Scripture from the book of Genesis through the book of Revelation. When Aaron and Miriam rebelled against Moses, the Lord defended Moses with these words: *"If there is a prophet among you, I, the LORD, make Myself known to him in a vision; I speak to him in a dream" (Numbers 12:6).*

Before we can fully appreciate what Abram saw, allow me to give you a short synopsis of who he was.

Abram was a Semite, a descendant of Shem, Noah's son. He lived in the city of Ur, where his father was an idol merchant. God called Abram out from his country through the commands and promises of Genesis 12 with the intention of making him the father of the Hebrew nation:

Now the LORD had said to Abram: "Get out of your country, from your family and from your father's house, to a land that I will show you. I will make you a great nation; I will bless you and make your name great; and you shall be a blessing. I will bless those who bless you, and I will curse him who curses you; and in you all the families of the earth shall be blessed." (vv. 1–3)

Acts 7:2–3 refers to this appearance of *"the God of glory"* to Abram while he was still in Mesopotamia shortly after the destruction of the

Tower of Babel, which is documented in Genesis 11. God was about to intervene in the life of Abram in a manner that would forever change his future and the future of mankind. While Genesis 11 was about the futile ploys of man, Genesis 12 is about the eternal plans of God for Abram, the Jewish people, and the nations of the world.

This glorious appearance of God to mankind was the first recorded since the expulsion of Adam and Eve from the Garden. After centuries of continued disobedience, the Lord chose a man among the world's idolaters who would be faithful to respond to His revelation and teach His precepts to his descendants (Proverbs 22:6). From this point forward, Abram and his seed are the major focus of Scripture.

Arthur W. Pink states, "The Lord's commands are rarely accompanied with *reasons* but they are always accompanied with *promises*, either expressed or understood."[3] Genesis 12 is no exception. God Almighty used the phrase "I will" five times within the sevenfold blessing to emphasize that He meant what He said, and as is His nature, the Lord has fulfilled every one of His declarations.

The first "I will" referred to the future state of Israel, which is now known as the crown jewel among all nations. The Jewish people have blessed the nations despite the efforts of many to eradicate them.

Through the centuries, they have miraculously survived the wicked plans of dictators, despots, psychopathic Caesars, expulsions, pogroms, and mass executions, all of which were an attempt to wipe them off the face of earth. However, no matter how vicious and horrific the campaigns, the Jewish people have survived and blessed humanity by scripting the Word of God and by giving us the patriarchs—Abraham, Isaac, and Jacob, the Old Testament prophets, and the First Family of our faith—Mary, Joseph, and Jesus. Christianity certainly owes a debt of gratitude to the Jewish people. Judaism does not need Christianity to explain its existence; however, Christianity cannot explain its existence without Judaism!

The Jewish people have also blessed the nations of the world in practical ways through their innovative medical discoveries, frontline high-tech advancements, pioneering agricultural developments, and advanced military technology—all while surrounded by a swarm of enemies obsessed with their eradication. And as God promised, Abraham's name is honored among Jews, Christians, and Muslims alike.

The decline and demise of nations in both ancient and modern times, which plagued Israel and tormented the Jewish people, can be directly attributed to God's "I will" promise to *"curse him who curses you" (Genesis 12:3)*. Here are just a few examples recorded in history.

The Assyrians invaded Israel (722 BCE) and instigated the first Jewish diaspora, forcing the Hebrew people to assimilate into their society. Soon after, Assyria fell to its ardent enemies: the Babylonians (612 BCE). Today, ancient Assyria is composed of parts of Iraq, Turkey, Iran, and Syria—all of which are war-torn countries marching toward the mountains of Israel and the judgment of God in the coming Gog and Magog Wars.

The Babylonians under Nebuchadnezzar conquered Jerusalem (586 BCE), destroyed the First Temple, and exiled the Jewish people to Babylon. They soon fell to Cyrus the Great, king of Persia (539 BCE). King Cyrus blessed the Jewish people, as foretold by the prophet Isaiah, and allowed the exiled Jews to return to their Promised Land from Babylon. Cyrus allowed a form of Jewish home rule in Jerusalem and decreed the rebuilding of the Jewish temple (Isaiah 44:28).

The effect of King Cyrus's blessing upon the Jewish people continued for over one hundred years, until 411 BCE, when a Persian by the name of Bagoas was made governor of Jerusalem. During his ruthless tenure, he tormented the Jews by levying burdensome taxes and desecrating their temple. Within the course of time, the evil Bagoas became the true ruler of Persia by governing through weak puppet-kings such as King Darius III.

Bagoas attempted to poison King Darius, as he had murdered the previous kings, but instead was forced to drink the poison himself. Soon after, Alexander the Great destroyed the Persian Empire (332 BCE) and conquered Judea.

The promise of God's curse on anti-Semitism continued. After the Greeks besieged the Jewish people and desecrated their holy altar, they were in time conquered by Rome (63 BCE). Rome viciously oppressed and tortured the Jewish people, and under the siege of Titus destroyed the Second Temple. The Germanic leader, Odoacer, overthrew the last of the Roman emperors (476 CE).

Modern nations have not circumvented the curse of Genesis 12, nor will they in the future. Prior to the Inquisition and the edict for the expulsion of the Jews in 1492, Spain was considered the first global superpower. But in less than two hundred years following this anti-Semitic edict, which forced the Jews to convert or leave the country within twelve days, Spain became fully bankrupt.[4] This marked the beginning of the end of Spanish imperialism. Spain is now considered a "fifth-state nation" among the European Union and is currently facing its worst financial and economic crisis in the last fifty years.[5]

Germany was in ruins after igniting the furnace of the vilest of Jewish propaganda, persecution, and pogroms, which culminated in the Final Solution through the monstrous death camps where over six million Jews perished at the hands of so-called Christians. German soldiers bowed at the feet of the Virgin Mary and then went out and threw her descendants alive into the gas chambers.

Has Germany recovered from the aftermath of their attempted annihilation of the Jewish people?

A recent article from the Gatestone Institute stated, "Mass migration from the Muslim world is fast-tracking the Islamization of Germany, as evidenced by the proliferation of no-go zones, Sharia courts, polygamy and child marriages. Mass migration has also been responsible for a host of social disruptions, including jihadist attacks, a migrant rape epidemic, a public health crisis, rising crime and a rush by German citizens to purchase weapons for self-defense—and even to abandon Germany altogether."[6] The curse continues.

At its peak, the British Empire was the world's foremost global power. By 1922, it was the largest empire in history, governing over one-quarter of the earth's total land area. However, the United Kingdom no longer governs any major locale in the world other than England, Scotland, Wales, and Northern Ireland.

The British Empire lost its world dominance when it violated its trust with the Jewish people through actions such as expelling the Jews from England, failing to vote for Israeli statehood at the United Nations, and for its continued anti-Semitic legislation of Boycott, Divestment, and Sanctions (BDS) against Israeli products and businesses.

I want to clearly state that America is no exception to God's promise of Genesis 12:3 with regard to our conduct toward the Jewish people and their Covenant homeland. Our nation has historically been a haven of hope for God's chosen people by becoming their safe harbor following the terrorizations of the Spanish Inquisition and the horrors of the European Holocaust. As a result, we were supernaturally blessed as a young and fledgling country because we blessed the Jewish people, especially after recognizing Israel's statehood in 1948.

However, during his tenure as president, Barak Obama deliberately put daylight between America and our only democratic ally in the Middle East. This orchestrated gap increased with the signing of the traitorous Iran Deal, which was a blatant betrayal of our nearly seventy years of friendship with Israel.

This alarming "deal" was nothing more than a nuclear accommodation of radical Islam, which threatened not only the safety of the Jewish people but also the welfare of the free world. By obliging Iran, Obama seriously risked Israel's future while the entire infrastructure of the Iranian nuclear weapons program remained intact.

Iran's chants of "Death to America" and "Death to Israel" are expressions of intent! Obama's relief sanctions kept alive the maniacal dreams of Iran for a nuclear holocaust for Israel and the Jewish people.[7] Remember, God's promise, *"I will curse those who curse you,"* also applies to America.

Instead of insisting that the survival of Israel was nonnegotiable, President Obama pandered to radical Islamist theocrats who daily threaten to wipe the Jewish people off the map. Ultimately, America betrayed the trust of the Jewish state, and as a consequence of this and other fundamentally disloyal actions against Israel, America lost its status as a respected world leader largely because our allies can't trust us and our enemies don't fear us.

However, God in His infinite mercy has given America an opportunity to reverse the curse with our current administration under the leadership of President Trump, who has pledged to stand by Israel and the Jewish people. Millions of Christians and I pray that our country continues to make every effort to restore and strengthen our relationship with Israel. I have said it before, and it bears repeating—those nations that have come against the Jewish people are in the boneyard of human history while the State of Israel lives and prospers. God's promises never fail!

SET APART

We must remember that Almighty God will have nothing to do with an idolatrous people or nation. God demands that His people be set apart to Him. The Creator of heaven and earth has great plans for His Covenant Land and His people: *"And you shall be holy to Me, for I the LORD am holy, and have separated you from the peoples, that you should be Mine" (Leviticus 20:26).*

God has not changed, and His precepts remain the same. The promise of Genesis 12 continues in verse 7, when God gave the land to Abram. The Lord used a variety of ways to bring Abram into his sevenfold blessing; however, Abram first needed to be completely separated from his idolatrous past, his family, and his country.

In Genesis 13, there was an argument between the herdsmen of Abram and those of his nephew Lot. Abram divided the grazing land and gave Lot the opportunity to choose the best real estate for himself, and then the two parted ways. As a result, Abram's final separation from his past, his father's house, and his relatives was complete.

It is significant to note that Lot's name meant "veil." In other words, no matter how close Abram and his nephew were, Lot was an *impediment* that prevented Abram from *seeing* his inheritance, and from achieving God's destiny for his life.

Abram was now in a place of divine separation where God could fully bless him. The Lord reaffirmed to Abram what He promised in Genesis 12: the giving of the land to him and his descendants forever. Bible history proves that what you are willing to walk away from will determine what God can bring you to. Abram walked away from Ur, his idolatry, his family, and all else God had commanded him to leave behind. Because of his obedience, Abraham became one of the most prosperous and revered men in history.

MELCHIZEDEK

Lot was now living in Sodom, and during this time in history, King Chedorlaomer of Elam, who followed in the way of Nimrod and Babel, conquered the lands as far west as Canaan and exercised authority over its southeastern part.[8] The five local kings of these regions, after paying tribute to him for twelve years, rebelled, but within a short time, Chedorlaomer and his three collaborating kings crushed their uprising.

During the battle, Chedorlaomer's legions plundered the region of the Dead Sea and took Lot captive. Abram came to Lot's rescue in the first war ever mentioned in Scripture and, in doing so, delivered the kings of Sodom and Gomorrah and their allies.

After the victory of the war of Genesis 14, Melchizedek, the king of Salem, who was also the priest of the Most High God (Hebrews 7:1), blessed Abram: *"Blessed be Abram of God Most High, Possessor of heaven and earth; and blessed be God Most High, who has delivered your enemies into your hand" (Genesis 14:19–20)*. Once the blessing was given, Abram presented *"a tithe of all" (v. 20)* to Melchizedek.

Melchizedek represents the foreshadowing of the millennial glory of Christ as he meets Abram upon his return from the slaughter of the kings, while Lot signifies the Jewish remnant during the tribulation period. So will it be when our Lord returns to usher in the Millennium. He will overthrow the Beast and his forces in this same *"King's Valley" (v. 17)*, deliver Israel out of their hands, and bless the descendants of Abraham. And just as Abram acknowledged the authority of Melchizedek by paying him tithes, so will Israel acknowledge their divine Melchizedek and claim Him as their Priest and King.[9]

Abram, after his meeting with Melchizedek, brought back the spoils of battle and was met by the king of Sodom, who suggested that Abram give him the prisoners of war but keep the *"goods"* that were seized in the conquest. However, Abram had made a promise to the Lord Most High and refused to keep anything—*"from a thread to a sandal strap" (v. 23)*—so as to prevent the king of Sodom or anyone else from taking credit for Abram's God-given blessing of victory and prosperity (Genesis 12:2).

THE VISION

Now we enter into Genesis 15:

> *After these things the word of the* LORD *came to Abram in a vision, saying, "Do not be afraid, Abram. I am your shield, your exceedingly great reward." But Abram said, "Lord* GOD, *what will You give me, seeing I go childless, and the heir of my house is Eliezer of Damascus?" Then Abram said, "Look, You have given me no offspring; indeed one born in my house is my heir!"*
>
> *And behold, the word of the* LORD *came to him, saying, "This one shall not be your heir, but one who will come from your own body shall be your heir." Then He brought him outside and said, "Look now toward heaven, and count the stars if you are able to number them." And He said to him, "So shall your descendants be."*
>
> *And he believed in the* LORD, *and He accounted it to him for righteousness. (vv. 1–6)*

These verses introduce a number of first-used concepts in Scripture that transformed Abram's life and the lives of all who believe. A few of the more significant words or phrases are *"vision," "do not be afraid," "believed," "accounted,"* and *"righteousness."* To better understand the importance of these words, let us consider what they intended.

Why did the Lord speak to Abram through a vision? And why

was he afraid? Think of it: Abram led his meager squadron composed of 318 armed servants—the first IDF commandos—in a surprise night attack, gaining a supernatural victory against four kings and their seasoned armies. Chedorlaomer was dead, as were the other kings, Lot was liberated, and the riches that had been taken from Sodom and Gomorrah were recovered. Abram acknowledged that it was God who had divinely assisted in this triumph— *but what now?*

Abram feared that the successors of the four kings would gather even larger armies in retaliation for his triumph over them, and he worried about whether God would deliver him once more. In order to comfort Abram, God appeared to him in a vision, saying, *"Do not be afraid, Abram. I am your shield, your exceedingly great reward"* *(Genesis 15:1).*

However, Abram had an even more desperate concern, which he presented to the Lord: *"Lord GOD, what will You give me, seeing I go childless?"(v. 2).* In the times of Abram, going childless meant his legacy would fade away, for "heirship is based upon sonship."[10]

At this time in Abram's life, he would have to leave all his possessions and honors to his trusted servant, who would become his heir by adoption. However, God, in His sovereignty, knew that He would make a covenant with Abram and have a relationship with his descendants even after the sins of Adam and Eve, the generations of Noah, and the Tower of Babel—therefore, God would give Abram the "son of promise" (see Galatians 4:22–23).

God's timing was crucial—He would wait until both Abram and Sarai were outside of their childbearing years (Hebrews 11:12). In doing so, God manifested His never-ending faithfulness and His miracle-working power once more. Just when Abram's dream seemed absolutely impossible—God showed up! Remember this truth: when you are down to nothing, God is up to something.

In answer to Abram's deeper-rooted fear, Jewish scholars teach that the Lord comforted Abram through two prophetic experiences—in a vision and by speech:

He brought him outside and said [God's Spoken Word], "Look [physical vision] now toward heaven, and count the stars if you are able to number them." And He said [God's Spoken Word] to him, "So shall your descendants be [prophetic vision]." (Genesis 15:5)

The combination of these two events (physical and prophetic visions) confirmed that God's promise of protection would not only comfort Abram but also his descendants whenever they were confronted with impending danger.[11] How did Abram respond? Abram *"believed in the LORD, and He [God] accounted it to him [Abram] for righteousness" (v. 6).*

Abram did not allow Almighty God power to be limited by his own natural mind; rather, he had confidence in God's Spoken Word—God said it, and he believed it! Abram grew both in his faith *in* God and in his obedience *to* God. And the Almighty acknowledged Abram's great trust with a binding and unbreakable covenant.

Derek Prince describes God's next step perfectly: "The final commitment of God to do whatever He's promised is in a covenant. Once God has made a covenant, there is nothing more He can do to commit Himself."[12] The interaction between God and Abram in the next few verses led to a remarkable covenant ceremony that stood at the time it was made, still stands today, and will stand throughout eternity.

Remember this truth: God will always perform what He promises.

TYPES OF COVENANTS

In order to appreciate the magnitude of the irrevocable agreement God was about to enter into with Abram, we must have a clear understanding of the types of covenants found in the Bible. First, God's covenants are *literal*, and any covenant pertaining to Israel is *eternal*, with the exception of one—the Mosaic covenant, which was to continue only until the coming of the "Promised Seed,"[13] our Lord and Savior Jesus Christ.

There are two forms of covenants: conditional and unconditional.

A conditional covenant is a two-sided agreement in which a proposal is made between two parties and is characterized by a qualifier—"if you will, then I will." Man's compliance or failure to keep his part of the agreement may result in either his blessing or his curse.

There are several covenants presented in Scripture, some major, some minor; however, I will refer to only six. Two of these are conditional: the covenant with Adam in the Garden of Eden (Genesis 2:15–17) and the covenant made between God and the nation of Israel at Mount Sinai (Exodus 19–24).

An unconditional covenant is a one-sided promise and solely depends upon the integrity of God for its fulfillment. It is a sovereign act of God. In it, He completely commits Himself to bring to pass specific blessings and conditions for the people with whom He has made a covenant.

As mentioned in the beginning of this chapter regarding Genesis 12:1–3, this type of covenant is characterized by the principle of God's *"I will,"* which emphasizes His resolve to do as He said.

There may be terms God asks the participant to meet within the covenant, but they *do not* alter the unconditional character of it, nor are they the basis of God fulfilling His promises of blessings. An unconditional covenant is made possible by the unmerited grace of God.[14]

The remaining four covenants are conditional:

- Noahic (Genesis 9:1–17)
- Abrahamic (Genesis 12:1–2, 7; 13:14–17; 15:1–21; 17:1–21; 22:15–18)
- Davidic (2 Samuel 7:8–16)
- New (Hebrews 8:6–13)

COVENANTS WITH ISRAEL

The unique nature of the unconditional covenants with Israel, aside from their literal meaning, is that they either have been or will be fulfilled; therefore, an unconditional covenant is in no way restricted or altered by time.

Once sealed, the contents of the covenant may go into effect immediately while some may go into effect in the near future, or certain provisions may come to fruition in the distant prophetic future that has yet to be fulfilled.

Another distinct nature of unconditional covenants is that they were exclusively entered into with one people:

> . . . who are Israelites, to whom pertain the adoption, the glory, the covenants, the giving of the law, the service of God, and the promises; of whom are the fathers and from whom, according to the flesh, Christ came, who is over all, the eternally blessed God. Amen. (Romans 9:4–5)

Paul underscored this fact in Ephesians 2:11–12 by declaring that Gentiles were considered *"strangers from the covenants."* Our hope as Christians is found in the following verse, *"But now in Christ Jesus you who once were far off have been made near by the blood of Christ"* (v. 13).

It is also important to reemphasize that these unconditional covenants were not and will not be withdrawn or revoked because of Israel's disobedience. These covenants are solely dependent upon the faithfulness of God for fulfillment.

ABRAHAMIC COVENANT

Now we arrive to Abram's vision of Genesis 15, which would lead to what is known as the Abrahamic covenant. This covenant is an eternal covenant—a binding and unconditional contract between God and man (Genesis 17:7, 13, 19; 1 Chronicles 16:17; Psalm 105:10).

The word *covenant* in Hebrew, *b'rit*, means a formal agreement or pact. The Hebrew verb meaning to "seal a covenant" literally translates "to cut." To "cut a covenant" implies the shedding of blood as part of the confirmation of the agreement.

God chose to "cut covenant" with Abram in this manner, which conveys the magnitude of the pact they entered into. If the Abrahamic covenant is the foundation of the things to come, then the knowledge of its details is essential to understanding its message.

> So He said to him, "Bring Me a three-year-old heifer, a three-year-old female goat, a three-year-old ram, a turtledove, and a young pigeon." Then he brought all these to Him and cut them in two, down the middle, and placed each piece opposite the other; but he did not cut the birds in two. And when the vultures came down on the carcasses, Abram drove them away.
>
> Now when the sun was going down, a deep sleep fell upon Abram; and behold, horror and great darkness fell upon him. Then He said to Abram: "Know certainly that your descendants will be strangers in a land that is not theirs, and will serve them, and they will afflict them four hundred years. And also the nation whom they serve I will judge; afterward they shall come out with great possessions. Now as for you, you shall go to your

fathers in peace; you shall be buried at a good old age. But in the fourth generation they shall return here, for the iniquity of the Amorites is not yet complete."

And it came to pass, when the sun went down and it was dark, that behold, there appeared a smoking oven and a burning torch that passed between those pieces. On the same day the LORD *made a covenant with Abram, saying:*

"To your descendants I have given this land, from the river of Egypt to the great river, the River Euphrates—the Kenites, the Kenezzites, the Kadmonites, the Hittites, the Perizzites, the Rephaim, the Amorites, the Canaanites, the Girgashites, and the Jebusites." (Genesis 15:9–21)

Let us study certain key words and phrases used within the covenant to paint a word picture of what transpired between God and Abram. Jewish scholars state that the covenant which is recorded in Genesis 15 is a "permanent bond between two parties, symbolizing a friendship so close that they are like a single body and that each is as responsible for the other as for himself. . . . The two parties entering into the covenant are to be as one body, each ready to risk danger if necessary to help the other."[15]

- *"Bring Me"*: signifies that the sacrifice belonged exclusively to God and would have the status of an irrevocable oath.
- *"a three-year-old heifer, a three-year-old female goat, a three-year-old ram"*:
  1. Both Christian and Jewish scholars agree that the three years of each animal's life reflect the perfection of the sacrifice at its peak of maturity and strength.
  2. God commanded Abram to take the animals to seal the covenant and to give the additional status of an

irrevocable oath. The sacrifices were God's symbols of atonement. They represented the offerings that God would one day establish for the Israelites to make amends for their sins.

3. The heifer is referenced several times in Scripture as a sacrificial offering for the purification from sin as mandated by God through the Mosaic law (Numbers 19:1–10; 1 Samuel 6:7–12; Job 21:10; Isaiah 7:21). The heifer was sacrificed on the most sacred of all the Hebrew holidays—the Day of Atonement (Yom Kippur). (Leviticus 16; Numbers 29:7–11).

4. Similarly, the goat signified the sin offering presented by an individual on the Day of Atonement (Leviticus 4:28; 16:15).

5. The ram is linked to the Levitical guilt offerings connected with consecration (Leviticus 8:1–10).[16]

- *"a turtledove, and a young pigeon"*: The turtledove is one of the smaller members of a species of birds also referred to as pigeons. Genesis 15:9 is the first time a turtledove is referred to in Scripture. Later, Levitical law would dictate that a pair of turtledoves or young pigeons was allowed as a sacrificial substitute for those who were too poor to provide a lamb.[17] A pair of these birds was offered by Mary in sacrifice at her purification (Luke 2:24).

  Because of its habit of pairing for life and its fidelity to its mate, the turtledove was a symbol of purity and an appropriate offering for the Abrahamic Covenant. Biblical scholars compare these birds to Israel because, like doves, they would be preyed upon by their enemies and yet would remain loyal to the God of Abraham.

The regular migration of the turtledove and its return in the spring is mentioned by Jeremiah and King Solomon and is significant to prophecy:

Even the stork in the heavens knows her appointed times; and the turtledove, the swift, and the swallow observe the time of their coming. But My people do not know the judgment of the LORD. (Jeremiah 8:7)

For lo, the winter is past, the rain is over and gone. The flowers appear on the earth; the time of singing has come, and the voice of the turtledove is heard in our land. (Song of Solomon 2:11–12)

The dove is described in Scripture as a symbol of the Holy Spirit, and I believe, after my personal in-depth study of Scripture over the last sixty years, that the Lord will return to His own in the spring when *"the voice of the turtledove is heard in our land."*

- *"cut them in two, down the middle, and placed each piece opposite the other"*: God is setting the stage for a "covenant-cutting" ceremony, similar to many contemporary cultures of the Near East. The sacred nature of this bond was attested to by the shedding of lifeblood.

- *"when the vultures came down on the carcasses, Abram drove them away"*: The birds of prey symbolize the nations of the world that would attempt to assimilate the seed of Abraham into foreign cultures and beliefs from generation to generation. In extreme cases, these enemies would also attempt to utterly exterminate Abraham's seed. By driving the predators away, Abram was protecting the spiritual tie between the Almighty and the future of Israel.

- *"a deep sleep fell upon Abram; and behold, horror and great darkness fell upon him"*: Abram's mind needed to be free to grasp the radical revelation he was about to receive. God isolated Abram's thoughts, bringing him into a "wholly yielded state."[18] This "deep sleep" was the same sleep with which God sedated Adam in the Garden of Eden to create Eve. In this case, the "deep sleep" prophetically reveals the birth of a nation (Israel) that would ultimately bring forth God's Only Begotten Son.

  Pink asserts that God further showed Abram he would not inherit the land during his natural life; instead, he must go to the grave and in due time inherit it together with the Promised Seed. In his awaking from this sleep, Abram received a "veiled promise of resurrection from the dead."[19] Bottom line: the way to Abram's inheritance was through death and resurrection— a type and shadow of our own redemption through the death and resurrection of Christ.

  This deep sleep also represented the tribulations that lay ahead for Abram's descendants. God revealed to Abram the darkness and bitterness of the future Hebrew exiles through the fourfold expressions of "horror," "darkness," "great," and "fell." This manifestation, which overtook Abram's spirit, referred to the four ancient kingdoms listed in the book of Daniel (chapters 2 and 7).

  The "horror" depicts Babylon, "darkness" represents Media-Persia, "great" refers to Greece, and "fell" symbolizes Rome. God forewarned Abram that if Israel sinned, the people would be kept in subjugation and exiled from their land by these

kingdoms. The Lord then plainly told Abram that their possession of the Promised Land would still come, but only after
their Egyptian exile.[20]

- *"your descendants will be strangers in a land . . . and will serve*
  them, and they will afflict them four hundred years. And also the
  nation whom they serve I will judge; afterward they shall come
  out with great possessions. . . . Now as for you, you shall go to
  your fathers in peace. . . . But in the fourth generation they shall
  return here": These verses contain a sevenfold prophecy, all
  of which would be literally fulfilled. It foretells the time of
  Abram's descendants in the land of Egypt, their bondage, their
  redemption, and their return to Canaan.

  1. You will be strangers in another country (Egypt) (Psalms
     105:11–15).
  2. You will be slaves in Egypt (Exodus 1:8–14).
  3. You will be oppressed four hundred years (Exodus
     12:40–42).
  4. God will judge Egypt (Acts 7:6–8).
  5. Israel will come out with many possessions (Exodus
     3:21–22; 12:35–36).
  6. Abram will not live through this period of slavery
     (Genesis 25:7–8).
  7. In the fourth generation (four hundred years), Israel
     will return to the land (Exodus 6:26).

The Bible provides all the proof necessary to show how
each of these prophecies was fulfilled, as illustrated by the
above scriptures and many more, such as the following: Exodus
6:16–26 gives the genealogy of Levi, the third son of Jacob,

representing the first generation of those who entered Egypt. The second generation was Levi's son Kohath. The third generation was Amram, the son of Kohath, and the fourth generation was Aaron and Moses, who were described as *"the same Aaron and Moses to whom the LORD said, 'Bring out the children of Israel from the land of Egypt according to their armies'"* (Exodus 6:26).

- *"Now as for you, you shall go to your fathers in peace; you shall be buried at a good old age"*: The Lord was telling Abram that he would be spared all of the trials and tribulations that his people would endure.

- *"But in the fourth generation they shall return here, for the iniquity of the Amorites is not yet complete"*: The Amorites represented all the Canaanite nations. God revealed to Abram that the slavery of the Hebrews in Egypt, their exodus, and their conquest of the Promised Land were part of His long-term plan.

  It would take four hundred years for the sins of the Amorites to reach such magnitude until God saw fit to expel them from the land. Joshua's subsequent invasion of the Amorite nations was not an act of aggression but a fulfillment of God's promise. Genesis 15: *"And the LORD drove out from before us all the people, including the Amorites who dwelt in the land"* (Joshua 24:18).

- *"there appeared a smoking oven and a burning torch that passed between those pieces"*: The burning torch symbolized the glory of the Lord. Only God passed between the pieces, indicating that it was *His covenant* and He would assume full responsibility for its administration—Abram's only requirement was to believe.[21]

Think of it—the great I AM was making a covenant with *Himself*, based on His own integrity! The fulfillment of the covenant had nothing to do with the faithfulness of the Jewish people. Replacement theologians present the concept that this covenant was broken because of Israel's failure to keep it; therefore, the Church has replaced Israel in the economy of God. Nothing could be further from the truth.

God never lies or changes His mind; therefore, this irrevocable covenant depends solely on God fulfilling His part. Nothing man can do or say will ever change this eternal promise between God, Abraham, and the land—the ratification of Abraham's covenant is as "sure as the ongoing life of the Lord."[22]

- *"On the same day the LORD made a covenant with Abram"*: Here the Lord confirmed the boundaries of the Promised Land grant.[23]

THE ISHMAEL BLESSING—
WHO OWNS THE LAND?

The most pressing geopolitical crisis of our time is the Arab-Israeli dispute over who owns the Promised Land of Israel. The chasm between the Jews and Arabs began after Abram, at the urging of doubting Sarai, took Hagar as his concubine. Hagar immediately conceived Ishmael, and soon after, Hagar and Sarai began to despise each other (Genesis 16:5–6).

Abram's regretful decision to follow his wife's prodding, which led to the birth of Ishmael by Hagar, created enmity between the two women. This animosity is the root cause of the hostility that exists between Abraham's descendants (Arabs and Jews) to this day.

Some Arabs believe that because they too are the seed of Abraham, the Promised Land belongs to them. It is true that the Arab nations have Abraham as their father through Ishmael, and it is also true that he loved his firstborn and wanted him to be included in the covenant, pleading to God, *"Oh, that Ishmael might live before You!" (Genesis 17:18).*

How did God respond to Abraham's request? His answer was instant and resolute: *"No, Sarah your wife shall bear you a son, and you shall call his name Isaac; I will establish My covenant with him for an everlasting covenant, and with his descendants after him" (Genesis 17:19).*

Paul reiterated God's position in Galatians 4:

Now we, brethren, as Isaac was, are children of promise. But, as he who was born according to the flesh then persecuted him who was born according to the Spirit, even so it is now. Nevertheless what does the Scripture say? "Cast out the bondwoman and her son, for the son of the bondwoman shall not be heir with the son

*of the freewoman." So then, brethren, we are not children of the
bondwoman but of the free. (vv. 28–31)*

The Lord honored Abraham's request to bless Ishmael, for the
Bible records:

*And as for Ishmael, I have heard thee: Behold, I have blessed
him, and will make him fruitful . . . twelve princes shall he
beget, and I will make him a great nation. But my covenant
will I establish with Isaac, which Sarah shall bear unto thee at
this set time in the next year." (Genesis 17:20–21)*

Fast-forward to the twenty-first century, when the twelve princes
of Ishmael became part of the OPEC nations, which is one of the
wealthiest oil conglomerates on planet Earth. They are truly blessed
of God because of Abraham. The world's most heated geopolitical issue can be explained in two simple sentences: *One father had
two sons. One inherited the real estate, and the other inherited the oil.*
When you go to Israel, you are blessing Isaac; when you fill your car
with fuel, you are blessing Ishmael.

THE ULTIMATE SACRIFICE

During the most dramatic scene of Abram's vision, the Almighty's
divine presence, represented by a *"burning torch,"* passed between
the cut halves of the sacrificial animals. It was at this time that God
chose to bind Himself to a unilateral obligation. This one divine
act constituted the ratification of the everlasting covenant He made
with Abram.

*And it came to pass, when the sun went down and it was dark,
that behold, there appeared a smoking oven and a burning torch*

that passed between those pieces. On the same day the Lord made
a covenant with Abram. (Genesis 15:17–18)

Abram was not required to perform this ritual for he had no obligation under the terms of the covenant. The *"smoking oven and a burning torch"* symbolized *one* single blazing fire—the Shekinah glory of God. This same *"cloud and thick darkness"* would appear *"as the smoke of a furnace"* at the revelation of the Torah (God's Word) to Moses in Exodus 19, and the *"torch"* was the *"fire"* that manifested on Mount Sinai (Deuteronomy 5:4). The Great I Am, Creator of heaven and earth, was the promising party within the covenant, and His oath was unconditional. This divine deed reflects one of the most beautiful truths in Scripture: God is the great Promise Keeper.

THE SIGN OF THE COVENANT

After thirteen years of silence, Abram was reminded that he must come to the end of himself before God could go further in sealing His covenant with him. By addressing Himself as *"I am the Almighty God"* or *"El Shaddai,"* He was pledging the covenant's fulfillment (Genesis 17:1).

This is the first time the term *El Shaddai* is used to refer to God in Scripture because He was and is sufficient in Himself to fulfill all that He promised. God would multiply Abram abundantly. He was and is the Life Giver who would restore reproductive ability to Abram and Sarai, for they were as good as dead!

Abram repented and demonstrated sincere humility and profound reverence by falling on his face in the presence of the Lord (v. 3). The next step in the fulfillment of Abram's divine destiny was the changing of his name. God gave Abram a new name—he would no longer be known as Abram or patriarch, but now he would be addressed as Abraham—the father of a multitude of nations (v. 5).

Think of it: every time Abraham spoke his own name or heard it spoken, he would be reminded of God's eternal promise.

When Abraham was ninety-nine years old and Sarah was eighty-nine, the Lord established the sign of the covenant through the act of circumcision. This physical symbol of Abraham's inclusion in God's irrevocable promise was such a significant milestone in the history of the Jewish people that the Torah precisely records it as occurring 2,047 years after creation.[24] His circumcision was a required preparatory procedure before the miraculous conception of Isaac, the "son of promise," could occur.

It was at this time that God reaffirmed His seven "I wills":

I will make you exceedingly fruitful; and I will make nations of you, and kings shall come from you. And I will establish My covenant between Me and you and your descendants after you in their generations, for an everlasting covenant, to be God to you and your descendants after you. Also I give to you and your descendants after you the land in which you are a stranger, all the land of Canaan, as an everlasting possession; and I will be their God. . . .

Then God said: "No, Sarah your wife shall bear you a son, and you shall call his name Isaac; I will establish My covenant with him for an everlasting covenant, and with his descendants after him. . . . But My covenant I will establish with Isaac, whom Sarah shall bear to you at this set time next year." (Genesis 17:6–8, 19, 21)

Remember this truth: God's promises are prophetically accomplished facts from the moment He speaks them into existence and are fully realized at His selected time. God's words are so sure in their fulfillment that when He declares in Genesis 17:5, *"I have made you a father of many nations*" and then again, in verse 7: "*to you and your descendants*"—it is as good as done!

Abraham's son Isaac, whom God clearly blessed, inherited the covenant in Genesis 26. It was then given to Jacob and his descendants in Genesis 32. Eventually, these descendants collectively became the "*children of Israel*" *(Exodus 6:26)* or the Jewish people, and the Promised Land is the land of Israel.

Please understand that the Abrahamic covenant is not just another relic of antiquity; it is the taproot to the Old Testament and the fulfillment of the New Testament—it is alive and well. J. Dwight Pentecost described God's covenant with Abraham and his descendants as the pillar on which the Holy Scripture stands:

> The eternal aspects of this covenant [Abrahamic], which guarantee Israel a permanent national existence, perpetual title to the land of promise, and the certainty of material and spiritual blessings through Christ, and guarantee Gentile nations a share in these blessings, determine the whole eschatological program of the Word of God.[25]

Abraham is the "*father of all those who believe*" *(Romans 4:11)*, and this fact is the foundation of the Judeo-Christian bond. The land of Israel, with its God-given boundaries, belongs exclusively to His Promised Seed. The Abrahamic covenant made by Almighty God with the Jewish people is not only eternal; it cannot be altered or amended by governments or mankind. And because of this certainty, Israel lives today, tomorrow, and forever, for as King David declared:

> *And who is like Your people, like Israel, the one nation on the earth whom God went to redeem for Himself as a people, to*

make for Himself a name—and to do for Yourself great and awesome deeds for Your land—before Your people whom You redeemed for Yourself from Egypt, the nations, and their gods? For You have made Your people Israel Your very own people forever; and You, LORD, have become their God. (2 Samuel 7:23–24)

The greatest legacy of the Abrahamic covenant is that it is the cornerstone of Israel's eternal relationship to God—all other Bible promises are based on this truth.

CHAPTER 11

DANIEL'S VISION— THE FOUR KINGDOMS

. . . and Daniel had understanding in all visions and dreams.
(Daniel 1:17)

F rom the beginning of time until we enter the dimension called eternity, where time shall be no more, Israel and the Jewish people have been and will continue to be God's prophetic timepiece. When major events take place that determine the destiny of mankind, God uses His Covenant nation to alert the world.

Many brilliant minds have devoted their life's work to the study of ancient biblical prophecies, the works of Christian and Jewish scholars, and even the prognostications of secular sources to better understand the time line of the End of Days. One such scientific genius was Sir Isaac Newton (1643–1727).

Newton is credited with astrophysical, mathematical, and scientific findings that include the invention of calculus, the construction of the first reflecting telescope, and of course the discovery of the laws of motion and gravity. However, few know that Newton was also a prominent Christian theologian who spent much time studying Bible prophecy.

He applied his unique scientific approach to studying Scripture, the Hebrew language, and the teachings of the Talmud, which is a compilation of Jewish oral law and stories. To Newton, science and faith were part of the same domain. He theorized that the Scriptures provided a "code" to the natural world. Newton believed that the study of God's Word was a type of science that, if properly interpreted, could predict what was to come.

One of the Hebrew texts Newton studied was the book of Daniel. He concluded that among the biblical prophets, Daniel was most distinct in order of time and should be used as the key to studying the End of Days.[1]

Josephus said that Daniel "not only predicted the future, like the other prophets, but specified when the events would happen."[2]

In order to better comprehend Daniel's writings, it is important to know a little of what happened to the Jewish people up to his time in history and how these events specifically affected Daniel's life. Therefore, the following is a simple overview of 1,555 years in Israel's history.[3]

ABRAHAM TO DANIEL

Some 290 years after God made the covenant with Abraham, the Jews entered into 430 years of Egyptian bondage.[4] Their captivity ended with their well-known exodus of 1440 BCE, when the Lord provided deliverance through His miraculous parting of the Red Sea. After a forty-year trek in the wilderness (Numbers 14:33; Exodus 16:35) under Moses's leadership, the mantle was handed to Joshua, who led the Israelites into a highly celebrated period in

Jewish history, beginning with their crossing of the Jordan into the Promised Land (Genesis 15:16; Joshua 3:1).

After Joshua came the golden age of Israel, which reached the pinnacle of its glory under the rule of King David (2 Samuel 5:3–3) and King Solomon (1 Kings 1:38–39). However, dissension reigned after the death of Solomon, dividing the nation of Israel into two parts: the Northern and the Southern Kingdoms (1 Kings 12:16, 19). This discord between the two kingdoms led to their turbulent and bloodstained decline, resulting in the eventual fall of Jerusalem in 586 BCE (2 Kings 24:10–16).

The northern ten tribes (Kingdom of Israel) chose national idolatry over obedience to God's Word. Consequently, they were the first to be captured by the Assyrians in 722 BCE. Then, in the course of time, the remaining two southern tribes (Kingdom of Judah) also embraced pagan worship and were conquered by the Babylonians in 586 BCE. This subjugation initiated King Nebuchadnezzar's forced deportation of the Jewish captives into Babylon (2 Kings 25:9–19; 2 Chronicles 36:18–19; Jeremiah 52:12–25; Daniel 1:1–21). These tragic events marked the end of the nation of Israel's first commonwealth.

Still, amid the carnage and decline of the Jewish nation, the seeds of hope remained alive for Israel's rebirth. Although the Assyrians completely absorbed the Northern Kingdom into its vast empire, the Babylonians chose not to colonize the conquered Kingdom of Judah. This meant Nebuchadnezzar permitted the Jewish remnant to stay in their land, maintain their identity, and continue to worship the One True God. Only the Creator of the Universe could have orchestrated this unique situation, guaranteeing the preservation of the roots of Judaism.

Therefore, this chapter in history, which recorded Israel as a nation—beginning with God's covenant promise with Abraham to the glorious reign of King David—had ended. What followed were seventy years of chaos and anguish for the Jewish people in Babylon. This significant time in Israel's history is simply referred to as the Exile.

THE EXILE

Thus Daniel continued [in Babylon] until the first year of King Cyrus. (Daniel 1:21)

The Assyrians were strategic warfare experts and were viciously aggressive in their dominance over their captured territories. They would forcibly remove the educated and influential upper class of the conquered nation and relocate them to other parts of their massive empire. By doing so, they ensured that the people in the seized lands would remain pacified.

Subsequently, the Assyrians would bring their own citizens to the conquered territory to settle there, which in turn displaced the captured remnant, triggering a domino effect as they lost their land and culture. Through this well-executed tactic of forced relocation and assimilation, the conquered people lost their God-given identity.

This integration policy caused the tribes of Israel that were part of the Northern Kingdom to scatter in small numbers throughout the massive Assyrian Empire. These peoples are referred to as the "Ten Lost Tribes of Israel" because they systematically disappeared from the pages of history. They silently and submissively assimilated into various ethnic communities throughout the Middle East, resulting in the abandonment of their Jewish identities, including Hebrew names, culture, and faith.

Unlike the Assyrians, when the Babylonians conquered the Kingdom of Judah, they relocated over ten thousand Israelites to *one* location: Babylon. Here the Jewish people were allowed to live in a separate community, providing them the opportunity to retain their identity and their religion, which was based on their belief in the God of Abraham, Isaac, and Jacob.[5]

After the siege of Jerusalem, Nebuchadnezzar confiscated many priceless temple implements, but he also took a far more valuable treasure: Judah's finest and brightest youth. These young men were taught by their fathers to be loyal to the Lord and observant to His laws. This biblically mandated instruction (Proverbs 3:3) would prove to be crucial for their survival during their time of testing in Babylonian captivity.

Nebuchadnezzar had no interest in destroying the Kingdom of Judah, though he did demand allegiance and subservience. He made great efforts in providing a Babylonian education in culture and religion for his elite captives. Nebuchadnezzar's calculated goal was to reprogram these young and bright Jewish minds through a three-year indoctrination within the "king's college."

Later, he planned to resettle these newly trained Hebrew leaders into the conquered territories as official representatives of the Babylonian government. With this deliberate strategy, it would be nearly impossible for the Kingdom of Judah to survive their future generation's assimilation into a pagan society.

Nebuchadnezzar's premeditated plan of integration, along with his suppression of the oppressed remnant, should have rationally led to Israel's extinction. However, we must remember that Israel was God's nation through His irrevocable covenant with Abraham and nothing—including displacement, integration and oppression—would erase what God had put in motion.

Within the despair of the Exile, the Great Architect of the ages was not only creating a path to survival for His chosen people; He was also laying the foundation for the imminent restoration of the nation of Israel. To help accomplish these tasks, God anointed and prepared a young man for royal ministry within King Nebuchadnezzar's college—Daniel, a Jewish captive from Jerusalem, who would become the "prince of the prophets."

THE BRIDGE TO ETERNITY

Daniel modestly described himself as a Jewish prisoner of war, a servant in Babylonian captivity. However, Daniel was so much more: he was an advisor to kings, the interpreter of dreams, a model of faith and courage, and a prophet of the future conquest and redemption. Most importantly, the accounts of his visionary insight would become one of the vital keys to understanding the End of Days for all generations.

Daniel, a contemporary of Jeremiah and Ezekiel, was credited with writing the book titled with his name, which in Hebrew means, "God is my judge" (Daniel 8:1; 9:2, 20; 10:2). Jesus trusted Daniel's insights by referring to them in His Olivet Discourse, which is recorded in Matthew 24, and His teaching on the signs of the times and the end of the age in Luke 21.

The events and prophecies presented within Daniel's writings were meant to encourage and comfort the Jewish people in exile through hope in the God of Israel. Jewish scholars teach that the "divine hand" was preparing the way for the exiles when He placed Daniel in the academy of the king's court. His writings, along with Christ's Olivet Discourse and the book of Revelation, would prove to be the anchors of the bridge to eternity for future generations.

A MATTER OF FAITH

The book of Daniel is divided into two parts. Part A is composed of chapters 1 through 6, which record Daniel's life and service in Babylon. Here, six vivid stories are presented in the third person and tell of Daniel's time of testing and God's miraculous intervention. These accounts reflect the faithfulness of God and attest to the righteous character of Daniel and his three friends: Shadrach, Meshach, and Abed-Nego.

Part B includes chapters 7 through 12 and chronicles four visions or revelations given to Daniel by God or His messenger. These narratives are set in first person and depict the Great Statue, the Four Beasts, the Seventy Weeks, and Daniel's Final Vision. Their message speaks of Israel's future, most of which has been fulfilled, and the End of Days, which has yet to be fully realized.

All that Daniel detailed in his writings was a testimony to the supernatural power of Israel's God. Everything that happened to Daniel and his friends while in exile was intended to separate them from God. Yet because of the Word embedded in their hearts, they remained loyal to the Almighty, and this faith-based allegiance became a beacon of light for generations to come.

For example, shortly after the four entered the king's college, their names were changed, a normal practice for Babylonian captives. The four young men were given Hebrew names at birth, which were derived from the names of God, while their new Babylonian names epitomized pagan gods. Daniel's name was changed to Belteshazzar, meaning "prince of the king." The Babylonians may have changed their names, but they could not change their commitment to Jehovah God. This test and others like it only galvanized their faith in the One True God of Israel.

Additionally, part of the daily regimen for those in the king's care included eating only the finest foods, but there was a problem— these items were first offered to idols as was the custom.[6] By consuming these delicacies, one would give allegiance to the gods of Babylon and not the God of Abraham.

Daniel and his friends refused the pagan offerings and persuaded the eunuch assigned to them to provide a simple diet of water and vegetables. Daniel and his young companions did not enter into a short-term fast—they abstained from eating meat for the duration of their captivity. God honored their allegiance and, inexplicable to their captors, their appearance was healthier than those who ate the rich royal foods offered to pagan gods.

Daniel never measured his God by the size of his problem; he had faith that the Lord would provide for his well-being in any situation. And for their faith, God rewarded Daniel and his friends: to Shadrach, Meshach, and Abed-Nego, God gave wisdom and knowledge; and to Daniel, He gave the gift of prophecy (Daniel 1:17).

Ask yourself these questions: Why were Daniel and his friends so adamant about remaining loyal to the God of Israel while in Babylon? Why were they willing to stand before a powerful king in a foreign land and boldly hold to their convictions at the risk of death?

The answer is simple: their fathers had faithfully taught them that there was only One True God. This doctrine has been the sacred foundation of the Jewish people since the genesis of time: *"Hear, O Israel: The LORD our God, the LORD is one!" (Deuteronomy 6:4).*

God chose Abraham to be the father and founder of Israel for one single reason:

> For I have known him, in order that he may command his children and his household after him, that they keep the way of the LORD, to do righteousness and justice. (Genesis 18:19)

Daniel and his friends recognized that the false gods of Nebuchadnezzar had the government's backing but not the approval of the Almighty.

By the same logic, why have our college and university campuses become cesspools of deception, rebellion, treason, and anti-Semitism? Why does anarchy reign in the streets of our cities? Why are there daily reports of mind-numbing acts of violence and murderous mayhem throughout America and the nations of the world? Why is idol worship rampant throughout the global media outlets? Why does this generation love itself more than its neighbor?

The answer to these questions is also simple: we no longer teach our children the ways of the Lord, nor do we seek His approval. Today's fathers do not impart the truth of God's Word into their families, nor do they speak blessings over their lives, leaving them defenseless and exposed to the floodgates of evil. In fact, many of today's fathers are absent from their homes—either physically, spiritually, or both.

Derek Prince describes the cultural downward spiral resulting from this parental and authoritarian neglect: "Men have failed in their basic responsibility and women have taken over the male role. The inevitable outcome, whether in a family, nation or civilization, can be summed up in one word: *confusion*."[7]

Fathers and mothers of this generation must return to the moral and spiritual instruction of their children, encouraged by these words from the Bible: *"Train up a child in the way he should go, and when he is old he will not depart from it" (Proverbs 22:6)*. Instead of teaching the Word of God to our children, we have taught them to worship the gods of our modern world, to include superheroes, pro athletes, actors, reality stars, and singing idols.

Many parents do not teach their children to make godly choices or allow them to suffer the consequence of bad ones. Today's generation is simply not held accountable. We have also failed to pass on the work ethic that previous generations passed to us. As a result, today's youth are looking for entitlements and handouts instead of taking pride in earning a living.

Remember this truth: our country's future does *not* depend on what the federal government does for our children, but it *does* depend on what we do, as parents, to teach our children the ways of God.

> *The fear of the LORD is the beginning of wisdom, and the knowl-edge of the Holy One is understanding. (Proverbs 9:10)*

While many of today's university students are demanding "safe spaces" to shelter their hurt feelings, Christians United for Israel (CUFI) is training brave young college campus advocates through-out America to stand up for the nation of Israel.[8]

These students are taught the importance of obeying the bibli-cal mandate to support Israel and the Jewish people through pro-grams such as the CUFI on Campus Bonhoeffer Fellowship. These same young men and women courageously stand on the front lines against the rising tide of anti-Semitism on their campuses—they are the young Daniels of this generation. They have discovered what the Lord requires of all of us:

> *He has shown you, O man, what is good; and what does the LORD require of you but to do justly, to love mercy, and to walk humbly with your God. (Micah 6:8)*

Daniel defied the king's commands to stop praying to God, and he faced death in the lions' den (Daniel 6:16). Shadrach, Meshach, and Abed-Nego were willing to walk into the fiery furnace instead of bowing to the golden image commissioned by Nebuchadnezzar (Daniel 3:21). Why? Because they believed that no matter the cir-cumstance, their God was able to deliver them. Since childhood, they had been trained in His mandates, which shaped in them an unequivocal faith that allowed them to prevail during times of trial.

My son, keep my words, and treasure my commands within you.
Keep my commands and live, and my law as the apple of your
eye. Bind them on your fingers; write them on the tablet of your
heart. (Proverbs 7:1–3)

Many of America's youth cannot withstand any form of testing. Instead, they have conformed to the current trends of this idolatrous society, losing their God-given identities as men and women, as citizens, and as Christians. Just as Daniel and the rest of Israel's elite youth were sent into Babylon's indoctrination program, so have the young minds of our generation been brainwashed with revisionist history and liberal Progressive propaganda wrapped in a package labeled "higher education." There is one stark difference: Daniel and his friends passed the test (Daniel 1:3–5, 19–20); the majority of our youth will not.

What can we do? We must launch a righteous revolution within our homes that begins with the father coming back into the God-given role of family leadership. We must disciple young mothers to stand in support of their husbands as together they lead their families. We must live by the following truth as we raise our children: *"The fear of the LORD is the beginning of wisdom, and the knowledge of the Holy One is understanding"* (Proverbs 9:10).

We must join in a righteous revolution that instills the Word of God into the hearts, minds, and souls of our children. It is the only way they will survive their time of testing. It is the only way the America we know will survive! Be assured that it is not a matter of *if* trials will come; it is only a matter of *when*!

Remember this truth: righteous power stems from righteous choices.

Daniel decided to stand with the Lord and not be tempted by

the greatest metropolis of his time, and God rewarded him with supernatural power. Daniel passed the test, and when it was time for him to graduate from the king's college, he was stronger in body and faith and had *"understanding in all visions and dreams" (Daniel 1:17)*. In short, Daniel became God's appointed messenger to his generation and for the future generations of the world.

The Lord of hosts rewarded the steadfast faith of this young sage by preparing him for far greater assignments. He would eventually serve as prime minister during Nebuchadnezzar's forty-four-year reign, and he would continue to serve as a highly respected and trusted leader under the rest of the Babylonian monarchs and subsequent rulers of the Medo-Persian Empire. Daniel continued his royal service "until the first year of King Cyrus" (Daniel 1:21).

Even though Daniel was trusted to lead the whole Medo-Persian Empire, I believe that one of Daniel's greatest missions was to show King Cyrus the two-hundred-year-old prophecies of Isaiah concerning the rebuilding of the temple and those of Jeremiah's foretelling the end of Babylonian captivity.

[The LORD] says of Cyrus, "He is My shepherd, and he shall perform all My pleasure, saying to Jerusalem, 'You shall be built,' and to the temple, 'Your foundation shall be laid.'" (Isaiah 44:28)

For thus says the LORD: After seventy years are completed at Babylon, I will visit you and perform My good word toward you, and cause you to return to this place. (Jeremiah 29:10)

Take a moment and imagine Daniel negotiating the liberation of his exiled brethren. It must have been an overwhelming joy for

Daniel to chart their path to redemption—a path that he himself would not walk.

THE OFFICE OF PROPHET AND SAGE

The word "prophet" or *navi* (nun-beit-yod-alef) in Hebrew is derived from the term *niv sefatayim* meaning "fruit of the lips," which emphasizes the prophet's role as a speaker.[9] While the gift of prophecy includes the capacity to see forthcoming events as revealed by God, a prophet exhibits far more qualities. The Bible portrays prophets as role models of righteousness; they are well learned and, most importantly, have a close relationship to God.

The Almighty appoints a prophet to speak on His behalf for the purpose of delivering His precise message or select teaching. It is the *Shekinah* or divine spirit of the Lord that rests upon a prophet or prophetess to accomplish the God-given task set before them.

The *Tanakh* or Hebrew Bible is composed of three sections: the Law (Torah), the Prophets (*Nevi'im*), and the Writings (*Ketuvim*). The book of Daniel is not included as part of the Prophets but rather the Writings. It is believed that Daniel had visions that were divinely inspired, and therefore he is considered a sage.[10]

Jewish scholars teach that there are two types of visions: prophecy and divine inspiration. A prophet studies the future and points out the opportunities for righteousness on life's journey. A sage looks into the past and shows how man can make way for God's healing presence and loving power in the choices he makes and the paths he follows. The prophet fortifies us with the gift of hope. The sage strengthens us with the gift of meaning.[11] Daniel did both.

He was led by divine inspiration and received power to take action, to speak wisdom, and to exhort. The book of Daniel includes visions and forthcoming revelations, which were not meant for the people of his time but were intended for future generations.[12] Daniel's writings, however, brought encouragement to his fellow captives and established positive examples of how to live the abundant life of a believer among unbelievers.

THE KING'S DREAM

Nebuchadnezzar favored Daniel and his three friends, keeping them within his palace until their appointed time. Four years after Daniel was taken captive, the king had a troubling dream that tormented him: *"Now in the second year of Nebuchadnezzar's reign, Nebuchadnezzar had dreams; and his spirit was so troubled that his sleep left him"* (Daniel 2:1). The king was so furious that none of his magicians, astrologers, or sorcerers could reveal and interpret his dream that he condemned them all to death—a sentence that would also include Daniel and his three friends.

Daniel learned of his imminent execution and requested more time to interpret the king's dream. He gathered his friends and went before God to ask for the meaning of the king's mysterious nightmare. The Almighty honored their request, and the *"secret was revealed to Daniel in a night vision"* (v. 19).

It is thought-provoking to note that the Lord sent a tormenting dream to a pagan king so that Daniel's supernatural powers could be revealed, establishing him as the voice of God in a godless society. There is no equal to the sovereign power and purpose of the Almighty!

I believe no chapter in the Bible is more detailed or extensive in presenting and understanding the things to come as the second chapter of Daniel. God's revelation produced a geopolitical panorama from Daniel's day to eternity. The king's dream was a symbolic prophecy depicting the future of the world.

Nebuchadnezzar's dream defines the theme of Daniel's book, which is "the superseding of the times of the Gentiles as rulers of the earth [specifically Israel] by an everlasting and universal kingdom which is to be established on earth by the God of Heaven which shall be everlasting and universal."[13]

I can see it now: The king sits on his throne, frozen with fear, sweat beads of suspense dripping from his face as he anticipates Daniel's next words. And there stands God's messenger, divinely inspired, confident in demeanor, strong in his faith, and bold in his courage as he enlightens this distraught ruler of Babylon's great empire.

Daniel presents God's divine revelation: The reign of Nebuchadnezzar's empire will be followed by four world empires, all of which will be destroyed by the "Stone cut out of a mountain without hands thus showing its supernatural origin."[14] Then God will establish a fifth kingdom that will endure forever.

Daniel describes the king's dream with exactness—a statue of a man composed of four metals (2:24–45). These metals symbolize the four Gentile empires that would sequentially rule over Israel, plus a fifth that would be established much later:

1. The head of gold represents the Babylonian Empire, which ruled 612–539 BCE.
2. The breast and crossed arms of silver is the Medo-Persian Empire, which would succeed Babylon in 539–332 BCE.
3. The belly and thighs of brass represent the Greeks, which followed the Medo-Persian rule in 332–63 BCE.
4. The legs of iron depict the Roman Empire, which ruled in 63 BCE–476 CE.
5. The feet and toes of iron and clay foreshadow the revised Roman Empire of the End of Days.

Daniel clearly describes the last portion of the king's dream speaks of a stone that destroys the metal statue:

Inasmuch as you saw that the stone was cut out of the mountain without hands, and that it broke in pieces the iron, the bronze, the clay, the silver, and the gold—the great God has made known to the king what will come to pass after this. The dream is certain, and its interpretation is sure. (Daniel 2:45)

The stone Daniel describes represents the Kingdom of God, which will suddenly appear, overrule, and destroy all earthly powers, no matter their strength. The Lord promised to strip the Gentiles of their domination over Israel, which they have had since Nebuchadnezzar conquered Zedekiah and destroyed Jerusalem in 586 BCE (2 Kings 25:4–9).

Can you imagine what the king felt when Daniel stood before him and clearly described every detail of his tormenting nightmare? Nebuchadnezzar immediately recognized that this young Hebrew had the accurate interpretation of the vivid image that haunted him. The king also acknowledged that Daniel's God was the *"God of gods,"* and as a reward for his service, Daniel and his three friends were promoted *"over the affairs of the province of Babylon"* (Daniel 2:46–49).

THE TIMES OF THE GENTILES

Daniel clearly described Gentile empires in his writings, and as I mentioned earlier, Jesus also referred to this period in His teachings. In Luke 21, the Rabbi from Nazareth was speaking to His followers about the signs of the times and the End of the Age: *"They will fall by the edge of the sword and will be taken as prisoners to all the nations.*

Jerusalem will be trampled on by the Gentiles until the times of the Gentiles are fulfilled" (v. 24 NIV). What was Jesus referencing?

The "times of the Gentiles" is the period of history when Gentile nations dominated the world—specifically Israel. Jesus declared that Jerusalem would be seized, its people dispersed, and then suffer subjugation under the rule of numerous Gentile nations. Their control would end with Jerusalem's reemergence. This prophecy was fulfilled when Jerusalem was reunified with the Covenant nation of Israel as an outcome of the Six Day War of 1967.

Once the "time of the Gentiles" ends, the messianic kingdom will arise and encompass the whole earth—and of His kingdom there will be no end (Isaiah 9:7; Daniel 2:44; 7:14; Luke 1:33).

VISION OF THE FOUR BEASTS

The last six chapters of the book of Daniel include visions and dreams, and the prophecies applicable to them. These visions and dreams occurred in the same time period of the first six chapters of the book and can find parallel imagery in both the books of Ezekiel (17:3) and Revelation (13:12).[15]

Daniel wrote down the relevant facts of his vision, which occurred fifty years after his exile and fourteen years before Babylon's fall (Daniel 7:1–8). This vision mirrors Nebuchadnezzar's dream, but with the use of animals. An important fact to note is that each of the nations represented in the great image of chapter 2 and the four beasts of chapter 7 were in force in Daniel's day and are still players on the world stage today.

In the first year of Belshazzar king of Babylon, Daniel had a dream and visions of his head while on his bed. Then he wrote down the dream, telling the main facts. Daniel spoke, saying,

"I saw in my vision by night, and behold, the four winds of heaven were stirring up the Great Sea." (Daniel 7:1–2)

Each of the beasts pictured in Daniel's vision represents four world powers and corresponds with the kingdoms of Nebuchadnezzar's image. The first beast is the lion (king of the animals) with an eagle's wings (king of the birds), each of which rightly represents the Babylonian Empire.

The second image is of a bear, symbolizing the Medes (ancient citizens of northwest Iran) and the Persians (modern-day Iran). The bear is raised on one side, indicating that the Persians had greater power than the Medes. The ribs in its mouth signify the three kingdoms that the Medo-Persians "devoured"—Babylon (part of modern-day Iraq), Lydia (part of modern-day Turkey), and Egypt.

The third beast is a swift leopard with four wings and four heads, representing Greece. The four wings symbolize the speed with which Alexander the Great conquered the entire known world. After Alexander's death, his kingdom was divided among his four generals, who led Macedonia (north central modern-day Greece), Egypt, Syria, and Thrace (parts of modern-day Turkey, Greece, and Bulgaria).[16]

The fourth and final beast is not named because he is incomparable to any other animal or human. This beast is described as *"dreadful and terrible, exceedingly strong" (Daniel 7:7)*. It has teeth of iron, which is the same metal that represented the Roman Empire in Nebuchadnezzar's image (Daniel 2:40). This beast also has ten horns; both the images in Daniel 2 and 7 represent a future kingdom with great power led by an evil ruler. These kingdoms will be reinvented as a form of New World Order, possibly evolving out of the European Union (Daniel 7:7).

Daniel then describes the "Ancient of Days" seated on His throne. This is God the Father, who will judge the kingdoms of this world (Daniel 7:9–10). Then Daniel witnesses *the Son of Man, coming in the clouds of heaven" (v. 13)*. This is Jesus Christ, our Blessed Redeemer, who will have dominion—He will rule the final kingdom that will last through eternity (vv. 13–14)!

DANIEL'S CALENDAR

Fast-forward: Daniel is now around eighty years old. According to several biblical time lines and dates associated with the Babylonian and Medo-Persian Empires, we can assume that he had been in Babylonian captivity for almost sixty years. Daniel was a faithful student of the Holy Scriptures before his exile and during, and was longing for the time when Jehovah would rebuild Jerusalem and its temple as He promised.[17] Daniel specifically reflected on Jeremiah's prophecy regarding the seventy years before Israel's redemption and their return to the holy city of Jerusalem:

This whole land will be a desolation and a horror, and these nations will serve the king of Babylon seventy years. (Jeremiah 25:11 NASB)

For thus says the LORD: After seventy years are completed at Babylon, I will visit you and perform My good word toward you, and cause you to return to this place. (Jeremiah 29:10)

Daniel believed that the time of Jeremiah's prophecy was ending, and so would Israel's Babylonian captivity. Yet there was no visible change in sight to confirm this promise. If I were Daniel, I would conclude that the sins of Israel had resulted in delaying or even annulling God's plan to return the Jews to Jerusalem. At this moment, he, like all believers, had a choice to make, lose hope or trust that the promise of the Lord would come to pass.

Daniel once again chose the safe haven of prayer in which to seek his answer. God the Father wants all His children to seek Him in prayer—to find refuge in prayer, to search for guidance and wisdom in prayer, and to hear His voice in prayer. Remember this truth: God's promises are often conditional to the actions of His people, and He has ordained prayer as one measure in which to communicate and accomplish His divine purpose.

I have always taught my congregation the importance of precise and detailed prayer. First, we must always pray according to God's Word, and second, we should pray with an exact and sincere regard for our need. This way when the provision comes, we have no doubt that it was God who answered our prayer. The Almighty is all-knowing, all-powerful, and ever-present, and He will give us the desires of our heart; however, He wants us to take the first step of faith through prayer.

Daniel presented an exemplary prayer that began with praise to God, repentance, and finally his specific petition for the restoration of his beloved Jerusalem (Daniel 9:4–19). Prayer and praise are the gateway to God the Father, and repentance is the key to answered prayer. Repentance has no doctrine or denomination—it is a gift for all mankind. Daniel did not assume to be faultless by way of a puffed-up attitude; instead, he willingly shared the guilt of his people.

Centuries later, it was God who had His only Son, the spotless Lamb, identify with our guilt in the Great Exchange at the cross: *"For He made Him who knew no sin to be sin for us, that we might become the righteousness of God in Him" (2 Corinthians 5:21).* The present-day church, which has been afforded so many blessings, must avoid any form of self-righteousness, for it demonstrates the same prideful attitude that caused the fall of Lucifer.

The evil one, knowing his time is short, will only increase his chaotic schemes against the body of Christ, and because of this increased warfare, arrogance should play no part in the believer's sincere exchange with God. The gateway to true intercession is the cry, "Lord Jesus, forgive me, for I have failed!" After all, who among us has not sinned against God at some time in our lives?[18]

AN ENCOUNTER OF
THE ANGELIC KIND

Daniel cried out to God and asked Him to fulfill the prophecy He had given Jeremiah. And it was in the midst of Daniel's heartfelt supplication that he received one of the most significant prophetic revelations of all time:

> Yes, while I was speaking in prayer, the man Gabriel, whom I had seen in the vision at the beginning, being caused to fly swiftly, reached me about the time of the evening offering. And he informed me, and talked with me, and said, "O Daniel, I have now come forth to give you skill to understand." (Daniel 9:21–22)

Daniel had a deep desire to know the truth about the future of the Jewish people in Babylonian captivity. Remember, it is not the *truth* that sets us free, but rather the knowledge and understanding of the truth, which produces liberty. Truth exists whether we are aware of it or not. The truth can stand inches from us, but it provides us no benefit without our knowledge of it.

Daniel had miscalculated Jeremiah's timetable, believing his people's captivity would *literally* last seventy years. He longed to discover the mystery of God's Word to Jeremiah concerning the Jewish people. He asked the Lord for wisdom and understanding and received much more than he anticipated. The angel Gabriel gave him a glimpse of the redemption of the Jewish people from the bondage of Babylon to Israel's final restoration under the Messiah.[19]

THE SEVENTY WEEKS

The Angel revealed the true meaning of Jeremiah's seventy-year prophecy to Daniel as instructed by God Himself.

Seventy weeks are determined for your people and for your holy city, to finish the transgression, to make an end of sins, to make reconciliation for iniquity, to bring in everlasting righteousness, to seal up vision and prophecy, and to anoint the Most Holy.

Know therefore and understand, that from the going forth of the command to restore and build Jerusalem until Messiah the Prince, there shall be seven weeks and sixty-two weeks; the street shall be built again, and the wall, even in troublesome times.

And after the sixty-two weeks Messiah shall be cut off, but not for Himself; and the people of the prince who is to come shall destroy the city and the sanctuary. The end of it shall be with a flood, and till the end of the war desolations are determined. Then he shall confirm a covenant with many for one week; but in the middle of the week he shall bring an end to sacrifice and offering. And on the wing of abominations shall be one who makes desolate, even until the consummation, which is determined, is poured out on the desolate. (Daniel 9:24–27)

The term *seventy weeks* has confounded many a Bible student, but it can best be understood with the phrase "seventy weeks of years." The interpretation of the word *week* is not a week of 7 days but a week of 7 years; therefore, the expression *seventy weeks* is referring to a time period of 490 years.

We read of similar calculations in Leviticus 23:15 concerning the Feast of Weeks (Pentecost or *Shavuot*), which is the celebration of the day God gave the Torah to Israel: *"And you shall count for yourselves from the day after the Sabbath, from the day that you brought the sheaf of the wave offering: seven Sabbaths shall be completed."*

This unique computation is also observed in Leviticus 25:8, which refers to the Year of Jubilee (a time of restoration) and seven-year (sabbatical cycles) rest for the land of Israel: *"And you shall count seven sabbaths of years for yourself, seven times seven years; and the time of the seven sabbaths of years shall be to you forty-nine years."*

Daniel believed that only two years of the conventional seventy-year time period remained. What he could not understand was how the remaining three world empires (Medo-Persian, Greek, and Roman) were to come and go within such a short time before the Jews could be restored to their "national existence."

Gabriel disclosed to Daniel that the seventy years was in truth a "type" of a longer time span. Everything God promised, as well as what the Jews longed for concerning Israel's future, were summed up with Gabriel's revelation of the "seventy weeks" as recorded in Daniel 9:24–27. Saint Peter describes this ultimate restoration as *"the times of restoration of all things, which God has spoken by the mouth of all His holy prophets since the world began"* (Acts 3:21).[20]

Bible scholar Clarence Larkin, who was published in 1929, long before the rebirth of the nation of Israel, believed the following:

The vision of the seventy weeks is not only an interpretation of "Prophetic Chronology" but it is the "Key" that unlocks the "Scriptures of Truth." It also discloses another important fact that the "Seventy Weeks" only cover the period when the Jews are dwelling in their own land, and does not cover the present period of their dispersion [the condition of the Jews at the time of Larkin] but takes up their history again when they return to their own land [the ingathering], thus covering the time from the going forth of the decree to "restore and rebuild Jerusalem" until the second coming of Christ.[21]

Rev. Larkin would not witness the prophesied rebirth of Israel (Isaiah 66:8); however, the ingathering of the Jews from their diaspora (the scattering into the nations of the world) had begun in his lifetime. The Jewish people began their return to their Promised Land in the late 1800s at the encouragement of Theodor Herzl's call to establish a Jewish state. The prophet Isaiah foretold this ingathering:

Fear not, for I am with you; I will bring your descendants from the east, and gather you from the west; I will say to the north, "Give them up!" And to the south, "Do not keep them back!" Bring My sons from afar, and My daughters from the ends of the earth. (Isaiah 43:5–6)

After the initial return to their Promised Land, the British government endorsed the establishment of a Jewish home in Palestine. This decision was made public in a letter from the British foreign secretary, Lord Arthur James Balfour, to Lord Walter Rothschild. The contents of this letter became known as the Balfour Declaration.

Foreign Office
November 2nd, 1917

Dear Lord Rothschild,

I have much pleasure in conveying to you, on behalf of His Majesty's Government, the following declaration of sympathy with Jewish Zionist aspirations which has been submitted to, and approved by, the Cabinet:

> *"His Majesty's Government view with favour the establishment in Palestine of a national home for the Jewish people, and will use their best endeavours to facilitate the achievement of this object, it being clearly understood that nothing shall be done which may prejudice the civil and religious rights of existing non-Jewish communities in Palestine, or the rights and political status enjoyed by Jews in any other country."*

I should be grateful if you would bring this declaration to the knowledge of the Zionist Federation.

Yours sincerely,
Arthur James Balfour [22]

However, the seventy-week countdown of Daniel 9 began long before the Balfour Declaration.

GOD'S PROPHETIC CLOCK

The angel Gabriel revealed to Daniel that Israel's refining judgments would come to an end and, at a certain time, the Messiah's everlasting righteousness would begin. Simply put: the computation of seventy weeks establishes the times governing Israel's destiny from its

Babylonian captivity to its rebirth as a nation until Messiah comes.

The duration of the complete seventy-weeks is divided into three periods for a total of 490 years:

1. The seven weeks (49 years)
2. The sixty-two weeks (434 years)
3. The one week (7 years)

As stated previously, these periods specifically deal with the Jewish people and Jerusalem—both part of God's prophetic clock.

The first period of the "weeks of years" begins with seven sevens, or forty-nine years. This period, dated from the decree of King Artaxerxes (444 BCE), allowed for the Jewish people to return to Israel from Babylon for the expressed commission of rebuilding Jerusalem (Nehemiah 2:1–8). This prophetic return culminated in the celebration of the Feast of Tabernacles (395 BCE).

The balance of the sixty-two sevens (434 years) ends with the triumphal entry of Christ into Jerusalem (32 CE).

The one remaining "week" or seven years has yet to be fulfilled, and will constitute the seven years of the Great Tribulation. It will be a time when the Antichrist makes a peace treaty with Israel, which will be violated after three and a half years, resulting in the righteous Jews fleeing to Petra in Jordan. There they will be preserved and protected by the hand of God for three and a half years until Messiah comes.

God's purposes for the seventy weeks are stated in verse 24:[23]

1. To annihilate man's first disobedience
2. To make an end to all sins against God
3. To make reconciliation for iniquity through the blood of Christ

4. To bring in everlasting righteousness

5. To seal the authenticity of vision and prophecy

6. To anoint the Most Holy—the coming Messiah

God the Father was once again leading His chosen people to their divine destiny. However, could He also have been making provisions for us—the Gentiles—within the seventy weeks?

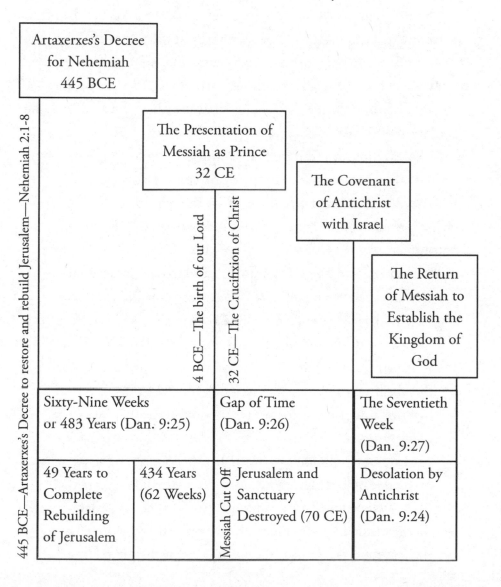

THE GENTILE EXPRESS

It is important to restate that the seventy weeks are not consecutive—there is a distinct gap of time between the sixty-ninth and seventieth weeks. Daniel 9:26 refers to two prophetic milestones; the death of Christ (33 CE) and the destruction of the temple (70 CE)—then God's prophetic clock stops.

Why did the clock stop ticking, and when will it begin again?

Remember, the seventy weeks refer solely to God's dealings with the Jewish people—the church of Jesus Christ is nowhere mentioned. Could it be that we occupy the time space—the gap between the sixtieth and seventieth week? What marked the beginning of the Church age, when will it end, and when will the seventieth week begin?

The Church was birthed at Pentecost, and its age will last until Christ raptures His bride into the Third Heaven.[24] Bible scholar Myer Pearlman quotes Louis C. Talbot's writing, which presents a perfect word picture of the time space we are referring to:

> Some years ago I was on a train . . . and for a while we ran on schedule, to the very minute. Then my train was sidetracked for two and a half hours. Finally, I asked the conductor why we were sidetracked all that while. He answered: "We are waiting for the express to go through." After a while, I heard the shrill whistle and saw the fast train whizz by. Then my own train was put back on the mainline, and on we went, according to schedule.
>
> I thought of God's train for Israel. For sixty-nine sevens of years His people ran according to schedule. Then their train was switched to a sidetrack, as it were, in order that the heavenly express might go through. From Pentecost to the Rapture, the gospel train of this age is on the main line.

One of these days, the journey will be over, and we shall be ushered into the presence of the Lord. Then the Jewish train will be put back on the main track.[25]

The Jewish nation has been placed on the sidetrack, awaiting the arrival and fulfillment of the "Gentile Express" (see Romans 11:25). There are those that refer to this sidetrack as a substitute for the Church. They teach the misguided doctrine of replacement theology or Supersessionism, which promotes the concept that the Church of Jesus Christ has replaced or superseded the Jewish people. This fallacy could not be further from the truth; this is in fact a *false doctrine.*

The deception of replacement theology believes that the first covenant (Old Testament) was supplanted by the new covenant (New Testament). Remember this truth: there is *one* Bible, and every word in the Holy Scriptures, beginning with Genesis 1:1 and ending with the "amen" of Revelation 22:20, is inspired by the Holy Spirit. The Old Testament is God's will *concealed,* and the New Testament is God's will *revealed*—every word is equally anointed, relevant, and eternally true.

The sidetracking of the Jewish nation has made space for the fast-tracking of the Gentile nation. This pause on the path to the ultimate redemption we all long for is God's grace in action and in no way violates His promise to the Jewish people.

If his sons forsake My law and do not walk in My judgments, if they violate My statutes and do not keep My commandments, then I will punish their transgression with the rod and their iniquity with stripes. But I will not break off My lovingkindness from him, nor deal falsely in My faithfulness. My covenant I will not violate, nor will I alter the utterance of My lips. Once

I have sworn by My holiness; I will not lie to David. His descendants shall endure forever and his throne as the sun before Me. It shall be established forever like the moon, and the witness in the sky is faithful. (Psalm 89:30–37 NASB)

The scourge of anti-Semitic persecution severely lashed Jewish backs through Pharaoh's slavery, Haman's gallows, Spain's inquisitions, and Hitler's Final Solution. Even before the Jewish people could recover from the vicious aftermath of the massacres of the pre- and post-war years, they must once again confront the rising tide of today's anti-Semitism in Europe, in the Middle East, and in the universities of America.

We, who were grafted into the blessings of Abraham, owe a great debt of gratitude to the Jewish people. Saint Paul wrote about this debt in the book of Romans: *"For if the Gentiles have been partakers of their [Jewish people] spiritual things, their [Gentiles'] duty is also to minister to them [Jewish people] in material things"* (15:27).

The Old Testament is the very solid foundation of our Christian faith. Remember this truth: Judaism does not need Christianity to explain its existence; Christianity, however, cannot explain its existence without Judaism.

THE PORTRAIT OF THE SON OF SATAN

Sometime in the immediate future, the bride of Jesus Christ will be taken from the earth in the *"twinkling of an eye" (1 Corinthians 15:52)*. Believers refer to this prophetic event as the Rapture of the Church (1 Thessalonians 4:16–17). However, I can assure you that those who are left behind will most likely call this phenomenon the "Great Disappearance."

This sudden departure of the Church will instantly take hundreds of millions of believers from the earth and subsequently out of the workplace. An immediate global economic crisis will result as a consequence of this sudden vacuum. Believers will not only be out of the workforce; we will not be paying taxes, attending universities, or buying goods and services.

Why is this significant? Remember that a European economic crisis promoted Adolf Hitler to absolute control over Germany and eventually most of Europe.

Enter the Antichrist.

Scripture declares that there will be one final, supremely evil, enormously powerful ruler who will dominate the human race. This ruler is the Antichrist—a person who has not yet been revealed in human history.

Daniel painted a vivid picture of the Antichrist in the last six chapters of his book. This ultimate antagonist will be a charismatic but immoral ruler who will come from the revised Roman Empire (Daniel 7:20). He was described as a willful king whose wicked powers originate from Satan, and his goal is to bring destruction to the world (v. 23).

Daniel referred to him as the little horn (Daniel 7:8) and a vile, self-exalting leader who will reign in deception (8:25). He further stated that the Antichrist is the *"prince who is to come" (9:26)* and the king who does as he pleases (11:36–45).

Isaiah called him the *"king of Babylon"* and *"Lucifer" (Isaiah 14:4, 12)*. Saint Paul recognized him as *"the lawless one" (2 Thessalonians 2:8),* and John the Revelator identified him as the rider on the white horse (Revelation 6:2) and the *"beast rising up out of the sea" (13:1–2)*.

Larkin describes the Antichrist as a "superman" that will appear as a great humanitarian posing as a friend to the nations of the world—especially the Jewish people. When in reality, this incarnate of evil will be the embodiment of all kinds of wickedness and blasphemy. He will persuade the masses that he has come to usher in the "golden age," as termed by the prophets, and the world will receive him as their messiah.[26]

The first thirty-five verses of Daniel's eleventh chapter covers approximately two hundred years, providing a succinct description of the Persian and Grecian Empires and the skirmishes of the kings of Syria and Egypt, and presenting an exposition of the Syrian king, Antiochus Epiphanes—the great persecutor of the Jewish people.

"The Illustrious," as he was called, established a federation of nations with one ruler and one world religion. Antiochus knew that the Jewish people would not abandon their faith in Jehovah, so consequently he banned Judaism and demanded conversion. He desecrated the temple with pig sacrifices, burned copies of the Torah, and demanded pagan worship by all Jews.

This was the Gentile world's first attempt to rob the Jewish people of their faith, but it would not be the last. While some Jews converted, thousands of the devoted suffered and died for their belief in the One True God of Israel.

The final verses in this chapter fast-forward to the End of Days and deal with the rise of the Antichrist, the Great Tribulation, Israel's deliverance, and the resurrection of the dead.[27]

THE FINAL WARNING

This is a time to remember that the Jewish people are people of destiny. They are called to lead the nations back to God. This divine calling is reason enough for Satan to target them for destruction in the book of Revelation.

Daniel was warned that the great persecution of the Jewish people in the *"time of the end" (Daniel 12:4)* will be much greater than previously suffered. However, there is hope—there is *always* hope! The Almighty promises to provide deliverance through His angel Michael!

Daniel's dream declares that after the time of trouble the wicked and the righteous will be raised. Those who are found *"written in the book"* will receive *"everlasting life"* and those who are not will spend eternity in *"shame and everlasting contempt" (12:1–2).* This is the first and only time the term *everlasting life* is used in the Old Testament—and it refers to the Jews, *not* the Church.

The book of Daniel ends with God's mandate to *"shut up the words, and seal the book until the time of the end" (12:4).* Why? Perhaps it is closed so that believers can lead righteous lives characterized by obedience, commitment, and faith, as Daniel did. And sealed so we do not dwell on the unknown but rather trust in the God of our salvation, Who will never fail or forsake us.

No matter the interpretation, no one can afford to ignore the life-transforming truths God has chosen to reveal to His people. The Lord's revelations have eternal significance for every soul. Myer Pearlman condenses the message of the book of Daniel with one profound statement:

> Throughout the chances and changes of this fleeing life, throughout political change and international upheavals—we can walk with the Eternal who never changes. And though we may not live to witness the final triumph in our own days, we can take leave of this life with the assurance that one day, God shall remake this troubled world after His own heart.[28]

CHAPTER 12

EZEKIEL'S VISION— THE FINAL GAME OF THRONES BEGINS

Now it came to pass in the thirtieth year, in the fourth month, on the fifth day of the month, as I was among the captives by the River Chebar, that the heavens were opened and I saw visions of God. (Ezekiel 1:1)

Since November 2016, television, newspaper, and social media outlets have paraded headlines screaming about the Russian hijacking of the US presidential election. Further headlines revolved around the FBI, the Obama Department of Justice, and the Clinton campaign colluding against President Trump in his presidential campaign. Most recently, there are allegations of the Russians hacking the Democratic National Committee (DNC). With the fake news environment that encompasses the world today—who the players are in these alleged events and where these assertions will lead—God only knows!

As truths are exposed, America appears to have a shadow government within our democratically elected government committed to bringing down the current administration. By any other definition, this is an act of treason. If this is the case, we owe an apology to President Richard Nixon, whose Watergate scandal pales by compassion.

Mark R. Levin, author and news commentator, has written,

I often wonder what Thomas Jefferson, George Washington, James Madison, John Adams, George Mason, Benjamin Franklin and the other Founders would think about today's America. . . . Surely they would object.

What will the future hold for our children and grandchildren? What will be left of our constitutional system? Will the Bill of Rights have the force of law? . . . How many will remember or care to learn about our founding principles, as concisely and brilliantly set forth in the Declaration of Independence? . . . What of civil society . . . ? Will it have frayed beyond repair? Will we have been conquered from within, as Thomas Jefferson, Joseph Story, and Abraham Lincoln feared might be our fate? Will we have avoided the doom of Athens and Rome? If we are honest with ourselves we must agree that the outcome is unclear.[1]

A GEOPOLITICAL SNAPSHOT

On the world front, we turn to North Korea, defended by China, courted by South Korea, and led by a murdering dictator who agreed to meet with President Trump one moment, then in the next breath threatened America with a nuclear blast that could turn New York City into a massive graveyard . . . only to finally meet with our president in Singapore for a "summit" that lasted a few hours.

Do not think for a minute that North Korean leader Kim Jong-Un has changed his agenda. He is just pulling a page out of the tactical propaganda journals used by Hitler, Yasser Arafat, and now President Hassan Rouhani of Iran—and that is: tell the world what they want to hear and continue planning for its destruction.

To restate, Iran was on the verge of bankruptcy in 2016 until President Obama bailed it out by releasing sanctions, thereby giving Iran access to over $100 billion. To add insult to injury, he sent an additional $1.7 billion in cash, using his executive power, thus avoiding a ratification fight in the Senate. These two radical dealings gave new life to a nation that is at the epicenter of global terrorism.

Make no mistake: Iran is a terror state whose citizens are programmed to swarm the streets shouting, "Death to America" and "Death to Israel," and they mean it! Iran's intentions are to rebuild the Persian Empire and control the Middle East, and perhaps the world, under its form of radical Islamic rule. When President Trump pulled out of the Iran nuclear deal, France, Germany, and Great Britain opposed the decision and opted to form an alliance in order to keep the deal—and they hope to get the backing of China and Russia.[2]

Russia, under the cunning leadership of former KGB officer Vladimir Putin, is methodically rebuilding the former USSR at a rapid pace, and no one is challenging his aggression. Putin perceives the European Union as a true strategic threat. His concern is that the potential reform of the participating countries will pull them away from Russia, thereby compromising their economy. His goal is to secure markets for Russian products and guarantee Russian jobs by creating a "Eurasian Union."[3] *So why is Russia interested in Israel?*

Putin is interested in Israel's warm water ports and natural gas resources. Russia recently signed an agreement with Syria in January

2017, where for forty-nine years, Russia is able to, at no cost, expand their presence and have sovereign control of their existing naval facility at the port of Tartus. The treaty states that Russia can keep eleven warships, including nuclear vessels at Tartus, with full privileges and "full immunity from civil and administrative jurisdiction of Syria."[4] By the end of 2017, Russia announced it was "forming a permanent grouping" at the Tartus naval facility as well as at its Hmeymim air base.[5]

Security analyst Daniel Nisman states, "The Russians have had varying levels of activity and personnel in Syria since the cold war."[6] Since Russia and Syria have been cooperating militarily as well as sharing intelligence for decades now, the Russians do not intend to leave the region any time soon and are ramping up for war in the Middle East.

In February 2018, a weaponized, unmanned drone originating from a base in Homs, Syria, was shot down by the IDF before it could reach its intended target. In May, I stood at the Israeli-Syrian border the day after the Quds Force (the overseas operations arm of Iran's Islamic Revolutionary Guard Corps) launched twenty missiles toward Judea and Samaria, just thirty short miles from Damascus.

IDF representative Lt. Col. Jonathan Conricus briefed our team and stated that four rockets were intercepted and destroyed by the Israeli Iron Dome aerial defense system, while sixteen others fell short of their targets. In response to the assault, Conricus said Israeli fighter jets struck seventy military targets belonging to Iran. The action, called "Operation House of Cards," nearly wiped out Iran's entire infrastructure in Syria. This, I might add, occurred with Putin's full knowledge and support.[7]

Together, Iran and Russia sponsor Hezbollah in Lebanon, which is a well-trained and equipped terrorist organization. Its written covenant pledges the slaughter of the Jewish people as their purpose for existence. Make no mistake; this terrorist organization, in addition to Hamas in Gaza, intends to eradicate the Jewish state. Israel may try to "draw the red lines" restricting the impact of Iran and Hezbollah in Syria—but it is Putin who is in control.[8]

A Hezbollah commander revealed in late 2016 that the relationship between Hezbollah fighters and Russian ground troops is "not a new development. He said Hizbullah and the 'cream of the Russian army,' specifically special forces and anti-tank missile (ATM) teams, had been fighting together in Aleppo for their mutual benefit. [The commander continued,] 'If you play with a good football team, you will learn something from them.'"[9]

Hezbollah's secretary general, Sheikh Hassan Nasrallah, declared, "What has been prepared for Israel differs from the battle we are fighting [in Syria] against the armed groups." What does he mean? Hezbollah is not going to just fight Israel in large formations, through conventional airstrikes, or with Russian tanks. Instead, it will also penetrate Israel's borders with small-unit configurations and specially trained cadres to conduct numerous and simultaneous ambushes and raids.[10] This is why Israel so fiercely defends and protects all of its borders.

Furthermore, as detailed earlier, Hezbollah has an arsenal of Iranian rockets ready to launch against Israel at a moment's notice. An online article found in Dahiya, a Lebanese pro-Hezbollah website, reported that the Syrian president Bashar al-Assad has ordered his army to build and camouflage missile silos to allow Hezbollah to increase its missile arsenal to five hundred thousand units in Syria alone.[11]

WHY SO MANY ROCKETS?

The well-known "Iron Dome," a mobile all-weather air defense system, currently protects Israel. The moment a rocket is launched toward Israel, the Iron Dome locks in on the incoming missile, computes its route, and immediately establishes whether it will hit a populated area. If so, a defensive missile is instantly fired, intercepting the incoming warhead, thereby blowing it up. According to an article in *Aviation Week*, Hezbollah launched 4,594 rockets in a fifty-day period from the Gaza Strip, and the Iron Dome destroyed all but 70 missiles, yielding a 90 percent success rate.[12]

However, the Iron Dome has an Achilles' heel. When we are talking about saving human lives, 90 percent is not good enough. The Dome can only process a limited number of incoming projectiles per minute, which is why Hezbollah has stockpiled over 150,000 rockets in Lebanon.

When the next war starts, Hezbollah will flood Israel's airspace with rockets and attempt to compromise the capability of the Iron Dome system. Their goal is to overwhelm the Dome at the same time they infiltrate Israel's borders with multiple incursions. If this happens, the results will be catastrophic.

This destructive strategy has already begun. At the end of May 2018, over 114 mortars and rockets were fired into Israel from Gaza in a twenty-four-hour period. This missile attack was the largest assault on Israeli civilians since the 2014 Gaza war, forcing over one million Israelis into bomb shelters. After hearing the piercing Red Alert sirens, warning of an incoming projectile, families had less than thirty seconds to get under cover.

The Iranian-backed terrorist groups Hamas and Palestinian Islamic Jihad issued a joint statement claiming "credit" for the attack on Israel. During the eight weeks of the Hamas-led riots along the Gaza-Israel border that I mentioned in a previous chapter, Hamas openly bragged that they would "tear down their fence just like we will tear out their [the Israeli's] hearts from their chests."[13]

ENTER RUSSIA ONCE AGAIN

In addition to funding Hezbollah, Iran also financially backs Hamas in Gaza and enables Hezbollah agents to train their operatives. However, this support has caused an internal dispute between radical Islamic conservatives and the Revolutionary Guard.

Enter Putin, who wants a Palestinian reconciliation, which would block a renewed partnership between Hamas and Iran. This settlement would satisfy the desires of Saudi Arabia, the United Arab Emirates (UAE), Jordan, and Egypt by "[healing] the rift between the Gulf states and Qatar, [forging] a unified position on the Syrian crisis and [ending] the Palestinian schism between Fatah [Palestinian National Liberation Movement] and Hamas."[14]

Why is this important? Zvi Bar'el, PhD, a highly credentialed Middle East affairs analyst, succinctly summarizes this scenario: "Jordan, Saudi Arabia, Egypt, Turkey and Israel all understand that the only great power capable of working a miracle in Syria is Russia. Thus each of them is now seeking guarantees from Moscow that its interests will be protected."[15]

Recently, President Putin and Israeli Prime Minister Netanyahu held talks in Moscow concerning Iran's presence in Syria. Netanyahu restated to Putin what has been understood from the start of the Iranian presence in the region, "Iran needs to leave Syria—that is not something new for you. . . ."[16] Israel has repeatedly stated that Assad's forces could remain at the border with Israel in exchange for the withdrawal of Iranian fighters from Syria.

Russia stated in June of 2018 that "Iranian forces and Hezbollah should withdraw from southern Syria, or else Syrian regime forces [Assad's government] would not be provided with any support [air coverage] from Russian forces in the upcoming battle in the province of Daraa."[17] Bottom line—the battle of Daraa did occur—

the Russians did supply air support and the Iranians are still in Syria.[18] Does this sound like KGB doublespeak? I am confident that the recent Helsinki summit between President Trump and Putin had as one of its talking points Russia's presence and purpose in Syria.

A major war in the Middle East is coming soon, and it will be massive. Israel will not have time, as it has in the past, to warn Palestinians who are caught in the crosshairs as a result of the terrorists using civilian locations to launch their rockets toward Jerusalem. There will be no time to win the global media war, which historically sides against Israel. There will be no time to fight the fake news that distorts the truth. For their survival, Israel must respond instantly either by immediate retaliation or by using the "first strike option," just as Moshe Dayan found it necessary to do at the start of the Six Day War.

Israeli intelligence officials have reported that weapons are hidden in mosques, schoolyards, and civilian houses, and Hamas's leadership war room is in a bunker beneath Gaza's largest hospital![19] As in previous wars, Hezbollah and Hamas will hide behind terrified women and children as they launch rockets from their homes into Israel.

If Israel *does not* respond swiftly and fiercely, they will suffer massive loss of life. Yet if they *do* respond aggressively, the global "blame Israel first" media will condemn the Israelis for bombing houses from which the rockets are being launched toward Israel.

The players are in place, and this coming war will be the birth pangs of the Gog and Magog Wars, as foretold by God to the prophet Ezekiel.

EZEKIEL'S CALL

Ezekiel, whose name means, "may God strengthen" in Hebrew, was the prophet of priestly descent and a contemporary of Jeremiah and Daniel. He was sent into Babylonian exile, along with ten thousand other captives, in 597 BCE—eleven years before the destruction of Jerusalem (Ezekiel 1:3; 2 Kings 24:14–16; Jeremiah 29:1).

Ezekiel was confronted by a divine vision of God's glory, which he vividly described as a great cloud coming out of the north. He saw a wheeled platform engulfed in a raging fire, carried by four living creatures, on which was enthroned the Lord's fiery majesty (1:1–28). Thus began Ezekiel's commission as a watchman, who would warn Israel of the devastating consequences of their wicked ways (3:17).

Jewish teachings state that Moses revealed what *could have been* and Ezekiel revealed *what was* (Exodus 6:2–8). Israel *could have been* the parchment upon which God's Word was written (Proverbs 3:1–4); *could have been* a living, breathing Torah scroll; *could have been* the living example that true wisdom and understanding was the product of the fulfillment of God's Word (Proverb 7:4).

Israel *could have been*, had they only heeded God's voice (Deuteronomy 28:1–14). Instead, they took their own path and walked in exile until the ingathering. Ezekiel witnessed the presence of the Lord depart from the Holy City and the Holy Temple (1 Kings 8:10; Ezekiel 10:18). Without God's Shekinah, Jerusalem lost its splendor, and the temple, although still beautiful, was empty of His glory.[20]

The Jewish people believed that the temple of God was insurance for their survival and their "sacrifices an antidote to the spiritual poison afflicting them." Not so. The temple and its service were a reflection of the people—if the nation was empty, then the temple was a mere shell; if their deeds were evil, then their sacrifices were an abomination to God.[21]

The Jewish people were now defenseless against Nebuchadnezzar's invasion and subsequent deportation to Babylon (2 Kings 24). The Lord commissioned Ezekiel to be the prophet to the exiles. His message was that one day, God Almighty would gather the Jewish people from the four corners of the earth and restore them to the land of Israel (Ezekiel 28:25). Once reunited with their covenant promise, they would never be removed again (Joel 3:16–21).

Ezekiel mourned the decline and destruction of Jerusalem. His vision encompassed the heavens, and his words revealed the rebirth of the Jewish nation. And it was Ezekiel whom Jehovah God chose to give His revelation of the final battles that would usher in earth's last empire.

THE FIVE Ws OF
THE GOG AND MAGOG WARS

There are five requests that I make of my executive assistant about every incoming phone call or invitation to speak. Those five questions I want answered are who, what, when, where, and why? When I return the call, the groundwork has been established for a clear and complete understanding of the pending conversation or decision.

Remember this truth: a clear understanding prevents a misunderstanding! So let us ask the five Ws concerning the Gog and Magog Wars.

Jewish and Christian students of the last days state that there is a king, whose name is Gog, who will rule over the nations of Magog (Ezekiel 38). Gog will gather these nations and cause them to rise up and overtake Israel. God Himself, who reigns supreme within His Eternal Kingdom, will exercise His retribution and miraculously defend Israel against the armies that come against the Jewish people (Ezekiel 38–39; Revelation 20:8). Ezekiel pronounced a prophecy to Gog where he described three events:

1. Gog's plan to thrust his mighty military armies against Israel (Ezekiel 38:10)

2. Jehovah's wrath overcomes Gog and Magog within His Covenant Land (Ezekiel 38:18-22; Joel 2:20; Zechariah 14)
3. Israel's seven-month cleansing of the devastating aftermath (Ezekiel 39:12)

Some Jewish theologians believe that Gog and Magog are a series of wars that includes the war in the "middle of the week," or three and a half years after the Antichrist negotiates a peace treaty with Israel (Daniel 9:27). The battle of Armageddon, the mother of all wars, happens seven years after the peace treaty. Once again, the hand of God will come against the invading armies who attack Israel.

1. Who Is Involved in This War?

Russia

It is widely believed among Bible scholars that Rosh is Russia. C. I. Scofield recognizes Meshach and Tubal as the Russian cities of Moscow and Tobolsk.[22] Magog, Tubal, and Meshach can be traced back to Genesis 10:1–2:

> Now this is the genealogy of the sons of Noah: Shem, Ham, and Japheth. And sons were born to them after the flood. The sons of Japheth were Gomer, Magog, Madai, Javan, Tubal, Meshech, and Tiras.

The names listed in Ezekiel 38 are the sons of Japheth.

> The word of the LORD came unto me, saying, Son of man, set thy face against Gog, the land of Magog, the chief prince of Meshach and Tubal, and prophesy against him. And say, Thus

saith the Lord GOD: Behold, I am against thee, O Gog, the chief prince of Meshach and Tubal. (vv. 2–3 KJV)

This is where the prophet Ezekiel is commanded by God Almighty to deliver a message against a man (Gog) and his kingdom (Magog). Certain anthropologists believe that Noah, Japheth, and their families migrated "to the north beyond the Caspian and Black Seas after the great flood, instead of going south, as did Shem, (the Shemites) and Ham, (the Hamites). Noah and Japheth then settled in the area of Rosh, which is modern-day Russia."[23]

Persia, Ethiopia, and Libya

The prophet Ezekiel stated that the following nations will join Russia, King of the North, in a massive military invasion of Israel: *"Persia, Ethiopia, and Libya are with them, all of them with shield and helmet"* (Ezekiel 38:5).

Persia is modern-day Iran. Do not confuse Persians with the Arabs of the Middle East. The Persians have been on the stage of world history since the sixth century BCE. They originated in central Asia, and under King Cyrus were the fourth empire in the Mediterranean, succeeding Egypt, Assyria and Babylon.

The Persian Empire was described in Daniel's vision (7:5) as one of the four global empires, which ruled over Israel and will come against them in the Gog and Magog Wars. However, they will be buried on the hills of Israel and join the other nations in the bone-yard of human history that have come against God's Chosen.

The Persians are brilliant, cunning, and artful masters of long-term planning. They underwent a successful coup d'état in 1921 that removed the ruling Qajar dynasty from power. Persia's name changed to Iran in 1935 at the prompting of Nazi associates of the Persian ambassador to Germany. Under the shah's new leadership, a more descriptive name, which better identified Persia and Germany's close alliance, was created. That name was "Iran," which mirrored the word *Aryan*.[24]

Later, in 1979, Iran's name became the Islamic Republic of Iran after the revolution put the radical Muslim Shiite supreme leader, Ayatollah Khomeini, in power.[25] Iran's republic continues to be an extremist, death-worshipping, religious dictatorship that threatens to use nuclear force against America and Israel at every opportunity. And to think that our American tax dollars are footing the bill for the impending nuclear cloud Iran wants to place over the freedom-loving nations of the world.

Ethiopia and Libya

J. Dwight Pentecost taught that Ethiopia and Libya represent two Arab states. Why? Moses fled Egypt after killing an Egyptian slave master (Exodus 2:15). He did not go south into African Ethiopia but into the Ethiopia of the Arabian Peninsula (Midian), and there he took a Semite Ethiopian woman as his wife. Therefore, when Ezekiel spoke of Ethiopia and Libya (a region west of the Nile), he was speaking of the Arab states around Israel.[26]

Germany and Turkey

In Ezekiel 38:6, we read about *"Gomer and all its troops; the house of Togarmah from the far north and all its troops."* Some identify Gomer as Germany. Josephus, the celebrated historian of the first century, noted that the Gomerites were identified with the Galatians, who inhabited what today is central Turkey.[27]

Josephus also provided an extensive listing of the nations, and in it are the sons of Gomer. Ashkenaz, Gomer's eldest son, founded the Ashkenazians (Germany), who were identified by the Greeks as Rheginians.[28]

"House of Togarmah" is in modern Turkey, located north of Israel. Germany and Turkey will also join the nations that will follow Russia in the massive land invasion of Israel in the Gog and Magog Wars.

2. What Will Ignite the Gog and Magog Wars?

Israel will make a seven-year peace treaty with the Antichrist, who forms a ten-nation pack following the collapse of the European Union. At this time, the EU will be in a state of chaos, both economically and socially, following the Rapture of the church.

Israel will be confident that these ten nations, comprising the revised Roman Empire in Europe, will give them complete protection from Russia and Iran. They will be sadly mistaken and deceived!

In three and a half years, this treaty will be broken by the Antichrist, who is known to the Jewish people as Amalek, the first recorded anti-Semite (Exodus 17:8). Israel will be attacked with a massive land invasion led by Russia and followed by Iran, Libya, Turkey, and Arab Islamic nations. Ezekiel prophesied concerning the leadership of Russia in 38:6, saying, *"Many people are with you."*

In recent years, Iran, Hezbollah, Syria, and Hamas have repeatedly attacked Israel. Europe's leadership is in disarray—the United Kingdom has left the European Union, and Germany is swamped with Islamic immigrants who are bringing utter chaos to the already fractured region. Angela Merkel, chancellor of Germany and leader of the European Union, said recently, "The world is coming apart at the seams."[29]

France is also unstable. Vicious radical Islamic terrorists are spilling French blood, using speeding trucks to kill and maim men, women, and children as they celebrate Bastille Day,[30] stabbing and killing two young innocent women at the Marseille Saint-Charles Train Station,[31] and gunning down concertgoers and café patrons, taking 130 lives and injuring 352 more.[32] The Jews of France are fleeing to Israel, America, and other nations of the world due to growing anti-Semitism in Europe, spurred by assaults such as the deadly Jewish market attack in Paris.[33]

Diana and I had the opportunity to go to Normandy, France, and visit Omaha Beach. This site and others like it were bloody battlefields during World War II. I walked the beaches where precious American soldiers were cut in half by machine gun fire. Others were blown to bits by the German guns coming from the cliffs overlooking the killing field of the beaches. History records that the waters of the sea were turned red with the blood of Allied soldiers fighting for the world's freedom. We must not forget their supreme sacrifice!

As we left the beach and walked through the pristine military cemeteries, which mark the graves of tens of thousands of America's sons who paid the ultimate sacrifice on the altar of freedom, tears ran down our faces. I looked at row after row of the final resting places of the fallen. I observed their ages; most were eighteen to twenty years of age, their hopes and dreams forever abandoned that ours might live.

I engaged our French tour guide in personal and detailed conversation. When he understood my knowledge of the geopolitical crisis in Europe, he made the following statement concerning France: "History is about to repeat itself. When Hitler came to power, the door of opportunity to leave France was opened only briefly. I'm leaving France soon before the flag of Islam flies over Paris."

3. When Will This Invasion Occur?

This is the final prophecy of Ezekiel concerning the Gog and Magog Wars. The birth pangs are increasing in intensity and frequency; the fulfillment of this prophecy continues:

After many days you will be visited. In the latter years you [Gog] will come into the land of those brought back from the sword and gathered from many people on the mountains of Israel, which had long been desolate; they [the Jewish people] were brought out of the nations, and now all of them dwell safely. . . . Then you [Russia] will come from your place out of the far north, you and many people with you, all of them riding on horses, a great company and a mighty army. You will come up against My people Israel like a cloud, to cover the land. It will be in the latter days that I will bring you against My land, so that the nations may know Me [the Lord God of Israel], when I am hallowed in you, O Gog, before their eyes. (Ezekiel 38:8, 15–16)

These verses tell the story! Especially verse 15: *"Then you [Russia] will come from your place out of the far north."* On September 15, 2015, Russia moved its military forces *"out of the far north"* into the Middle East, specifically Syria.

The *New York Times* headline read, "Russian Moves in Syria Widen Role in Middle East." Furthermore, Iran and Syria have had a strategic alliance ever since the start of the Iran-Iraq War in 1980. Russia and Iran are currently plotting the genesis of the Gog and Magog Wars that Ezekiel clearly stated shall be *"in the latter years"* *(38:8).*

In the Latter Years

"In the latter years" begins at the day of Pentecost (Acts 2:1). In chapter 11 ("Daniel's vision"), we also discussed this phrase as part of the Balfour Declaration of November 2, 1917, when foreign secretary Arthur James Balfour wrote an urgent letter to Britain's most distinguished Jewish citizen, Baron Rothschild, expressing the British

government's support for a Jewish homeland in Palestine. The letter became known as the Balfour Declaration.

This historic document opened the door for Ezekiel's prophecy to become reality: *"For I will take you from among the nations, gather you out of all countries, and bring you into your own land" (Ezekiel 36:24).*

"In the latter years" is when God supernaturally breathed upon the valley of dry bones, making Israel's physical rebirth possible.

> *Thus says the Lord GOD to these bones: "Surely I will cause breath to come into you, and you shall live." (Ezekiel 37:5)*

The word *breath* in Hebrew is *ruach*, meaning "spirit." When God created Adam, His physical man may have been perfect, but when God breathed His Spirit into him, Adam then became a living soul. There is no doubt that Ezekiel's prophecy referred to Israel becoming a living nation again: *"These bones are the whole house of Israel" (v. 11).*

The Jewish nation has been liberated from their Gentile graves. They are home; they do not occupy the land—they own the land of Israel! They are prospering and thriving in every dimension of life! Israel lives! Shout it from the housetops! Israel lives!

After almost two thousand years of wandering, the exiles have come home *"in the latter years,"* as prophesied by Ezekiel. The miracle of miracles happened May 14, 1948, when Prime Minister Ben-Gurion bounded up the steps of the museum in Tel Aviv to read the Declaration of Independence for the State of Israel as the world listened by radio in absolute shock and amazement. President Harry Truman recognized the Jewish state eleven minutes after it was read by Ben-Gurion.

I was eight years of age, sitting at our kitchen table in Channelview, Texas, listening to the radio with my father as this historic announcement was made. My father, a pastor and Bible scholar, seldom wept, but as we listened to the broadcast, tears ran down his face. I knew this event was earthshaking, although I did not know why.

I remember his words to this day: "Son, this is the most important prophecy of the twentieth century. It proves the words of the prophets and the promises of the Bible are absolutely true. The State of Israel has been reborn. Messiah is coming!"

"In the latter years," Israel's restoration to the land of Israel was prophesied by Rabbi Judah ben Samuel, who lived in Regensburg, Germany, during the twelfth and thirteenth centuries (1140–1217). Rabbi ben Samuel stated that God measures time in modules of fifty years, called "Jubilees." The Bible refers to the Jubilee in Leviticus 25:10–11:

> *And you shall consecrate the fiftieth year, and proclaim liberty throughout all the land to all its inhabitants. It shall be a Jubilee for you; and each of you shall return to his possession, and each of you shall return to his family. The fiftieth year shall be a Jubilee to you; in it you shall neither sow nor reap what grows of its own accord, nor gather the grapes of your untended vine.*

A Jubilee year in ancient Israel meant that all debts were forgiven, indentured servants were liberated, all lands were given back to the original owner, and the Promised Land was allowed to rest. Jubilee was a time when God Almighty poured out His blessings on Israel and the Jewish people. Rabbi ben Samuel's prophecy was as follows:

When the Ottomans (Turks) . . . conquer Jerusalem they will rule over Jerusalem for eight jubilees. Afterwards Jerusalem will become no-man's land for one jubilee, and then in the ninth jubilee it will once again come back into the possession of the Jewish nation—which would signify the beginning of the Messianic end time.[34]

Let's do the math! The first prediction was that the Turks would rule over Jerusalem for eight Jubilees or four hundred years. The Turks gained control of Jerusalem in 1517 and held power for exactly four hundred years until British forces led by General Allenby took control of Jerusalem on Hanukkah, December 17, 1917. Please note: the Turks took possession of Jerusalem three hundred years after Rabbi ben Samuel's death. This was an astonishingly accurate prophecy.

Rabbi ben Samuel's prophecy over Israel continues: "Afterwards Jerusalem will become no-man's land for one jubilee."

Under the British Mandate of 1917, Jerusalem was an international city and declared a "no-man's-land." Fifty years later, or one Jubilee, on June 17, 1967, the Israeli army reclaimed the city of Jerusalem during the Six Day War. Jerusalem was under Jewish control for the first time since the day the city was destroyed in 70 CE by General Titus and the Roman Legion. Another part of ben Samuel's prophecy was fulfilled.

The final part of his prophecy stated that one Jubilee following Jerusalem's reunification would begin the year of the "Messianic end time."

When you add fifty years to 1967, you have the year 2017. This was the year that Jerusalem celebrated a Jubilee year, or fifty years since it was reunited with the State of Israel. It was certainly a time when God Almighty poured out His blessings on Israel and the Jewish people.

Furthermore, on December 6, 2017, President Donald J. Trump recognized Jerusalem as the eternal and undivided capital of the state of Israel by announcing the move of the US embassy from Tel Aviv to the Holy City. On May 14, 2018, seventy years to the day that Israel was reborn as a nation, Diana and I were privileged to be in Jerusalem to witness biblical history in the making. I was honored to be asked by the US ambassador to Israel, David Friedman, to give the closing benediction:

> Our most gracious heavenly Father, God of Abraham, Isaac, and Jacob, the God who calls the stars by name and measures space with the span of His hand—King of the universe.
>
> We gather here today to thank You for the joy of living to see this glorious and historic day. We thank You for the State of Israel, the lone torch of freedom in the Middle East, who lives and prospers because of Your everlasting love for the Jewish people.
>
> It was You, O Lord, who gathered the exiles from the nations and brought them home again. It was You who made statehood possible.
>
> It was You that gave a miraculous victory in 1967 when Jerusalem reopened to worshippers of all faiths.
>
> Jerusalem is the city of God.
>
> Jerusalem is the heartbeat of Israel.
>
> Jerusalem is where Abraham placed his son on the altar on the Temple Mount and became the father of many nations.
>
> Jerusalem is where Jeremiah and Isaiah penned the principles of righteousness that became the moral foundations of Western civilization.

Jerusalem is where Messiah will come and establish a kingdom that will never end.

We thank You, O Lord, for President Donald Trump's courage in acknowledging to the world a truth established three thousand years ago, that Jerusalem is and always shall be the eternal capital of the Jewish people.

And because of that courage of our president, we gather here today to consecrate the ground upon which the United States embassy will stand, reminding the dictators of the world that America and Israel are forever united.

We thank You for our ambassador, David Friedman, and pray Your anointing upon him as he opens the doors to the US embassy to receive the nations of the world.

Let the word go forth from Jerusalem today . . . Israel lives!

Shout it from the housetops that Israel lives!

Let every Islamic terrorist hear this message—Israel lives!

Let it be heard in the halls of the United Nations—Israel lives!

Let it echo down the marble halls of the presidential palace in Iran—Israel lives!

Let it be known to all men that Israel lives because, "He that keepeth Israel [shall] neither slumber nor sleep" [Psalm 121:4 KJV].

As King David prayed three thousand years ago, we pray for the peace of Jerusalem and for all its inhabitants.

Let the name of the Lord be glorified today for the Defender of Israel today, tomorrow, and forever is here!

Can we all shout Hallelujah? Amen!

Prayer of Dedication for the US embassy
Jerusalem, Israel
May 14, 2018

Sadly, *"in the latter years"* is also the time when scientists produced nuclear weapons that have the power to turn the earth into a spinning graveyard in space. Einstein said of this time: "I know not with what weapons World War III will be fought, but World War IV will be fought with sticks and stones."

The Bible very clearly indicates there will be a nuclear war in the future for control over the city of Jerusalem, which was precisely described by the prophet in Zechariah 14:12:

> *And this shall be the plague with which the LORD will strike all the people who fought against Jerusalem: their flesh shall dissolve while they stand on their feet, their eyes shall dissolve in their sockets, and their tongues shall dissolve in their mouths.*

This word picture portrays what happens to the human body when exposed to the heat of a nuclear blast. Temperatures of such an explosion can reach those of the interior of the sun, or about one hundred million degrees Celsius.[35] With this devastating amount of blazing heat, it requires little imagination to visualize the words of the prophet Zechariah. The city of Hiroshima, Japan, experienced the horrific destruction of the first atomic bomb, but its aftermath pales in comparison to the incalculable lethal power of a nuclear bomb.

4. Where Will the Gog and Magog Wars Take Place?

Israel is surrounded by her enemies on three fronts—north, east, and south; therefore, the Gog and Magog Wars will happen throughout the nation of Israel.

> *The mountains shall be thrown down, the steep places shall fall, and every wall shall fall to the ground. "I will call for a sword*

against Gog throughout all My mountains," says the Lord GOD. *(Ezekiel 38:20–21)*

5. Why Is Russia Coveting Israel?

Theologians have debated this question for many years. Some say Russia is trying to gain more territory. *But why?* Look how vast Russia is geographically. Who needs a postage stamp–sized nation like Israel when you have such a mammoth landmass?

As I stated earlier, the Russians are clearly interested in Israel's natural gas resources. The *Wall Street Journal* stated that the recent offshore gas and oil discoveries in Israel are sufficient to meet Israel's gas needs for one hundred years.[36] Moscow is concerned that this massive discovery will threaten their manipulative supply of natural gas to Europe, which will negatively affect Russia's entire economy. This, however, is not the only reason for invasion: Russia also wants Israel's warm water ports.

I recently visited with a former Israeli intelligence officer, and I asked him why Russia wants to invade Israel. The officer used a standing global map to show me where Russia has its naval bases. He said, "Russia's navy is frozen in place for several months each year. For Russia to achieve military dominance in the Middle East and Europe it must find a warm water port to the oceans of the world."

I asked, "So how does Israel figure into global warm water ports?" I have been to Israel forty times and did not put together what he was about to say. The officer spun the globe to Israel's coastline, which borders the Mediterranean Sea with the Port of Haifa.

The Mediterranean Sea leads to the north and south Atlantic oceans. Going south from Haifa, the warm water takes you to the Red Sea, which leads to the Indian Ocean to the North Pacific and the oceans of the world. In one sentence, the officer captured why the nation of Israel is invaluable from a military perspective. The IDF officer said, "Israel is one of the few nations in the Middle East that has warm water access to the oceans of the world year-round. Russia must have this kind of access to those oceans for military dominance." Its target is Israel!

The warm water ports may be the goal of Israel's enemies, but oil is the hook in their jaw set by God Almighty (Ezekiel 38:4). Russia must have the natural resources and strategic port access to reclaim its position as a global superpower. No matter their purpose, the King of the universe will drag Russia and its anti-Semitic coalition to their graves in Israel instead.

Unwalled Villages

Ezekiel 38:9 describes the massive military invasion coming into Israel like a storm. In 38:10, Gog makes an evil plan to invade Israel,

> You [Gog] will say, "I will go up against a land [Israel] of un-walled villages; I will go to a peaceful people [Jews], who dwell safely, all of them dwelling without walls, and having neither bars nor gates." (Ezekiel 38:11)

Why is Israel referred to as *"a land of unwalled villages"*? Walls, then and now, are protection against invasion. At this time, concrete walls surround Israel to protect them from enemy sniper fire. But the Jewish people, who have been under ceaseless attack since the rebirth of their nation, will trust in the peace treaty they sign with the Antichrist so they can finally live without fear of destruction. They will pay a great price for trusting in man and their own abilities instead of their God.

The European Response

Ezekiel 38:13 reads, *"Have you come to take plunder? Have you gathered your army to take booty, to carry away silver and gold, to take away livestock and goods [oil and technology], to take a plunder?"* Doesn't this sound exactly like our previous state department that chose to ignore all signs of impending dangers?

They were known for asking supremely stupid questions like the ones in that verse: Have you come to take a spoil? Are you intending to do harm? Can we give you jet planes loaded with cash or perhaps repay an old loan with over a billion dollars in unmarked bills to help future invasions? Russia will thumb its nose at the European Union, ignore all inept world governments, and invade God's Covenant nation.

God's Response

Israel's enemies have formed a confederacy against it and for centuries boasted that they would *"cut them off from being a nation, that the name of Israel may be remembered no more" (Psalm 83:4).* This will happen—but not to Israel. God will make sure of that! King David prophesied about this exact situation in the second chapter of Psalms:

> *Why do the nations rage, and the people plot a vain thing? The kings of the earth set themselves, and the rulers take counsel together, against the LORD and against His Anointed, saying, "Let us break Their bonds in pieces and cast away Their cords from us."*
>
> *He who sits in the heavens shall laugh; the Lord shall hold them in derision. Then He shall speak to them in His wrath, and distress them in His deep displeasure: "Yet I have set My King on My holy hill of Zion."*

"I will declare the decree: The LORD has said to Me, 'You are My Son, today I have begotten You. Ask of Me, and I will give You the nations for Your inheritance, and the ends of the earth for Your possession. You shall break them with a rod of iron; You shall dash them to pieces like a potter's vessel.'"

Now therefore, be wise, O kings; be instructed, you judges of the earth. Serve the LORD with fear, and rejoice with trembling. Kiss the Son, lest He be angry, and you perish in the way, when His wrath is kindled but a little. Blessed are all those who put their trust in Him.

Jehovah, the King of the universe, the Defender of Israel, watches over His people night and day as He sits on His Holy Throne. When the Almighty looks from heaven and sees the Russian-Islamic armada storm His Land, He will shout out in laughter—the Lord of hosts has been waiting for this moment since Amalek fought against the Israelites (Exodus 17:8–16). *Then why would God allow Russia and their Gog and Magog hordes to invade Israel?*

The answer is clearly presented in Ezekiel's prophecy: God's righteous fury will pour out judgment and vengeance on all nations that have historically persecuted and slaughtered the Jewish people:

It will be in the latter days that I will bring you against My land, so that the nations may know Me, when I am hallowed in you, O Gog, before their eyes. (Ezekiel 38:16)

"And it will come to pass at the same time, when Gog comes against the land of Israel," says the Lord GOD, "that My fury will show in My face. For in My jealousy and in the fire of My wrath I have spoken." (Ezekiel 38:18–19)

God's Fury

The face of God is generally portrayed as one of absolute peace, tranquility, and love without limit. Ezekiel described God's face as enraged, nostrils flared, eyes blazing, incensed with the invasion of *"the apple of His eye"* by enemy nations and kings (Zechariah 2:8).

God's face is saying, "You weren't satisfied with the massacre of My people throughout the empires, while in exile, during the Inquisition, or during the Holocaust. Now you have come to the only place on earth I have created for Abraham's seed to live in safety and security to slaughter them! Today your blood will stain the soil of Israel that the world may know that I am God and turn to Me with their whole heart."

Jewish theologian Rabbi Solomon ben Isaac, more commonly referred to as "Rashi," also saw the Gog and Magog Wars as a time of reckoning for all the evils that the nations have perpetrated against Israel over the centuries. The armies of Magog are coming, and God Almighty is waiting for them with His day of retribution.

The nations of the world will watch the Russian-Islamic alliance lead a vast military invasion into the Holy Land, and it will appear that Israel is finished. However, this pagan and godless generation have completely forgotten the "God Factor."

The children of Israel have experienced the "God Factor" time and time again. When Moses led his people out of Egypt and through the desert, they were overcome by fear as six hundred of Pharaoh's fiercest chariots pursued them all the way to the banks of the Red Sea. The people cried out to Moses, saying, *"Because there were no graves in Egypt, have you taken us away to die in the wilderness?" (Exodus 14:11).*

What was God's response? He caused the Red Sea to part and His children walked *"into the midst . . . on the dry ground."* Then God told Moses, *"Stretch out your hand over the sea, that the waters may come back upon the Egyptians, on their chariots, and on their horsemen."* The result: *"Not so much as one remained"* (Exodus 14:19–22, 26, 28).

God has redeemed His people before, and He will do it again! While the nations of the world anxiously watch, as the Jewish people appear to be standing on the brink of annihilation, Almighty God is measuring every step of the invading armies as they march toward Israel. When their pagan feet touch its sacred soil, God's fury will be released:

> *For in my jealousy and in the fire of My wrath I have spoken: "Surely in that day there shall be a great earthquake in the land of Israel, so that the fish of the sea, the birds of the heavens, the beasts of the field, all creeping things that creep on the earth, and all men who are on the face of the earth shall shake at My presence." (Ezekiel 38:19–20)*

God is going to use the mountains around Israel to crush and bury its invaders by means of earthquakes. The Lord has used earthquakes throughout the history of man to communicate with those who refuse to obey His sovereign will. God is not in heaven saying to the tyrants of earth, "Let's make a deal." He is in heaven saying, "This is the deal!"

God used an earthquake to open the *"fountains of the great deep" (Genesis 7:11)*. This huge disturbance unbridled the global Flood. God's purpose was to renew the human race through the family of Noah.

God used an earthquake to destroy Sodom and Gomorrah (Amos 4:11). God used an earthquake to bring down the walls of

Jericho (Joshua 6:20). God used an earthquake at Calvary to testify to the Roman Empire that Jesus of Nazareth was indeed the King of the Jews (Matthew 27:51). An earthquake released Jesus from the tomb on the third day (Matthew 28:2). An earthquake released Paul and Silas from the prison in Philippi (Acts 16:26) to testify to all that they were men sent from God.

The earthquake of Ezekiel 38–39 that will crush Gog and his invaders is a supernatural disaster of colossal scale that will shock the world. This immense calamity will result in

1. The destruction of the invading armies (38:18–23)
2. God's greatness and holiness being seen among the nations (38:23)
3. The national atonement of Israel (39:25–29)

Then the Creator of the universe will declare,

And all men who are on the face of the earth shall shake at My presence. The mountains shall be thrown down, the steep places shall fall, and every wall shall fall to the ground. (Ezekiel 38:20)

Friendly Fire

God follows up His "welcome to Israel" earthquake with the tactic of friendly fire—which is when a military force mistakenly fires upon its own troops, causing casualties. The earthquake will fill the air with a thick black cloud of dust and dirt, and then *"every man's sword will be against his brother"* (Ezekiel 38:21).

Screams of terror coming from those falling into mass graves will confuse and disorient the enemy's armies, causing them to turn their weapons on each other. They will open fire at every sound they hear! Blood will flow, and legions will die because the very weapons intended for the slaughter of the Jewish people will now be used to execute God's judgment against their enemies.

This is not the first time God has used friendly fire to crush the enemies of Israel. Gideon was commanded by the Lord to have three hundred men blow trumpets and charge the enemies of Israel with pitchers filled with torches. Then *"The LORD set every man's sword against his companion throughout the whole camp" (Judges 7:22).* The Midianites killed each other! When invading armies come to call on the chosen people, God will once again open His combat manual and initiate "Operation Chaos."

Grand Finale

God created the world through His perfect plan and for His perfect purpose. And one purpose of creation is the sanctification of His Holy Name. God had Moses chisel it in stone so that Israel and the nations of the world would never forget the sanctity of the Great I AM (Exodus 3:14). In Ezekiel 38:22–23, we read about the grand finale, where God's name will be magnified and made known throughout the world:

> *And I will bring him [Gog] to judgment with pestilence and bloodshed; I will rain down on him, on his troops, and on the many peoples who are with him, flooding rain, great hailstones, fire and brimstone. Thus will I magnify Myself and sanctify Myself and I will be known in the eyes of many nations.*

There are many questions about these wars we do not have the answers to, but the following is what we do know based on God's infallible Word:

- One out of six of Israel's enemies will survive. Ezekiel writes, *"And I [God] will turn thee back, and leave but a sixth part of thee" (39:2 KJV).*
- It will take the Israelites seven years to burn the weapons of war (Ezekiel 39:9).
- The largest Russian graveyard on planet Earth will be located in the Valley of Hamon Gog (Ezekiel 39:11).
- It will take Israel seven months to bury the dead and cleanse the land (Ezekiel 39:12).
- Almighty God, Creator of heaven and earth, will call *"every feathered fowl, and to every beast of the field . . . upon the mountains of Israel, that ye may eat flesh, and drink blood" (Ezekiel 39:17 KJV).*
- The supernatural annihilation of the armies of Russia, Iran, Turkey, Germany, and Islamic nations will cause a spiritual awakening in the house of Israel (Ezekiel 39:22).
- God Almighty will have mercy upon the whole house of Israel (v. 25).

What is the common denominator that has driven the nations of the world to resent and resist the chosen people of God? The Jewish people, for millennia, have lifted high the torch of truth. Kings, queens, and dictators of the Kingdom of Darkness hate the light of God's truth. King David penned the evidence of this thought when he wrote, *"Thy word is a lamp unto my feet, and a light unto my path" (Psalm 119:105).*

There are only two kingdoms on earth and in eternity: the Kingdom of Light and the Kingdom of Darkness. From the beginning of Genesis until the End of Days, the Kingdom of Light will always prevail. We will all belong to one kingdom or the other—which will you choose?

For the first time in world history, the players of the Gog and Magog Wars are in place. Once these wars happen, the remnant armies that survived God's fury will join the King of the West and the Kings of the East and together they will begin their march toward the Valley of Megiddo for the war of global supremacy (Revelation 16:16).

THE FINAL GAME
OF THRONES

CHAPTER 13

SATAN'S THRONE

I will ascend into heaven, I will exalt my throne above the stars of God; I will also sit on the mount of the congregation on the farthest sides of the north; I will ascend above the heights of the clouds, I will be like the Most High. (Isaiah 14:13–14)

History most definitely repeats itself. The twentieth century saw the harbinger of the coming Antichrist: his name was Adolf Hitler. He is recorded in history as staining the earth with innocent blood, as did other megalomaniac monsters, such as Haman, Herod, Nero, Stalin, Mussolini, Tojo, Saddam Hussein, Assad, and Khamenei of Iran to name a few.

HITLER LIVES

The mere mention of Hitler's name triggers horrifying accounts of World War II, culminating in the slaughter of 6 million Jewish people. Since his cowardly suicide in 1945, more than 120,000 publications of his psychotic life have been written, and even now the ghost of Hitler walks across the nations of the globe, including America.

Steven Spielberg's intense and heart-wrenching movie *Schindler's List* brilliantly captured a glimpse of the Holocaust and the living hell it produced. I believe God Almighty put this artistic genius on the earth to create his graphic depiction of the unspeakable horrors committed against the Jewish people. The world must never forget the satanic evil of the Final Solution, the Nazi's code name for the systematic murder of Europe's Jewish population. This film should be required viewing for every student of the world in an attempt to eradicate the poisonous stream of anti-Semitism that still flows through our modern culture.

Although Hitler has been dead for over seventy-three years, you can still watch nightly documentaries that feature his mesmerizing speeches to throngs of spellbound Germans as they recite a perverted version of the Lord's Prayer: "Adolf Hitler, you are our great leader. We praise thee! Heil Hitler!"[1]

There are countless biopics on his weapons of war, works of art, connection to the occult, obsession with racial purity, the Third Reich (his personal empire), and of course his gruesome attempt to annihilate the Jewish people. Why are we still so obsessed with this diabolical madman?

The headline in a March 2018 *New York Times* world news section screamed, "Indian Children's Book Lists Hitler as a Leader 'Who Will Inspire You.'" The publisher "came under fire . . . for including Hitler in a children's book about world leaders who have 'devoted their lives for the betterment of their country and people.'"

"'This description would bring tears of joy to the Nazis and their racist neo-Nazi heirs,' [responded] Rabbi Abraham Cooper, associate dean of the Simon Wiesenthal Center, an international Jewish human rights organization. . . . On the book's cover, a stony-faced Hitler is featured alongside . . . Mahatma Gandhi, Nelson Mandela and India's prime minister, Narendra Modi."[2]

Make no mistake: the tactic of the radical extremists is to place a monster like Hitler in the company of respectful leaders to confuse impressionable young minds concerning this human devil, his methodical extermination of six million Jews, and the bloody war that killed fifty-two million people. We say, "Never again"; but anti-Semitism *is* happening again!

Remember this truth: there is soon to appear on the earth an unequivocally depraved barbarian far worse than Adolf Hitler. The Bible calls him the Antichrist—the Beast and the chief son of Satan. His evil empire will engulf and enslave the world and his deeds will make Adolf Hitler look like a choirboy. But before he reveals his true nature, the Antichrist will offer peace in our time once again.

Destruction Through False Peace

The offer of peace is not a new tactic for world dominance. Hitler manipulated the peace process as a weapon of war just as the Antichrist will do in the near future:

And through his policy also he [the Antichrist] shall cause craft [deceit] to prosper in his hand; and he shall magnify himself in his heart, and by [false] peace shall destroy many [Great Tribulation]: he shall also stand up against the Prince of princes [Christ]; but he shall be broken without hand. (Daniel 8:25 KJV)

Later in the book of Daniel we read, *"He shall confirm a covenant with many for one week [seven years]"* (9:27).

On September 30, 1938, the Munich Pact was signed between Great Britain's prime minister, Neville Chamberlain; French premier Édouard Daladier; Italy's leader, Benito Mussolini; and Germany's chancellor, Adolf Hitler. This pact allowed Hitler to enter Czechoslovakia unhindered, fulfilling his goal of German expansion.[3]

Prime Minister Chamberlain was willing to sacrifice the people of Czechoslovakia to avoid another world war—it was his "land for peace" agreement. Chamberlain flew home to London victoriously waving the signed peace treaty, proclaiming, "This means peace in our time." However, it was Hitler's ploy, intended to seduce the British into complacency. Hitler even duped the German people into believing there would be peace in November 1938:

> Circumstances have forced me [Hitler] to almost only speak of peace for decades. It was only through the continued emphasis on the German desire for peace and peaceful intentions that it was possible to give the German people the arms that were always a requirement for the next step.[4]

The "peace treaty" was actually a blatant act of deception devised by a demonized megalomaniac whose lust to destroy and control Europe knew no limits. Hitler continued his ruse for fraudulent peace via the 1939 Hitler-Stalin Pact, which allowed him to invade Poland while the Russians looked the other way. "Before the signing of the non-aggression pact, President Franklin D. Roosevelt warned Stalin that 'it was as certain as that the night followed the day that as soon as Hitler had conquered France he would turn on Russia and it would be the Soviets' turn next.'"[5]

By the following summer, war was declared between France, Britain, and the Axis powers. Germany had a massive head start in the war effort due to the territory and resources it had seized in Eastern Europe. Then on June 22, 1941, Hitler broke his treaty with Stalin and launched one of the largest surprise attacks in the history of warfare. By the time the war ended, more than twenty million

Russian soldiers and civilians alone had been killed due to Hitler's so-called peace process.

The man who saved England, and arguably Western civilization, from this evil incarnate was Sir Winston Churchill. He saw through Hitler's charade. With a voice of a lion, he roared at those who thought negotiating with Hitler was a plausible tactic to maintain peace. Churchill thundered, "You cannot reason with a tiger when your head is in his mouth."[6]

When most in the British Parliament wanted to collaborate with Adolf Hitler at the beginning of World War II in 1940, Winston Churchill issued instead a call to arms in his first speech after being appointed prime minister of Great Britain. While the armies of the Third Reich were treading across Europe in an unrelenting quest to conquer as much of it as possible, Churchill instinctively recognized that appeasement was not the answer to Hitler's aggression.

The survival of Great Britain was at best uncertain, yet Churchill managed to unite his people when he bellowed before Britain's legislative body, "You ask, what is our aim? I can answer in one word. It is victory, victory at all costs, victory in spite of all terror, victory, however long and hard the road may be; for without victory, there is no survival."[7]

Once again, we are walking toward a similar skyline where one will appear out of Europe, a charismatic, multilingual political superstar who will lead a ten-nation coalition. This false messiah will enter into a seven-year peace treaty with the State of Israel and his motive will be like that of Hitler—to conquer the nations of the world and set up his own empire.

Peace, One Piece at a Time

The leaders of the world have been attempting to broker peace in the Middle East since before Israel was reborn as a nation. Every major politician in the West wants the Middle East peace treaty notch on their belt. Some American negotiators have become so obsessed with reaching a deal that they have not considered the cost.

The problem is that all the concessions for peace in the Middle East to this point in history have been made by Israel. While the Arab nations say they want peace with Israel, in reality they only want it *one piece of land at a time* and will not be content until they control all of Israel to include Jerusalem.

The question arises, What kind of peace treaty will the Antichrist negotiate that will cause the geopolitically savvy leaders of Israel to sign? How will the Antichrist deceive them?

Why not offer a seven-year peace treaty that will promise the Jewish people total control of Israel, to include the Temple Mount? Why not include the authorization of the building of the Third Temple? What about offering Israel complete jurisdiction over all the holy sites? I can assure you that this cunning man of deception will offer the moon! It will not matter what the Antichrist offers or what Israel accepts, because the Great Deceiver does not intend to keep the pact anyway—peace was never his objective.

Doubtless, once the treaty is signed, the Antichrist will receive the Nobel Peace Prize after he is deluged with global praise from the United Nations and the world media. Even some of the Jewish people will believe that this "man of peace" is the Messiah. However, this lawless ruler has two main goals: present himself as God and destroy the nation of Israel and the Jewish people.

This promise of seven years of peace is, in reality, part of the Antichrist's calculated tactic—it will become his vehicle for war. The treaty (Daniel 9:27; Revelation 11:1) and the ten-nation federation (Daniel 2:40–44; Revelation 17:12) that the Antichrist will lead are mentioned by Daniel and John the Revelator. They foretell of the Antichrist's breach of this ill-famed accord exactly forty-two months after it is made and his ensuing military attack on Israel.

Charismatic Deception

One of the most celebrated film clips of the Third Reich is of Adolf Hitler standing on a massive platform surrounded by the German high command, his voice booming like claps of thunder, as thousands of Nazi soldiers scream, "Heil Hitler." Historians may give Hitler high marks as a public speaker, but his oratory skill does not explain the mesmerizing effect he had on the masses.

Men and women wept uncontrollably and hysterically shouted praise while they assembled by the hundreds of thousands to hear him rant. It was as if they were spellbound as they listened to the pseudosavior of Germany.

In my book *The Three Heavens*, I detail Hitler's involvement with the occult and his close association with Dietrich Eckart, who was a committed occultist. It was Eckart who "trained Hitler in self-confidence, projection, persuasive oratory, body language and ranting discord." It was not "by his own power" that Hitler deceived millions, nor will it be by the Antichrist's own power that he captivates the masses.[8] *"His [the Antichrist's] power shall be mighty, but not by his own power" (Daniel 8:24)*, and he will have Satan's ability to deceive and bring nations to submission with his oratory:

> *And he [the Antichrist] was given a mouth speaking great things and blasphemies, and he was given authority [by Satan] to continue for forty-two months. (Revelation 13:5)*

THE FORESHADOWERS

There have been many foreshadowers of the Antichrist who have slithered through the pages of history: Nimrod, Pharaoh, Nebuchadnezzar, the Roman Caesars, and Antiochus Epiphanes, just to name a few. These vile men had many things in common with the Antichrist:

- They rebelled against God and His authority.
- They persecuted and murdered the chosen people at will.
- They erected images of themselves for self-seeking adulation.

Adolf Hitler perfectly fit this list of wickedness—he too can be described as a forerunner of the Antichrist. After his ascension to power in 1933, Hitler required German schoolchildren to recite a prayer that equated Hitler with Christ. Hitler, like Satan and the Antichrist, craved praise and worship.

Historian Joseph J. Carr records, "Nazism was no mere political movement of racist gangsters and misfits, as is commonly believed, but rather, it was an occultic religion in which Adolf Hitler was the Messiah, Heinrich Himmler the High Priest and the blood-drenched men of the SS Death's Head Formation the clergy."[9]

Hitler thought himself to be god and the Third Reich his kingdom. His National Socialist Party was more than a mere political movement—it was a formal faith with rituals, rites, doctrine, scripture, and a messiah. Nazism was an evil New World Order. Hitler's reign of destruction, dispensed by his evil hordes, will pale in comparison to the demonic triune that will participate in the Final Game of Thrones.

DEMONIC TRIUNE

One of Satan's desires is to emulate God. A prime example of this obsession is his defilement of the Holy Trinity. God's Trinity consists of the Father; Jesus Christ, the Son; and the Holy Spirit. Their sacred union is defined by righteousness, truth, and life. The Holy Trinity refers to the one God who exists in three coequal and coeternal Persons—no one and nothing can emulate this. The "unholy triune" is completely opposite and consists of Satan, the Antichrist, and the False Prophet. These evil entities depict pure wickedness, deception, and death. They are three separate beings who have no essential unity—two of which are human beings.

Satan

Satan's fixation to be *"like the Most High" (Isaiah 14:14)*, which I detailed in my book *The Three Heavens*, began in the midst of heaven. Here are some key facts I have compiled:

- God created an inexpressibly beautiful angel named Lucifer. He was a cherub and the overseer of the Garden of God. He was also wise, the most glorious of all the angels, and the worship leader in paradise (Third Heaven).
- Lucifer displayed such splendor and radiance that he was called *"son of the morning" (Isaiah 14:12). Lucifer* is the English translation of the Hebrew name *helel,* which means "to shine" or "to bear light." He reflected the magnificent majesty of God's radiance. Ezekiel vividly depicted Lucifer:

> *Thus says the Lord GOD: "You were the seal of perfection, full of wisdom and perfect in beauty. You were in Eden, the garden of God; every precious stone was your covering. . . . The workmanship of your timbrels and pipes was prepared for you on the day you were created. You were the anointed cherub who covers; I established you; you were on the holy mountain of God; you walked back and forth in the midst of fiery stones." (28:12–14)*

- Lucifer's wings "covered" the place where God's glory was manifested in His heavenly temple, just as the cherubim in the tabernacle of Moses covered the mercy seat and the place where the visible glory of God appeared (Exodus 37:9). So what went wrong? It was by his own confession that Lucifer made a declaration of defiance:

You have said in your heart: "I will ascend into heaven, I will exalt my throne above the stars of God: I will also sit on the mount of the congregation. . . . I will ascend above the heights of the clouds, I will be like the Most High." (Isaiah 14:13–14)

- Five times Lucifer said, *"I will."* He lusted for God's throne, and in his self-centeredness, he became dissatisfied with his position, exalted though it was. Lucifer was consumed by his desire to be worshipped, an ambition that will be temporarily satisfied when he gives power to the man of sin—the Antichrist (2 Thessalonians 2:3; Revelation 13:4).

As penalty for Lucifer's rebellion, God banished him from the Third Heaven. In that instant, the chief cherub was no longer the "bearer of light"—he would forever be called Satan. The beautiful Lucifer was no more. Once banished, the rebel of all rebels established his throne in the Second Heaven, where he and his fallen angels rule over all the kingdoms of the world, for the Word of God declares that *"the whole world lies under the sway of the wicked one" (1 John 5:19).*

The Scriptures reveal many of the names given to Satan based on his evil nature:

- The accuser (Job 1:6; Zechariah 3:1–2; Revelation 12:10)
- The tempter (Matthew 4:3)
- The ruler of demons (Matthew 12:24)
- The strong man (Mark 3:27)
- Beelzebub (Luke 11:15)

- A murderer (John 8:44)
- The father of lies (John 8:44)
- The ruler of this world (John 14:30)
- The prince of the air (Ephesians 2:2)
- The power of death (Hebrews 2:14)
- Adversary the devil (1 Peter 5:8)
- A roaring lion (1 Peter 5:8)
- The wicked one (1 John 5:19)
- The angel of the bottomless pit (Revelation 9:11)
- The great dragon (Revelation 12:9)
- The serpent of old (Revelation 12:9)

Since the time of his fall until now, the wicked one has attempted to foil God's plan of redemption by destroying His chosen line from which our Messiah comes. There was Cain, who *"was of the wicked one" (1 John 3:12)*, and there was the evolution of universal disobedience that caused God to redeem mankind through Noah (1 Peter 3:19–20), whose lineage included Abraham, Isaac, and Jacob—the fathers of God's chosen people. It is within Satan's evil nature to direct his hostility toward God's faithful remnant.

The serpent's goal was to thwart the Father's plan of redemption, but he failed! This ages-long conflict will reach its climax when an angel from heaven seals Satan in the abyss for one thousand years (Revelation 20:1–3).

Jesus knows where Satan's throne is; He referred to it in the letter to the church of Pergamos (Revelation 2:12–17). If there is a throne, there is an empire.

The Antichrist

The second entity of the demonic triune is the Antichrist. The Scriptures are replete with descriptions that capture his nefarious nature:

- The little horn, with *"eyes like the eyes of a man"* (Daniel 7:8)
- A prince who is to come, who *"shall destroy the city and the sanctuary"* (Daniel 9:26)
- The one who makes desolate *"on the wing of abominations"* (Daniel 9:27)
- A foolish shepherd *"who will not care for those who are cut off"* (Zechariah 11:15–17)
- The son of perdition: *"the man of sin"* (2 Thessalonians 2:3–10)
- The lawless one, *"according to the working of Satan"* (2 Thessalonians 2:8–9)
- The rider on the white horse who *"went out conquering and to conquer"* (Revelation 6:2)
- The beast out of the sea, *"and on his heads a blasphemous name"* (Revelation 13:1–2)

The Little Horn

The prophet Daniel called the Antichrist "the little horn," speaking of his obscurity among the larger horns of Daniel 8:9. This description aptly fits Hitler as well: *"And out of one of them came a little horn which grew exceedingly great toward the south, toward the east, and toward the Glorious Land."*

Who would have ever believed that a man as insignificant as Adolf Hitler could rise to global power from such absolute obscurity in such a short period? Carr writes, "Physically, Hitler was colorless and unimpressive enough to make one wonder how he could inspire the 'ideal' Nordic beast of his SS formations, much less an entire nation."[10]

He stood only five foot nine, and he had dark hair and a pasty, pale complexion—a far cry from the blond-haired, blue-eyed Nordics that were being exalted as the super race. If it were not for his crazed eyes that seemed to be ablaze, he would have been lost in an average crowd. He was not even physically fit to meet the qualifications for admission to his own SS!

However, Hitler was just a type of the Antichrist to come. I believe this disciple of evil is alive on planet Earth, awaiting his day of satanic anointing. He will come onto the world stage and deceive the world as the prince of peace and within three and a half years morph into the son of Satan. He will be shot in the head and recover miraculously. The Antichrist will immediately turn on the Jewish people with a demonic rage to rob, kill, and destroy.

The Bible teaches that in the end times, right after the Rapture, the greatest political leader in the history of mankind will emerge. After rising to power through diplomatic cunning and deceit, and after three and a half years, he will launch a military campaign that will end in his acquiring *"authority . . . over every tribe, tongue, and nation" (Revelation 13:7)*. His empire will be the most extensive in world history, encompassing the entire globe, and his rule will be the most demonic the world has ever experienced—it will exceed all previous world empires.

> *Then I stood on the sand of the sea. And I saw a beast [Antichrist] rising up out of the sea [the world], having seven heads and ten horns, and on his horns ten crowns [leaders of ten nations], and on his heads a blasphemous name. (Revelation 13:1)*

The prophet Daniel described a creature similar to John the Revelator's beast. Both come out of the nations, and they are unique from any other beast known to man. Daniel's beast represents the Roman Empire, and John's beast, the revised Roman Empire, which will embody the characteristics of the four previous world empires. Both beasts have ten horns, which symbolize ten kings or a federated government of ten nations.

At an appointed time, the Beast of Revelation 13 is going to have three of the ten leaders killed, leaving only seven heads. He will place the fallen leaders' crowns on his head and will increase his power as the dynamic, charismatic, and visionary leader of the revised G7. This savior-like figure will astound the masses with his innate skill to solve the world's seemingly insurmountable problems. However, as the Antichrist consolidates his satanic supremacy, his true nature will be revealed.

He will emerge as a demonically empowered individual who hates God and is determined to annihilate those who believe in Him—both Jews and Christians. For this reason, he is identified as the Antichrist (1 John 2:18), for he will stand against God, the Father of Abraham, Isaac, and Jacob, and His anointed one, Jesus Christ.

The Bible teaches that many Jewish people will accept the Antichrist as a great political leader and diplomat. They will put their trust in him as the guarantor of peace in the Middle East. But the moment he reveals himself halfway through the Tribulation by blaspheming God, the righteous Jews will revolt. They will reject him as Messiah, and this willful king (Daniel 11:36) will respond with vehemence by attempting to annihilate them—the spirit of Haman and Hitler will live again.

I believe that just as the Maccabees revolted against the abominations of Antiochus Epiphanes, a righteous Jewish revolution will rise up against the Antichrist, ending in him suffering a mortal wound to the head: *"And I saw one of his heads as it were wounded to death; and his deadly wound was healed: and all the world wondered after the beast"* (Revelation 13:3 KJV).

This incident will lead to one of Satan's greatest deceits—the Antichrist will shockingly survive and present himself anew to the world as the living god. Then he will set up his image in the Third

Temple in Jerusalem and demand that the world worship him. Those who do not accept his new one world religion will be *beheaded.*

The Son of Perdition

Saint Paul called the Antichrist the son of perdition and described him as *"the mystery of lawlessness"*:

> *Let no one deceive you by any means; for that Day will not come unless the falling away comes first, and the man of sin is revealed, the son of perdition [Antichrist], who opposes and exalts himself above all that is called God or that is worshiped, so that he sits as God in the temple of God, showing himself that he is God. . . .*
>
> *For the mystery of lawlessness [the spirit of Antichrist] is already at work; only He [the Holy Spirit] who now restrains will do so until He is taken out of the way [the Rapture]. And then the lawless one will be revealed, whom the Lord will consume with the breath of His mouth [Revelation 19:15] and destroy with the brightness of His coming. The coming of the lawless one is according to the working of Satan, with all power, signs, and lying wonders, and with all unrighteous deception among those who perish, because they did not receive the love of truth, that they might be saved. (2 Thessalonians 2:3–4, 7–10)*

What exactly does the term *mystery of lawlessness* mean? The Antichrist is the illegitimate claimant to the throne of Christ. Satan, being the ultimate impersonator, is determined to desecrate what God has made holy. Jesus Christ is described as the *"mystery of godliness,"* which is God manifested in the flesh (1 Timothy 3:16).

The Son of God was born of a virgin by the power of the Holy Spirit (Luke 1:35). The son of perdition will be conceived by the power of Satan, who is attempting to emulate Jesus's supernatural birth. Our all-knowing Father in heaven foretold Satan's future when He rebuked the serpent in the Garden of Eden: *"And I will put enmity between you [Satan] and the woman, and between your seed [Antichrist] and her Seed [Jesus Christ]" (Genesis 3:15).*

Therefore, the term *mystery of lawlessness* or *the lawless one* means "wickedness incarnate." The Antichrist is called the "man of lawlessness" or "man of sin" because it is his nature. His very life is characterized by blasphemous sin against God. [11]

But until that day when Jesus Christ returns, it is Satan's offspring, the Antichrist, who will bring a reign of terror upon the earth that it has never seen before.

Nature of the Antichrist

Bible scholar A. W. Pink says of the coming Antichrist, "Across the varied scenes depicted by prophecy there falls the shadow of a figure at once commanding and ominous. Under many different names like the aliases of a criminal, his character and movements are set before us."[12]

The following are a few of the characteristics that define the nature of the Antichrist:

- A warmonger, a man of bloodshed and deceit (Psalm 5:6)
- A *"deceitful and unjust man"* (Psalm 43:1)
- A worker of deceit (Psalm 52:2)
- His words are *"smoother than butter"* (Psalm 55:21)
- Boastful (Daniel 7:8)
- Strong-willed; demands his own way and arrogantly speaks against the Almighty (Daniel 7:25)
- Mighty, *"but not by his own power"* (Daniel 8:24)
- Has no *"desire of women"* (Daniel 11:37)

- Possessed by Satan, just as Judas was (Luke 22:3)
- Will be *"after the working of Satan with all power and signs and lying wonders"* (2 Thessalonians 2:9)
- Has Satan's power and authority (Revelation 13:2)
- Speaks arrogant words and blasphemies (Revelation 13:5)

The immoral and depraved character that the Antichrist displays is best summed up in the names assigned to him in the Holy Scriptures:

- The insolent king (Daniel 8:23)
- The vile person (Daniel 11:21)
- The willful king (Daniel 11:36)
- The worthless shepherd (Zechariah 11:17)
- The abomination (Matthew 24:15)
- The man of sin (2 Thessalonians 2:3)
- The son of perdition (2 Thessalonians 2:3)
- The Beast (Revelation 13:1)

Christ versus the Antichrist

At every point in the Bible, the Antichrist is the antithesis of Jesus Christ. Pink continues: "The word *Antichrist* has a double significance. Its primary meaning is one who is *opposed* to Christ; but its secondary meaning is one who is *instead* of Christ. He will attempt to become another Christ, a pretender to the name of Christ. The Antichrist will set himself up as the true Christ, but he will be the Devil's counterfeit."[13] It is not hard to fathom how even the elect will be deceived (Matthew 24:24).

The Scriptures provide several references illustrating how the Antichrist is a counterfeit of Jesus Christ. Here are but a few examples:

CHRIST	THE ANTICHRIST
Christ was despised and afflicted (Isaiah 53:3).	The Antichrist will be admired and lauded (Revelation 13:3–4).
Jesus makes an everlasting peace covenant with Israel (Ezekiel 37:26).	The Antichrist makes a seven-year peace treaty with Israel, which he breaks (Daniel 9:27).
Jesus Christ was resurrected from the dead (Matthew 28:6).	The Antichrist will miraculously recover from a fatal wound to the head (Revelation 13:3, 14).
Christ came to save (Luke 19:10).	The Antichrist will come to destroy (Daniel 8:24).
Christ came from heaven (John 6:38).	The Antichrist will come from the bottomless pit (Revelation 11:7).
Christ came in His Father's name (John 5:43).	The Antichrist will come in his own name (John 5:43).
Christ came to do His Father's will (John 6:38).	The Antichrist will come to do his own will (Daniel 11:36).
Christ is the Good Shepherd (John 10).	The Antichrist will be the evil shepherd (Zechariah 11:16, 17).
Christ is the truth (John 14:6).	The Antichrist will be *"the lie"* (2 Thessalonians 2:11).
Jesus Christ is part of the Holy Trinity (Father, Son, and Holy Spirit) (Matthew 28:19).	The Antichrist is part of a demonic triune (Satan, the Antichrist, and the False Prophet) (Revelation 13).
Christ is the mystery of godliness, God manifested in the flesh (1 Timothy 3:16).	The Antichrist will be the "mystery of lawlessness," Satan manifested in the flesh (2 Thessalonians 2:7–9).

CHRIST	THE ANTICHRIST
The Lord's name is exalted in all the earth (Psalm 148:13).	The Antichrist will exalt himself above all (2 Thessalonians 2:4).
Jesus mandates men to only worship God (Matthew 4:10).	The Antichrist seduces men to worship Satan (Revelation 13:4).
Christ seals His servants' foreheads with God's name (Revelation 7:3; 14:1).	The Antichrist forces his followers to be branded with his counter mark (666) on their foreheads or right hands (Revelation 13:16–18).
Christ is Lord of lords and King of kings (Revelation 17:14).	The Antichrist will be given authority by Satan over the ten kings (2 Thessalonians 2:9; Revelation 17:12–13).
Jesus Christ will descend from heaven, riding a white horse (Revelation 19:11).	The Antichrist rides on the white horse of the Apocalypse (Revelation 6:2).
Jesus Christ is crowned with many crowns (Revelation 19:12).	The Antichrist has ten horns with ten crowns (Revelation 13:1).
God will establish Christ's throne (2 Samuel 7:12–14; Psalm 132:11).	The Antichrist will sit on Satan's throne (Revelation 13:2).
Christ will reign over His Eternal Kingdom (Revelation 11:15).	The Antichrist will have a temporary kingdom (Revelation 17:17).

The False Prophet

The third entity of the demonic triune is the "second beast," or the False Prophet. Satan charges him with the malevolent mission of leading the masses in the worship of the Antichrist. He is the antithesis of the Holy Spirit.

Then I saw another beast [False Prophet] coming up out of the earth, and he had two horns like a lamb and spoke like a dragon. And he exercises all the authority of the first beast [Antichrist] in his presence, and causes the earth and those who dwell in it to worship the first beast. . . . He [False Prophet] performs great signs, so that he even makes fire come down from heaven on the earth in the sight of men. And he deceives those who dwell on the earth by those signs which he was granted to do in the sight of the beast. (Revelation 13:11–14)

Based on the Scriptures, this "beast" will be a globally renowned religious figure who will control the world for seven years during the Great Tribulation. He will call fire from heaven and cause a statue of the Antichrist to speak, convincing the nations of the world that Satan's messiah is the living god. Just as the Third Reich's propaganda machine vaulted Hitler to power, the False Prophet will catapult the Antichrist to the throne of his evil empire.

Satan is now a step closer to fulfilling one of his eternal pursuits—the utter destruction of God's chosen people. He hates God and therefore hates the Jewish people. What God establishes, the Great Adversary opposes. Satan may have his battle plans drawn, but the God of Israel has decided on the battle site—the Valley of Megiddo. This is the setting for the bloodiest military battle humanity has ever seen—Armageddon.

CHAPTER 14

THE APOCALYPSE

Write the things which you have seen, and the things which are, and the things which will take place after this. (Revelation 1:19)

Who can judge time in terms of eternity? Only God Himself. In the first portion of this book, I presented a short synopsis of over 1,550 years of biblical history from the time of Abraham to Daniel. Now I will take you on a brief journey from here to eternity—from the End of Days to time without end.

Abraham, Jeremiah, Ezekiel, Daniel, Joel, Amos, and Zechariah were shown visions of the future, including the End of Days. However, one man stands out as having "unveiled" the impending events leading to the Final Game of Thrones—his name is John the Revelator.

The last of John's five manuscripts included in the Bible is the book of Revelation. It is often referred to as the "Apocalypse," or the "unveiling." Revelation deals with eschatology, or "a study of the last days" pertaining to the imminent conclusion of the world as we know it. More importantly, it is the fulfillment of the purposes of God.

God the Father reveals the final book of the Bible to His Son, Jesus Christ. Christ makes its message known to *"His angel" (Revelation 1:1)*, who then unveils it to the apostle John on the Island of Patmos. Fundamentally, God is the Author and John is His scribe.

The Lord emphasized the importance of knowing the *things to come* in this passage: *"Blessed is he who reads and those who hear the words of this prophecy, and keep those things which are written in it; for the time is near" (Revelation 1:3).*

God's perfect will and revelation of truth are found throughout His Word—it is the protoplasm of life. God's Word is a training in righteousness; it is medicine for the sick, peace for a troubled heart, direction for the wayward soul, and encouragement to the hopeless—it is everything His children will ever need to lead a victorious life. It is no wonder that the Enemy of God—the Great Deceiver—has devised a campaign to mock this sacred Book.

We are supposedly living in a time of enlightenment—the Information Age[1]—but exactly whose information are we receiving? In a recent *Gentlemen's Quarterly* (*GQ*) magazine article titled "21 Books You Don't Have to Read," the Holy Bible was listed as number twelve. Novelist Jesse Ball writes:

> The Holy Bible is rated very highly by all the people who supposedly live by it but who in actuality have not read it. Those who *have* read it know there are some good parts, but overall it is certainly not the finest thing that man has ever produced.[2]

Remember this truth: God's truth always transcends that of man, and His Word declares:

All Scripture is given by inspiration of God, and is profitable for doctrine, for reproof, for correction, for instruction in righteousness, that the man of God may be complete, thoroughly equipped for every good work. (2 Timothy 3:16–17)

The Word of God is greater than all other books as the blazing sun is greater than a single candle on a child's birthday cake, as the oceans of the earth are greater than a dripping faucet, or as Mount Everest is greater than a grain of sand. The Bible is not a good book—it is *The Book* by which all other books are judged.

The history of the world has proven repeatedly that mankind has been at odds with the Creator since the days of Adam and Eve. Yet what few realize is that the Architect of the ages is not swayed by our failings—instead, He has fashioned a plan of ultimate redemption through the glorious and triumphant return of His Son, which is the core event for the book of Revelation.

THE THINGS YOU HAVE SEEN

Man has been anticipating the end of time for centuries, yet never before have so many prophetic events been fulfilled leading to the Rapture of the Church, the appearance of the Antichrist, and the second coming of Christ to the earth. As John unfolds the revelation of the End of Days, we can begin to connect the dots of what is soon to come.

The first section of the book of Revelation deals with what John witnesses as a follower of Jesus. He attempts to portray the Lord and His profound majesty by describing Him as the one *"who is and who was and who is to come . . . the Alpha and the Omega, the Beginning and the End" (Revelation 1:4, 8)*. Because of the righteous deeds John personally witnessed Christ accomplish, he declared His Master to be the Conqueror of death, the Ruler of the nations, and the resurrected Savior of the world (Revelation 1:5; John 4:42).

This "beloved disciple" dropped his nets by the shores of Galilee as a teenager and followed the Rabbi from Nazareth. John later played a vital role in the expansion of the early church. His writings are intended to give the reader an understanding of Christ through His works and words. And in turn, those who believe in Him will *"have [eternal] life in His name" (John 20:31).*

Jesus called John and his older brother, James, the *"Sons of Thunder" (Mark 3:17),* most likely because of their fervent passion and steadfast loyalty for the things of God (Mark 9:38; Luke 9:54). The two brothers, along with Peter, where chosen by Christ to be in His inner circle (Matthew 17:1). The Scripture refers to John as the disciple *"whom Jesus loved,"* so much so that the Lord asked him to watch over His mother, Mary, after His death (John 13:23; 19:27).

John saw firsthand Jesus turn water into wine (John 4:46), he witnessed the healing of the lame man at the pool of Bethesda (John 5:9), and he was there when Jesus miraculously fed the multitudes by the Sea of Galilee (John 6:13). John was the only disciple to witness Christ's crucifixion (John 19:30), and he visited with the Lord following His supernatural resurrection (John 21:14). John received the power of the Holy Spirit in Jerusalem along with Christ's mother Mary and the other believers who gathered in the Upper Room when the New Testament church was born in the wind and fire of Pentecost (Acts 2:4).

After Christ's ascension, Herod continued to persecute the church through imprisonment and death, causing believers to scatter outside of Jerusalem (Acts 12:1–17). John found temporary refuge in Ephesus but was eventually captured by the Roman emperor Domitian and exiled to the island of Patmos (Revelation 1:9). It was here that Christ visited John and gave to him the book of Revelation.

THE THINGS THAT ARE

As John begins his account, he describes the Holy Trinity—God the Father, sitting on His throne; Jesus, one like the Son of Man; and the Seven Spirits, which embody the presence of the Holy Spirit (Isaiah 11:2; Acts 10:38; Revelation 1:4). He also sees seven lampstands and seven stars, which symbolize the seven churches of Asia Minor and their pastors (Revelation 1:12, 16).[3]

The second portion of John's book deals with the letters Christ addresses to these churches. Think of it as Christ the Author and John the "Postman of Patmos."[4] The churches were located in Ephesus, Smyrna, Pergamos, Thyatira, Sardis, Philadelphia, and Laodicea. Every church is defined by its traits, all but one are commended, some are reproved, and all are given a promise.

The promises given to the seven churches are also afforded to every believer in Christ (Revelation 2–3). These promises include:

- Access to the Tree of Life (2:7; 22:14)
- The victor's crown (2:10; 3:11)
- A new name (2:17)
- Power to rule over nations (2:26)
- An everlasting place in the Book of Life (3:5)
- Deliverance from the Great Tribulation (3:10)
- Sharing in the throne of Christ (3:21)

THE THINGS THAT WILL TAKE PLACE

The third and final section of the book of Revelation begins with Christ opening the door of eternity to His faithful disciple. It is here that John sees the throne room of God (Revelation 4).

You have heard me say that man cannot fully describe the glory and grandeur that awaits every believer in heaven. I am certain that even John, who actually caught a glimpse of this splendor, still paints a pale portrait of the beauty that surrounds the heavenly throne of the Almighty (1 Corinthians 2:9; Revelation 4:1–11).

Twenty-Four Elders

John first sees twenty-four elders seated on individual thrones around the throne of God. These men represent the twelve Old Testament Patriarchs (twelve sons of Jacob) and the New Testament apostles. The white robes they are wearing reflect their righteousness (Revelation 3:18), and the crown of life on their heads depicts their victory over death (Revelation 2:10). These elders are in heaven now and will worship Him who sits on the throne, singing the song of Moses and the song of the Lamb (Revelation 4:9–10; 15:3; see Deuteronomy 32:1–43).

The Rapture of the Church

At this point in John's account of what he witnessed in heaven, I must pause and interject the most important event that will occur for all the faithful believers in Christ Jesus. Let us engage in our five Ws exercise to summarize this highly anticipated event called the Rapture.

What is the Rapture? It is a date known only to God when, in a *"twinkling of an eye,"* the Church of Jesus Christ will be taken from this earth and united with our Lord and Savior in heaven (1 Corinthians 15:52).

Who will participate? All believers in Christ, living and dead, will meet the Lord Jesus in the air. The dead in Christ will rise first, and the living will be *"caught up together"* with them and be with the Lord forever (1 Thessalonians 4:17).

When will it happen? The timing of the Rapture is highly debated; however, I will answer this question based on my personal conviction. Christ promised to deliver believers from the *"hour of trial"* also known as the Tribulation that is soon to come upon the earth (Revelation 3:10; see also 1 Thessalonians 5:9). John's account in Revelation largely addresses a time when God will pour out His divine wrath on those who rejected the gospel of Jesus Christ.

Our Lord is a Promise Keeper who does not lie; therefore, I believe the Rapture of the Church will take place before the beginning of the seven-year Tribulation—the time of unparalleled trouble and suffering on earth (Revelation 4:1). Dake says, the "church will continue to hinder lawlessness until the Rapture. And then the Antichrist will be revealed."[5]

Where will the Rapture take place? This phenomenon will be a worldwide occurrence. All who are in Christ Jesus will be taken up with Him *in the cloud* and will ascend into the Third Heaven (1 Thessalonians 4:16–17).

Why will the Rapture happen? The bride of Christ is preventing the wrath of God from being executed on the ungodly. Once the righteous in Christ are gone, those left behind will encounter the power of lawlessness, which is presently being *restrained* by the Holy Spirit. Saint Paul taught that *"the mystery of lawlessness"* will be *unconstrained* by the Holy Spirit when He ascends to heaven with the believers (2 Thessalonians 2:7).

At that very moment, empty cars will careen down the highway, their drivers and occupants absent. Homes of believers will be suddenly vacant, with supper dishes on the dining table, food bubbling in the microwave, and water running in the sink. Instantly people will be frantically looking for their loved ones on all social media outlets, and the headlines the next morning will read, "THE GREAT DISAPPEARANCE—MILLIONS MISSING!"

In the following months, churches will be overflowing with despondent people who have realized, all too late, that God's Word is true. The world will spiral out of control and will enter a time simply known as the Tribulation. The Scriptures repeatedly warn of the Rapture and the time of trouble that follows. Even Jesus taught on this season several times, during His prophecy seminar (Matthew 24:1–36), in the parable of the ten virgins (Matthew 25:1–13), right before His ascension into heaven (Acts 1:7), and at the Mount of Olives with four of His disciples:

> *But of that day and hour no one knows, not even the angels in heaven, nor the Son, but only the Father. Take heed, watch and pray; for you do not know when the time is. It is like a man going to a far country, who left his house and gave authority to his servants, and to each his work, and commanded the door-keeper to watch. Watch therefore, for you do not know when the master of the house is coming—in the evening, at midnight, at the crowing of the rooster, or in the morning—lest, coming suddenly, he find you sleeping. And what I say to you, I say to all: Watch! (Mark 13:32–37)*

The Judgment Seat of Christ

Every one of us will face a day of judgment—either the Judgment Seat of Christ (the judgment of the righteous) or the Great White Throne of Judgment (the judgment of the unrighteous). According to Scripture, *"it is appointed for men to die once, but after this the judgment"* (Hebrews 9:27).

After the Rapture of the Church, the righteous will appear before the Judgment Seat of Christ. God Almighty will judge us for the lives that we lived on earth. This judgment does not qualify us for heaven—we are already there. It will determine the kind of reward we will receive for the life we led.

> *For we must all appear before the judgment seat of Christ, so that each one may be recompensed for his deeds in the body, according to what he has done, whether good or bad. (2 Corinthians 5:10 NASB)*

Jesus Christ will judge us based on our personal words and deeds. It is here that *"the fire will test each one's work, of what sort it is" (1 Corinthians 3:11–15).* Believers will be judged and rewarded in part on how faithfully we served Christ (1 Corinthians 9:4–27; 2 Timothy 2:5), how well we obeyed God's mandates (Deuteronomy 28:1–14; 1 Peter 4:17), whether we were part of the Great Commission (Matthew 28:18–20), and how we triumphed over sin (Romans 6:1–4).

Christians will receive one of five different crowns: the victor's crown (1 Corinthians 9:25–27), the crown of life (Revelation 2:10), the crown of glory (1 Peter 5:2–4), the crown of righteousness (2 Timothy 4:8), and the crown of rejoicing, also called the soul winners' crown (1 Thessalonians 2:19–20).[6]

Think of it—we will all stand before God Almighty and answer for every word, thought, and deed. I ask, are you ready to give an account to God for your life?

Marriage Supper of the Lamb

Once the bride of Christ (the blood-bought church) is adorned in her wedding robe and crowns, the Bridegroom, Jesus Christ, will welcome the wedding guests to the marriage supper. In Revelation 19:9, John is told to write, *"Blessed are those who are called to the marriage supper of the Lamb!"* These are the saints of past and future ages. You will see Old Testament saints such as Abel, Seth, Enoch, Noah, Abraham, Job, Moses, David, and the prophets in attendance.

It will be a truly magnificent occasion, beyond the power of words to describe. Imagine the guests passing through the gates of splendor and onto the streets of heaven lined with mansions of glory. They will then enter the banquet hall of the King of kings and sit at the table of the marriage supper of the Lamb—the Messiah, the Son of David, the Son of Abraham—Jesus Christ, our Redeemer. Hallelujah to the Lamb!

Then, at the end of seven years, the marriage supper will move locations as the King of kings returns to earth. The blood-bought Church of Christ and the Old Testament saints will be part of this massive army mounted on white horses traveling faster than the speed of light through space and time.

This royal mounted heavenly host will fly over Petra where for three and a half years the hand of God has protected the Jewish people from the Antichrist. Those coming with Christ will see the city of Jerusalem. They will look on Mount Calvary where our Redeemer died for the sins of the world. They will see the Mount of Olives, where Jesus will return to establish His Kingdom that will never end. They will see the Antichrist and his army that have gathered at Armageddon.

The Scroll

The apostle John beheld God sitting on His throne in all of His majesty, holding a scroll stamped with seven seals. He then sees Christ take the scroll from His Father's hand, for He is the only One worthy to open the manuscript. John witnesses all who surrounded the throne bow down and sing a new song before the Lamb of God (Revelation 5:8–10).

The lamb is significant in both the New and Old Testaments. Abraham assured Isaac that the Lord would provide a lamb for his sacrifice (Genesis 22:8). The blood of the Passover lamb was offered as a sacrifice for Israel's redemption from Pharaoh's bondage (Exodus 12:12–13). This liberation was a type and shadow of God's redemptive plan for all humanity from the spiritual bondage of sin through the sacrifice of His Son on the cross (John 1:35–36; 11:25–26; 1 Peter 1:19).

John mentions the Lamb repeatedly within his writings and refers to Him as the Lion of the Tribe of Judah (Revelation 5:5; see Genesis 49:8–10) and the Root of David (Revelation 22:16; see Isaiah 11:1–10; Romans 15:12), signifying His identity as the messianic King (John 4:25–26). He also describes the Lamb as having seven horns, symbolizing the Lord's strength and power, and seven eyes, representing His perfect wisdom and understanding (Revelation 5:6).

Seven in Judaism represents creation, blessings, completeness, and perfection. The Bible is filled with events and images associated with the number seven. Aside from the length of creation, the first verse of Genesis consists of seven Hebrew words; the Sabbath is on the seventh day, and many Jewish feasts are seven days long.

The land of Israel was mandated to rest every seventh year, the menorah in the Temple has seven branches, and the walls of Jericho fell after the Israelites encircled it for seven days.[7] Christ used the imagery of sevens throughout the book of Revelation. John referred to four successive judgments represented by seven seals, seven trumpets, seven thunders, and seven bowls. These judgments are part of the Great Tribulation. It is a time when God pours out His righteous anger on those who have rejected His Son.

This period is marked by God's fury, Israel's longing for the coming Messiah, and the preparation of Christ's return. Repeatedly, John uses the phrase *God's wrath* to describe this turbulent seven-year period.

Silence and the Seventh Seal

The Lord, through the prophets, promised that judgment would come, and now it is here. Appropriately, there is half an hour of stone silence in heaven as the Lord opens the seventh seal, pulls back the curtain of time, and shows the Church the judgments He will execute upon the nations of the world.

Imagine a quiet so intense that not even your own breathing is heard. Then suddenly, after thirty minutes of absolute stillness the

	Seals (Revelation 6:1–8:6)		
	White Horse (Antichrist)	Red Horse (War)	Black Horse (Famine)
	Trumpets (Revelation 8:7–11:19)		
Symbol	Hail, fire, blood	Burning mountain	Star falls from heaven
Result	1/3 of Earth's vegetation destroyed	1/3 of the sea turns to blood	1/3 of rivers become contaminated
	Bowls (Revelation 15:1–16:21)		
Symbol	Foul sores	Seas become blood	Rivers become blood
Result	Those with mark of the Beast are afflicted	All sea creatures die	Those who killed martyrs must drink blood

prayers of the saints who have been crying out for vengeance break the silence. And then *"… there were noises, thunderings, lightnings, and an earthquake"*—all happening at once, ushering in a synchronized cacophony of cataclysmic proportions (Revelation 8:5).

The *"sounding of the trumpets and the pouring out of the vials"* are revealed when Christ opens the seventh seal. With the sounding of the seven trumpets, (Revelation 11:15), seven angels are given seven vials or bowls containing God's wrath (15:7; 16:1), which are His verdict on those who have rejected His Son, tormented the saints, and worshipped the Antichrist.

The first four trumpets announce earthly disasters that will cause massive destruction upon the earth (Revelation 8:7–13). The fifth trumpet describes a "star" falling from heaven—this is Satan. He

Pale Horse (Death)	Souls under the altar (martyrdom)	Natural, physical calamity (fear upon all men)	Silence
Heavenly bodies are struck	First "Woe"	Second "Woe"	Third "Woe"
1/3 of light is lost	Plague of terrible locusts	1/3 of mankind is killed	
Sun becomes scorching	Darkness	Euphrates river dried Up	Thunder, lightning, earthquake
Those burned by the sun blaspheme God	Great pain inflicted on those who follow the Beast	Wicked nations of the Earth gather at Armageddon	God's fierce wrath upon Babylon

is given the key to the bottomless pit, which he opens, and out springs a smoke so dense that even the sun is darkened by its intensity (Revelation 9:1–2).

Coming from this blinding smoke is a horde of demons that resemble huge, scorpion-like creatures. Satan will lead these instruments of misery as they afflict humanity so severely that even the rich and powerful, whose bodies are covered with agonizing sores, cry out for death as a means to relieve their suffering (Revelation 9:3–6).

Whereas the fifth trumpet brought torture and torment, the sixth produces death. At a very precise time, the sound of the sixth trumpet will release four angels, whose assignment is to kill one-third of mankind (Revelation 9:14). The severity of human suffering during the Great Tribulation is beyond the mind of man to fathom.

Remember this truth: the only thing that equals the love of God is the wrath of God. The Almighty will direct His righteous anger on those who refuse to repent *"of the works of their hands, that they should not worship demons, and idols of gold, silver, brass, stone, and wood, . . . their murders or their sorceries or their sexual immoralities or their thefts" (Revelation 9:20–21).*

This time of travail is a precursor to Christ's millennial reign.

The Two Witnesses

Once the Antichrist comes to power, his evil reign will not be hindered However, not everyone will fall under his demonic spell. Among the many who refuse to submit to the Antichrist's subjugation will be two invincible witnesses sent by God to torment him. John does not identify who they are; however, many Bible scholars believe they are Elijah and Enoch, the only two people who were taken to heaven from this earth without experiencing death.

It is as if God were preparing them for a great assignment. The prophet Malachi clearly identified Elijah as one of them, and Enoch is the only other man who was translated without dying (Genesis 5:24; 2 Kings 2:11; Malachi 4:5; Hebrews 11:5).

These two witnesses will be filled with the Holy Spirit and will testify of God's glory (Zechariah 4:6). They will prophesy within the city of Jerusalem and perform great miracles. God will supernaturally protect them by giving them the power to kill their enemies with the fire that comes from their mouths. For three and a half years, no harm will prevail against these two witnesses until their mission is complete.

Then the Antichrist will kill Elijah and Enoch, leaving their bodies exposed on the streets of Jerusalem without proper burial, to be seen by the entire world on global television and "shared" by millions through social media. The people of the earth will celebrate their murder for three and a half days, until God raises them from the dead and they ascend to heaven. The awesome power of God will strike fear in the hearts of every person on earth after their resurrection. Within an hour, a great earthquake will take place, destroying a tenth of the city, killing seven thousand people (Revelation 11:1–15).

The 144,000—the Sealed of Israel

John describes four angels originating from the four corners of the earth, holding the four winds. They represent God's total control over all He has created. They are commanded not to sound their trumpets until the fifth angel marks the foreheads of the righteous with the seal of the living God, protecting them from death at the hand of the Antichrist (Revelation 7:1–3; 14:1).

This seal is the *"Father's name" (Revelation 14:1)* placed on their foreheads, visible to all—just as the mark of the Beast (666) will be seen on the foreheads or right hands of those who bow down to the Antichrist (Revelation 13:8; 14:9).

Saint Paul referred to this *"remnant according to the election of grace" (Romans 11:5).* They number 144,000—composed of 12,000 from each of the twelve tribes of Israel. Reverend Clarence Larkin makes a very important point about the tribes of Israel that are chosen. The tribes of Dan and Ephraim were not included in the 144,000; instead, the tribes of Joseph and Levi are (Revelation 7:7, 8).

Why? Because the Lord promised that any *"man or woman or family or tribe"* who introduced idolatry into Israel would be set apart from the other tribes and blotted out from under heaven (Deuteronomy 29:18–21). Both Dan and Ephraim allowed pagan worship when they worshipped the golden calves (1 Kings 12:25–30). The God of Abraham, Isaac, and Jacob does not forget a promise—He fulfills this promise when He chooses this select group.[8]

The Tribulation and the Great Tribulation

Following the Rapture of the Church, there will be a revival of the Roman Empire (federation of European states), generating great evil in the world (Revelation 17:3–13). At the Lord's chosen time, the Antichrist (Daniel 7:8; 2 Thessalonians 2:3; Revelation 11:7; 13:1; 19:20) will come onto the world stage and enter into a seven-year Middle East peace treaty with Israel, signaling the beginning of the Tribulation (Daniel 9:27).

The Tribulation is a future, seven-year period of unspeakable horror that can be best described as "hell on earth." It is a time when God will unleash His wrath on all those who have rejected Him and the gospel of the Kingdom. The Tribulation is also described as the Day of the Lord (Isaiah 2:12; 13:6–9; Joel 2; 1 Thessalonians 5:2; Zephaniah 1:14; Acts 2:20) and as a day of trouble, wrath, and distress (Deuteronomy 4:30; Ezekiel 7:19; Zephaniah 1:15; Romans 2:5).

The Antichrist will betray Israel in the *"middle of the week,"* exactly three and a half years after signing his peace treaty with them (Daniel 9:27). This demarcation is when the Antichrist will be revealed to the world as the son of Satan. The "lawless one" will ban Jewish sacrifices in the temple and exalt himself as the head of a New World Religion (Revelation 13:11–15).

These incidences signify the beginning of the Great Tribulation, when Satan, the Antichrist, and the False Prophet (the demonic triune) will rule their evil empire and the wrath of God will greatly intensify (Daniel 7:25). Please note that the Tribulation represents the full seven-year period, while the Great Tribulation specifically denotes the second half.

Christ expressly distinguishes the horrific impact of the Great Tribulation from any other time of trials: *"For then there will be great tribulation, such as has not been since the beginning of the world until this time, no, nor ever shall be" (Matthew 24:21).*

The Great Tribulation Saints

John then sees a large number of people from all nationalities before the throne of God. They represent the saints who have been martyred during the Great Tribulation (Revelation 7:9, 14), who were killed after declining the mark of the Beast (Antichrist) and refusing to worship his image in the temple of Jerusalem.

All the angels, the twenty-four elders, and the *"four living creatures" (Revelation 7:11)* will fall prostrate worshipping the God of our salvation, crying:

Amen! Blessing and glory and wisdom, thanksgiving and honor and power and might, be to our God forever and ever. Amen. (Revelation 7:12)

Again, those of us who have accepted Christ as Savior will have been taken up with Christ in the Rapture prior to the Tribulation. The apostle John refers to this highly debated event in Revelation 3:10: *"Because you have kept My command to persevere, I also will keep you from the hour of trial which shall come upon the whole world, to test those who dwell on the earth."*

The Four Horsemen of the Apocalypse

John the Revelator is told to *"come and see"* (Revelation 6:1) as the Lamb opens the first four seals, which reveal four riders on four horses.

The first rider sits on a white horse, wears a crown, and represents the world ruler of the false peace movement. He is the Antichrist. The second rider holds a great sword and straddles a red horse; he symbolizes worldwide warfare and bloodshed. The next rider carries a pair of scales and rides a black horse. He embodies severe scarcity, poverty, and lack. The forth rider sits on a pale horse; he represents death, which will strike one-third of the earth's population through famine, pestilence, and the attack of wild beasts, which are all represented by the previous three seals.

The fifth seal reveals an altar upon which the martyrs cry out for God's righteous judgment upon the enemies of His people. Please note that the Rapture of the Church occurs before these seals are revealed. These martyrs represent those individuals who are saved after the resurrection of the dead in Christ.

They will be killed for their faith by the Antichrist after the Rapture and before the opening of the fifth seal, which takes place three and a half years into the Great Tribulation. The great harlot of Revelation 17 will take the lives of these martyrs while she reigns in coregency with the ten kings of the revised Roman Empire (Revelation 7:9–15).

The sixth seal represents earth-shattering natural disasters, which will herald the second coming of the Lord. They include great earthquakes, the darkening of the sun, the moon becoming as blood, the stars falling from the sky, and mountains and islands that will be moved from their natural position.

Some of these phenomena are described in other books of the Bible:

> *For the stars of heaven and their constellations will not give their light; the sun will be darkened in its going forth, and the moon will not cause its light to shine. (Isaiah 13:10)*

> *The sun shall be turned into darkness, and the moon into blood, before the coming of the great and awesome day of the LORD. (Joel 2:31)*

> *But the day of the Lord will come as a thief in the night, in which the heavens will pass away with a great noise, and the elements will melt with fervent heat; both the earth and the works that are in it will be burned up. (2 Peter 3:10)*

The Battle of Armageddon

God chose the nation of Israel to provide the source of divine truth on this earth for the generations to come. Through Israel, the Almighty gave mankind His sacred Word, the Patriarchs, the prophets, and our Redeemer, Jesus Christ. Because Satan hates what God establishes, the spirit of anti-Semitism has prevailed through the ages in an effort to destroy this thread of redemption.

At the beginning of the seven years of Tribulation, Satan's

messiah will make a treaty with Israel that will ensure their national security and allow them to rebuild their temple (Daniel 9:27; Ezekiel 38:8, 11). At the halfway mark of the Tribulation, Gog and Magog will invade the land of Israel. God Almighty will destroy the invading Gog and Magog armies, killing five out of six combatants, demonstrating to the world that He is the mighty Shield of Israel—the One True God of Abraham, Isaac, and Jacob (Ezekiel 38–39; Daniel 9:27; 11:40–41; Ezekiel 39:2; Psalms 18:2).

The Antichrist will then break his treaty with the Jewish people and take over Jerusalem, establishing the throne of his evil empire in the Third Temple. He, with the help of the False Prophet, will erect his image in the temple and demand that the world worship him as God. This is the *"abomination of desolation" (Matthew 24:15)*. The Jewish people, recognizing the Antichrist for who he is, will flee Judea and be sheltered by the hand of God in Petra, marking the last half of the Tribulation (Matthew 24:15–16).

There are two major wars fought during the seven years of the Tribulation. The first is the Gog and Magog Wars of Ezekiel 38–39, and the second is the Battle of Armageddon, which happens at the end of the Tribulation in the Valley of Megiddo.

The armies of the King of the West (the Antichrist), representing a vast military armada, and the Kings of the East (China), with a marching army of two hundred million, will march down the dry riverbed of the Euphrates to reach Israel and face off in the mother of all wars (Revelation 9:16).

The Battle of Armageddon begins with the Antichrist and the Kings of the East meeting on the battlefield of the Valley of Jezreel in Israel (Revelation 16:16). When the Kings of the West and East open fire with all their weapons of war, the Bible states, *"Blood came out . . . up to the horses' bridles, for one thousand six hundred furlongs [184 miles]" (Revelation 14:20)*. This battle ends not with an invasion from the north, south, east, or west, but with an invasion from heaven.

Christ will return to earth riding on a magnificent white horse, ushering in the final triumph over the enemies of Israel. The army riding with Him is mounted on white horses and clothed in pure white linen. Jesus Christ will come to rule the earth with a rod of iron as He establishes the theocracy of the Final Kingdom.

The Second Coming of Christ

John records the amazing revelation of the Second Coming with the words, *"Now I saw heaven opened . . ." (Revelation 19:11).* When translated in the Greek, this phrase literally means that when Christ returns to earth, this gateway to and from heaven will open, and will remain open, for all eternity. It reminds us of Jacob's ladder, with the angels ascending into heaven and descending to earth at will (Genesis 28:12).

How long will it take to go from heaven to earth and back again in our supernatural bodies? According to the length of Daniel's prayer, it will only be a matter of seconds:

> *Now while I was speaking, praying, and confessing my sin and the sin of my people Israel, and presenting my supplication before the LORD my God for the holy mountain of my God, yes, while I was speaking in prayer, the man Gabriel, whom I had seen in the vision at the beginning, being caused to fly swiftly, reached me . . . . "At the beginning of your supplications the command went out, and I have come to tell you, for you are greatly beloved." (Daniel 9:20–23)*

The Scriptures are replete in offering the purposes of Christ's return to earth. He will come to:

- Fulfill His promise (Zechariah 14:4; Matthew 25:31; Acts 1:9–11)
- Gather and restore His people (Isaiah 43:5–6; Jeremiah 30:10; 33:6–9; Ezekiel 36:24–38; 37:1–28)
- Judge the nations for their wickedness (Matthew 25:31–46; Revelation 19:2)
- Resurrect the dead who refused the mark of the Beast (Daniel 12:1–4; Revelation 20:4–6)
- Reign as the King of kings (Revelation 19:6)

Judge, Warrior, and Lord. The apostle John, who was an eyewitness to the Lord's ascension, now records His triumphant return:

Now I saw heaven open, and behold, a white horse. And He who sat on him was called Faithful and True, and in righteousness He judges and makes war. His eyes were like a flame of fire, and on His head were many crowns, He had a name written that no one knew except Himself. He was clothed with a robe dipped in blood, and His name is called The Word of God. And the armies in heaven, clothed in fine linen, white and clean, followed Him on white horses. Now out of His mouth goes a sharp sword, that with it He should strike the nations. And He Himself will rule them with a rod of iron. He Himself treads the winepress of the fierceness and wrath of Almighty God. And He has on His robe and on His thigh a name written: KING OF KINGS AND LORD OF LORDS. (Revelation 19:11–16)

Christ's position on a white horse signifies His conquest in battle (Revelation 6:2; see also Psalm 45:4). He is first the Conqueror over death, hell, and the grave. Second, He is the Conqueror of Satan and his evil empire and the enemies of Israel. Jesus appears in this scriptural setting as Judge, Warrior, and Lord. His judgment is indicated by His *"eyes . . . like a flame of fire,"* and He is bearing many crowns, declaring His absolute power and Lordship (Revelation 19:12).

A Robe Dipped in Blood. Having been in the ministry for sixty-plus years, I have heard Revelation 19:13—*"He was clothed with a robe dipped in blood"*—explained in many ways. Some say that this is the blood of Christ shed for the remission of sins at the cross. However, I do not agree with that statement based on the writings of the prophet Isaiah.

First, Isaiah posed the question:

Who is this who comes from Edom, with dyed garments from Bozrah, this One who is glorious in His apparel, traveling in the greatness of His strength? (Isaiah 63:1)

Then the answer was given:

"I who speak in righteousness, mighty to save."
Why is Your apparel red, and Your garments like one who treads in the winepress?
"I have trodden the winepress alone, and from the peoples no one was with Me. For I have trodden them in My anger, and trampled them in My fury; their blood is sprinkled upon My garments, and I have stained all My robes. For the day of vengeance is in My heart, and the year of My redeemed has come."
(Isaiah 63:1–4)

When we think of Jesus, we do not consider Him vengeful. It was not an act of retribution when He was on the cross but an act of absolute love. He forgave the thief who was next to Him, and even on behalf of those guilty of His crucifixion, He pleaded, *"Father, forgive them for they know not what they do" (Luke 23:34).*

Jesus Christ forgave the Romans who entered into a Calvary conspiracy to kill him. He even forgave the handful of Pharisees in Pilate's courtyard who hated Him for saying, *"I say to you that tax collectors and harlots enter the kingdom of God before you" (Matthew 21:31).*

What Isaiah is describing is the greatest destruction that earth will ever see. Scores will be destroyed at Armageddon. The One who treads the winepress with His garments splattered and soaked in crimson blood is the description of God's day of vengeance upon the enemies of Israel at the Battle of Armageddon.

The Winepress. John the Revelator describes God's winepress:

> *And another angel came out from the altar, who had power over fire, and he cried with a loud voice to him who had the sharp sickle saying, "Thrust in your sharp sickle and gather the clusters of the vine of the earth, for her grapes are fully ripe." So the angel thrust his sickle into the earth and gathered the vine of the earth, and threw it into the great winepress of the wrath of God. And the winepress was trampled outside the city [Jerusalem], and blood came out of the winepress, up to the horses' bridles, for one thousand six hundred furlongs." (Revelation 14:18–20)*

John is saying that the armies of the Antichrist are surrounding the city of Jerusalem. They are the *"clusters of the vine,"* which are *"fully ripe."* What they don't realize is that God is waiting for them! Every commander and every soldier in that army is about to experience the winepress of God in His version of *The Grapes of Wrath.*

The prophet Zechariah declared, *"Behold, the day of the LORD cometh [Day of Judgment] . . . [when] I will gather all nations against Jerusalem to battle . . . and fight against those nations"* (14:1–3 KJV).

King David spoke of God's protection over His people: *"As the mountains surround Jerusalem, so the LORD surrounds His people [the Jewish people] from this time forth and forever"* (Psalms 125:2).

Moses prophesied that the hand of God will annihilate the invading armies of Israel: *"For He will avenge the blood of His servants, and render vengeance to His adversaries; He will provide atonement for His land and His people"* (Deuteronomy 32:43).

One of God's top priorities in these bloodbaths called the Gog and Magog Wars and Armageddon is to destroy the enemies of Israel. These wars are the day God's vengeance is released against those who sought to destroy His chosen people. God's retribution has come for the Jewish people who have suffered so much for their steadfast faith.

It is important for Christians to comprehend the depths of God's love for the Jewish people. God called Israel *"My son, My firstborn"* (Exodus 4:22). The Jewish people are a chosen people; they are a Covenant people; they are a cherished people. God made this promise to all of us concerning the Jewish people: *"I will bless those who bless you, and I will curse him who curses you"* (Genesis 12:3).

Buzzards will consume the bloated corpses of the armies that will come against God's people. Their lifeless bodies will stretch across the great span of the battlefield known as Armageddon. This is a testimonial of God's ultimate fury on the nations of the world who persecuted the nation of Israel and the Jewish people (Ezekiel 39:17–20; Revelation 19:17).

Why is God doing this? He answers in Ezekiel 39:22, 29:

"So the house of Israel shall know that I am the LORD their God from that day forward. . . . And I will not hide My face from them anymore; for I shall have poured out My Spirit on the house of Israel," says the Lord GOD.

The bodies of kings, captains, commoners, and horses will become a banquet for the birds of prey, fulfilling the prophecy of Jesus: *"For wherever the carcass is, there will the eagles be gathered together"* (Matthew 24:27–28).

The Authority of God's Word. As Jesus Christ, mounted on His white horse, circles over the battlefield of Armageddon with the heavenly host, He opens *"His mouth [and out] goes a sharp sword, that with it He should strike the nations"* (Revelation 19:15).

The Spoken Word of God based on the will of God is an awesome force. The Bible says that Jesus *"will consume with the breath of His mouth and destroy with the brightness of His coming"* (2 Thessalonians 2:8).

It was the authority of God's Word that created the heavens and the earth. It was the authority of Jesus' Spoken Word that healed the sick, raised the dead, and caused demons to tremble.

Now comes the grand finale, demonstrating the awesome power of God's Spoken Word. Jesus will open His mouth and utterly destroy the armies of the Antichrist and of the Kings of the East. It is here that the blood will flow up to the bridle of a horse for 184 miles. This is God's day of vengeance against the enemies of Israel.

The Seventy-Five Day Interval. According to the prophet Daniel, there is a literal seventy-five-day interval between the second coming of Christ and the official inauguration of the Kingdom of God. Daniel explained this gap in time:

*And from the time that the daily sacrifice is taken away, and the abomination of desolation is set up, there shall be one thousand two hundred and ninety days. Blessed is he who waits, and comes to the **one thousand three hundred and thirty-five days**. (Daniel 12:11–12)*

Revelation 11:3 states, *"And I will give power to my two witnesses, and they will prophesy **one thousand two hundred and sixty days**, clothed in sackcloth."* The difference between 1,335 days and 1,260 days creates the 75-day interval between Christ's return to the Mount of Olives and the end of the Tribulation, which means the official beginning of the Millennial Age. So what will happen in those 75 days?

There is no exact timeline; however, somewhere during this 75-day period it is clear that the Lord is getting Israel's house in order.

1. He will remove the abomination of desolation from the temple.
2. He will cast the Antichrist and the False Prophet alive into the lake of fire (Revelation 19:20).
3. He will bind Satan and cast him into the bottomless pit (Revelation 20:2–3).
4. He will execute the judgment of the Gentiles (Matthew 25:31–46).
5. The Old Testament saints will be resurrected (Isaiah 26:19; Daniel 12:2).
6. The Tribulation saints will be resurrected (Romans 14:10; 2 Corinthians 5:10; Revelation 20:4).
7. The Marriage Feast of the Lamb will take place (Revelation 19:9).

Bible scholar John Phillips beautifully describes that next step in the Final Game of Thrones:

> The remnant of the Jews and the redeemed of the Jews and the redeemed from among the Gentiles will go into the millennial kingdom, the nucleus of the New Kingdom. The millennial kingdom will be worth waiting for.[9]

CHAPTER 15

THE MILLENNIAL REIGN

And I saw thrones, and they sat on them, and judgment was committed to them. Then I saw the souls of those who had been beheaded for their witness to Jesus and for the word of God, who had not worshiped the beast or his image, and had not received his mark on their foreheads or on their hands. And they lived and reigned with Christ for a thousand years. (Revelation 20:4)

During the seven years of the Tribulation, a global evangelism campaign will take place. This time of testimony begins with the 144,000 Jewish evangelists of Revelation 7, who are protected from the Antichrist with the seal of God's Name on their foreheads. How will these 144,000, chosen from the twelve tribes of Israel, come to the knowledge of Christ? By supernatural revelation.

They will have an encounter with the Lord similar to that of the apostle Paul on the road to Damascus. Here Christ arrested the brilliant yet antagonistic Pharisee with His presence, blinding him, and then sent him to Ananias for healing before being commissioned to preach the gospel (Acts 9:1–20). Thereafter, Paul established the New Testament church and shook the Roman Empire with the power of the good news of Jesus Christ.

Beside these 144,000 evangelists, God will release three angels, giving them the assignment of *"flying in the midst of heaven, having the everlasting gospel to preach to those who dwell on the earth—to every nation, tribe, tongue and people"* (Revelation 14:6).

Add to this avalanche of evangelism the two witnesses, Elijah and Enoch, who were taken up to heaven thousands of years earlier without experiencing death. The last promise God made to the Jewish people in the final chapter of the last book of the Old Testament was the promise of Elijah: *"Behold, I will send you Elijah the prophet before the coming of the great and dreadful day of the LORD"* (Malachi 4:5).

Elijah and his companion, Enoch, will have awesome supernatural power during their evangelism tour. If someone tries to harm them, fire will come from their mouths and cremate their attackers. They will have power to cause drought and famine and perform miracles.

Planet Earth has never seen such an awesome demonstration of God's power from any previous evangelist. Countless numbers of people will convert after hearing their testimony and remembering the sudden disappearance of millions of people because of the Rapture of the Church of Jesus Christ.

THE JUDGMENT OF THE NATIONS

The Judgment of Nations (all Gentile nations) will immediately follow the return of Christ to earth and occur before the start of His millennial reign. This is when Jesus Christ will execute His judgment on earth:

"Behold, the days are coming," says the LORD, "that I will raise to David a branch of righteousness; a King [Jesus Christ] shall reign and prosper, and execute judgment and righteousness in the earth." (Jeremiah 23:5)

What is the basis for this judgment? Jesus Christ is calling the people of all nations to give an account of how they treated the Jewish people, as recorded in Matthew 25:31–46. Those who blessed the Jewish people will hear, *"Come, you blessed of My Father, inherit the kingdom prepared for you from the foundation of the world" (v. 34).*

Where is the Jewish connection? Listen to the words of Jesus in verse 40:

And the King [Jesus] will answer and say to them, "Assuredly, I say to you, inasmuch as you did it to one of the least of these My brethren [Jewish people], you did it to Me."

Before the cross, Jesus never called the Gentiles "My brethren." It was not until His death that His precious blood wrote the adoption papers on the parchment of His flesh and made the outcast Gentiles His very own (Ephesians 2:12).

What happens to those who witnessed the suffering of the Jewish people throughout the ages and did nothing? Listen to the words of the Rabbi from Nazareth: *"And these [who did nothing to help the suffering Jews] will go away into everlasting punishment" (Matthew 25:46).*

Remember what God told Abraham the first time He spoke to him thousands of years ago: *"I will bless those who bless you, and I will curse him who curses you" (Genesis 12:3).* This mandate is still in the books of heaven. Allow me to ask you a very important question: What are you doing to bless the house of Israel?

Israel and the Jewish people were at the epicenter of prophecy from the moment God made His Covenant with Abraham, and they will remain so throughout eternity. All other nations and celebrated cities will fall by the wayside, but Israel and Jerusalem will live forever.

The late theologian John Walvoord clearly summarized the purpose and effect of the Judgment of the Nations:

The sheep [righteous] who have manifested their faith in Christ under trying circumstances by befriending a Jew are now rewarded by being ushered into the millennial kingdom with its blessings of Christ's righteous rule and beneficent care over all who trust in Him. By contrast, the goats [unrighteous] who followed the course of this world and undoubtedly participated in the persecution of the Jewish people as well as neglecting their acts of kindness now come under the divine judgment which they justly deserve, and are cast into everlasting fire.[1]

SATAN BOUND
FOR A THOUSAND YEARS

Before the glorious millennial reign of perfect peace, Satan is bound in chains and cast into *"the bottomless pit"* for a thousand years.

Then I saw an angel coming down from heaven, having the key to the bottomless pit and a great chain in his hand. He laid hold of the dragon, that serpent of old, who is the Devil and Satan, and bound him for a thousand years; and he cast him into the bottomless pit, and shut him up, and set a seal on him, so that he should deceive the nations no more till the thousand years were finished. But after these things he must be released for a little while. (Revelation 20:1–3)

It will only take one angel, at God's direction, to imprison Satan—*"the prince of the power of the air" (Ephesians 2:2)* and the *"god of this age" (2 Corinthians 4:4)*. Think about it . . . *one angel!* Why should that encourage you? Because the Bible clearly states that every believer has at least *two angels* as their security escort at all times.

For He [God Almighty] shall give His angels [more than one] charge over you, to keep you [defend] in all your ways. In their hands they shall bear you up, lest you dash your foot against a stone. You shall tread upon the lion and the cobra, the young lion and the serpent you shall trample underfoot. (Psalm 91:11–13)

God Almighty gives His angels charge over you! They are created to protect you, defend you, and minister to you. We serve an awesome heavenly Father! When the serpent comes to torment you with doubt, strife, disease, and hardship, imagine him chained in the bottomless pit so deep that he cannot see the Light that imprisoned him. He is finished for the next one thousand years.

THE JEWISH ELECT

As soon as Jesus Christ sets His foot on the Mount of Olives, He is going to gather His chosen ones from all over the earth. *"And He will send His angels with a great sound of a trumpet, and they will gather together His elect from the four winds, from one end of heaven to the other" (Matthew 24:31)*. Who are "His elect"? They are the Torah-believing Jewish people.

Observant Jews do not recognize Jesus as Messiah because, according to the teachings of Paul in Romans, chapters 9 through 11, the Jewish people have been judicially blinded by the hand of God to the identity of Jesus as Messiah. God has done this in order for the Gentiles to have their day of salvation (Romans 11:25).

Those who teach that the Church has replaced the Jewish people in the eternal plan of God are promoting a false doctrine. Listen to Paul: *"I say then, has God cast away His people [Jewish people]? Certainly not! For I also am an Israelite, of the seed of Abraham, of the tribe of Benjamin"* (Romans 11:1).

Paul's logic is clear. He classifies himself as completely Jewish with a threefold certification. He continues his argument, stating that if God is still using him, then He will use the rest of the Jewish people as well.

As a side note, when Jesus returns to earth, He will be introduced as the Lion of Judah. *Judah* is the root word from which we get the word *Jew*. Jesus was born a Jew from the tribe of Judah. He ministered as a Rabbi from Nazareth. When Jesus comes to earth a second time, He remains a Jew and He will identify Himself with His Jewish brethren. The Jewish people have not been replaced by anyone, and they will be front and center in the millennial reign. Saint Paul succinctly presented the evidence:

> *What then? Israel has not obtained what it seeks; but the elect have obtained it, and the rest [Jewish people] were blinded. . . . For I do not desire, brethren, that you should be ignorant of this mystery [judicial blindness of the Jews concerning Christ's true identity], lest you be wise in your own opinion, that blindness in part [of the Messiah] has happened to Israel until the fullness of the Gentiles has come in.* (Romans 11:7, 25)

The blindness of Israel happened as a judicial act by the hand of God. The phrase *has happened to* occurs in the active voice as an act that ensued from outside the Jewish people's own effort or control. Their blindness or loss of sight is restricted only to the aspects of the death, burial, and resurrection of Jesus Christ. Again, the purpose of this judicious blinding is so that salvation could come to the Gentiles.

Romans 11:28 reads, *"Concerning the gospel they are enemies for your sake, but concerning the election they are beloved [of God Almighty] for the sake of the fathers."* The "enemies" refer to the Pharisees who were persecuting Christians in Paul's day, and the "fathers" are Abraham (the father of all who believe), as well as Isaac and Jacob.

Paul warns Gentile Christians who boast of their relationship with God through the death, burial, and resurrection of Jesus Christ: *"Do not boast against the branches [Jewish people]. But if you [Gentiles] do boast, remember that you do not support the root [Abraham and his seed], but the root supports you"* (Romans 11:18).

I have stated repeatedly and state it again—Judaism does not need Christianity to explain its existence, but Christianity cannot explain its existence without Judaism. It will be the "elect," the righteous observant Jewish person of Matthew 24:31, who will recognize Jesus as Messiah when He returns.

MESSIAH'S REIGN

The *Millennium* literally refers to the era of one thousand years when Christ begins His kingship on earth shortly after His victory at Armageddon. Satan has been locked in the abyss, and there is no earthly theocratic kingdom aside from Christ's. Why will this era take place?

How can the curse be repealed; how can death be overcome; how can all the fearful evils pertaining to man and nature be removed; how can the unspeakably great blessings be obtained: all of which are to be realized in this Kingdom under Messiah's reign.[2]

The millennial reign exists solely on Christ and the fulfillment of His Word.

The prophets Isaiah, Jeremiah, and Ezekiel recorded the words of the Lord concerning His triumphant return and His joyous reign!

Now it shall come to pass in the latter days that the mountain of the LORD's house shall be established on the top of the mountains, and shall be exalted above the hills; and all nations shall flow to it. . . .

He shall judge between the nations, and rebuke many people; they shall beat their swords into plowshares, and their spears into pruning hooks; nation shall not lift up sword against nation, neither shall they learn war anymore. (Isaiah 2:2, 4)

"Behold, the days are coming," says the LORD, "that I will perform that good thing which I have promised to the house of Israel and to the house of Judah: 'In those days and at that time I will cause to grow up to David a Branch of righteousness; He shall execute judgment and righteousness in the earth. In those days Judah will be saved, and Jerusalem will dwell safely. And this is the name by which she will be called: THE LORD OUR RIGHTEOUSNESS.'" (Jeremiah 33:14–16)

Then they shall dwell in the land that I have given to Jacob My servant, where your fathers dwelt; and they shall dwell there, they, their children, and their children's children, forever; and My servant David shall be their prince forever. Moreover I will make a covenant of peace with them, and it shall be an everlasting covenant with them; I will establish them and multiply them, and I will set My sanctuary in their midst forevermore. My tabernacle also shall be with them; indeed I will be their God, and they shall be My people. The nations also will know that I, the LORD, sanctify Israel, when My sanctuary is in their midst forevermore. (Ezekiel 37:25–28)

THE GOVERNMENT OF
THE MILLENNIAL KINGDOM

The millennial kingdom will be a theocracy, as it was in the days before the reign of King Saul, when Israel was under the direct government rule of God Himself (1 Samuel 9:16–17; 10:1). In addition to reigning over Israel, Christ is also King of kings over the entire earth, including the Gentiles (Psalm 72:8).

The prophet Isaiah declared, *"For unto us a Child is born, unto us a Son is given; and the government will be upon His shoulder. And His name will be called Wonderful, Counselor, Mighty God, Everlasting Father, Prince of Peace"* (9:6).

The promise of an Eternal Kingdom was spoken to Mary by the angel Gabriel:

Then the angel said to her, "Do not be afraid, Mary, for you have found favor with God. And behold, you will conceive in your womb and bring forth a Son, and shall call His name JESUS. He will be great, and will be called the Son of the Highest; and the Lord God will give Him the throne of His father David. And He will reign over the house of Jacob forever, and of His kingdom there will be no end." (Luke 1:30–33)

Christ alone will rule with the Word of God and a rod of iron:

Now out of His mouth goes a sharp sword, that with it He should strike the nations. And He Himself will rule them with a rod of iron. He Himself treads the winepress of the fierceness and wrath of Almighty God. (Revelation 19:15)

THE SIZE OF THE ROYAL LAND GRANT

The Lord God of Israel holds the title deed of the Promised Land, and He has transferred the ownership to Abraham, Isaac, and Jacob and their descendants forever. Then God recorded the deed in the Holy Scriptures to be witnessed by the world.

God made two promises to Abraham concerning the nation of Israel:

1. The promise of becoming a great nation (Genesis 12:1–3; 13:16; 15:5; 17:7; 22:17–18)
2. The promise that the land of Israel was an everlasting inheritance (Genesis 12:7; 13:14–17; 15:18–21)

The Royal Land Grant given by God to Abraham and his descendants extended from the *"river of Egypt [Nile] to the great river, the River Euphrates" (Genesis 15:18)*, from Hamath, northeast of Damascus, to Kadesh on the south[3] (Ezekiel 48:1–29). The land promise includes all the land Israel now owns, plus Judea and Samaria (West Bank), Gaza, parts of Egypt, Syria, Lebanon, and Iraq (Genesis 15:18–21). The Covenant Land promised to the Jewish people is literal and unconditional and will be fulfilled in the millennial reign.

The Palestinian claim to Israel is without merit. Those who call themselves Palestinians today are actually descendants of Arabs who lived in the land referred to as Palestine. But where did the name *Palestine* originate? It is derived from the Egyptian/Hebrew word *peleshet*, or "wanderers."[4] The Egyptians used this term in a derogatory reference against the Hebrew children who came to live in their country during the great famine of Joseph's time. The Egyptians feared Abraham's people as they grew into a great multitude (Exodus 1:7–11).

Once again, the demonic spirit of anti-Semitism reared its ugly head, but the God of Abraham, Isaac, and Jacob used a man named Moses to lead them out of Egyptian bondage and back into the Promised Land.

Later, a quasi form of the word *Palestine* appears in the fifth century BCE when the Greek historian Herodotus called the area *Palaistin*.[5] In the second century CE, the Romans quashed the revolt of Shimon Bar Kokhba and as a result created a new Roman province from the merger of Roman Syria and Roman Judaea. In an attempt to sever any Jewish ties with the land of Israel, the Romans, under Emperor Hadrian, renamed the area *Palaestina*.[6]

Centuries later under the Ottoman Empire, the territory south of Syria was *unofficially* designated as Palestine until 1914. After World War I, during the British Mandate (1920–1948), the same territory was *officially* labeled by the British as Palestine and included present-day Israel and present-day Jordan. Incidentally, the international press only labeled *Jews* as Palestinians and not Arabs before Israel's independence in 1948.[7]

Prior to 1948, the British government established the Royal Commission of Inquiry (1936) under the leadership of Lord Robert Peel to investigate the causes of unrest among Arabs and Jews. The findings of the Peel Commission substantiate the Jewish claim to the Covenant Land of Israel:

The Jewish nation was presented as the only nation linked to the land by a historical presence and religious connections. The Commission argued that it was only in the land of Palestine that the Jewish people could achieve political freedom. The Report notes that the Jewish people are indigenous to the Land of Israel/Palestine because of their historical presence in the land. For example, the Commission described in detail the flourishing and influential Jewish community in Safed in the Sixteenth Century.[8]

The Palestinian refugee debate began shortly after the Arab-Israeli war of 1948, when five Arab armies consisting of Egypt, Lebanon, Syria, Iraq, and Saudi Arabia invaded the State of Israel just hours after President Truman recognized it as a state. At the direction of their Arab leaders, over 750,000 Palestinian Arabs fled their homes to avoid the war. They had the assurance of returning soon once the Arab armies defeated the new Jewish state.

Instead, the Lord God of Israel intervened on behalf of His people and miraculously delivered them from their enemies. The Palestinian claim to any part of the land of Israel is nothing more than political propaganda, which is what the Jewish people have had to contend with for centuries.

The Covenant God made with King David gave him a royal dynasty that would rule over His Kingdom forever. When Jesus Christ, the Son of David, sits on His throne on the Temple Mount in Jerusalem during the millennial reign . . . this Covenant will be fulfilled. Our God is *the* Promise Keeper!

JERUSALEM:
THE HOLY CITY OF THE FUTURE

Jerusalem is so much more than the eternal capital of the State of Israel. The Scriptures are filled with descriptions and stories that reflect why it holds such a special place in God's heart and why millions from around the world seek refuge behind its gates:

- Jerusalem is where Abraham placed his son Isaac on the altar on Mount Moriah (Temple Mount) (Genesis 22:2, 9).
- Jerusalem is where King David conquered the city from the Jebusites (1 Chronicles 11:4).
- Jerusalem is where God has placed His Name (2 Chronicles 6:6).
- Jerusalem is where the angel of the Lord destroyed Sennacherib and his army of 185,000 when they threatened to destroy the Holy City (2 Kings 19:35).
- Jerusalem is the City of God (Psalms 48:1–2, 8).
- Jerusalem is the city from which living waters will flow (Zechariah 14:8).
- Jerusalem is where Jesus Christ introduced Himself as Messiah (Matthew 21:7–11).
- Jerusalem is where Jesus was crucified for the sins of the world (Luke 23:33; 24).
- Jerusalem will be the seat of government from the millennial reign into eternity (Revelation 20:4).

THE TEMPLE

The Third Temple will be rebuilt per the specifications found in Ezekiel chapters 40 through 44. Then, after the return of Messiah at the start of the Millennium, the Aaronic priesthood is reestablished and the sons of Zadok will officiate and offer sacrifices once more.

"But the priests, the Levites, the sons of Zadok, who kept charge of My sanctuary when the children of Israel went astray from Me, they shall come near Me to minister to Me; and they shall stand before Me to offer to Me the fat and the blood," says the

Lord GOD. "They shall enter My sanctuary, and they shall come near My table to minister to Me, and they shall keep My charge." (Ezekiel 44:15–16)

THE MILLENNIAL BLESSINGS AND FEASTS

Scripture describes this thousand-year period as one like no other since the Garden of Eden. It will be a time when the land of Israel will be fully restored (Joel 3:18), man and nature will live together in peace (Isaiah 11:6–9), and humanity will once again live long, healthy lives (Zechariah 8:4; see also Ezekiel 47:12).

There will also be a great blessing afforded specifically to the Jewish people during the millennial reign. After centuries of abuse, ridicule, and bigoted hatred, they will be celebrated and sought after. God's love and favor for His Chosen will finally be recognized by all the nations on earth:

Yes, many peoples and strong nations shall come to seek the LORD of hosts in Jerusalem, and to pray before the LORD. . . . In those days ten men from every language of the nations shall grasp the sleeve of a Jewish man, saying, "Let us go with you, for we have heard that God is with you." (Zechariah 8:22–23)

The teachings of the God of Abraham, Isaac, and Jacob will be a major theme during this time of peace: *". . . to the house [the Jewish people] of the God of Jacob; He will teach us His ways, and we shall walk in His paths.' For out of Zion the law shall go forth, and the word of the LORD from Jerusalem"* (Micah 4:2).

Gentile believers from the nations of the world will *"grasp the sleeve"* of the Jewish people and ask about the foundations of the *true faith.* What is the *true faith?* It is what Christianity was meant to be devoid of Babylonian paganism, which is still very much a part of modern-day Christianity. *True faith* is the pure precepts of Judaism, as revealed to Moses by God on Mount Sinai, enriched by God's grace and unmerited favor through the death and resurrection of Jesus Christ, His only begotten Son.

What is meant by the phrase *grasp the sleeve*? The word *sleeve* refers to the Hebrew word *tallith*, or "prayer shawl." What is a prayer shawl? It is a garment worn by observant Jews to specifically fulfill biblical precepts. Gentile believers will learn that Jesus wore one the entirety of His adult life—while He taught His followers, healed the sick, gave sight to the blind, and raised Lazarus from the dead. Jesus was buried wearing a prayer shawl that was found after His resurrection, neatly folded in the place where His body had been laid (John 20:7). He will return wearing one, as He *is* the fulfillment of the law (Numbers 15:38–40; Matthew 5:17).

Additionally, there will be two feasts observed forevermore: Passover (Exodus 12:1–14) and the Feast of Tabernacles (Zechariah 14:16). Gentile believers will want to learn the true meaning of the feasts of the Lord since they play such an important role during the millennial reign—and the Jewish people will teach them.

The word *feast* in Hebrew means "a set or appointed time." The feasts are like a dress rehearsal, offering a portrait of God's prophetic plan. The combined seven feasts, divinely instituted shortly after the people of Israel were delivered from the slavery of Egypt, would be a spiritual blueprint of what lies ahead for Israel, Jerusalem, and the rest of the world.

The majority of Gentile believers are ignorant to the importance of the feasts and will seek out their Jewish brethren for instruction and interpretation of these *appointed times*. Remember this truth: everything God will do, He has already done. Gentile believers will need a teacher, and the Jewish people will be delighted to share the Jewish roots of Christianity as found in God's Word.

SATAN LOOSED

As the curtain of time on the glorious millennial reign of Jesus Christ draws to a close, the angel who put Satan in the *"bottomless pit" (Revelation 20:1–3)* will turn him loose to deceive the nations of the world.

> *Now when the thousand years have expired, Satan will be released from his prison and will go out to deceive the nations which are in the four corners of the earth. (Revelation 20:7–8)*

After a millennium without stress, worry, or wars, why would God allow this monster to be released upon the earth once again? There can only be one answer. Despite all God has the ability to do, He will never force someone to believe in Him. All mankind is given free will. The Word reminds us that it is required of every person to *"choose for yourselves this day whom you will serve" (Joshua 24:15)*.

God releases Satan from the bottomless pit so that those who have not had the opportunity to exercise their free will of choosing between good or evil will do so. The millions who have been born during this time still have the same sinful Adamic nature as all who were born before, as the late J. Vernon McGee described perfectly:

> The human heart alone remains unchanged under these circumstances and many will turn their backs on God and will go after Satan. . . . This rebellion following the Millennium reveals how terrible the heart of man is. . . . We just cannot bring our old nature into subjection to God.[9]

When Satan is loosed from his prison, people from all nations of the earth will believe his lies and follow him back to the gates of hell. It seems impossible to fathom that after a thousand years of glorious peaceful living, many will choose to turn their backs on God and heed Satan instead, but it will happen. So great is the sinful nature of man that even in the clear triumph of the gospel, Satan leads many into a hopeless rebellion.

Who can understand what drives men to sin? For those who are living in earthly bodies, even as we are now, the law of sin is like the law of gravity. No matter how much we want to rise above it, it draws us down. Romans 8:7 says, *"The carnal mind is enmity against God; for it is not subject to the law of God, nor indeed can be."* It is only through the power of Christ that we can rise above sin at all.

Since sin will still have a foothold in creation, it must be eradicated. It is at the end of the thousand-year reign of Christ when the final conflict between God and Satan will take place. Unfortunately, just as men failed in previous ages, mankind will fail during this period as well. Though most will obey Christ, millions will rebel against God and His righteousness.

Remember that the millennial reign of Christ will be a time similar to the Garden of Eden. And just as Adam and Eve, who were placed in a perfect environment created by God Almighty, chose to sin, so will mankind choose the same during Christ's reign. Even under ideal circumstances—an abundant earth, no sickness, and no war—the human heart will prove that it remains unchanged unless regenerated by the power of Christ. Sadly, many will turn their backs on the God who has sustained them and follow the evil one.[10]

Notice that Revelation mentions Gog and Magog in this verse describing the final conflict, but this is not part of the same Gog and Magog Wars described in Ezekiel 38–39. J. Vernon McGee believed that "the rebellion of the godless forces from the north will have made such an impression on mankind that after one thousand years, the last rebellion of man bears the same label— Gog and Magog." Just as we have called two conflicts World War I and World War II, the people of that time could call this last battle Gog and Magog II.[11]

When the glorious millennial reign has ended, Satan will gather the largest army ever assembled to war against Jesus Christ and the Jewish nation. These rebellious armies will advance against Jerusalem, where Jesus rules and reigns from the Temple Mount.

> *Now when the thousand years have expired, Satan will be released from his prison and will go out to deceive the nations which are in the four corners of the earth, Gog and Magog, to gather them together to battle, whose number is as the sand of the sea. They went up on the breadth of the earth and surrounded the camp of the saints and the beloved city. (Revelation 20:7–9)*

There they will learn that rebellion against God always ends in destruction. To purge creation of the evil effects of sin finally and forever, the Almighty will destroy the earth with great heat and fire. Moreover, this conflict will end swiftly and victoriously, because the Great I AM is ready to destroy Satan and his hordes forevermore! Saint Peter described this complete obliteration of the earth: *"The heavens will pass away with a great noise, and the elements will melt with fervent heat; both the earth and the works that are in it will be burned up"* (2 Peter 3:10).

God Almighty will consume all the people who fought against Jerusalem. However, what about Satan?

> *And fire came down from God out of heaven and devoured [annihilated] them. The devil [Satan], who deceived them, was cast into the lake of fire and brimstone where the beast and the false prophet are. And they will be tormented day and night forever and ever. (Revelation 20:9–10)*

"Tormented day and night forever and ever." This statement clearly establishes the fact that there is no end to eternity. At this time, the Antichrist (the Beast) and the False Prophet are still in the lake of fire, in constant anguish. This eternal inferno was prepared specifically for Satan and his fallen angels (Matthew 25:41), not to consume them, but to punish them for all eternity. Dear reader, if you do not know Christ as Savior and ignore this warning—you will spend eternity with this demonic triune!

The Enemy—the one who has tormented, tempted, and tested Christians and Jews through the ages of time—will be permanently bound; however, today he still roams the earth, seeking to rob, kill, and destroy.

At the end of the Millennium, those who chose to side with Satan will be destroyed. God will bring an end to rebellion, and all who participated, human and immortal, will face judgment and be confined to eternal hell and torment. God Almighty will then create a new heaven and a new earth that will last for all eternity.[12]

THE GREAT WHITE THRONE JUDGMENT

The final rebellion of Satan prepares the way for the Great White Throne Judgment. The theme of this judgment is the eternal destiny of those who did not make the Rapture of the Church. The Bible says, *"And as it is appointed for men to die once, but after this the judgment"* (Hebrews 9:27). Those appearing before this judgment are coming to be officially sentenced to everlasting punishment.

Clarence Larkin describes those who will participate:

> The Church is not in this judgment, nor is Israel, for both have been already judged. . . . This [judgment] is after the Millennium when Christ shall sit on the Great White Throne.

. . . In this judgment, "Death" and "Hell" are personified. By "Death," we are to understand the "Grave," which holds the "body" until the resurrection. By Hell the compartment of the underworld or Hades where the souls of the wicked dead remain until the resurrection of the wicked. That both Death and Hell are cast into the lake of fire signifies that Death and Sin will not be found on the New Earth.[13]

There are two resurrections—the resurrection of the just and that of the unjust: *"I have hope in God, which they themselves also accept, that there will be a resurrection of the dead, both of the just and the unjust" (Acts 24:15).*

The resurrection of the just takes place in three phases. The first phase was at Calvary when men came out of their graves and were seen in the city of Jerusalem. The second phase will be the Rapture of the Church. The third phase will occur at the end of the Tribulation, when martyred saints are taken into heaven (Daniel 12:2; Revelation 20:4). All men, both righteous and unrighteous, will experience a resurrection day.

In John 5:27–29, Jesus Christ says that the Father:

has given Him [Christ] authority to execute judgment also, because He is the Son of Man. Do not marvel at this; for the hour is coming in which all who are in the graves will hear His voice and come forth—those who have done good, to the resurrection of life, and those who have done evil, to the resurrection of condemnation.

After the resurrection of the unjust, John describes the throne where their sentencing takes place:

Then I saw a great white throne and Him who sat on it, from whose face the earth and the heaven fled away. And there was found no place for them. And I saw the dead, small and great, standing before God, and books were opened. And another book was opened, which is the Book of Life. And the dead were judged according to their works, by the things which were written in the books. The sea gave up the dead who were in it, and Death and Hades delivered up the dead who were in them. And they were judged, each one according to his works. Then Death and Hades were cast into the lake of fire. This is the second death. (Revelation 20:11–14)

Notice that God has two sets of books, for John the Revelator says, *"books were opened."* There is the Book of Life, which contains the name of every person who accepted Jesus Christ while they were on the earth. When the wicked dead approach the Great White Throne Judgment, God will first look for their names in the Book of Life, and obviously, they will not be found.

Then He will open the "books" that are His written records of every word, thought, and deed of the wicked.[14] John describes what happens next: *"And anyone not found written in the Book of Life was cast into the lake of fire"* (Revelation 20:15).

Either your name is in the Book of Life or it is not. You can receive Christ in this life, or you can choose to follow Him in the Tribulation at the cost of having your head cut off by the Antichrist. It is *your* choice.

If you choose to do neither, you will be made to account for every word, thought, and deed of your life as you stand at the Great White Throne Judgment. Following this judgment, you will be formally sentenced to spend eternity in the lake of fire.

It is *your* choice. I want to be perfectly clear—this is not a future fable I am describing—this is fact. Every one of us is going to spend eternity somewhere: either with God, the Son, and the Holy Spirit in the New Jerusalem, or in the lake of fire with the unholy triune—Satan, the Antichrist, and the False Prophet. But until this time comes, the Great Deceiver is still seeking whom he will devour.

Imagine Satan in the lake of fire, cursing the glory of God and mocking those he has fooled to follow him. His only reward is the damned souls that will share in the torment of his eternal home. His only regret is that he did not win the Final Game of Thrones.

Satan's Final Song

Long ago, I planned in my embodied pride,
That today I would reign as king.
But where is my kingdom, where is my crown?
Is the bitter song I sing.

What bliss have I won through my evil designs?
What pleasure in my soul-wrecking plan?
I hoped to conquer both Heaven and Earth,
But have won nothing more than man.

Where are my princes, my legions of imps,
And the millions of souls I have won?
My chains and my torment are greater by far,
Because of the evil I've done.

Come on, all you dupes, you millions of men,
Who heeded my wishes like fools;

Take your share of the vexing chains,
Under Him who in Triumph rules.

You have lived and died for my wretched cause,
Your souls are eternally marred;
You shall see no more than glimpses of the Light
Of Heaven, from which you are barred.

Then cast your despair, my friends, to the winds,
As the echo of silence replies,
You will feel henceforth the deeper degrees,
Of the Hell within which we lie.

—Author Unknown[15]

I pray you will chose the path to redemption that will lead you to the Eternal Throne of the Living God and not be one of the many who will follow Satan into eternal damnation.

As the millennial reign comes to an end, God will create His new heaven and His new earth:

But the heavens and the earth which now exist are kept in store
by the same word, reserved for fire until the day of judgment and
perdition [destruction] of ungodly men. . . . But the day of the
Lord [judgment] will come as a thief in the night, in which the
heavens will pass away with a great noise, and the elements will
melt with fervent heat; both the earth and the works that are in
it will be burned up. (2 Peter 3:7, 10)

Once this purification by fire has been completed, the New Jerusalem will descend from the Third Heaven, and God the Father will set up His Eternal Throne and establish the Final Kingdom.

CHAPTER 16

THE FINAL THRONE

"Heaven is My throne,
And earth is My footstool.
Where is the house that you will build Me?
And where is the place of My rest?" (Isaiah 66:1)

We live in an information age, yet I believe we are one of the most uninformed generations in the history of humanity when it comes to the knowledge of the truth. We listen to "fake news," we refuse to read books, and we allow historical revisionists to hijack the foundational truths of our nation's birth.

Reality TV has made voyeurism a family pastime. We watch YouTube tirades and consider Facebook the Holy Grail, yet we don't know how to communicate with our loved ones across the dinner table. Scientists can split the atom, create deadly chemical weapons, and build nuclear missiles of war in an effort to secure world power.

We know how to use complicated electronic gadgetry, children can fly a plane via virtual video games, and radical terrorists can create deadly bombs with internet blueprints.

Yet all this high-tech information is a recipe for disaster if we refuse to recognize the veracity of God's Word: *"The entirety of Your word is truth, and every one of Your righteous judgments endures forever" (Psalms 119:160).*

If you do not believe Genesis 1:1, then you will not believe the balance of God's Word. However, if you *do* believe God's Word, then you can look at the past, the present, and into the future with absolute confidence and certainty.

THE AGES OF AGES

Prophecy scholar Clarence Larkin refers to the "Creative Ages" of Genesis as the "Alpha Ages" and the "End of the Ages" of Revelation as the "Omega Ages." When time as we know it ceases, the "Eternal Ages," or the "Ages of the Ages," will begin.

This is what the apostle Paul called the *"ages to come"* in his letter to the Ephesians (2:7). John, in the book of Revelation, said that Satan, the Beast, and the False Prophet shall be tormented day and night forever and ever (Revelation 20:10), or through the "Ages of the Ages." And during this same period, the servants of God shall reign in the new earth (Revelation 22:5).

God only knows what the "Ages of Ages" will reveal; however, believers will experience the glorious things He has planned.[1] The "Ages of Ages" will usher in the Final Throne!

THE NEW EARTH

God's purging fire will destroy man's rebellious social order for the last time. This divine cleansing will mark the end of sin's contamination of the world. The apostle John opens his book by pulling back the veil of eternity through Christ's revelation, and he closes it by describing a *"new heaven and a new earth"*: *"I saw a new heaven and a new earth, for the first heaven and the first earth had passed away. Also there was no more sea" (Revelation 21:1).*

The seas that were created in Genesis 1:2 will be put back into heaven and in the center of the earth, where they originated. The earth will be "renewed to its original state as before the fall of Lucifer and before the first rebellion of the earth against God." The world's new water source will come from rivers, lakes, and small seas.[2]

> His dominion shall be *"from sea to sea, and from the River to the ends of the earth." (Zechariah 9:10)*
>
> And in that day it shall be that living waters shall flow from Jerusalem, half of them toward the eastern sea [Dead Sea] and half of them toward the western sea [Mediterranean]; in both summer and winter it shall occur. (Zechariah 14:8)
>
> And he showed me a pure river of water of life, clear as crystal, proceeding from the throne of God and of the Lamb. (Revelation 22:1)

The new earth will have everything you will ever need. However, there are things you will not find there:

- No tears: *"And God will wipe away every tear from their eyes"* (Revelation 21:4)
- No death: *"there shall be no more death"* (21:4)
- No mourning: *"nor sorrow, nor crying"* (21:4)

- No pain: *"no more pain, for the former things have passed away"* *(21:4)*
- No curse: *"there shall be no more curse,"* forever conquered through the cross of Christ *(22:3)*
- No night: *"for the Lord God gives them light"* *(22:5)*
- No sin: *"anything that defiles, or causes an abomination or a lie"* *(21:27)*

God has eradicated all evil: *"But the cowardly, unbelieving, abominable, murderers, sexually immoral, sorcerers, idolaters, and all liars shall have their part in the lake which burns with fire and brimstone, which is the second death"* *(Revelation 21:8)*.

THE NEW JERUSALEM

The pinnacle of God's eternal plan for mankind is a new heaven and a new earth. The old has passed away. Sin and decay are no more. God promises *"he who overcomes"* *(Revelation 21:7)* an inheritance in an eternal paradise with Christ Jesus.

We will live forever in the Final Kingdom, worshipping God Almighty as He sits on His Eternal Throne in the new city of Jerusalem. The New Jerusalem will be a city of celestial origin. It is the city Jesus told His followers He is preparing for them in heaven (John 14:2).

For me, this is one of the most exciting descriptions in the book of Revelation. I can imagine it in the theater of my mind—the heavens opening, and this perfect, foursquare city in all its glory descending onto the new earth. It will be established in the center of the Promised Land. What a remarkable sight!

The New Jerusalem will have many unique traits, for John the Revelator takes the time to describe its appearance, its foundations, the buildings, its location, its measurements, its materials, and its rulers. One of the most important truths about this beautiful city is that God the Father, Jesus Christ the Son, and the Holy Spirit will dwell there (Revelation 21:22; 22:17).

Seven Characteristics of the New Jerusalem

1. It will be known by many names, among them are:
   - The Holy City (Isaiah 52:1; Revelation 21:2)
   - The tabernacle of God (Psalm 46:4; Revelation 21:3)
   - The city of the living God (Hebrews 12:22)
   - My Father's house (John 14:2)
2. God is the Architect, the Builder, and the Owner (Revelation 21).
3. The glory of God and the light of the Lamb will illuminate it (v. 23).
4. It will be made of gold and precious stones (vv. 18–21).
5. It will have walls and foundations (vv. 12–14).
6. It will have twelve gates of solid pearl and twelve streets made of pure, transparent glass-like gold (v. 21).
7. There will be no temple there, *"for the Lord God Almighty and the Lamb are its temple" (v. 22).*

New Tree of Life

The original Tree of Life was in the midst of the Garden of Eden (Genesis 2:9). The new earth will have a new Tree of Life, whose leaves will be for the healing of the nations, preserving the lives of all who live in the Final Kingdom.

It will bear twelve variety of fruits—one for every month: *"In the middle of its street, and on either side of the river, was the tree of life, which bore twelve fruits, each tree yielding its fruit every month. The leaves of the tree were for the healing of the nations" (Revelation 22:2).*

Who Will Inhabit the New Earth?

According to John the Revelator, the inhabitants of the new earth will be angels (Revelation 21:12), the redeemed of Israel (v. 12), the Church of Jesus Christ (v. 14), and the *"nations of those who are saved" (v. 24)*.

However, the most important inhabitants are the members of the Holy Trinity—God Himself, His Son, and the Holy Spirit: *"And I heard a loud voice from heaven saying, 'Behold, the tabernacle of God is with men, and He will dwell with them, and they shall be His people. God Himself will be with them and be their God'" (Revelation 21:3)*.

Finis Dake says of the Trinity and the new earth, "The Father, the Son and the Holy Spirit will reign together throughout all eternity, as before the rebellion, which made it necessary for them to take separate parts in the creation and redemption of all things."[3]

The heavenly city has the glory of God and the throne of God, and those who dwell there shall see His face (Ezekiel 43:7; Revelation 22:4). The Great I AM will dwell among His people forever, which is the final realization of the eternal plan of God for man and the earth.

Who Will Be King?

Several empires and kings have walked across the stage of history. They have conquered men and nations and taken their seat on gilded thrones. Through the centuries, thrones have been fought over and toppled, ascended to and sat upon, and the majority have passed away.

A throne symbolizes power and authority over kingdoms and empires. Subjects throughout the world have bowed, knelt, and prostrated themselves before them. Listed below are some the most renowned rulers who have held a throne throughout history.[4] Additionally, I have compiled a list of the largest empires recorded in history based on the amount of land they conquered.[5]

1. Genghis Khan (Mongolia)
2. Alexander the Great (Greece)
3. Tamerlane (Uzbekistan)
4. Attila the Hun (Austria/Germany)
5. Charlemagne (France)
6. Pharaoh Thutmose III (Egypt)
7. Ashoka the Great (India)
8. Cyrus the Great (Media and Persia)
9. Ch'in Shih Huang (China)
10. Augustus Caesar (Rome)

| No. | THE EMPIRES | Size of Empire by Land Mass | | TIME PERIOD | TOTAL REIGNING YEARS |
		Million Miles^2	% of World Land Mass		
1	British	13.01	22%	1497–1997 CE	500
2	Mongolian	9.15	16%	1206–1368 CE	162
3	Russian	9.15	15%	1721–1917 CE	196
4	Spanish	7.72	13%	1492–1899 CE	407
5	Qing Dynasty	5.68	10%	1636–1912 CE	276
6	Yuan Dynasty	5.41	9%	1279–1368 CE	89
7	Umayyad Caliphate	5.02	8%	756–1031 CE	275
8	Abbasid Caliphate	4.29	7%	750–1258 CE	508
9	Portuguese	4.02	6.5%	1415–1999 CE	584
10	Rashidun Caliphate	3.0	6%	632–661 CE	29
11	Roman Empire (Western and Eastern)	1.43	2.85%	27–476 CE 476–1453 CE	449 977
12	Ottoman	695,000 mi^2	1.2%	1299–1922 CE	623
13	Holy Roman (Germany)	302,881 mi^2	0.53%	962–1806 CE	844

To be considered an empire, an expanse of land must be led politically by a monarch, an emperor, or an oligarchy. Aside from this leadership model, the only other thing these empires and rulers have in common is that each of them disappeared.

However, there is One who was, and is, and is to come. He will take His kingship on the Final Throne in His Eternal Kingdom. There is only one throne and one King—the Almighty God, Creator of heaven and earth. The throne of God is where He manifests His power and great glory, declaring His absolute sovereignty. *"Your throne, O God, is forever and ever; a scepter of righteousness is the scepter of Your kingdom" (Psalms 45:6).* He is God Almighty, the Great I AM, the Alpha and Omega, who sits upon His throne and is:

- Majestic and worthy of honor: *"[Jesus] has sat down at the right hand of the throne of God" (Hebrews 12:2).*
- Perfect justice: *"Righteousness and justice are the foundations of His throne" (Psalms 97:2).*
- Holy: *"God reigns over the nations; God sits on His holy throne" (Psalm 47:8).*
- Worthy of praise: *"But You are holy, enthroned in the praises of Israel" (Psalm 22:3).*
- Pure: *"And in their mouth was found no deceit, for they are without fault before the throne of God" (Revelation 14:5).*
- Eternal life: *"And he showed me a pure river of water of life, clear as crystal, proceeding from the throne of God and of the Lamb" (Revelation 22:1).*
- Grace: *"Let us therefore come boldly to the throne of grace, that we may obtain mercy and find grace to help in time of need" (Hebrews 4:16).*

My dear friend Derek Prince described one of the most splendid scenes that will surround the Throne of the Living God. It is the praise of His people:

> What a beautiful revelation that is—when we realize that the throne God sits upon is the praises of His people. God is Holy. God is a King. He's the King of kings and Lord of lords. We do not make Him a King by praising Him, but we offer Him the throne, which is His due.
>
> You see, Jesus said: "When two or three are gathered together in My name, there am I in the midst." His presence in our midst is guaranteed. It depends upon His faithfulness, not our response. But when He comes in our midst—as the King of kings and the Lord of lords—it's very right and appropriate that we respond to Him as a King.
>
> As a King, He merits a throne; nothing else becomes Him. And it is our privilege to offer Him the throne. When we praise Him, when we exalt Him, when we sing praises and glorify His Name and extol His majesty, then we are acknowledging His Kingship and we are responding in a way that is appropriate. We are offering Him a throne to sit upon—the throne of our praises.[6]

One day all creation will bow to the majesty of God's throne (Philippians 2:9–11). The regal beings surrounding the throne will lay their crowns before God and say, *"You are worthy, O Lord, to receive glory and honor and power" (Revelation 4:11).*

The Bible presents a perfect and complete circle. Everything that God created in the Garden of Eden, after several thousand years of blood, tears, and suffering, has returned to be an exact replica of paradise—what God intended all along. We will live in a realm where there will be no more death, nor sorrow, nor suffering. There will be no pain, for the former things have all passed away. I ask you, will you be there?

One of the greatest preachers and soul winners of all time was a prince of the gospel named Charles Haddon Spurgeon. Over a century ago, he presented a sermon at Metropolitan Tabernacle on the throne of God. The following is the call to salvation he offered the hearer. I could think of no better way to end this book than to afford you, the reader, the same opportunity.

We do not suppose that a man is shooting at a target if he does not look that way; nor can we imagine that a man's ambition is fixed on heaven if he has no heavenward thoughts or aspirations. The pilgrim turns his steps towards the place he is desirous to reach. . . . Till the day breaks and the shadows flee away, let us wait for the Bridegroom's appearing, and the home-bringing of the bride. As virgins that look forward to the marriage day let us keep our lamps trimmed, and see to it that there is oil in our vessels, lest when the cry is heard, "The Bridegroom cometh" any of us should need to nurse the dimly-burning spark, or despairingly cry, "Our lamps are gone out." Let us all be ready that we may go in through the gates into the city.

Some of you, alas! are not able to feel the joy which this subject excites in our breasts. You cannot take delight in the throne of God and of the Lamb. God grant you may. Come, now, to the throne of grace with open confession and secret contrition. It is the throne of God, who knows the nature of your sin; it is the throne of the Lamb, who bore the penalty of sin, and can put it away. Come to the throne of the Lamb that was slain. I entreat you to come now. So shall you find peace and reconciliation, and you shall be made meet to enter into the joy of your Lord.[7]

If you are presently experiencing a time of tears, a time of suffering and sorrow, there is hope for the troubled heart. Remember: we are moving ever closer toward the perfection that God has created for the righteous. The King of kings is preparing for the appointed time when He will set up earth's last empire—on the new earth, in the New Jerusalem, reigning forevermore on His Final Throne.

"Surely I am coming quickly." Amen. Even so, come, Lord Jesus! *(Revelation 22:20)*

THE ETERNAL THRONE

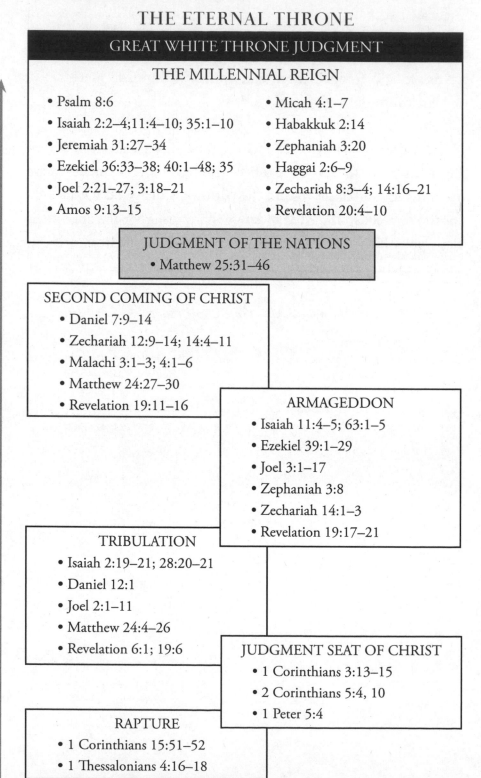

GREAT WHITE THRONE JUDGMENT

THE MILLENNIAL REIGN

- Psalm 8:6
- Isaiah 2:2–4;11:4–10; 35:1–10
- Jeremiah 31:27–34
- Ezekiel 36:33–38; 40:1–48; 35
- Joel 2:21–27; 3:18–21
- Amos 9:13–15

- Micah 4:1–7
- Habakkuk 2:14
- Zephaniah 3:20
- Haggai 2:6–9
- Zechariah 8:3–4; 14:16–21
- Revelation 20:4–10

JUDGMENT OF THE NATIONS
- Matthew 25:31–46

SECOND COMING OF CHRIST
- Daniel 7:9–14
- Zechariah 12:9–14; 14:4–11
- Malachi 3:1–3; 4:1–6
- Matthew 24:27–30
- Revelation 19:11–16

ARMAGEDDON
- Isaiah 11:4–5; 63:1–5
- Ezekiel 39:1–29
- Joel 3:1–17
- Zephaniah 3:8
- Zechariah 14:1–3
- Revelation 19:17–21

TRIBULATION
- Isaiah 2:19–21; 28:20–21
- Daniel 12:1
- Joel 2:1–11
- Matthew 24:4–26
- Revelation 6:1; 19:6

JUDGMENT SEAT OF CHRIST
- 1 Corinthians 3:13–15
- 2 Corinthians 5:4, 10
- 1 Peter 5:4

RAPTURE
- 1 Corinthians 15:51–52
- 1 Thessalonians 4:16–18

EARTH'S
LAST EMPIRE

NOTES

SECTION ONE: ALL ROADS LEAD TO JERUSALEM

My Jerusalem

1 Yehuda Amichai, "Jerusalem, 1967," in *The Poetry of Yehuda Amichai*, ed. Robert Alter (New York: Farrar, Straus and Giroux, 2015), 88.

Chapter 1

1 Simon Sebag Montefiore, *Jerusalem: The Biography* (New York: Alfred A. Knopf, 2011), xix.

2 Rabbi Jill Jacobs, in an article for the website My Jewish Learning, explains, "While we speak often of 'the Midrash,' there is no single book with this title, but only a series of compilations composed and edited over the course of more than a millennium. These works are generally categorized as either *halachic* (legal) or *aggadic* (narrative). . . . One of the works that best exemplifies this intermingling of legal and narrative material is Midrash Tanhuma, a collection of stories, discussions of specific laws, and rabbinic homilies, all connected with the five books of the Torah and named for Rabbi Tanhuma, the first character to appear in the collection." Adapted from Jill Jacobs, "Midrash Tanhuma," My Jewish Learning, accessed June 16, 2018, https://www.myjewishlearning .com/article/midrash-tanhuma/.

3 Midrash Tanhuma, Kedoshim 10.

4 Teddy Kollek, *Jerusalem: Policy Papers 22* (Washington, DC: Washington Institute for Near East Policy, 1990), 19–20.

5 Eric H. Cline, *Jerusalem Besieged: From Ancient Canaan to Modern Israel* (Ann Arbor: University of Michigan Press, 2004), 311.

6 Israel Ministry of Foreign Affairs, "Jerusalem 3000: When Did King David Conquer Jerusalem?" MFA Archive, June 2, 1993, http://www.israel.org/MFA/MFA-Archive/1993/Pages/JERUSALEM%203000-%20When%20did%20King%20 David%20conquer%20Jerusa.aspx.

7 William G. Dever, *Who Were the Early Israelites and Where Did They Come From?* (Grand Rapids, MI: Eerdmans, 2003).

8 Israel Ministry of Foreign Affairs, "Israel's War of Independence (1947–1949)," About Israel: History, accessed June 16, 2018, http://mfa.gov.il/MFA/AboutIsrael/History /Pages/Israels%20War%20of%20Independence%20-%201947%20-%201949.aspx.

9 JIMENA, "Jewish Refugees from Arab Countries: Country Profiles," Jews Indigenous to the Middle East and North Africa, http://www.jimena.org/jimena-country-by-country/.

10 Meir Loewenberg, "What Happened on the Original Yom Yerushalayim in 1967?" Behind the News in Jerusalem, http://israelbehindthenews.com/happened-original -yom-yerushalayim-1967/14682/.

11 Jewish Virtual Library, "The Six-Day War: Background and Overview/The Stunning Victory," accessed June 16, 2018, http://www.jewishvirtuallibrary.org/background-and -overview-six-day-war. (Jewish Virtual Library hereafter cited as JVL.)

12 Howard M. Sachar, *A History of Israel: From the Rise of Zionism to Our Time* (New York: Knopf, 2007), 676; CAMERA (Committee for Accuracy in Middle East Reporting in America), "Immediate Aftermath: The 3 No's of Khartoum," The Six-Day War, accessed June 18, 2018, http://www.sixdaywar.org/content/khartoum.asp.

13 UN General Assembly, Resolution 3379 (30), Elimination of All Forms of Racial Discrimination, November 10, 1975, 83–84, https://documents-dds-ny.un.org/doc /RESOLUTION/GEN/NR0/000/92/IMG/NR000092.pdf?OpenElement.

14 CNN Library, "Camp David Accords Fast Facts," CNN, last updated September 3, 2017, https://www.cnn.com/2013/08/23/world/meast/camp-david-accords-fast-facts /index.html.

15 William E. Farrell, "Sadat Assassinated at Army Parade as Men amid Ranks Fire into Stands: At Least 8 Killed," *New York Times*, October 7, 1981, https://archive.nytimes .com/www.nytimes.com/learning/general/onthisday/big/1006.html.

16 Peter Bergen, "The Cleric Who Altered the Course of Modern History," CNN, February 19, 2017, https://www.cnn.com/2017/02/19/opinions/9-11-spiritual-guide-dies-bergen/.

17 JVL, "Israel's Wars and Operations: Operation Opera—Raid on Iraqi Nuclear Reactor/ Diplomacy Fails," accessed June 18, 2018, http://www.jewishvirtuallibrary.org /operation-opera-raid-on-iraqi-nuclear-reactor.

18 Dario Leone, "Operation Opera: How 8 Israeli F-16s Destroyed an Iraqi Nuclear Plant 33 Years Ago Today," *Aviationist* (blog), June 7, 2014, https://theaviationist.com/2014 /06/07/operation-opera-explained/.

19 JVL, "First Lebanon War: Background and Overview/Burgeoning Violence," accessed June 18, 2018, http://www.jewishvirtuallibrary.org/background-and-overview-of-first -lebanon-war.

20 Henry Kissinger, "From Lebanon to the West Bank to the Gulf," *Washington Post*, June 16, 1982, accessed June 28, 2018, https://www.washingtonpost.com/archive/politics /1982/06/16/from-lebanon-to-the-west-bank-to-the-gulf/76008a90-a029-4bc3-88b9 -ece961df8a22/?utm_term=.7b8b414229c4.

21 JVL, "First Lebanon War: Israeli Civilian Casualties on the Lebanese Border," accessed June 18, 2018, http://www.jewishvirtuallibrary.org/israeli-civilian-casualties-on-the -lebanese-border-1985-1999.

22 Michael Omer-Man, "This Week in History: Operation Moses Begins, *Jerusalem Post*, November 19, 2010, www.jpost.com/Features/In-Thespotlight/This-week-in-History -Operation-Moses-begins.

23 Michael Slackman, "Some Palestinian Jordanians Lose Citizenship," *New York Times*, March 13, 2010, https://www.nytimes.com/2010/03/14/world/middleeast/14jordan .html; Hussein bin Talal, "Address to the Nation," English translation of speech delivered in Amman, Jordan, July 31, 1988, http://www.kinghussein.gov.jo/speeches_letters.html.

24 JVL, "Terrorism against Israel: Comprehensive Listing of Fatalities," accessed June 18, 2018, http://www.jewishvirtuallibrary.org/comprehensive-listing-of-terrorism -victims-in-israel.

25 Rich Valkanet, "Bible Timeline," Bible Hub, accessed June 18, 2018, Biblehub.com /timeline/.

26 Brian Whitaker, "The Mitchell Report: End the Violence Now, So That Peace Talks Can Start Again," *Guardian*, May 21, 2001, https://www.theguardian.com/world/2001/may /22/israel1.

27 Dona J. Stewart, *The Middle East Today: Political, Geographical and Cultural Perspectives* (New York: Routledge, 2009), 165.

28 Sharon Otterman, "Middle East: The Road Map to Peace," Council on Foreign Relations, February 7, 2005, www.cfr.org/backgrounder/middle-east-road-map-peace.

29 Israel Ministry of Foreign Affairs, "Declaration of the Establishment of the State of Israel," May 14, 1948, www.mfa.gov.il/mfa/foreignpolicy/peace/guide/pages /declaration%20of%20establishment%20of%20state%20of%20israel.aspx.

30 Daniel Ayalon, "In Gaza, a Test Case for Peace," *Washington Post* Opinions, July 20, 2005, http://www.washingtonpost.com/wp-dyn/content/article/2005/07/19/AR2005071901552.html.

31 Human Rights Watch, "Why They Died: Civilian Casualties in Lebanon during the 2006 War," *Human Rights Watch* 19, no. 5(E) (September 2007), www.hrw.org/reports/2007/lebanon0907/lebanon0907webwcover.pdf.

32 Aaron Klein, "Israeli Strike in Syria Eliminates Reviled Perpetrator of Attack 'So Sickening' Details 'Give Pause to Israel's Enemies," Breitbart, December 20, 2015, http://www.breitbart.com/jerusalem/2015/12/20/israeli-strike-in-syria-eliminates-reviled-perpetrator-of-attack-so-sickening-details-give-pause-to-israels-enemies/.

33 Dudi Cohen, "Iran Honors Murderer Samir Kuntar," Ynetnews, January 30, 2009, https://www.ynetnews.com/articles/0,7340,L-3664187,00.html.

34 Ali Hashem, "How Will Nasrallah Retaliate for Death of Hezbollah Leader in Syria?" Lebanese-Canadian Coordinating Council, December 24, 2015 (news release from Al-Monitor, December 23, 2015), http://eliasbejjaninews.com/archives/34153/ali-hashem-how-will-nasrallah-retaliate-for-death-of-hezbollah-leader-in-syria/.

35 JVL, "Operation Cast Lead: IDF Soldiers Killed, accessed June 19, 2018, http://www.jewishvirtuallibrary.org/idf-soldiers-killed-during-operation-cast-lead.

36 Jodi Rudoren and Isabel Kershner, "Israel's Search for 3 Teenagers Ends in Grief," *New York Times*, June 30, 2014, www.nytimes.com/2014/07/01/world/middleast/Israel-missing-teenagers.html.

37 COGAT, "Hamas Terror Tunnels—Built with Gazans' Stolen Money," Coordination of Government Activities in the Territories, May 18, 2017, http://www.cogat.mod.gov.il/en/Our_Activities/Pages/Hamas-Terror-Tunnels-18.5.17.aspx.

38 "Cement Intended for Gaza Reconstruction Ends Up on Black Market," *Algemeiner*, December 3, 2014, https://www.algemeiner.com/2014/12/03/cement-intended-for-gaza-reconstruction-ends-up-on-black-market/.

39 "Israeli Humanitarian Operations: Aid to the Gaza Strip (June 2010-Present)," Jewish Virtual Library, https://www.jewishvirtuallibrary.org/israeli-humanitarian-aid-to-the-gaza-strip.

40 JVL, "Israel's Wars and Operations: Operation Protective Edge/Statistics," accessed June 19, 2018, http://www.jewishvirtuallibrary.org/operation-protective-edge.

41 US Department of State, "Joint Comprehensive Plan of Action," accessed June 19, 2018, https://www.state.gov/e/eb/tfs/spi/iran/jcpoa/.

42 Prime Minister's Office, "The Nuclear Deal with Iran: Questions and Answers about the Nuclear Deal with Iran," accessed June 19, 2018, http://www.pmo.gov.il/English/Pages/Iran.aspx.

43 James S. Robbins, "The Iran Nuclear Deal Was the Worst Deal Ever. No Wonder Donald Trump Nixed It," *USA Today*, May 8, 2018, www.usatoday.com/story/opinion/2018/05/08/Iran-nuclear-deal-worst-donald-trump-column/589828002/.

44 Alexander Fulbright, "Iranian Drone Shot Down in Northern Israel in February Was Armed with Explosives," *Times of Israel*, April 13, 2018, www.timesofisrael.com/iranian-drone-shot-down-in-northern-israel-in-february-was-armed-with-explosives/.

45 Yaniv Kubovich and Noa Shpigel, "Israel Shoots Down Syrian Drone Infiltrating 10 Kilometers into Israeli Airspace," *Haaretz*, July 11, 2018, https://www.haaretz.com/israel-news/israel-shoots-down-drone-infiltrating-from-syria-1.6267047.

46 Michael Bachner and TOI Staff, "Hamas Said to Offer Israel Long-Term Ceasefire in Gaza," *Times of Israel*, May 7, 2018, www.timesofisrael.com/hamas-said-to-offer-israel-long-term-ceasefire-in-gaza-report/.

47 Reuters, "Israeli Fire Kills Palestinian During Protest at Gaza Border," *New York Post*, April 5, 2018, www.nypost.com/2018/04/05/israeli-fire-kills-palestinian-during-protest -at-gaza-border/.

48 Tamara Pileggi and TOI Staff, "PA Warned Paris That Gaza Border Clashes Financed by Iran—Report," *Times of Israel*, June 5, 2018, https://www.timesofisrael.com/pa-warned -paris-that-gaza-border-clashes-financed-by-iran-report/.

Chapter 2

1 Edward Flannery, *The Anguish of the Jews: Twenty-Three Centuries of Anti-Semitism* (Mahwah, NJ: Paulist, 1985), 295.

2 Dagobert D. Runes, *The War Against the Jew*, epigraph (New York: Philosophical Library, 1968), xxv.

3 "31 Countries Adopt New Definition of Anti-Semitism that Includes Anti-Zionism," *Tower*, June 3, 2016, http://www.thetower.org/3462-31-countries-adopt-new-definition -of-anti-semitism-that-includes-anti-zionism/.

4 Martin Lockshin, "Haman's Antisemitism: What Did He Not Like about the Jews?" TheTorah.com, March 8, 2017, https://thetorah.com/hamans-antisemitism-what -did-he-not-like-about-the-jews/.

5 Elon Gilad, "The Revolt of the Maccabees: The True Story behind Hanukkah," *Haaretz*, December 10, 2014, https://www.haaretz.com/jewish/.premium-maccabean-revolt-the -true-story-1.5343197.

6 Flannery, *Anguish of the Jews*, 13.

7 Ibid., 8.

8 Josephus, *The Jewish War*, trans. G. A. Williamson (Harmondsworth: Penguin, 1959).

9 Jewish Virtual Library (www.jewishvirtuallibrary.org) and Rabbi Eisen. Eisen serves as senior rabbinical lecturer at the Orthodox Union (OU) Jerusalem World Center, where he has taught for thirty years. His lecture series include completed studies of Ethics of the Fathers, The Kuzari and Guide of the Perplexed series in early Biblical commentaries, Talmudic Aggadah, and classic Jewish thought and philosophy. For over twenty years, he also taught Talmud and Midrash, with a special focus on Jewish thought philosophy at Yeshivat Hakotel's Foreign Students and Israeli Hesder programs. Rabbi Eisen has also been a Torah lecturer in the Israel Defense Forces (IDF) Rabbinate Torah Lecture Corps (reserves), and has also volunteered as a board member of Operation Dignity, a relief organization on behalf of the former residents of Gush Katif, after their expulsions. More recently he has been involved in "building bridges" with the Christian community through lectures and informal meetings in Israel, North America, and Europe, as well as via the Internet (especially through Yeshivath Sharashim).

10 Bruce L. Shelley, "325 The First Council of Nicea," *Christian History* 28 (1990), www.christianitytoday.com/history/issues/issue.../325-first-council-of-nicea.html.

11 From the Letter of the Emperor to all those not present at the Council, found in Philip Schaff and Henry Wallace, *Nicene and Post-Nicene Fathers*, second series, vol. 1 (New York: Cosimo, 2007), 524.

12 Erin Doom, "Dating Easter: A Concise History of the Division," Eighth Day Institute, May 4, 2015, https://www.eighthdayinstitute.org/dating_easter_a_concise_history _of_the_division.

13 Ignatius of Antioch, Epistle to the Magnesians, chap. 8–10.

14 Justin Martyr, "Dialogue with Trypho" chaps. 16, 21, in *Saint Justin Martyr: The First Apology, The Second Apology, Dialogue with Trypho, Exhortation to the Greeks, Discourse to the Greeks, The Monarchy or The Rule of God*, trans. Thomas B. Falls, *The Fathers of the Church*, vol. 6 (Washington, DC: Catholic University of America Press, 2008), 172, 178.

15 Attributed to John Chrysostom, quoted by Rabbi Ken Spiro, "History Crash Course #46: Blood Libel," Aish.com, September 29, 2001, http://www.aish.com/jl/h/cc /48951151.html.

16 Charlotte Elisheva Fonrobert, "Jewish Christians, Judaizers, and Christian Anti-Judaism", chap. 10 in *Late Ancient Christianity, A People's History of Christianity*, vol. 2 (Minneapolis, MN: Fortress Press, 2005).

17 John Chrysostom, *Against the Jews* 1:5, in "Early Church Fathers—Additional Texts," ed. Roger Pearse, Tertullian.org, http://www.tertullian.org/fathers/chrysostom_adversus _judaeos_01_homily1.htm.

18 Augustine, *Confessions* 12.14

19 *Oxford Dictionary of Byzantium*, ed. Alexander P. Kazhdan (New York: Oxford University Press, 1991), s.v. "Codex Theodosianus."

20 History, "Pope Urban II Orders the First Crusades," www.history.co.uk/this-day-in -history/27-november/pope-urban-ii-orders-the-first-crusades.

21 S. Grayzel, *The Church and the Jews in the 13th Century*, 1966.

22 Madeleine Schwartz, "The Origins of Blood Libel," *The Nation*, January 28, 2016, www .thenation.com/article/the-origins-of-blood-libel/.

23 Itamar Marcus, "Islam's War Against the Jews: Quotes from the Palestinian Authority," Aish.com, July 21, 2001, http://www.aish.com/jw/me/48883732.html.

24 Martin Luther, *On the Jews and Their Lies* (1543), quoted in "Anti-Semitism: Martin Luther—'The Jews and Their Lies," Jewish Virtual Library, accessed June 22, 2018, https://www.jewishvirtuallibrary.org/martin-luther-quot-the-jews-and-their-lies-quot.

25 Jeanne Favret-Saada, "A Fuzzy Distinction: Anti-Judaism and Anti-Semitism (An excerpt from Le Judaisme et ses Juifs)," *HAU: Journal of Ethnographic Theory* 4, no. 3 (Winter 2014), https://www.journals.uchicago.edu/doi/full/10.14318/hau4.3.021.

26 John Calvin, quoted in *The Calvin Handbook*, ed. Herman J. Selderhuis, trans. Henry J. Baron (Grand Rapids, MI: Eerdmans, 2009), 146.

27 John Calvin, quoted in "Anti-Semitism of the 'Church Fathers,'" Yashanet, accessed June 25, 2018, http://www.yashanet.com/library/fathers.htm.

28 Barbara Newman, *The Passion of the Jews of Prague: The Pogrom of 1389 and the Lessons of a Medieval Parody Church History 81:1* (March 2012), 1–26.

29 "Jewish Ghetto, Venice: History of the Jewish Ghetto," Sacred Destinations, accessed June 23, 2018, http://www.sacred-destinations.com/italy/venice-ghetto.

30 Anna Foa, *The Jews of Europe after the Black Death* (Berkeley: University of California Press, 2000), 146.

31 "Jewish Massacre Denounced: East Side Mass Meeting Plans to Help Victims of Russians in Kishinev," *New York Times*, April 28, 1903, 6.

32 John Doyle Klier, *Russians, Jews, and the Pogroms of 1881–1882* (New York: Cambridge University Press, 2011), 58.

33 Wilhelm Marr, *The Victory of Judaism over Germanism: Viewed from a Nonreligious Point of View*, 8th ed., trans. Gerhard Rohringer (Bern: Rudolph Costenoble, 1879), accessed June 23, 2018, http://www.kevinmacdonald.net/marr-text-english.pdf.

34 United States Holocaust Memorial Museum (hereafter cited as USHMM), *Holocaust Encyclopedia*, s.v. "Protocols of the Elders of Zion," accessed June 23, 2018, www.ushmm .org/wlc/en/article.php?ModuleId=10007058.

35 Ibid.

36 "Audio: Hitler and the Jews," History, BBC, accessed June 23, 2018, http://www.bbc.co .uk/history/worldwars/genocide/hitler_audio.shtml.

37 USHMM, *Holocaust Encyclopedia*, s.v. "Anti-Jewish Legislation in Prewar Germany," accessed June 23, 2018, https://www.ushmm.org/wlc/en/article.php?ModuleId =10005681.

38 Jeremy Noakes and Geoffrey Pridham, eds., *Documents on Nazism 1919–1945* (NY: Viking, 1975), 463–67; *Encyclopaedia Judaica*, vol. 15: Nat–Per, eds. Fred Skolnik and Michael Berenbaum, s.v. "Nuremberg Laws" (Farmington Hills, MI: Macmillan Reference, 2007), https://ketab3.files.wordpress.com/2014/11/encyclopaedia-judaica-v-15-nat-per.pdf.

39 USHMM, *Holocaust Encyclopedia*, s.v. "Antisemitic Legislation 1933–1939," accessed June 23, 2018, https://www.ushmm.org/wlc/en/article.php?ModuleId=10007901.

40 USHMM, *Holocaust Encyclopedia*, s.v. "Kristallnacht," accessed June 23, 2018, https://www.ushmm.org/wlc/en/article.php?ModuleId=10005201#seealso.

41 "Extract from the Speech by Hitler, January 30, 1939," SHOAH Resource Center, Yad Vashem, accessed June 23, 2018, http://www.yadvashem.org/odot_pdf/Microsoft%20Word%20-%201988.pdf.

42 David B Green, "This Day in Jewish History // 1939: Hitler Makes First Call for Jews' 'Annihilation,'" *Haaretz*, January 30, 2014, https://www.haaretz.com/jewish/premium-1939-hitler-makes-first-call-for-jews-annihilation-1.5316931.

43 "Reading 20: The Voyage of the *St. Louis*," from Margot Stern Strom, *Holocaust and Human Behavior*, chap. 7 (Brookline, MA: Facing History and Ourselves National Foundation, 1994), a teaching resource on Facing History and Ourselves (website), accessed June 23, 2018, https://www.facinghistory.org/holocaust-and-human-behavior/chapter-7/voyage-st-louis. See also "Reading 15: World Responses to Kristallnacht," https://www.facinghistory.org/holoaust-and-human-behavior/chapter-7/world-responses-kristallnacht.

44 "U.S. Policy During the Holocaust: The Tragedy of *S.S. St. Louis*," Jewish Virtual Library, accessed June 23, 2018, https://www.jewishvirtuallibrary.org/the-tragedy-of-s-s-st-louis.

45 USHMM, *Holocaust Encyclopedia*, s.v. "Voyage of the St. Louis," accessed June 23, 2018, https://www.ushmm.org/wlc/en/article.php?ModuleId=10005267.

46 Aish.com staff, "German Expansion and War," Holocaust Studies, Aish.com, December 31, 1969, http://www.aish.com/ho/o/48955271.html.

47 "Why Did the League of Nations Fail to Keep the Peace in the 1930s?" Modern World History \ International Relations 1900–1939, Marked by Teachers, accessed June 23, 2018, http://www.markedbyteachers.com/gcse/history/why-did-the-league-of-nations-fail-to-keep-peace-in-the-1930-s.html.

48 Christopher Klein, "History Stories: The Secret Hitler-Stalin Pact," August 22, 2014, History, www.history.com/news/the-secret-hitler-stalin-pact-75-years-ago.

49 "Timeline of Events: After 1945," USHMM, accessed June 23, 2018, https://www.ushmm.org/learn/timeline-of-events/after-1945.

50 "Reichstag Speech: January 30, 1939; Timeline of Events 1939–1941," USHMM, accessed June 23, 2018, https://www.ushmm.org/learn/timeline-of-events/1939-1941/hitler-speech-to-german-parliament.

51 Michael Berenbaum, "Wannsee Conference," *Encyclopaedia Britannica*, accessed June 23, 2018, www.britannica.com/event/Wannsee-Conference.

52 "Section 1: Nazi Camps," in Tony Joel and Mathew Turner, "Week 7: The 'Auschwitz Experience' and Other Settings of Mass Death and Devastation," Contemporary Histories at Deakin, accessed June 25, 2018, https://blogs.deakin.edu.au/holocauststudents/wp-content/uploads/sites/48/2014/03/WEEK-7__FINAL.pdf.

53 Some suggested resources are: Franklin H. Littell, *The Crucifixion of the Jews* (New York: Harper & Row, 1975); Edward Flannery, *The Anguish of the Jews: Twenty-Three Centuries of Anti-Semitism* (Mahwah, NJ: Paulist, 1985); Dagobert D. Runes, *The War Against the Jew* (New York: Philosophical Library, 1968).

54 Raul Hilberg, "The Destruction of the European Jews: Precedents," chap. 1 in *Holocaust: Origins, Implementation, Aftermath*, ed. Omer Bartov (New York: Routledge, 2000), 25.

55 Laura Bult, "Nobel Peace Prize Winner Elie Wiesel's Best Quotes on Survival, Activism and Humanity," *New York Daily News*, July 2, 2016, http://www.nydailynews.com/news /world/elie-wiesel-quotes-survival-spirituality-humanity-article-1.2697132.

56 From an interview with Carol Rittner and Sandra Myers, *The Courage to Care: Rescuers of Jews During the Holocaust* (New York: New York University Press, 1986), 2.

Chapter 3

1 Kenneth Marcus, "The Horror of Holocaust Denial," Louis D. Brandeis Center, June 3, 2014, http://brandeiscenter.com/the-horror-of-holocaust-denial/.

2 Adapted from "Holocaust Denial: Denial Forms," Auschwitz-Birkenau: Former German Nazi Concentration and Extermination Camp, accessed June 25, 2018, http://auschwitz .org/en/history/holocaust-denial/denial-forms.

3 United States Holocaust Memorial Museum (hereafter cited as USHMM), *Holocaust Encyclopedia*, s.v. "Introduction to the Holocaust," https://www.ushmm.org/wlc/en /article.php?ModuleId=10005143.

4 "Extract from the speech by Hitler, January 30, 1939," SHOAH Resource Center, Yad Vashem, accessed June 23, 2018, http://www.yadvashem.org/odot_pdf/Microsoft %20Word%20-%201988.pdf.

5 Katie, "December 12th 1941: Adolf Hitler Announces Extermination of the Jews," This Day in History, *Today in History* (blog), December 13, 2011, http://todayinhistory .tumblr.com/post/14168048136/december-12th-1941-adolf-hitler-announces.

6 Julius Streicher, from an article in *Der Stuermer*, November 4, 1943, quoted in "Nuremberg Trial Defendants: Julius Streicher," Jewish Virtual Library (hereafter cited as JVL), accessed June 25, 2018, https://www.jewishvirtuallibrary.org/nuremberg-trial -defendants-julius-streicher.

7 "Gas Chambers and Crematoria: The Nazi Murder Machine Operated at Peak Efficiency," Aish.com, December 31, 1969, http://www.aish.com/ho/o/Einsatzgruppen -The-Killing.html.

8 Ibid.

9 The History Place, "Biographies of Nazi Leaders: Adolf Eichmann," accessed June 25, 2018, www.historyplace.com/worldwar2/biographies/eichmann-biography.htm.

10 Ibid.

11 Louis Bülow, "Rudolf Hoess, Death Dealer of Auschwitz," Auschwitz.dk, accessed June 25, 2018, http://www.auschwitz.dk/hoess.htm.

12 Ibid.

13 Ibid.

14 Ibid.

15 "A Description of the Mass Murder of Jews in the Gas Chambers of Auschwitz," excerpted from Autobiografia Rudolfa Hössa, komendanta obozu oświęcimskiego, Warsaw, 1989, 202–3, http://en.auschwitz.org/lekcja/12_miejsce_pamieci/kurs/s405 /fragmenty.pdf.

16 Eric Lichtblau, "The Holocaust Just Got More Shocking," Sunday Review, *New York Times*, March 1, 2013, https://www.nytimes.com/2013/03/03/sunday-review/the -holocaust-just-got-more-shocking.html.

17 USHMM, *Holocaust Encyclopedia*, s.v. "Jewish Population of Europe in 1933: Population Data by Country," https://www.ushmm.org/wlc/en/article.php?ModuleId=10005161.

18 Ibid., s.v. "Jewish Population of Europe in 1945," https://www.ushmm.org/wlc/en /article.php?ModuleId=10005687.

19 Mark Weber, "Wilhelm Höttl and the Elusive 'Six Million,'" *Journal of Historical Review* 20, no. 5/6 (September/December 2001): 25.

20 Raul Hilberg, *The Destruction of the European Jews*, 3rd ed. (New Haven, CT: Yale University Press, 2003). First published 1961 by Quadrangle Books (Chicago).

21 Lucy S. Dawidowicz, *The War against the Jews* (New York: Holt, Rinehart and Winston,1975).

22 Wolfgang Benz, *Dimension des Völkermords: Die Zahl der jüdischen Opfer des Nationalsozialismus* (Munich: Dtv,1996).

23 Adolf Eichmann, "Eichmann's Own Story, Part 2: 'To Sum It All Up, I Regret Nothing,'" *Life*, December 5, 1960, 161, https://books.google.com/books?id=900EAAAAMBAJ &pg=PA46&source=gbs_toc_r&cad=2#v=onepage&q=I%20regret%20nothing&f=false.

24 History Place, Adolf Eichmann.

25 Ibid.

26 Kate Connolly, "'Accountant of Auschwitz' Goes on Trial in Germany," *Guardian*, April 21, 2015, US edition, https://www.theguardian.com/world/2015/apr/20/former -auschwitz-death-camp-guard-oskar-groning-on-trial-germany; see also Matthias Geyer, "An SS Officer Remembers: The Bookkeeper from Auschwitz, Part 2: Counting the Money of the Dead," trans. Christopher Sultan, *Spiegel* Online International, May 9, 2005, http://www.spiegel.de/international/spiegel/an-ss-officer-remembers-the -bookkeeper-from-auschwitz-a-355188-2.html.

27 Associated Press, "'Accountant of Auschwitz' Oskar Groening Loses Prison Appeal," CBS News, December 29, 2017, https://www.cbsnews.com/news/nazi-accountant-of -auschwitz-oskar-groening-loses-prison-appeal/.

28 Ed Wight, "Hall of Shame," *The Sun*, January 31, 2017, www.thesun.co.uk/news /2750293/nazi-ss-guards-auschwitz-concentration-camp/.

29 Laurence Rees, *Auschwitz: The Nazis & the "Final Solution"* (London: BBC Books, 2005).

30 USHMM, *Holocaust Encyclopedia*, s.v. "Ohrdruf," accessed June 25, 2018, https://www .ushmm.org/wlc/en/article.php?ModuleId=10006131.

31 "U.S. Policy During WWII: U.S. Army & the Holocaust," JVL, accessed June 25, 2018, https://www.jewishvirtuallibrary.org/u-s-army-and-the-holocaust.

32 *Holocaust Encyclopedia*, s.v. "Ohrdruf."

33 Nicholas Lemann, "The Murrow Doctrine: Why the Life and Times of the Broadcast Pioneer Still Matter," *New Yorker*, January 23, 2006, https://www.newyorker.com /magazine/2006/01/23/the-murrow-doctrine.

34 "Extract from the Nuremberg Trial," Buchenwald (Germany), JewishGen (website), https://www.jewishgen.org/ForgottenCamps/Camps/BuchenwaldEng.html.

35 Holocaust Education & Archive Research Team, "Buchenwald Concentration Camp," Holocaust Research Project, accessed June 25, 2018, http://www .holocaustresearchproject.org/othercamps/buchenwald.html.

36 "Ed Murrow Reports from Buchenwald—April 15, 1945," Media Resource Center Moffitt Library, UC Berkeley, accessed June 26, 2018, http://www.lib.berkeley.edu /MRC/murrowbuchenwaldtranscript.html.

37 Erwin Lutzer, quoted in Pastor Rudy, "Will It Happen Again?" *Cape May County Herald*, September 19, 2014, http://www.capemaycountyherald.com/opinion/columns/article _f189573a-7d3a-5e91-a3da-88690fde657b.html.

38 Judi Heit, "Adelaide Hautval," *Heroines of the Resistance* (blog), September 17, 2015, http://resistanceheroines.blogspot.com/2015/09/adelaide-hautval-1906-1988.html.

39 Yad Vashem, "Dr. Adelaide Hautval," The Stories of Six Righteous among the Nations in Auschwitz: Flickers of Light, accessed June 26, 2018, http://www.yadvashem.org/yv/en /exhibitions/righteous-auschwitz/hautval.asp.

40 Ibid.

41 Roddie's Code: Be the Hero, "The Story of Master Sergeant Roddie Edmonds," accessed June 26, 2018, http://www.roddieedmonds.com/bio/.

42 Jewish Telegraphic Agency, "American Soldier Named Righteous among the Nations for First Time," December 2, 2015, https://www.jta.org/2015/12/02/news-opinion /united-states/american-soldier-named-righteous-among-the-nations-for-first-time.

43 Ibid.

44 Judaism 101, Sh'ma.

45 Peter Longerich, *Holocaust: The Nazi Persecution and Murder of the Jews* (New York: Oxford University Press, 2010).

46 Gerhard SP and Spiegel, "How Denmark Saved Its Jews from the Nazis," ABC News, November 3, 2013, https://abcnews.go.com/International/denmark-saved-jews-nazis /story?id=20750027.

47 Michael Ignatieff, "Denmark and the Holocaust: One Country Saved Its Jews. Were They Just Better People?" Aish, May 24, 2014, http://www.aish.com/ho/i/Denmark --the-Holocaust.html.

48 Rabbi Israel Ba'al Shem Tov, quoted in David Silberklang, "More Than a Memorial: The Evolution of Yad Vashem," *Yad Vashem Quarterly Magazine*, Special Commemorative Edition (Fall 2003), 7.

Chapter 4

1 Theodor Herzl, *The Jewish State* (*Der Judenstaat*), trans. Sylvie D'Avigdor (American Zionist Emergency Council, 1946), quoted in Jewish Virtual Library (hereafter cited as JVL), "Texts Concerning Zionism: *The Jewish State*," https://www.jewishvirtuallibrary. org/quot-the-jewish-state-quot-theodor-herzl; Britannica Educational Publishing, *Judaism: History, Belief, and Practice*, ed. Matt Stefon (New York: Rosen Education Service, 2011), 346.

2 David Brog, "The Jews Come Home," chap. 3 in *Reclaiming Israel's History: Roots, Rights, and the Struggle for Peace* (Washington, DC: Regnery, 2017), 61–82.

3 "The Mandate for Palestine," Israel Ministry of Foreign Affairs, http://www.mfa.gov.il /mfa/foreignpolicy/peace/guide/pages/the%20mandate%20for%20palestine.aspx.

4 "The Weizmann-Feisal Agreement," Israel Ministry of Foreign Affairs, http://www.mfa. gov.il/mfa/foreignpolicy/peace/mfadocuments/pages/the%20weizmann-feisal %20agreement%203-jan-1919.aspx.

5 Jacqueline Shields, "Pre-State Israel: Arab Riots of the 1920s," JVL, https://www .jewishvirtuallibrary.org/arab-riots-of-the-1920-s.

6 Richard Bass, *Israel-Palestine for Critical Thinkers* (self-pub., 2015), 56.

7 Ibid., 60.

8 Jacqueline Shields, "Pre-State Israel: Arab Riots of the 1920s," JVL, https://www .jewishvirtuallibrary.org/arab-riots-of-the-1920-s.

9 Ibid.

10 Ibid.

11 "The Holocaust: The Mufti and the führer," JVL, https://www.jewishvirtuallibrary.org /the-mufti-and-the-f-uuml-hrer.

12 "Israeli War of Independence: Background & Overview," JVL, https://www .jewishvirtuallibrary.org/background-and-overview-israel-war-of-independence.

13 Ibid.

14 JIMENA: Jews Indigenous to the Middle East and North Africa, http://www.jimena .org/.

15 David Patterson, "The Muslim Brotherhood and the Evolution of Jihadist Antisemitism," January 17, 2018, Flashpoint 50, Institute for the Study of Global Antisemitism and Policy, https://isgap.org/flashpoint/the-muslim-brotherhood-and-the-evolution-of -jihadist-antisemitism/.

16 Ibid.

17 "The Muslim Brotherhood" (white paper), The Investigative Project on Terrorism, http:// www.investigativeproject.org/documents/misc/135.pdf.

18 Ibid.

19 See "Timeline of Ancient Israel" at TimeMaps, https://www.timemaps.com/civilizations /ancient-israel/.

20 "Palestine Liberation Organization: The Original Palestine National Charter (1964)," JVL, https://www.jewishvirtuallibrary.org/the-original-palestine-national-charter-1964.

21 Ibid.

22 "Israel's Wars & Operations: Operation Isotope (May 1972)," JVL, https://www .jewishvirtuallibrary.org/operation-isotope.

23 "Munich Olympic Massacre: Background & Overview (September 1972)," JVL, https:// www.jewishvirtuallibrary.org/background-and-overview-munich-olympic-massacer.

24 "Israel's Wars & Operations: The Entebbe Rescue Operation (July 1976)," JVL, https:// www.jewishvirtuallibrary.org/the-entebbe-rescue-operation.

25 "First Lebanon War: Background & Overview (1982–1985)," JVL, https://www .jewishvirtuallibrary.org/background-and-overview-of-first-lebanon-war.

26 David Daoud, "On the Roots and Branches of Shi'a Anti-Semitism," Tower, September 2015, http://www.thetower.org/article/on-the-roots-and-branches-of-shia-anti-semitism/.

27 Ibid.

28 "Hezbollah: Overview," Counter Extremism Project, https://www.counterextremism .com/threat/hezbollah#overview.

29 Ibid.

30 Ibid.

31 Badih Chayban, "Nasrallah Alleges 'Christian Zionist' Plot," Daily Star (Lebanon), October 23, 2002, http://www.dailystar.com.lb/News/Lebanon-News/2002/Oct-23 /21779-nasrallah-alleges-christian-zionist-plot.ashx.

32 Fred Fleitz, "Secret Ransom Payment Is More Evidence of the Enormous Fraud of the Iran Deal," National Review, August 3, 2016, https://www.nationalreview.com/2016/08 /iran-ransom-payment-proves-obama-clinton-iran-deal-fraud/.

33 Ian Mount, "The U.S. Sent Another $1.3 Billion to Iran after Hostages Were Released," Fortune, September 7, 2016, http://fortune.com/2016/09/07/us-iran-billion-hostages -arms-deal/.

34 Jerusalem, February 9, 2018 Rockets, Missiles and More; Predicting the Third Lebanon War.

35 "Iran to Host 'Hourglass Festival' in Anticipation of Israel's Destruction within 25 Years," Tower, March 1, 2018, http://www.thetower.org/iran-to-host-hourglass-festival-in -anticipation-of-israels-destruction-within-25-years/.

36 Aaron Bandler, "Ayatollah Khamenei Tweets That Israel Is a "Cancerous Tumor.' Israel Claps Back," Jewish Journal, June 4, 2018, http://jewishjournal.com/news/israel/234736 /ayatollah-khamenei-tweets-israel-cancerous-tumor-israel-claps-back/.

37 "Iran Prepares to Boost Uranium Enrichment Capacity," TRT World, June 6, 2018, https://www.trtworld.com/mea/iran-prepares-to-boost-uranium-enrichment -capacity-18001.

38 "PM Netanyahu Reveals the Iranian Secret Atomic Archive," Israeli PM YouTube channel, April 30, 2018, https://youtu.be/pkihrV4cZLE.

39 Patterson, "Muslim Brotherhood."

40 "ISIS: Overview," Counter Extremism Project, https://www.counterextremism.com
    /threat/isis#overview.

41 "Hamas: Background & Overview," JVL, https://www.jewishvirtuallibrary.org
    /background-and-overview-of-hamas.

42 Richard Bass, *Israel for Critical Thinkers* (CUFI Edition, 2006), pgs 87–91. Copyright ©
    Richard Bass, info@forcriticalthinkers.com.

43 Ibid., 96.

44 "Hamas War Tactics: Attacks from Civilian Centers," JVL, https://www
    .jewishvirtuallibrary.org/jsource/images/hamastactics.pdf.

45 Dan Williams and Nidal al-Mughrabi, "Gazans Send Fire-Starting Kites into Israel;
    Minister Threatens Lethal Response," Reuters, June 5, 2018, https://www.reuters.com
    /article/us-israel-palestinians-kites/gazans-send-fire-starting-kites-into-israel-minister
    -threatens-lethal-response-idUSKCN1J127C.

46 Judah Ari Gross, "Despite Concerns, Senior IDF Technology Officer Says Anti-Kite
    Drones a Success," *Times of Israel*, June 8, 2018, https://www.timesofisrael.com/disputing
    -news-report-colonel-declares-idfs-anti-kite-drones-a-success/.

47 "Tenuous Cease-Fire Reached in Gaza after IDF Pounds Hamas Posts," Israel Hayom,
    July 15, 2018, http://www.israelhayom.com/2018/07/15/tenuous-cease-fire-reached
    -in-gaza-after-idf-pounds-hamas-posts/.

48 "PM: Anyone Who Attacks Israel Will Meet Forceful Counterattack," Israel Hayom,
    July 15, 2018, http://www.israelhayom.com/2018/07/15/pm-anyone-who-attacks-israel
    -will-meet-forceful-counterattack/

49 Lahav Harkov, "Palestinians Increase Payments to Terrorists to $403 Million," *Jerusalem
    Post*, March 6, 2018, https://www.jpost.com/Arab-Israeli-Conflict/Palestinians
    -increase-payments-to-terrorists-to-403-million-544343.

50 Raphael Ahren, "'Pandemic' of Anti-Semitism Taking Shape Worldwide, Even Threatens
    America, Warns Top US Jewish Leader," *Times of Israel*, February 27, 2017, https://www
    .timesofisrael.com/pandemic-of-anti-semitism-taking-shape-worldwide-even-threatens
    -america-warns-top-us-jewish-leader/, emphasis added.

51 "Anti-Semitic Incidents Surged Nearly 60% in 2017, According to New ADL Report,"
    Anti-Defamation League, February 27, 2018, https://www.adl.org/news/press-releases
    /anti-semitic-incidents-surged-nearly-60-in-2017-according-to-new-adl-report.

52 Ahren, "'Pandemic' of Anti-Semitism Taking Shape Worldwide.

53 Reprise to "Sixteen Going on Seventeen" by Oscar Hammerstein in the theatrical (not
    film) version of *The Sound of Music*, http://www.thepeaches.com/music/composer
    s/hammerstein/SixteenGoingOnSeventeen.htm.

54 Commentary on "Watchman," BibleGateway, https://www.biblegateway.com/resources
    /encyclopedia-of-the-bible/Watchman.

55 Commentary on Isaiah 62:6, "Who shall never be silent by day or by night," The Israel
    Bible, https://theisraelbible.com/bible/isaiah/chapter-62.

56 Yehuda Bauer, quoted in "Voice of the Jewish News: Thou Shalt Not Be a Bystander,"
    Jewish News Online, January 28, 2016, http://jewishnews.timesofisrael.com/voice-of
    -the-jewish-news-thou-shalt-not-be-a-bystander/.

SECTION TWO: THE EMPIRES

Chapter 5

1 Peter Davidson, *Atlas of Empires: The World's Great Powers from Ancient Times to Today*
   (East Petersburg, PA: CompanionHouse Books, 2018), from the introduction.

2 "Ancient Rome," UShistory.org, Independence Hall Association, accessed June 12, 2018, http://www.ushistory.org/civ/6.asp.

3 "The Fall of the Roman Empire," UShistory.org, Independence Hall Association, accessed June 12, 2018, http://www.ushistory.org/civ/6f.asp.

4 Michael Frassetto et al., "Roman Catholicism," *Encyclopedia Britannica*, last updated May 17, 2018, https://www.britannica.com/topic/Roman-Catholicism.

5 "Holy Roman Empire," *Almanach de Saxe Gotha*, accessed June 11, 2018, http://www .almanachdegotha.org/id131.html.

6 Ibid.

7 Dariusz Kasprzak, "The Theological Principles Underlying Augustine's 'City of God,'" *Theological Research* 1 (2013): 104, http://dx.doi.org/10.15633/thr.153.

8 Stephen L. Baehr, "From History to National Myth: *Translatio Imperii* in Eighteenth-Century Russia," *Russian Review* 37, no. 1 (1978): 1, http://www.jstor.org/stable/128360.

9 Spyridon Flogaitis, *The Evolution of Law and the State in Europe: Seven Lessons* (Portland, OR: Hart, 2014), 10.

10 "Holy Roman Empire," *Saxe Gotha*.

11 Ibid.

12 "The Origins of Anti-Semitism," Alpha History, accessed June 14, 2018, http:// alphahistory.com/holocaust/origins-of-anti-semitism/.

13 "Medieval anti-Semitism," Alpha History, accessed June 14, 2018, http://alphahistory .com/holocaust/medieval-anti-semitism/.

14 David B. Green, "Holy Roman Emperor Orders All Jewish books—Except the Bible—Be Destroyed," *Haaretz*, August 19, 2013, https://www.haaretz.com/jewish/this-day -an-emperor-rounds-up-books-1.5322641.

15 Katy Gibbons, "Five of the Most Violent Moments of the Reformation," The Conversation, January 20, 2017, http://theconversation.com/five-of-the-most-violent -moments-of-the-reformation-71535.

16 David B. Green, "1670: The Holy Roman Emperor Banishes the Jews from Austria," *Haaretz*, March 1, 2015, https://www.haaretz.com/jewish/.premium-1670-austrian -jews-banned-1.5330064.

17 David B. Green, "1802: Jews Ask Holy Roman Empire to Upgrade Them to Citizens," *Haaretz*, November 15, 2013, https://www.haaretz.com/jewish/.premium-1802-jews -seek-german-rights-1.5290758.

18 "Holy Roman Empire," *Saxe Gotha*.

19 "Napoleon Bonaparte," Jewish Virtual Library, accessed June 14, 2018, http://www .jewishvirtuallibrary.org/napoleon-bonaparte.

20 Gemma Betros, "The French Revolution and the Catholic Church," *History Review*, no. 68 (December 2010), https://www.historytoday.com/gemma-betros/french-revolution -and-catholic-church.

21 Michael Adkins, "North German Confederation (1866–1871): History," Dead Country Stamps and Banknotes, accessed June 14, 2018, http://www.dcstamps.com/north -german-confederation-1866-1871/.

22 David Kaiser, "Treaty of Versailles," *The Reader's Companion to Military History*, ed. Robert Cowley and Geoffrey Parker (New York: Houghton Mifflin, 1996), 488–89 (hereafter cited as *Reader's Comp.*; citations refer to the 2001 paperback ed.); Gideon Rose, "Reparations," *Reader's Comp.*, 385–86.

23 "Encyclopedia Judaica: Emancipation: Germany," Jewish Virtual Library, American-Israeli Cooperative Enterprise (AICE), http://www.jewishvirtuallibrary.org/emancipation.

24 Elizabeth Vlossak, "Alsace-Lorraine: Alsace-Lorraine between France and Germany, 1871–1914," International Encyclopedia of the First World War, last updated October 21, 2016, https://encyclopedia.1914-1918-online.net/article/alsace-lorraine.

25 "Understanding the Kulturkampf," History, Unan Sanctam Catholicam, accessed June 14, 2018, http://www.unamsanctamcatholicam.com/history/79-history/394 -kulturkampf.html.

26 "The Attack on the Social Democrats," German Empire: The Making of the Empire, Encyclopedia Britannica, accessed June 14, 2018, https://www.britannica.com/place /German-Empire#ref339177 (hereafter cited as German Empire, Britannica).

27 "Foreign and Colonial Policy," German Empire, Britannica.

28 "The Fall of Bismarck," German Empire, Britannica.

29 BBC, "Wilhelm II (1859–1941)," History: Historic Figures, accessed June 14, 2018, http://www.bbc.co.uk/history/historic_figures/wilhelm_kaiser_ii.shtml.

30 United States Holocaust Memorial Museum, "The Weimar Republic," Holocaust Encyclopedia, accessed June 14, 2018, https://encyclopedia.ushmm.org/content/en /article/the-weimar-republic.

31 Michael H. Kater, "Everyday Anti-Semitism in Prewar Nazi Germany: The Popular Bases," Yad Vashem Studies 16 (1984): 129–59, https://www.yadvashem.org/odot_pdf /Microsoft%20Word%20-%203261.pdf.

Chapter 6

1 Michael Novak, On Two Wings: Humble Faith and Common Sense at the American Founding (San Francisco: Encounter Books, 2002), 5–13.

2 Novak, On Two Wings, 34–39.

3 See James Madison's argument in Federalist No. 47, in Alexander Hamilton, James Madison, and John Jay, The Federalist Papers, ed. Clinton Rossiter (New York: Mentor Books, 1961), 269.

4 Alexis de Tocqueville, Democracy in America, trans. George Lawrence, ed. J. P. Mayer (New York: Harper & Row, 1969), 292.

5 For a discussion of the structural features of the three branches of government, see Jeffrey K. Tulis, The Rhetorical Presidency (Princeton, NJ: Princeton University Press, 1987), 41–45.

6 The Federalist Papers is the best place to start to understand the Framers' vision for the American presidency. Hamilton's quote can be found in No. 75.

7 Federalist, No. 70.

8 This discussion is based heavily on the work of Stephen Skowronek, who first articulated this understanding of American history as a series of partisan regime cycles. See Stephen Skowronek, The Politics Presidents Make: Leadership from John Adams to George Bush (Cambridge, MA: Belknap Press, 1993); and Stephen Skowronek, Presidential Leadership in Political Time: Reprise and Reappraisal (Lawrence, KS: University Press of Kansas, 2008).

9 On the early American party system, see Richard Hofstadter, The Idea of a Party System: The Rise of Legitimate Opposition in the United States, 1780–1840 (Berkeley: University of California Press, 1969).

10 For a detailed account of early American party politics, see Richard P. McCormick, The Presidential Game: The Origins of American Presidential Politics (New York: Oxford University Press, 1982).

11 For a thorough look at Jacksonian politics, see Gerard N. Magliocca, *Andrew Jackson and the Constitution: The Rise and Fall of Generational Regimes* (Lawrence, KS: University Press of Kansas, 2007).

12 John C. Calhoun, "On the Oregon Bill," speech delivered in the Senate of the United States, June 27, 1848.

13 Abraham Lincoln referenced this quote by Indiana senator John Pettit in his "Speech at Peoria, Illinois," October 16, 1854.

14 Lincoln, "Speech at Peoria."

15 "Republican Party Platform of 1856," June 18, 1856, The American Presidency Project: Political Party Platforms, http://www.presidency.ucsb.edu/ws/index.php?pid=29619.

16 Scott v. Sandford, 60 U.S. (19 How.) 393 (1856).

17 Alexander H. Stephens, "Corner-Stone Speech," Savannah, GA, March 21, 1861.

18 The most complete exploration of Theodore Roosevelt's political philosophy is Jean M. Yarbrough, *Theodore Roosevelt and the American Political Tradition* (Lawrence, KS: University Press of Kansas, 2012).

19 For a thorough account of Wilson's place in Progressive politics, see Ronald J. Pestritto, *Woodrow Wilson and the Roots of Modern Liberalism* (Lanham, MD: Rowman & Littlefield, 2005).

20 Calvin Coolidge, "The Inspiration of the Declaration" (speech), July 5, 1926.

21 On the Great Depression, see Amity Shlaes, *The Forgotten Man: A New History of the Great Depression* (New York: Harper Perennial, 2008). On Roosevelt's transformation of the executive branch, see Sidney M. Milkis, *The President and the Parties: The Transformation of the American Party System Since the New Deal* (New York: Oxford University Press, 1993).

Chapter 7

1 "Remarks of President Donald J. Trump—As Prepared for Delivery: Inaugural Address," Washington, DC, January 20, 2017, https://www.whitehouse.gov/briefings-statements/the-inaugural-address/.

2 Goldwater's own political philosophy is most succinctly expressed in Barry Goldwater, *The Conscience of a Conservative* (Shepherdsville, KY: Victor, 1960).

3 A succinct discussion of these differences can be found in Paul Gottfried and Thomas Fleming, *The Conservative Movement* (Boston: Twayne, 1988). The most comprehensive history of the post-war conservative movement is George H. Nash, *The Conservative Intellectual Movement in America Since 1945* (Wilmington, DE: ISI Books, 2006).

4 For a comprehensive account of the period leading up to Reagan's victory, see Steven F. Hayward, *The Age of Reagan: The Fall of the Old Liberal Order, 1964–1980* (New York: Forum, 2001).

5 On the idea of a culture war and cultural realignment, see James Davison Hunter, *Culture Wars: The Struggle to Define America* (New York: Basic Books, 1991).

6 Scott v. Sandford, 60 U.S. (19 How.) 393 (1856); Roe v. Wade, 410 U.S. 113 (1973).

7 "Ronald Reagan, 'Evil Empire Speech' (8 March 1983)," Voices of Democracy, http://voicesofdemocracy.umd.edu/reagan-evil-empire-speech-text/.

8 On Reagan's presidency, see Andrew E. Busch, *Ronald Reagan and the Politics of Freedom* (Lanham, MD: Rowman & Littlefield, 2001). See also Steven F. Hayward, *The Age of Reagan: The Conservative Counterrevolution, 1980–1989* (New York: Crown Forum, 2009).

9 See transcript of "Saddleback Civil Forum on the Presidency," in which Pastor Rick Warren interviewed then Senator Barack Obama during the 2008 presidential race (August 16, 2008), http://transcripts.cnn.com/TRANSCRIPTS/0808/16/se.02.html.

10 David Remnick, "Going the Distance: On and Off the Road with Barack Obama," *New Yorker*, January 27, 2014, https://www.newyorker.com/magazine/2014/01/27 /going-the-distance-david-remnick.

11 On the polarization in American politics and its source in the 1960s, see James E. Campbell, *Polarized: Making Sense of a Divided America* (Princeton, NJ: Princeton University Press, 2016).

12 Shannon, Pettypiece, "Trump Signs $1.5 Trillion Tax Cut in First Major Legislative Win," Bloomberg, December 22, 2017, https://www.bloomberg.com/news/ articles/2017-12-22/trump-signs-1-5-trillion-tax-cut-in-first-major-legislative-win.

13 "The Employment Situation: December 2000," Bureau of Labor Statistics, January 5, 2001, https://www.bls.gov/news.release/history/empsit_01052001.txt.

14 "Conscience Protection Act: What It Is and Why It's Needed," Speaker Paul Ryan's Press Office (July 12, 2016), https://www.speaker.gov/general/conscience-protection-act-what -it-and-why-it-s-needed.

15 "Mairead McArdle, "U.S. Pulls Out of 'Biased' UN Human Rights Council," *National Review*, June 19, 2018, https://www.nationalreview.com/news/united-states-pulls-out-of -united-nations-human-rights-council/.

16 Yair Lapid, "The U.N. and Antisemitism: 10-Year Report Card," *The Jerusalem Post*, July 12, 2018, https://www.jpost.com/Opinion/The-UN-and-antisemitism-10-year-report -card-562377.

Chapter 8

1 For more detail on this subject, see John Hagee, *Three Heavens: Angels, Demons and What Lies Ahead* (Nashville: Worthy, 2015).

2 Flavius Josephus, "Concerning the Tower of Babylon, and the Confusion of Tongues," bk. 1, chap. 4, in *The Antiquities of the Jews*, in *The Genuine Works of Flavius Josephus*, William Whiston, ed. (Halifax: William Milner, 1849), 30.

3 "Bible Verses about Semiramis," Bible Tools, https://www.bibletools.org/index.cfm /fuseaction/topical.show/RTD/cgg/ID/770/printer/friendly.

4 Shaul Wolf, "The Life and Times of Nimrod, the Biblical Hunter," Chabad.org, https:// www.chabad.org/library/article_cdo/aid/3162874/jewish/The-Life-and-Times-of -Nimrod-the-Biblical-Hunter.htm.

5 Source of quote unknown, though widely attributed to Alexander Hislop, *The Two Babylons*, 2nd American edition (Neptune, NJ: Loizeaux Brothers, 1959), 5, 24.

6 Wilhelm J. Woldaardt, "The Story of Nimrod as It Relates to Christmas and Easter," email message to Hebraic Heritage Newsgroup, January 12, 1999, http://www.hebroots .org/hebrootsarchive/9901/9901_q.html.

7 "Historical Pictures of Christianity: Babylonian Priests Migrate," http://historical .benabraham.com/html/babylonian_priests_migrate.html.

8 Socrates Scholasticus, *Ecclesiastical History*, bk. 5, chap. 22.

9 Isabel Hernández, "Meet the Man Who Started the Illuminati," *National Geographic History*, November 1, 2016, https://www.nationalgeographic.com/archaeology -and-history/magazine/2016/07-08/profile-adam-weishaupt-illuminati-secret-society/.

10 Ibid.

11 Elizabeth Entenmen, "List of Illuminati Members," Complex, www.complex.com/life /list-of-illuminati-members/baron-Adolph-von-knigge.

12 Martha Gill, "What Is the Illuminati? You Asked Google—Here's the Answer," *Guardian*, November 22, 2017, https://www.theguardian.com/commentisfree/2017/nov/22/what -is-illuminati-google-autocomplete.

13 Christian Tomuschat, ed., *The United Nations at Age Fifty: A Legal Perspective* (The Hague: Martinus Nijhoff, 1995), 77.

14 Attributed to Dietrich Bonhoeffer. For more on his life, see Eberhard Bethge and Victoria Barnet, ed., *Dietrich Bonhoeffer: A Biography* (Minneapolis: Fortress Press, 2000).

15 Ibid.

16 Peter Pry, "Welcome to the Nuclear Blackmail of Putin's 'New World Order,'" *The Hill*, March 7, 2018, thehill.com/opinion/national-security/377183-welcome-to-the-nuclear -blackmail-of-putins-new-world-order.

17 United Nations, "European Union Indispensable Partner of United Nations, Ready to Build Cooperative New World Order, Its Top Diplomat Tells Security Council," Meetings coverage: Security Council 7935th meeting, May 9, 2017, https://www.un.org /press/en/2017/sc12814.doc.htm.

18 Ibid.

19 "Russian President Dmitry Medvedev Pulls New World Currency from His Pocket," *Telegraph*, July 10, 2009, https://www.telegraph.co.uk/finance/currency/5796892 /Russian-President-Dmitry-Medvedev-pulls-new-world-currency-from-his-pocket.html.

20 "G7 statement: Mnuchin asked to convey 'unanimous concern and disappointment,'" Reuters, June 2, 2018, https://www.reuters.com/article/g7-summit-finance/g7-statement -mnuchin-asked-to-convey-unanimous-concern-and-disappointment-idUSW1N1R3026.

21 Leika Kihara and Gernot Heller, "U.S. Isolated at G7 Meeting as Tariffs Prompt Retaliation," Reuters, June 1, 2018, https://www.reuters.com/article/us-usa-trade/u-s -isolated-at-g7-meeting-as-tariffs-prompt-retaliation-idUSKCN1IX478.

22 Freedom-channel, "A New World Order and a New World Currency in 2018?," Steemit, https://steemit.com/money/@freedom-channel/a-new-world-order-and-a-new-world -currency-in-2018.

23 Ibid.

24 MSN, "Who's Stockpiling Gold?" (slideshow), slides 26 (China) and 25 (Russia), https://www.msn.com/en-us/money/markets/this-is-who-owns-most-of-the-worlds -gold/ss-BBGmtjN?fullscreen=true#image=22.

25 Freedom-channel, "New World Currency."

26 MSN, "Who's Stockpiling?," slides 27–31.

27 Conrad Hackett and David McClendon, "Christians Remain World's Largest Religious Group, but They Are Declining in Europe," Pew Research Center, April 5, 2017, http:// www.pewresearch.org/fact-tank/2017/04/05/christians-remain-worlds-largest-religious -group-but-they-are-declining-in-europe/.

SECTION THREE: FROM AMALEK TO ARMAGEDDON

Chapter 9

1 Adapted from Riley Winters, "The Ancient Roots of Doomsday Prophecies and End of the World Beliefs," Ancient Origins, January 15, 2015, https://www.ancient-origins.net /history/ancient-roots-doomsday-prophecies-and-end-world-beliefs-002571.

2 "Ancient Jewish History: The Assyrians (1170-612 BCE)," Jewish Virtual Library, https:// www.jewishvirtuallibrary.org/the-assyrians.

3 Mark Strauss, "Ten Notable Apocalypses That (Obviously) Didn't Happen, *Smithsonian*, November 12, 2009, https://www.smithsonianmag.com/history/ten-notable-apocalypses -that-obviously-didnt-happen-9126331/.

4 John Roach, "End of World in 2012? Maya 'Doomsday' Calendar Explained," *National Geographic*, December 20, 2011, https://news.nationalgeographic.com/news/2011/12 /111220-end-of-world-2012-maya-calendar-explained-ancient-science/.

5   Jack Schofield, "The Millennium Bug: Special Report," Money We Spent, *Guardian*, US edition, January 4, 2000, https://www.theguardian.com/technology/2000/jan/05/y2k.guardiananalysispage.

6   Marissa Fessenden, "People Have Always Been Obsessed with the End of the World," Smart News, *Smithsonian*, September 8, 2015, https://www.smithsonianmag.com/smart-news/people-have-always-been-obsessed-end-world-180956525/.

7   Ibid.

8   Ibid.

9   Ibid.

10 David Ross, editor, "The Edict Expulsion," Britain Express, www.britainexpress.com/History/medieval/expulson-jews.htm.

11 Adapted from Martin Ralph DeHaan, *Signs of the Times* (Grand Rapids, MI: Zondervan, 1951), 168–69.

12 J. Dwight Pentecost, *Prophecy for Today: God's Purpose and Plan for Our Future*, rev. ed. (Grand Rapids, MI: Discovery House, 1989), 16.

13 Derek Prince, *Foundational Truths for Christian Living: Everything You Need to Know to Live a Balanced, Spirit-Filled Life* (Lake Mary, FL: Charisma House, 2006), 22–23.

14 "353 Prophecies Fulfilled in Jesus Christ," According to the Scriptures, http://www.accordingtothescriptures.org/prophecy/353prophecies.html.

15 Brian H. Edwards, *Nothing but the Truth: The Inspiration, Authority and History of the Bible Explained* (Darlington, UK: Evangelical Press, 2006), 116–43.

16 J. Barton Payne, *Encyclopedia of Biblical Prophecy: The Complete Guide to Scriptural Predictions and Their Fulfillment* (Ada, MI: Baker, 1980).

17 Alan Dershowitz, *The Case for Israel* (Hoboken, NJ: John Wiley, 2003), 30–33.

18 "Main Indicators," Central Bureau of Statistics, accessed July 2, 2018, http://www.cbs.gov.il/reader/cw_usr_view_Folder?ID=141.

19 John Hagee, ed., *Prophecy Study Bible* (Nashville, TN: Thomas Nelson, 1997).

20 Edward Reese, ed., *Chronological Bible* (Nashville, TN: Regal, 1977); Hagee, *Prophecy Study Bible*; Clarence Wagner, "Zechariah's Eight Visions for Israel," http://www.ldolphin.org/zechwagner/.

Chapter 10

1   Adapted from Hersh Goldwurm, *Daniel: A New Translation with a Commentary Anthologized from Talmudic, Midrashic, and Rabbinic Sources*, Artscroll Tanach Series (Brooklyn: Artscroll Mesorah, 1979), xxiv.

2   Ibid.

3   Arthur W. Pink, *Gleanings in Genesis* (Chicago: Moody Press, 1922), 142.

4   Richard Cavendish, "Spanish Bankruptcy," *History Today*, November 11, 2007, https://www.historytoday.com/richard-cavendish/spanish-bankruptcy.

5   Habibur Rahman, Ramón Sanguino Galván, and Ascensión Barroso Martínez, "Economic Recession in Spain: Exploring the Root Causes, Consequences and Recoveries for the Sustainable Economic Growth," Science and Education Publishing, October 26, 2017, http://pubs.sciepub.com/ijefm/5/2/5/.

6   Soeren Kern, "The Islamization of Germany in 2016: 'Germany Is No Longer Safe," January 2, 2017, Gatestone Institute International Policy Council, https://www.gatestoneinstitute.org/9700/germany-islamization.

7   James S. Robbins, "The Iran Nuclear Deal Was the Worst Deal Ever. No Wonder Donald Trump Nixed It," *USA Today*, May 8, 2018, https://www.usatoday.com/story/opinion/2018/05/08/iran-nuclear-deal-worst-donald-trump-column/589828002/.

8   Charles Kingsley, "Abraham's Faith," in *Twenty-Five Village Sermons* (Literature Network, 2012; first published 1854), http://www.online-literature.com/charles-kingsley/village -sermons/12/. This book was converted from its physical edition to the digital format by a community of volunteers.

9   Pink, *Gleanings in Genesis*, 162–63.

10 Ibid., 166.

11 Meir Zlotowitz, *Bereishis/Genesis*, Artscroll Tanach Series (Brooklyn: ArtScroll Mesorah, 1986), 504.

12 Derek Prince, "God's Covenant with Abraham," https://www.derekprince.org/Articles /1000085415/DPM_USA/Archive_of_UK/Keys/Relationships/Relationship_with_God /Gods_Covenant_with.aspx.

13 J. Dwight Pentecost, *Things to Come: A Study in Biblical Eschatology* (Grand Rapids, MI: Zondervan, 1958), 69.

14 Adapted from Ibid., 68.

15 *Bereishis*, ArtScroll Tanach Series, vol. 1(a), (Brooklyn, NY: Mesorah Publications, Ltd., 1969), 519–20, note 1.

16 Pink, *Gleanings in Genesis*, 169.

17 "Birdwatching from a Christian Perspective: Birds of the Bible," *Lee's Birdwatching Adventures Plus* (blog), https://leesbird.com/bb/.

18 Finis J. Dake, *Dake's Annotated Reference Bible–KJV* (Lawrenceville, GA: Dake, 2014), 20.

19 Pink, *Gleanings in Genesis*, 170.

20 Zlotowitz, *Bereishis/Genesis*, 524.

21 *The Nelson Study Bible: NKJV* (Nashville, TN: Thomas Nelson, 1997), 27.

22 Ibid., 29.

23 Clarence Larkin, "Royal Grant to Abraham" (chart), in "The Jews: Dispensational Truth," chap. 9, Blue Letter Bible, https://www.blueletterbible.org/study/larkin/dt/09.cfm#c41.

24 *The Chumash*, ArtScroll Stone Edition (Brooklyn, NY: Mesorah Publications, Ltd., 1998), 72, note 17.

25 Pentecost, *Things to Come*, 71.

Chapter 11

1   Aron Heller, "Sir Isaac's Jewish Writings Enter the 21st Century," *Times of Israel*, February 19, 2012, https://www.timesofisrael.com/sir-isaacs-jewish-writings-enter -the-21st-century/.

2   Flavius Josephus, *Antiquities of the Jews* (Book X, Chapter 11, section 7), Internet Sacred Text Archive, http://sacred-texts.com/jud/josephus/ant-10.htm.

3   "General Timeline Abraham to Nehemiah," accessed July 3, 2018, http://livingstonesclass .org/Archive/Daniel%20Introduction.pdf.

4   "What Is the Basic Timeline of the Old Testament?" Compelling Truth, accessed July 3, 2018, https://www.compellingtruth.org/Old-Testament-timeline.html.

5   "The Jewish Temples: The Babylonian Exile (597–538 BCE)," Jewish Virtual Library, https://www.jewishvirtuallibrary.org/the-babylonian-exile.

6   Tom Bradford, Old Testament Studies (Lesson 4, Daniel 1, cont.), Torah Class, http:// www.torahclass.com/old-testament-studies-tc/1816-old-testament-studies-daniel/1385 -lesson-4-daniel-ch-1-cont.

7   Derek Prince, *Husbands and Fathers: Rediscover the Creator's Purpose for Men* (Grand Rapids, MI: Chosen Books, 2000), 28.

8   See "What We Do," CUFI on Campus, https://www.cufioncampus.org/about.

9 Tracey R. Rich, "Prophets and Prophecy," Judaism 101, accessed July 20, 2018, http://www.jewfaq.org/prophet.htm

10 Yehuda Shurpin, "Why Isn't the Book of Daniel Part of the Prophets?: The Difference between Prophecy and Divine Inspiration," Chabad, https://www.chabad.org/library/article_cdo/aid/1735365/jewish/Why-Isnt-the-Book-of-Daniel-Part-of-the-Prophets.htm.

11 Lewis Eron, "Prophets and Sages," Reconstructing Judaism, https://www.reconstructingjudaism.org/dvar-torah/prophets-and-sages.

12 *The William Davidson Talmud*, Megillah 14a, Sefaria, https://www.sefaria.org/Megillah.14a?lang=bi.

13 W. C. Stevens, *The Book of Daniel* (Camp Hill, PA: Christian Publications, 1915), 41.

14 Clarence Larkin, *The Book of Daniel* (Glenside, PA: Rev. Clarence Larkin Estate, 1990; first published 1919), 50.

15 *The Woman's Study Bible: NKJV*, 2nd ed. (Nashville, TN: Thomas Nelson, 2006), 1089.

16 *NKJV Study Bible*, 2nd ed. (Nashville, TN: Thomas Nelson, 2007), 1349.

17 Adapted from Myer Pearlman, *Daniel Speaks Today* (Springfield, MO: Gospel Publishing House, 1943), 81.

18 Ibid., 82–83.

19 John F. Walvoord, *Daniel: The Key to Prophetic Revelation* (Chicago: Moody Press, 1971), 214–16.

20 Adapted from Pearlman, *Daniel Speaks*, 85.

21 Larkin, *The Book of Daniel*, 176.

22 Jennifer Rosenberg, "The History of the Balfour Declaration," ThoughtCo, updated June 11, 2018, https://www.thoughtco.com/balfour-declaration-1778163.

23 Joseph Benson, *Commentary of the Old and New Testament* (New York: Carlton and Porter, 1857).

24 John Hagee, *The Three Heavens* (Nashville, TN: Worthy, 2015).

25 Pearlman, *Daniel Speaks*, 87–88.

26 Clarence Larkin, *The Greatest Book on 'Dispensational Truth' in the World*, chap. 19 (self-pub., 1920).

27 Pearlman, *Daniel Speaks*, 99.

28 Ibid., 118.

Chapter 12

1 Mark R. Levin, *Rediscovering Americanism: And the Tyranny of Progressivism* (New York: Threshold Editions, 2017), 1, 238.

2 "German FM: Europe 'Very United' on Decision to Stay in Iran Deal," Radio Free Europe/Radio Liberty, updated May 23, 2018, https://www.rferl.org/a/us-pompeo-determined-to-stop-iran-nuclear-nonnuclear-threats/29245754.html.

3 Uri Friedman, "Putin's Playbook: The Strategy Behind Russia's Takeover of Crimea," *Atlantic*, March 2, 2014, https://www.theatlantic.com/international/archive/2014/03/putins-playbook-the-strategy-behind-russias-takeover-of-crimea/284154/.

4 Tass, "Moscow Cements Deal with Damascus to Keep 49-Year Presence at Syrian Naval and Air Bases," January 20, 2017, http://tass.com/defense/926348; "New Russia-Syria Accord Allows up to 11 Warships in Tartus Port Simultaneously," Deutsche Welle. January 20, 2017, https://www.dw.com/en/new-russia-syria-accord-allows-up-to-11-warships-in-tartus-port-simultaneously/a-37212976.

5 "Moscow Moves to Make Military Presence in Syria Permanent," *Times of Israel*, December 27, 2017, https://www.timesofisrael.com/moscow-moves-to-make-military-presence-in-syria-permanent/.

6 Inna Lazareva, "Russian Spy Base in Syria Used to Monitor Rebels and Israel Seized," *Telegraph*, October 8, 2014, https://www.telegraph.co.uk/news/worldnews/europe/russia/11148857/Russian-spy-base-in-Syria-used-to-monitor-rebels-and-Israel-seized.html.

7 Matthew RJ Brodsky, "Russia Is Reaping the Benefits of Israel's Actions in Syria," *National Interest*, May 20, 2018, http://nationalinterest.org/feature/russia-reaping-the-benefits-israels-actions-syria-25897.

8 Anshel Pfeffer, "Israel Struggles to Draw New Red Lines in Russia's Syria Playground," Analysis, *Haaretz*, February 11, 2018, https://www.haaretz.com/middle-east-news/syria/.premium-israel-struggles-to-draw-new-red-lines-in-russia-s-syria-playground-1.5806718.

9 IHS Jane's, "Hizbullah's Expanded Role in Syria Threatens Israel," an analysis report from HIS Jane's Military and Security Assessments Intelligence Centre, 2017, http://www.janes.com/images/assets/885/68885/Hizbullahs_expanded_role_in_Syria_threatens_Israel.pdf.

10 Ibid.

11 MEMRI, "Pro-Hizbullah Lebanese Website: Hizbullah Has 70,000 Iranian Missiles across Syria Ready to Launch into Israel; in a Year It Will Have 500,000," Special Dispatch No. 7328, February 12, 2018, https://www.memri.org/reports/pro-hizbullah-lebanese-website-hizbullah-has-70000-iranian-missiles-across-syria-ready.

12 Alon Ben David, "Iron Dome Blunts 90% of Enemy Rockets," *Aviation Week*, September 1, 2014, http://aviationweek.com/defense/iron-dome-blunts-90-enemy-rockets.

13 CUFI Talking Points, "More Rockets Fired into Israel over the Past 24 Hours Than During Past 3 Years," Christians United for Israel, https://www.cufi.org/cufi-talking-points-more-rockets-fired-into-israel-over-the-past-24-hours-than-during-past-3-years/.

14 Zvi Bar'el, "Russia Seeks Hamas-Fatah Reconciliation in Order to Save Assad, Weaken Iran," Haaretz, September 13, 2017, https://www.haaretz.com/middle-east-news/palestinians/.premium-russias-next-potential-victory-hamas-fatah-reconciliation-1.5450299.

15 Ibid.

16 Sabra Ayres and Noga Tarnopolsky, "Netanyahu Meets Putin in Russia to Discuss Syria, Iran, Security Issues," *Los Angeles Times*, July 11, 2018, http://www.latimes.com/world/middleeast/la-fg-russia-israel-putin-netanyahu-20180711-story.html.

17 Saeed Abdelrazek and Atef Abdul Latif, "Syria: Moscow Links Southern Battle to Iran's Withdrawal," *Asharq Al-Awsat*, June 5, 2018, https://aawsat.com/english/home/article/1290581/syria-moscow-links-southern-battle-iran%E2%80%99s-withdrawal.

18 Zaman Al Wasl, Agencies, "Russian Air Strikes Hit Daraa as Talks Fail," Zaman Al Wasl, July 4, 2018, https://en.zamanalwsl.net/news/article/36002/.

19 Steve Erlanger, "A Gaza War Full of Traps and Trickery," *New York Times*, January 10, 2009, https://www.nytimes.com/2009/01/11/world/middleeast/11hamas.html.

20 Adapted from Moshe Eisemann, *Yechezkel/Ezekiel*, Artscroll Tanach Series (Brooklyn: ArtScroll Mesorah, 1989), xx.

21 Ibid. xv.

22 "Ezekiel 38," *Scofield Reference Notes*, 1917 ed., Bible Study Tools (website), https://www.biblestudytools.com/commentaries/scofield-reference-notes/ezekiel/ezekiel-38.html.

23 J. Dwight Pentecost, *Prophecy for Today: An Exposition of Major Themes in Prophecy* (Grand Rapids, MI: Zondervan, 1961), 107–8.

24 Ehsan Yarshater, "Communication," *Iranian Studies* 22, no. 1 (1989): 62–65, https://www.jstor.org/stable/4310640?seq=1#page_scan_tab_contents.

25 "History of Iran: Islamic Revolution of 1979," Iran Chamber Society, http://www
.iranchamber.com/history/islamic_revolution/islamic_revolution.php.

26 Pentecost, *Prophecy for Today*, 108.

27 Josephus, *Antiquities* 1.6.1.

28 Bodie Hodge, "Josephus and Genesis Chapter Ten: A Wonderful Stepping-Stone,"
Answers in Genesis, November 18, 2009, https://answersingenesis.org/genesis/josephus
-and-genesis-chapter-ten/.

29 Nick Miller, "Angela Merkel Proposes Partial Burqa Ban ahead of German Election,"
Sydney Morning Herald, December 7, 2016, https://www.smh.com.au/world/angela
-merkel-proposes-partial-burqa-ban-ahead-of-german-election-20161207-gt5gth.html.

30 Associated Press, "Nice Truck Attack Claims 86th Victim," *Star Tribune* (Minneapolis,
MN), August 19, 2016, https://web.archive.org/web/20160821175505/http:/www
.startribune.com/nice-truck-attack-claims-86th-victim/390715371/.

31 Angelique Chrisafis, "Man Shot Dead by French Army after Killing Two People at
Marseille Train Station," *Guardian*, October 1, 2017, https://www.theguardian.com
/world/2017/oct/01/french-police-operation-under-way-at-marseille-train-station.

32 Eleanor Steafel, "Paris Terror Attack: Everything We Know on Saturday Afternoon,"
Telegraph, November 21, 2015, https://www.telegraph.co.uk/news/worldnews/europe
/france/11995246/Paris-shooting-What-we-know-so-far.html.

33 Griff Witte, "In a Kosher Grocery Store in Paris, Terror Takes a Deadly Toll," *Washington
Post*, January 9, 2015, https://www.washingtonpost.com/world/europe/paris-kosher
-market-seized-in-second-hostage-drama-in-nervous-france/2015/01/09/f171b97e-97ff
-11e4-8005-1924ede3e54a_story.html?utm_term=.45094e12a036.

34 "12th-Century Rabbi Predicted Israel's Future," World Net Daily, November 11, 2012,
http://www.wnd.com/2012/11/12th-century-rabbi-predicted-israels-future/.

35 "Thermal Radiation," Effects of Nuclear Weapons, Atomic Archive, http://www
.atomicarchive.com/Effects/effects7.shtml.

36 Charles Levinson and Guy Chazan, "Big Gas Find Sparks a Frenzy in Israel,"
Wall Street Journal, updated December 30, 2010, https://www.wsj.com/articles
/SB10001424052970204204004576049842786766586.

SECTION FOUR: THE FINAL GAME OF THRONES

Chapter 13

1 Joseph J. Carr, *The Twisted Cross* (Shreveport, LA: Huntington House, 1985), 39.

2 Kai Schultz, "Indian Children's Book Lists Hitler as Leader 'Who Will Inspire You,'"
New York Times, March 18, 2018, https://www.nytimes.com/2018/03/17/world/asia
/india-hitler-childrens-book.html.

3 Daryl Worthington, "The Munich Pact," New Historian, September 30, 2014, http://
www.newhistorian.com/munich-pact/1340/.

4 Ian Kershaw, "The Führer Myth: How Hitler Won Over the German People," Spiegel
Online, January 30, 2008, http://www.spiegel.de/international/germany/the-fuehrer
-myth-how-hitler-won-over-the-german-people-a-531909-3.html.

5 Christopher Klein, "The Secret Hitler-Stalin Pact," History Stories, History, August 22,
2014, https://www.history.com/news/the-secret-hitler-stalin-pact-75-years-ago.

6 A line from the movie *Darkest Hour*, as reported by Navnee Likhi in "One Man Who
Took a Stand," *Tribune* (Chandigarh, India), December 10, 2017, http://www
.tribuneindia.com/news/spectrum/entertainment/one-man-who-took-a-stand/510703
.html.

7   Winston Churchill, "Blood, Toil, Tears and Sweat, 1940," National Churchill Museum, accessed July 17, 2018, https://www.nationalchurchillmuseum.org/blood-toil-tears-and -sweat.html.
8   John Hagee, *The Three Heavens* (Franklin, TN: Worthy, 2015), 164.
9   Carr, *Twisted Cross*, 13.
10 Ibid.
11 John F. Walvrood, Chapter 8 The Revelation of the Man of Sin http://walvoord.com /article/177
12 Arthur W. Pink, *The Antichrist* (Grand Rapids: Kregel, 1923; 1988), 9.
13 Ibid., 62.

Chapter 14

1   Manuel Castells, *The Information Age: Economy, Society and Culture*, 3 vols. (Cambridge, MA: Wiley-Blackwell, 1999).
2   "21 Books You Don't Have to Read," *GQ*, April 19, 2018, https://www.gq.com/story /21-books-you-dont-have-to-read.
3   Finis J. Dake, *Dake's Annotated Reference Bible–KJV* (Lawrenceville, GA: Dake, 2014), 501.
4   G. A. Hadjiantoniou, *The Postman of Patmos: The Letters to the Seven Churches of Revelation* (Grand Rapids, MI: Zondervan, 1961).
5   Dake, *Annotated Reference Bible*, 405.
6   Clarence Larkin, *Dispensational Truth, or God's Plan and Purpose in the Ages* (1920; repr., Brattleboro, VT: Echo Point, 2015), 110; Hagee, *Three Heavens*, 270–75.
7   Adapted from Geoffrey Dennis, "Judaism and Numbers," My Jewish Learning, accessed July 18, 2018, https://www.myjewishlearning.com/article/judaism-numbers/.
8   Clarence Larkin, *The Book of Revelation* (Glenside, PA: Rev. Clarence Larkin Estate, 2004), 66.
9   John Phillips, *Exploring the Book of Daniel: An Expository Commentary* (Grand Rapids, MI: Kregel, 2004), 222–23.

Chapter 15

1   John F. Walvoord, *The Nations in Prophecy* (Grand Rapids, MI: Zondervan, 1967), http://walvoord.com/book/export/html/318.
2   Geo. N. H. Peters, *The Theocratic Kingdom of Our Lord Jesus: The Christ, as Covenanted in the Old Testament, and Presented in the New Testament* (New York: Funk & Wagnalls, 1884), 3:220.
3   See map, Clarence Larkin, "Royal Grant to Abraham" (chart), in *The Jews: Dispensational Truth*, chap. 9, Blue Letter Bible, https://www.blueletterbible.org/study/larkin/dt/09 .cfm#c41.
4   David Abulafia, *The Great Sea: A Human History of the Mediterranean* (New York: Oxford University Press, 2011), 55.
5   Anson F. Rainey, "Herodotus' Description of the East Mediterranean Coast," *Bulletin of the American Schools of Oriental Research*, no. 321 (February 2001), 57–63, https://www .jstor.org/stable/1357657.
6   Louis H. Feldman, "Some Observations on the Name of Palestine," *Hebrew Union College Annual* 61 (1990): 19, https://www.jstor.org/stable/23508170.
7   Noah Rayman, "Mandatory Palestine: What It Was and Why It Matters," *Time*, September 29, 2014, http://time.com/3445003/mandatory-palestine/; "Israel: Origins of the Name 'Palestine,'" Jewish Virtual Library, https://www.jewishvirtuallibrary.org

/origin-of-quot-palestine-quot; "British Palestine Mandate: History and Overview (1922–1948)," Jewish Virtual Library, https://www.jewishvirtuallibrary.org/history -and-overview-of-the-british-palestine-mandate.

8   Shaul Bartal, "The Peel Commission Report of 1937 and the Origins of the Partition Concept," *Jewish Political Studies Review* 28, no. 1/2 (Spring 2017): 54, https://www .jstor.org/stable/44510475. See also: William R. W. Peel, et al., "Zionism," in chap. 1, "The Historical Background," *Palestine Royal Commission Report*, 11–15, https:// biblio-archive.unog.ch/Dateien/CouncilMSD/C-495-M-336-1937-VI_EN.pdf; General Council (Va'ad Leumi) of the Jewish Community of Palestine, *Three Historical Memoranda, submitted to* the United Nations Special Committee on Palestine, 5707/1947 (Jerusalem: Hasman Press, 1947), 56–60; Bernard Lewis, "Studies in the Ottoman Archives–I," *Bulletin of the School of Oriental and African Studies, University of London* 16, no. 3 (1954): 469–501, https://www.jstor.org/stable/608618.

9   J. Vernon McGee, *Thru the Bible: 1 Corinthians–Revelation*, vol. 5 (Nashville, TN: Thomas Nelson, 1983), 1058.

10 John Hagee, *The Battle for Jerusalem* (Nashville, TN: Thomas Nelson, 2001), 244–47.

11 J. Vernon McGee, *Revelation Chapters 14–22: The Prophecy* (Nashville, TN: Thomas Nelson, 1991), 152.

12 Hagee, *Battle for Jerusalem*, 244–47.

13 Clarence Larkin, The Book of Revelation, Rev. Clarence Larkin Estate, Glenside, Pennsylvania, 1919, p 193.

14 John Hagee, ed., "Top 20 Questions: 15. What is the Great White Throne Judgment?," *NKJV Prophecy Study Bible* (Nashville, TN: Thomas Nelson, 1997), 1597.

15 Adapted from Finis Jennings Dake, *God's Plan for Man* (1949; Lawrenceville, GA; Dake Bible Sales, 1981), 1009.

Chapter 16

1   Adapted from Clarence Larkin, *The Book of Revelation* (Glenside, PA: Rev. Clarence Larkin Estate, 2004), 209.

2   Finis Jennings Dake, *God's Plan for Man* (1949; Lawrenceville, GA: Dake Bible Sales, 1981), 987.

3   Ibid.

4   Conn Iggulden, "Ten of the Greatest: Historical Conquerors," *Mail Online*, September 4, 2010, http://www.dailymail.co.uk/home/moslive/article-1308014/Ten-greatest -Historical-conquerors.html.

5   Numbers 1–10 taken from Abby Rogers, "The 10 Greatest Empires in the History of the World," *Business Insider*, November 9, 2011, http://www.businessinsider.com/the-10 -greatest-empires-in-history-2011-9; nos. 11–13 based on Google searches on land masses based on empires territories.

6   Derek Prince, "A Throne for the King," devotional on Facebook, May 19, 2018, https:// www.facebook.com/dpmlegacy/posts/10156535190977975.

7   Charles Haddon Spurgeon, "The Throne of God and of the Lamb," sermon no. 1576, delivered at Metropolitan Tabernacle, Newington (1881), *Metropolitan Tabernacle Pulpit: Volume 27: Sermons Preached and Revised in 1881* (repr., Pasadena, TX: Pilgrim Publications, 1975); available for viewing online at The Spurgeon Center for Biblical Preaching at Midwestern Seminary, https://www.spurgeon.org/resource-library/sermons /the-throne-of-god-and-of-the-lamb#flipbook/.

ABOUT THE AUTHOR

JOHN HAGEE is the founder and senior pastor of Cornerstone Church in San Antonio, Texas, a non-denominational evangelical church with more than 22,000 active members. He is the author of forty books including several *New York Times* bestsellers. Pastor Hagee is known for his support of Israel and his teachings on prophecy with such books as *The Beginning of the End, Jerusalem Countdown, In Defense of Israel, Four Blood Moons,* and *The Three Heavens*. John Hagee is the founder and chairman of Christians United for Israel (CUFI) with over 4.3 million members. His television and radio outreach spans America and the nations of the world.

IF YOU ENJOYED THIS BOOK, WILL YOU CONSIDER SHARING THE MESSAGE WITH OTHERS?

Mention the book in a blog post or through Facebook, Twitter, Pinterest, or upload a picture through Instagram.

Recommend this book to those in your small group, book club, workplace, and classes.

Head over to facebook.com/JohnHageeMinistries, "LIKE" the page, and post a comment as to what you enjoyed the most.

Tweet "I recommend reading #EarthsLastEmpire by @PastorJohnHagee // @worthypub"

Pick up a copy for someone you know who would be challenged and encouraged by this message.

Write a book review online.

WORTHY®
PUBLISHING

Visit us at worthypublishing.com

twitter.com/worthypub

worthypub.tumblr.com

facebook.com/worthypublishing

pinterest.com/worthypub

instagram.com/worthypub

youtube.com/worthypublishing